PUBLICATIONS OF THE PENNSYLVANIA GERMAN SOCIETY

VOLUME XXVIII
1994

OLEY VA
THE

OLEY VALLEY HERITAGE
COLONIAL YEARS 1700-1775

BY PHILIP E. PENDLETON

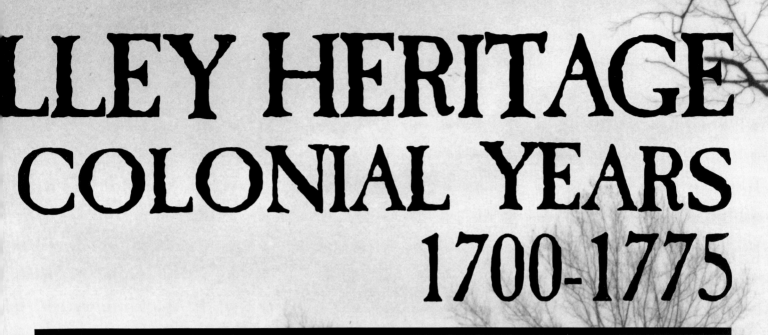

BIRDSBORO, PENNSYLVANIA
THE PENNSYLVANIA GERMAN SOCIETY
OLEY, PENNSYLVANIA
THE OLEY VALLEY HERITAGE ASSOCIATION
1994

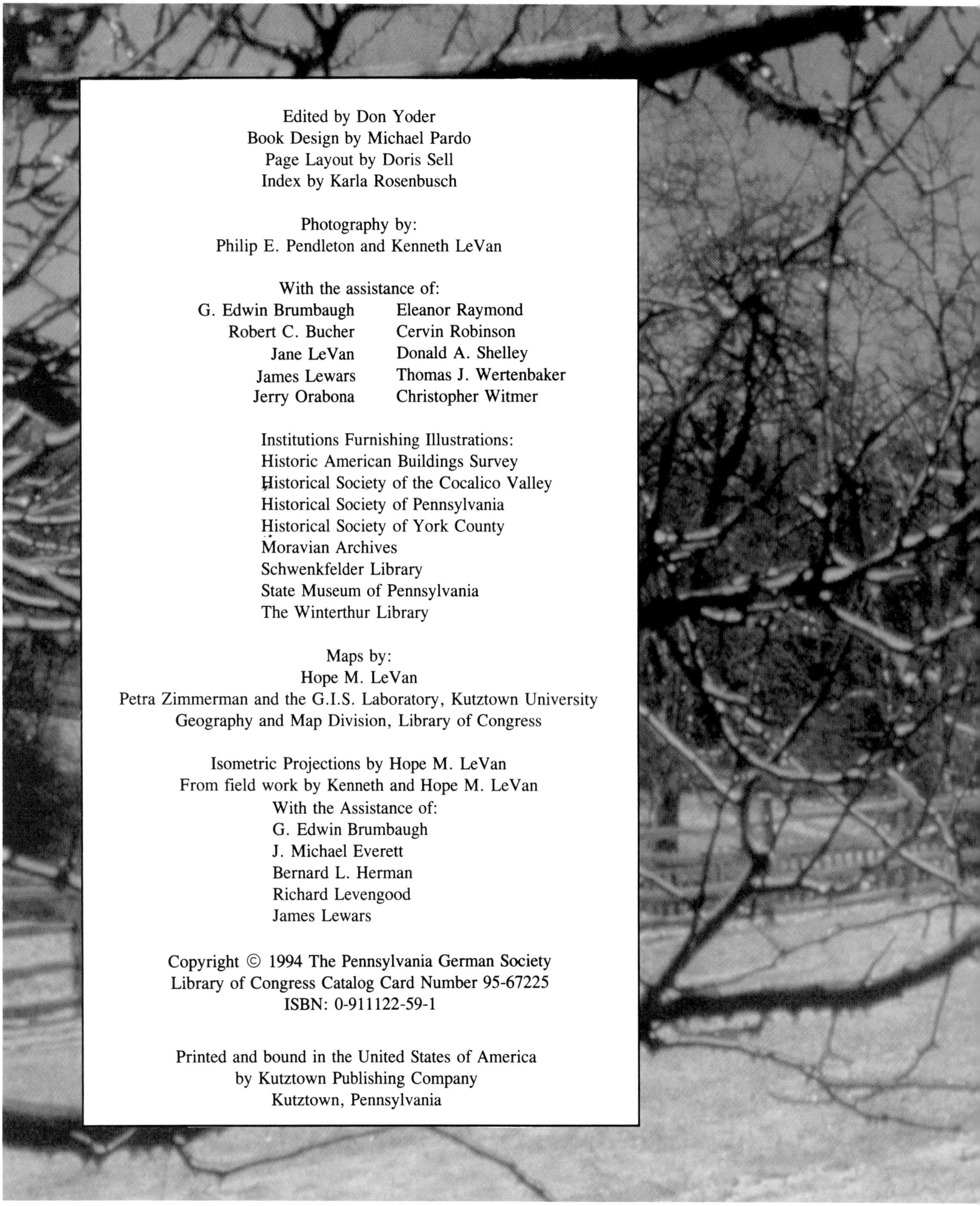

Edited by Don Yoder
Book Design by Michael Pardo
Page Layout by Doris Sell
Index by Karla Rosenbusch

Photography by:
Philip E. Pendleton and Kenneth LeVan

With the assistance of:

G. Edwin Brumbaugh	Eleanor Raymond
Robert C. Bucher	Cervin Robinson
Jane LeVan	Donald A. Shelley
James Lewars	Thomas J. Wertenbaker
Jerry Orabona	Christopher Witmer

Institutions Furnishing Illustrations:
Historic American Buildings Survey
Historical Society of the Cocalico Valley
Historical Society of Pennsylvania
Historical Society of York County
Moravian Archives
Schwenkfelder Library
State Museum of Pennsylvania
The Winterthur Library

Maps by:
Hope M. LeVan
Petra Zimmerman and the G.I.S. Laboratory, Kutztown University
Geography and Map Division, Library of Congress

Isometric Projections by Hope M. LeVan
From field work by Kenneth and Hope M. LeVan
With the Assistance of:
G. Edwin Brumbaugh
J. Michael Everett
Bernard L. Herman
Richard Levengood
James Lewars

Copyright © 1994 The Pennsylvania German Society
Library of Congress Catalog Card Number 95-67225
ISBN: 0-911122-59-1

Printed and bound in the United States of America
by Kutztown Publishing Company
Kutztown, Pennsylvania

TO THE PEOPLE OF TODAY'S
OLEY VALLEY COMMUNITY —
STEWARDS OF AN IRREPLACEABLE HERITAGE

CONTENTS

FOREWORD	9
INTRODUCTION	10

CHAPTER 1: THE LAND — 13

European Roots of Oley Valley Settlers	15
Migration of Settlers into the Oley Valley	16
The Oley Huguenots	20
Patterns of Settlement	23
Claiming Land	24
Relations Between the Settlers and the Lenape Indians	25
Notes	27

CHAPTER 2: THE ECONOMY — 29

Agricultural System Based on Wheat	29
Agricultural Implements	32
The Agricultural Year	32
Careless Husbandry	34
Herds, Flax Patches, Orchards, and Gardens	34
Artisans and Mills: Integral to Agriculture	37
Open for Business	40
Export Industry: Merchant Mills, Paper Mills, and Ironworks	41
Growth of Complexity in Local Economic Life	43
Means of Exchange and Credit	47
Cash Settlement Requested	48
Servants and Slaves	48
Philadelphia Newspaper Advertisements for Runaway Servants from the Oley Valley	51
Conclusion	52
Notes	53

CHAPTER 3: THE ARCHITECTURAL LANDSCAPE — 55

Construction	56
Vernacular House Types	67
Anglo-Pennsylvanian House Types	68
The Stove-Room House: A Pennsylvania German House Type	70
Palladian-Influenced House Types	73
The Domestic Material Environment	83
House-Mills and Ancillary Houses	84
Barns and Outbuildings	94
The Larger Farmstead	97
Mill Buildings	98
Conclusion	98
Real Estate	99
Notes	101

CHAPTER 4: SOUL	103
The New Born	106
Other German Sectarian Groups	109
Early German Reformed and Lutheran Activity	109
The Moravians	111
George DeBenneville	118
Lutheran and German Reformed Congregations	119
The Church of Sweden and the Church of England	121
Muhlenberg's Journals: The Hearts of the People	126
The Society of Friends	126
Quaker Meeting Documents	131
Conclusion	132
Notes	133

CHAPTER 5: COMMUNITY	135
Family	135
Departed Wives	137
Relations Among Nationalities: "Good Neighboring"	137
Local Government	140
Stolen	143
Road and River	143
Oley Township Supervisors of Highways Record, 1774-1775	148
Conclusion	149
Notes	150

APPENDIX 1: Colonial-Period Schools in the Oley Valley	152
APPENDIX 2: Colonial-Period Ministers and Preachers in the Oley Valley	153
APPENDIX 3: County-Level Officials Resident in the Oley Valley during the Colonial Period	154
APPENDIX 4: Noteworthy Colonial-Period Buildings in the Oley Valley	155
APPENDIX 5: Architectural Glossary	157
APPENDIX 6: Isometric Projections of Oley Valley House Types	167
APPENDIX 7: Known Heads of Households and Single Freemen Residing in the Oley Valley 1701-1741	176
APPENDIX 8: Township Zone Maps for 1725, 1750, and 1775, Showing Businesses, Social Organizations, and Nationalities	179
APPENDIX 9: Township Zone Maps for 1725, 1750, and 1775, with Property Ownership Key	186
APPENDIX 10: Daniel Boone Homestead	207
BIBLIOGRAPHY	208
ACKNOWLEDGMENTS	219
SUBJECT INDEX	221
PERSONAL NAME INDEX	226
SOCIETY OFFICERS AND BOARDS OF DIRECTORS	232

OLEY VALLEY HERITAGE

FOREWORD

"America began here." This statement has frequently been made of our Commonwealth of Pennsylvania, where to a greater degree than in New England or much of the South, a variety of ethnic, cultural, and religious groups settled alongside each other and worked out their relationships as neighbors.

The Oley Valley—one of Pennsylvania's earliest settlements, along with Skippack, Goshenhoppen, Conestoga, and Tulpehocken—is a prime example of this American mixture of population and ideas. Settled at the very beginning of the eighteenth century by Swedes who had moved up the Schuylkill River from Philadelphia, then later by Palatines and Swiss, French Huguenots, and English and Welsh Quakers, the larger Oley area, which eventually constituted the colonial townships of Oley, Amity, and Exeter, soon began the process of adjustment and acculturation between British Isles and Continental European cultures, along with Lenape Indians who were still in the area, and also some blacks. In the colonial period, Oley was indeed a microcosm of America, bristling with difference but also with accommodation.

Philip E. Pendleton, a preservationist who currently lives in Baltimore, has deep roots in Berks County, where he was born and educated. While working some years ago for the Berks County Conservancy, he began the present book at the request of the Oley Valley Heritage Association, which supported his research. Using every available source—court and church records, personal papers, autobiographies and letters, descriptions by travelers who visited the area, and above all, extensive field work and photography of the surviving colonial-period farmsteads, his project eventually took shape as a full length "biography" of the Oley Valley and its people. Detailed chapters cover the early settlement history of the area, the economic system, architecture, religious patterns, and the development of community organization. Maps of the area in 1725, 1750, and 1775 show every surveyed tract and farm, with the names of the owners, as well as locations of mills, taverns, churches, roads, creeks, and rivers.

Above all, the photographs, many taken by the author, others from such agencies as the Historic American Buildings Survey at the Library of Congress, provide a graphic picture of the Oley Valley architectural landscape, and insight into the ways in which Berks County settlers arranged and managed their everyday lives.

The book will appeal to all those interested in American colonial history; genealogy; regional architecture; Pennsylvania German culture; religious patterns of early Pennsylvania (with all their complexities and tensions); the development of industry, mills, and trade as part of the economic network of colonial Pennsylvania; and the gradual growth of community organization and community spirit.

"One out of many." With its continuing agricultural tradition, its active churches, and its firm sense of identity, the Oley Valley today is a prime example of how the American right to be different has been respected and cherished over almost three centuries. We thank and compliment the Oley Valley Heritage Association and its officers for supporting this book from the very beginning, and for joining the Pennsylvania German Society in its publication.

June 1, 1994

**Don Yoder, Editor
Pennsylvania German Society**

OLEY VALLEY, OCTOBER, 1994
Country road leading to a mountain farm.
Photo by Jerry Orabona.

INTRODUCTION

In eastern Berks County, Pennsylvania, lies a picturesque valley, historically an agricultural community, known as Oley. The fertile land of the Oley Valley is studded with old stone buildings, many of them erected in the 1700s. The Oley area was the earliest part of Berks County to be settled by Europeans, beginning in the first decade of the eighteenth century. The apparent richness of the soil of Oley Valley so enticed the early pioneers that they passed by some twenty to thirty miles of unsettled Pennsylvania country to claim this land.

During the colonial period (i.e., from 1700 to 1775 in reference to the Oley Valley settlement), European people of several different nationalities took up residence in the valley: Swedes, Germans, Swiss, English, Welsh, Huguenots, and others. In the years prior to American independence the valley community was established, its system of agriculture developed, its religious gatherings nurtured, and many of its homesteads built, in forms that would set the pattern of life in Oley for generations to come. Although social relations were not without contentious incident, a notable characteristic of this pattern of community life was the amicable interplay among the various groups of settlers, learning from one another and cooperating to attain shared goals.

The Oley Valley has long been considered an "historic place." The many surviving eighteenth- and early nineteenth-century buildings, as well as the valley's innate natural beauty, have drawn Sunday drivers and architectural historians alike since the onset of the automobile age, perhaps longer. Local antiquarians and church historians have celebrated the oft contentious religious ferment among the valley's early European inhabitants. In 1983, Oley Township was nominated to the National Register of Historic Places as an Historic District, the first rural municipality in America to be listed in its entirety. This action followed a three-year study of the township and its well-preserved historic landscape by the Rural Project organization of the National Trust for Historic Preservation. The Oley Valley Heritage Association, which commissioned the present work as an element in its ongoing program for preservation and education, grew out of the vital local volunteer effort that carried out the nomination.

This history will look at many events and personalities in the colonial period of the Oley Valley. Other earlier chroniclers, such as Peter G. Bertolet, Morton L. Montgomery, P. C. Croll, J. Bennett Nolan, John Joseph Stoudt, John E. Eshelman, and J. Taylor Hamilton, have scrutinized these events, but this history will consider these events and personalities (as well as other people and matters) from a social-historical perspective.

In recent years, the work of folklife students, archaeologists, geographers, demographers, anthropologists, art and architectural historians, and other scholars of the human past has impelled historians to broaden the scope of their investigations far beyond their traditional account of political and religious institutions and events. With the conviction that the human story encompasses all human experience, that changes in the nature of domestic and economic aspects of family life have affected that story just as surely as have wars and the drafting of constitutions, scholars have sought and grasped historical meaning in the day-to-day world of our forebears. Every possible aspect of human life—work, play, love, family bonds, religion, and the material world (including buildings, furniture, clothing, food, tools, farm fields, and whatever else)—all these and more have become grist for the historian's mill. Rich historical evidence awaits pursuit in the records left for practically all American communities by church pastors, tax collectors, courts, and the keepers of real estate and probate records. Besides these official sources, there are personal and family papers including letters, diaries, and account books. These documents, as well as the testimony evident in old buildings and other surviving (if obscured) features on the landscape, show that in reality every place is an "historic place."

This work looks at the Oley Valley in the colonial period from the perspective of everyday life. It seeks to shed light on the commonplace experience of these particular early Americans. Of special note is the manner in which the Oley Valley colonists created and maintained a community comprising people of different European nationalities and religious faiths. Early Mid-Atlantic localities with mixed populations, such as Oley, set the pattern for a uniquely American community life, a pattern that later generations carried across the nation.

Underlying all the research for this work is the comprehensive investigation of colonial-period property ownership records for all the real estate within the study area. The extent of the study area was determined by the application of the place name "Oley" in these early land records and in such other early sources as petitions for township or road creation, other court records, and church records. In conducting the research it was found that colonial-period inhabitants used the place name Oley to refer to an area much larger than present-day Oley Township. Completion of comprehensive research on real estate ownership enabled the identification of all landowning inhabitants, which in turn facilitated the use of probate records such as estate inventories and a variety of other sources, including church records and period newspapers. Investigation of taxation records added the names of non-landowners for these purposes. One result of this comprehensive research was the compilation of a series of sequential maps that illustrate the development of the valley settlement through the period.

The narrative text is organized in five chapters. The first depicts the establishment of the Oley Valley settlement. The other four examine the topical areas of economic life, architectural landscape, religious life, and family and community. The intended scheme of the work was a progression from the most basic material aspects of life upward to those concerning people's loftier aspirations. Since the chapter on community seemed most forthrightly to present the central themes of the book—American cultural development and the relations between cultural

OLEY VALLEY HERITAGE

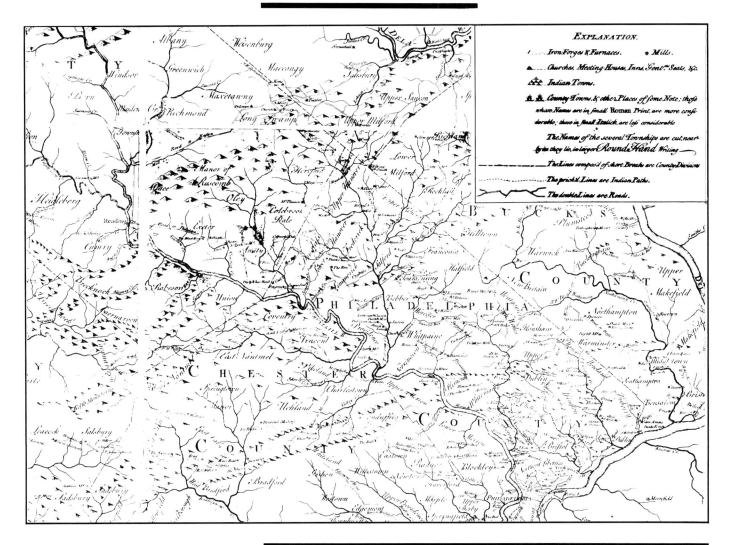

groups—that chapter was selected to close the text. The reader, of course, is free to "dip in" as he or she pleases. The chapter on religion perhaps most nearly presents a straightforward narrative of the valley settlement.

Adjustments have been made to names and quotations from documents in the interest of readability and comprehensibility. The spelling and punctuation in quotations from period sources is rendered in modern form.

The names of German-speaking settlers (i.e., those born or with ancestral roots in the German-speaking region of central Europe) are consistently given in Germanic form, for example, "Johannes Joder" instead of "John Yoder." With allowance for this germanizing, the form of a surname employed in the text is the predominant spelling that appears in period documents. The names of the valley's colonial-period inhabitants were spelled with dizzying variation by clergy, government clerks, neighbors serving as local officials or scriveners, and even, over time, by some inhabitants themselves. Illiterate people were at the mercy of others in this regard. Most German speakers generally gave their names in Germanic form when affixing their signatures, though their names usually ap-

THE OLEY VALLEY SETTLEMENT, 1759: A Period View
This detail from Nicholas Scull's map of the Province of Pennsylvania shows a selection of most prominent establishments in the valley that was perhaps influenced by the surveyor-cartographer's own Anglo-Pennsylvanian background, though these were also located along the most important thoroughfares: Exeter Meeting, Pine Forge, wealthy ironmaster William Bird's house (a "gentleman's seat"), William Boone's Gristmill, Edward Drury's Store (housed in a rented building on William Boone's property), John Hughes's Tavern, the White Horse Tavern, and the Black Horse Tavern. Whether or not Scull was in error regarding the name at that date, the latter location became better known as Black Bear.

"An Account of the Distances from the City of Philadelphia," printed in 1754 by William Bradford of Philadelphia, gave the following distances from the Philadelphia County Courthouse along the road to Reading (a "perch" being the same as a rod, or sixteen-and-a-half feet, with eighty making a quarter-mile):

To Baltzer Cressman's [The White Horse], 40 miles, 0 quarters, 0 perches

Drury's, 47 miles, 1 quarter, 78 perches

The Mariner's Compass [Hughes's Tavern], 49 miles, 0 quarters, 42 perches

Courtesy, Geography and Map Division, Library of Congress.

peared in English form in deeds, tax assessment lists, and other legal documents. The use of German name-forms for all German-speaking inhabitants aids in the reader's identification of whether a person mentioned is a German speaker or an English speaker.

Chapter 1

THE LAND

THE DANIEL BOONE HOMESTEAD STATE HISTORIC SITE, Exeter Township
Photo by Philip E. Pendleton.

The Oley Valley is situated entirely within Berks County, Pennsylvania. The valley's western edge lies about two miles east of the city of Reading, the county seat, and its southeast corner is approximately thirty miles northwest of Philadelphia. The valley is a distinct topographical entity, as either a drive through it or a glance at a relief map will show. The valley comprises a definite, separate region in the perception of local people, due to its topography and history.

The greater Oley Valley takes the rough shape of an upside-down T. It is divided into two sections, north and south. The northern or upper section, a bowl-shaped depression, is the part more properly called "Oley." The name, conferred by the local Lenape Indians, means both "hole" and "kettle" in their language. The valley floor here is fertile limestone soil of the finest quality, the basis for centuries of agricultural prosperity. The northern section of the valley lies on a north-south axis and measures approximately seven miles long by four-and-a-half miles wide. Modern Oley Township contains about three-fourths of the northern Oley Valley within its bounds. The adjoining townships of Pike, Earl, Amity, Exeter, and Alsace hold a small part of the northern section.

The Schuylkill River runs through the southern or lower part of the valley, so that this latter section comprises an intersection of the Oley Valley with the river valley. Most of the soil of the southern part of the Oley Valley is a less fertile red shale. The southern section represents the bar in the inverted T, aligned east-to-west, and is approximately eleven miles long by four-and-a-half miles wide. On the northern bank of the Schuylkill, about five-sixths of modern Amity Township and three-fourths of Exeter Township are encompassed within the southern section of the Oley Valley, as well as a small part of Douglass Township and the entirety of the borough of Saint Lawrence. To the south of the Schuylkill, Union, Robeson, and Cumru townships each contain a portion of the southern Oley Valley, and the borough of Birdsboro lies entirely within that portion. Between the two sections of the larger valley lies a range of low broad ridges, running from west to east across Exeter and Amity townships, which more or less defines the divide between the two sections.

In human society the northern and southern sections of the Oley Valley were closely linked throughout the colonial years. The settlers of both areas tended to be economically successful by the standards of the province at large. But the divergent physical natures of the two areas, the fertile soil of the northern valley superior to that of the southern valley, do appear to have resulted in a noticeable measure of socioeconomic divergence. The settlers of the northern section seem to have had a tendency to sink their roots somewhat deeper than those who homesteaded in the southern section. The fine soil evidently drew the northern settler families to stay longer, and develop their properties more rapidly and more fully. The greater prosperity of the people of the northern area, and their families' longer persistence, can be seen in the vernacular architecture of the two sections. More substantial houses, two-story structures constructed of stone, and more of them, were built earlier in the upper section of the Oley Valley.

OLEY VALLEY HERITAGE

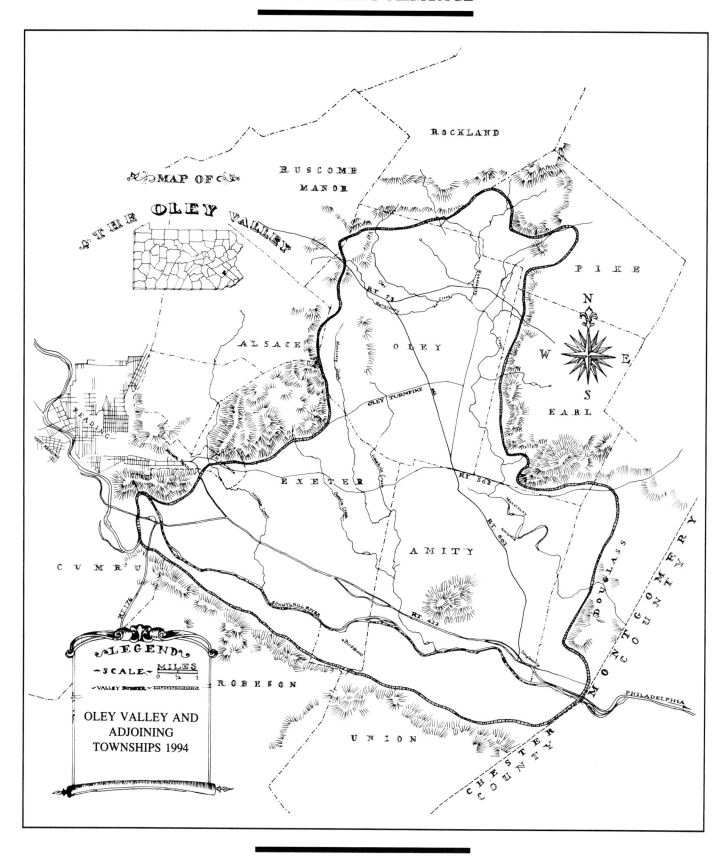

THE OLEY VALLEY
The area in Berks County, Pennsylvania, researched extensively for this work, in its modern geographical context.
Map by Hope M. LeVan.

THE LAND

EUROPEAN ROOTS OF OLEY VALLEY SETTLERS

The migration of European people into the Oley Valley began in the first years of the eighteenth century. By the onset of the American Revolution in 1775, settlers had transformed the valley from a sparsely inhabited, near-wilderness domain of the Lenni Lenape to one of prosperous farms, ironworks, mills, and craftsworks.

Predominant among the earliest arrivals in the valley were people of British, Swedish, and Netherlandic origin who had been born in America and who moved to the Oley Valley from earlier settled communities. German-speaking people, mostly recent immigrants from Europe, were soon present as well; in 1775 they would outnumber the other inhabitants of European origin by almost three to one.

Movement into the Oley Valley during the 1700s, whether from older American settlements or from across the Atlantic, was one small current in a vast and complex pattern of migration among the peoples of northwestern Europe that went on through the seventeenth and eighteenth centuries. The motive of native-born, English-speaking Americans in coming to the valley was a simple search for economic opportunities that were lacking in their by then well-developed home places. Emigration from the German-speaking region of Europe was a somewhat more complicated matter.

The opening phase of German immigration to Pennsylvania (1683-1727) produced an irregular trickle of immigrants. This trickle did, however, produce the German-speaking pioneers who established the Pennsylvania German settlement of Oley Valley in the 1710s and 1720s. The majority of pre-1727 German immigrants to Pennsylvania were seekers of the religious freedom that had been offered to Germans by William Penn in 1681. Many migrants were sectarians, such as the Mennonites, shedding the oppressive rule of Lutheran or Reformed princes. Some were members of visionary and pietist groups. A few were "church people" (i.e., members of the Lutheran or Reformed churches), fleeing persecution by rulers of other persuasions. What is now called Germany was not a sovereign nation during this period. It was a collection of hundreds of principalities and city-states of widely varying size, most of them petty sovereignties within the Holy Roman Empire.

Germany had been in a state of tumult ever since the outbreak of the Thirty Years' War in 1618. By the cessation of that dreadful conflict, waged largely on German soil, war and famine had reduced the German population about one-third. Particularly hard hit was the Rhineland (a region, not a political entity), which would emerge as the major source region of German emigration to Pennsylvania. The Palatinate, the largest polity of the Rhineland, alone would contribute about half the German emigrants to Penn's colony. In the aftermath of the great war the Rhineland states invited Protestant settlers from France, Alsace, and Switzerland to relocate and to help rebuild the area from the devastation of the war. Swiss migrants became especially numerous, both among those who came into the region and among those who later left for the New World. During the late 1600s and early 1700s, unfortunately, the people of the Rhineland were beset by repeated French invasions, domestic religious oppression, and an intermittent series of unusually severe winters that led to famine. These were encouragements to emigrate, but restrictions on such movement, imposed by rulers fearing renewed depopulation, kept the number of departures from 1683 to 1727 at a generally low rate.

The movement of Swiss, Alsatian, and French families into the Rhineland, where they mingled and intermarried with the Rhinelanders and with one another for the space of a generation or so before making the move to Pennsylvania, made the region somewhat a staging area for European emigration to America. This melding imparted a rich mixture of cultural influences to those who made the transatlantic voyage.

The years from 1727 to 1775 saw massive emigration by German-speaking people to Pennsylvania. Those German settlements already established in Penn's province were inundated by waves of countrymen who went on to expand the area of predominantly German population far beyond its 1727 extent. Most of these arrivals were "church people" (i.e., adherents of the Lutheran and Reformed or Calvinist faiths), not sectarians. Lack of religious freedom in Germany, though hardly absent from the roster of emigrants' complaints, was no longer a significant motive in emigration. The continued warfare in Germany and general governmental oppression do appear to have been factors encouraging emigration, but the most significant force driving the mass movement was an economic one. The Rhineland and adjoining areas now were crowded, with a resulting constriction of opportunity for most persons. Recognizing the overpopulation, rulers permitted more citizens to leave.

The volume and composition of German-speaking immigration to Pennsylvania varied during the great movement of 1727-1775. For the first two decades or so (1727-1748) the immigrants tended to be families traveling together, generally consisting of young or middle-aged parents with several children, the latter frequently adolescents or young adults. Historian Marianne Wokeck estimates the number of migrants at about one thousand per year.[1] Some families were able to bring significant resources with them to the new country. With or without funds for investment, the open American landscape provided opportunity for families with plenty of hands to work, and the German-speaking immigrants of this period tended to prosper.

The brief span of six years from the beginning of 1749 to the end of 1754 was the time of the most intense immigration, with the flow of humanity averaging nearly six thousand people per year. Particularly severe economic conditions in the German-speaking region pushed potential emigrants to leave. A specialized shipping business, consisting of several merchant firms operating in the port of Rotterdam in Holland, had grown up in response to the migration. These businessmen pulled potential emigrants to the embarkation port with offers of credit for the cost of the voyage. The credit often would have to be "redeemed" by a period of bound (unfree) labor in Pennsylvania. The migrants of the six peak years tended to be somewhat younger, poorer, and less often traveling in family groups than those who had gone before.

In 1755 the German-speaking migration fell off dramatically, due to disruption by the Seven Years' War (or French and Indian War, as generally known in

OLEY VALLEY HERITAGE

MOUNCE JONES HOUSE, 1716, Amity Township
An example of the hall-parlor type, the house is a property of the Historic Preservation Trust of Berks County, which has reclaimed Berks County's oldest known standing house from a state of ruin.
Photo by H. Winslow Fegley, 1911. Courtesy, Schwenkfelder Library.

MIGRATION OF SETTLERS INTO THE OLEY VALLEY

The European pioneers of the Oley Valley came in parties of varying size. Some settlers came as part of a large group consisting of two or more households with some preexisting relationship. The group members might be related to one another, or may have come from the same community. Settlers coming in this manner were a pivotal element in settlement. Their clusters of homesteads became nuclei around which other people located. Some people came as individual family households. Although settlers migrating in groups predominated in the first two decades, families arriving alone later came to outnumber the group members. Nuclear families often were accompanied by grown but unmarried siblings of one or both of the parents. In the early years few men and fewer women came unaccompanied. It took more than one pair of hands to get a farmstead going. But after 1750 lone laborers and indentured servants, people of little or no means, arrived in numbers.

Four significant groups of families, who settled together in the Oley Valley as virtual small self-contained communities, have been identified. The first to arrive consisted of some "Ancient Swedes" (as they called themselves) from the Philadelphia vicinity, descendants of the vanquished colonists of the New Sweden colony along the lower Delaware River Valley. The first of the Swedes, Magnus Jonasson (generally called Mounce Jones), settled by the Schuylkill River, in the southeastern part of the valley, by 1704. Jonasson stood at the center of the Swedish group of settlers, most of whose members were directly related to him by blood or marriage. These included the Yocom, Huling, and Lycon families.

America). In 1756 the migration practically ceased until the coming of peace in 1763. From the latter date until 1775 the migration continued, at the same rough average of a thousand people per year as had prevailed between 1727 and 1748. The participants in the late-colonial phase of the migration, however, were overwhelmingly young, single men and women of little or no means, bound to endure a term of servitude when they landed in the New World.

THE LAND

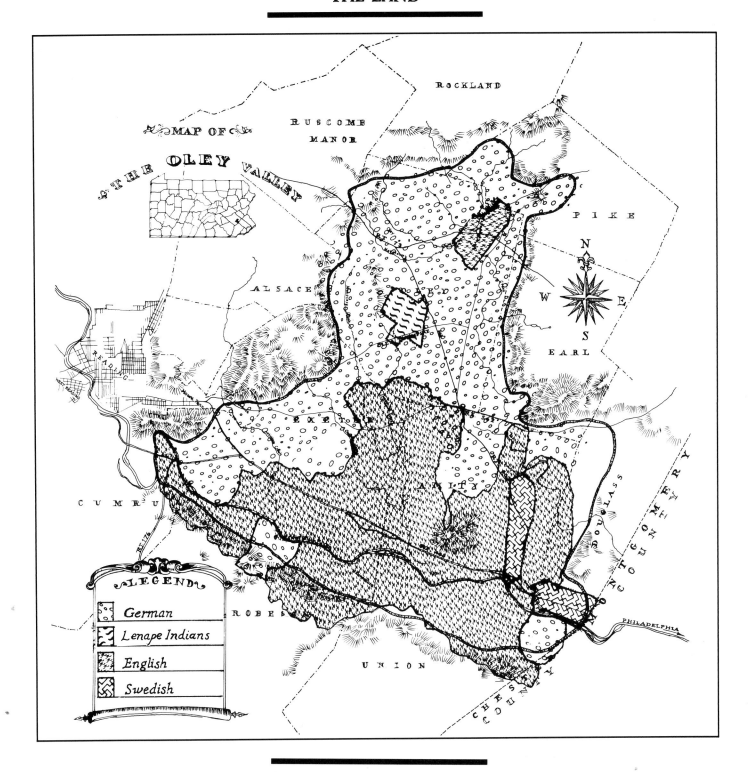

AREAS WITHIN THE OLEY VALLEY
Inhabited by the Various Nationality Groups, 1750
By this date the valley settlement was characterized by a limited degree of intermingling of the homesteads of the nationalities, a tendency not depicted in this generalized rendering.
Map by Hope M. LeVan, from computerized cartography by Petra Zimmermann and the G. I. S. Laboratory, Kutztown University, Kutztown, Pennsylvania.

OLEY VALLEY HERITAGE

CORNELIUS DEHART HOUSE (Darra House), Circa 1760, Enlarged Circa 1825-1850, Amity Township
The original section to the left, with intact pent roof and pent eaves, was constructed as an example of the stove-room type. The section to the right is representative of the four-over-four or Pennsylvania farmhouse type.
Photo by Philip E. Pendleton.

Magnus Jonasson and his wife Ingabo donated the land for Molatton Church (later Saint Gabriel's Church), which functioned between 1719 and 1753 as a sort of unofficially interdenominational congregation for Swedish Lutherans, German Lutherans, and Anglicans. An influential coparishioner and fellow member of the cluster of Swedish settlers was Andrew Robeson, a Scot whose wife Mary was a Delaware Valley Swede. Formerly the chief justice of the Supreme Court of the province of Pennsylvania, the wealthy Robeson moved to the southern Oley Valley in 1714. His evident intention was to provide a solid economic footing for his many offspring by participating in the early development of this promising new settlement.

By 1708 the Swedes had been joined in the Amity Township vicinity by the first elements of a migration from Monmouth County and neighboring areas of central New Jersey. These people included Netherlanders (i.e., from the Netherlands or Holland), Scots, and Anglo-Americans of New England heritage. Prominent in this group were the DeHart, Winter, Bord, Sadowski, Campbell, Warren, and Lincoln families.

The next significant group of settlers was a large group of acquainted or related families from the Palatinate, including some families of Swiss derivation and some of at least partial French extraction. The first of these people settled in the northern part of the Oley Valley by 1712. It is likely that most or perhaps all of these pioneers were members of the perfectionist "New Born" sect. Families constituting this large cluster of migrants, or who soon arrived and intermarried with them, appear to have included those of Baumann, Bertolet, Levan, DeTurk, Joder (spelled Yoder today), Kühlwein, Huffnagel, Schenkel, Keim, Schneider, Hoch (anglicized as High), Ballie, Peter, Herbein, Weber (anglicized as Weaver), Kersten (later shortened to Kerst), Aschmann, Ritter, and Kauffmann.[2] The presence of the French families (and exaggeration of the proportion of French ancestry among the people) has led over the years to frequent reference to this group of settlers as the "Oley Huguenots."

Quaker families from Gwynedd and Abington meetings outside Philadelphia, led by the Boone family, composed the last of the four identified settler groups. They began arriving in 1718, choosing to settle along Monocacy Creek, below the Oley Valley proper. The Welsh families of Hughes and Ellis were also prominent in this group.

To say that each of these groups of people "came to the valley together" is actually an oversimplification. It is unlikely that in any of these four cases all the households arrived as one great unit. Instead, just a few households came at first, to be joined later by others from the home vicinity, drawn by the pioneers' reports. Although the first members of the New Jersey group arrived by 1708, others from the same vicinity came as late as 1729, possibly later. This phenomenon of people coming much later to join friends or relations already established was probably equally common in regard to families that settled in the valley. Pierre Bertolet, for example, settled in Oley about 1720.

THE LAND

MORDECAI LINCOLN HOUSE, 1733, Enlarged Circa 1760, Exeter Township
A frontal view. The addition, similar in plan to the original section, is to the left.
Photo by Philip E. Pendleton.

JOHANNES JODER HOUSE, 1741, Enlarged 1782 and Circa 1820, Oley Township
The west wing, the lower structure to the right, of two-story double-cell plan, was added in 1741. The center section (the three rightmost bays on the larger block) was rebuilt in 1782; its foundation antedates 1741, and thus represents the oldest surviving part of the building. "Bay," a useful term for describing a building, refers to a spatial unit on the facade as defined by a window or door opening.
Photo by Kenneth LeVan.

OLEY VALLEY HERITAGE

MAUGRIDGE-DETURK HOUSE (Daniel Boone Homestead), Circa 1752-1755, Enlarged Circa 1770-1775, Exeter Township The architectural centerpiece of the Daniel Boone Homestead State Historic Site. The four-bay main section, to the right, was built on a hall-parlor plan by William Maugridge, as an addition to a much smaller house. The earlier dwelling had been constructed for Squire Boone circa 1730, probably of log. When Johannes DeTurk, Jr., rebuilt the section to the left circa 1770-1775, he made use of Boone's foundation. DeTurk also installed a German jamb-stove arrangement.
Photo by Cervin Robinson, 1958. Courtesy, The Historic American Buildings Survey, Prints and Photographs Division, Library of Congress.

Six years later his brother Jean arrived with his family and purchased a homestead not far from that of Pierre.

Other early settlers of the valley, however, regarding their making the move to Oley, do not appear to have been associated with any of the four major groups named above. Many families came entirely on their own. Sometimes just two or three related or acquainted families settled together. Johann Jacob Rodt and Johann Theodorick Greiner arrived in Amity Township from Bonfeld (a village in the Palatinate) in 1717. As far as is known, Rodt and Greiner were friends, not relatives. They pooled their money and bought a three-hundred-acre tract straddling Manatawny Creek from English settler Henry Gibson, comprising the back acreage of Gibson's five-hundred-acre property. They then parted their new estate, employing the creek as their division line.

A variation on the small knot of families that came together was the family that comprised a virtual clan, with several related households settling next to each other. An example is the extended family of Quaker ironmaster Thomas Rutter, who came to the valley in 1715 to establish Pine Forge, Pennsylvania's first ironworks. Although Rutter probably had the capital to bring along some skilled English ironworkers, it is possible that he, his three sons Thomas, Joseph, and John, and his son-in-law Samuel Savage furnished most of the necessary mine, forest, and forge labor during the initial, experimental years.

THE OLEY HUGUENOTS

Isaac DeTurk, along with Jean LeDee (both came to Oley about 1709-1712), Pierre Bertolet (came by 1720), Jean Bertolet (1726), Abraham Levan (by 1727), and Isaac Levan (by 1730), composed the original "Oley Huguenots," early settlers of French Protestant heri-

THE LAND

tage celebrated in local legend. The Bertolet family originated in the French-speaking part of Switzerland, and so would not, strictly speaking, be considered Huguenots by scholars of the French Calvinist movement. The place of origin in France for the other families is not known. The echo of Near Eastern regions in the names DeTurk and Levant (as the name Levan was spelled in early Pennsylvania documents) raises the possibility that these families had earlier been engaged in trade between France and the Near East. The French merchant class contributed disproportionately to the ranks of the French Huguenots. These families had been living in Germany for varying lengths of time before coming to Pennsylvania, germanizing to some extent via marriage and cultural assimilation. Family members called themselves "Huguenots" in the early nineteenth century, however, and elderly ones recalled that their parents had spoken French in the home. The name Levant was modified to Levan during the eighteenth century.

The preacher George DeBenneville was born in England to parents who were French Protestant refugees. Possible additional Oley Valley families of French origin include those of DelaPlank (often shortened to DePlank or Plank), Ballie, Barto, Herbein, Huyet, and Lebo. The valley families of Fischer, Keim, and Schneider may have originated in Alsace. The Alsatians of about 1700 were not "Frenchmen." Although always open to some French cultural influence, the Alsatians were the German-speaking inhabitants of their own independent state until its conquest by the French king Louis XIV in 1681. In subsequent years many Protestant Alsatians left the province to take refuge in other parts of the German-speaking region, and eventually Pennsylvania. The number of early Oley settlers who were of French or Alsatian extraction appears to have been greatly exaggerated by early twentieth-century antiquarians in reaction to the then prevalent anti-Kaiser sentiment.

ABRAHAM LEVAN HOUSE, Circa 1753, Oley Township
A large, steep-roofed example of the stove-room type.
Photo by Robert C. Bucher, 1962. Courtesy, Robert C. Bucher.

OLEY VALLEY HERITAGE

PETER BALLIE HOUSE, Circa 1725-1742, Oley Township
Front and rear views. This evident early house, built by Peter Ballie as his primary dwelling, exhibits the bank siting and independent access to cellar characteristic of the Pennsylvania German ancillary house. The leftmost bay on the frontal view represents a later addition, as does the rear lean-to structure. The original first-floor plan was a two-room version of the stove-room type. The board-sheathed gable end, similar to those in log-constructed buildings but unknown in other stone Oley Valley buildings, would seem to be evidence of an early date. Surprisingly, some years ago this structure was incorporated into that of a larger modern house.
Photos by G. Edwin Brumbaugh, circa 1931. Courtesy, The Winterthur Library: Joseph Downs Collection of Manuscripts and Printed Ephemera.

THE LAND

PATTERNS OF SETTLEMENT

Settlement did not develop throughout the valley at a uniform rate. Some places drew the attention of settlers and land dealers before others. The upper valley, with its fertile limestone soil, was an early target for both German and English people, though a large centrally positioned area of the upper valley remained vacant of European homesteads longer than adjacent areas. The acquisition of the finest soil was not the highest priority for every early settler when selecting a homestead site. Other attributes that attracted early occupation included waterpower potential, adjacency to the Schuylkill River (ensuring access to transportation before the creation of a decent system of roads), and immediate security of title. The latter quality could be obtained by buying land in Amity Township, which originated as one large property called the Swedes' Tract. The entire township was granted by William Penn to a group of Delaware Valley Swedes, most of whom sold their land in turn rather than settling it themselves. Due to the presence of these beneficial features, lands along the Schuylkill, along Monocacy Creek, and in Amity were settled concurrently with the more fertile upper valley in the 1710s and 1720s. Most of the western arm of the lower valley, however, located in modern Exeter Township, awaited claiming until the 1730s.

As the settlement of the Oley Valley proceeded, neighborhoods formed according to nationality. The English-speaking settlers, including the Swedes, concentrated in the less fertile lower valley. The Germans started out as the minority among the valley's inhabitants, but by 1750 they had become the larger of the two main groups of colonists. They fanned out all over the valley, their homesteads eventually mingling with those of the English to some extent. The nationalities' differing patterns of settlement had little to do with preferences for types of soil, as some historians have suggested.[3] The pattern evolved as it did due to the selection of sites made by certain influential early-arrived English-speaking families, namely the Jonassons (or Joneses, as they became known) and the Boones. As the first Europeans to settle, the Jonassons chose land on the Schuylkill at the valley's southeastern entrance. Meanwhile the entrepreneurially inclined Boones selected a chain of potential waterpower sites along Monocacy Creek

JACOB KAUFFMANN HOUSE, 1766, Oley Township
A large and relatively late embodiment of the stove-room type. The house is especially noteworthy for its lack of alteration within. The wing partially visible to the left was constructed in the nineteenth century.
Photo by Cervin Robinson, 1958. Courtesy, The Historic American Buildings Survey, Prints and Photographs Division, Library of Congress.

OLEY VALLEY HERITAGE

JOSEPH BOONE HOUSE, 1765, Amity Township
With its cut-stone principal facade, this is a particularly refined example of the double-parlor house type, even without its original pent roof. The absence of the pent is marked by the belt of rubble stonework.
Photo by Philip E. Pendleton.

suitable for mills and tanyards. The bailiwicks of the Jones and Boone families became the foci of settlement by English-speaking people, a trend strongly reinforced by these families' patronage of the local congregations of the Church of Sweden and of the Society of Friends, respectively. Magnus (or Mounce) and Ingabo Jonasson donated, around 1719, the land for Molatton Church (today Saint Gabriel's Protestant Episcopal Church), a congregation in which Anglicans, Swedish Lutherans, and German Lutherans cooperated. The Boones began holding Quaker worship in their homes around 1721, and George, Jr., and Deborah Boone gave the land for a meetinghouse in 1726.

The homestead sites selected by individual Anglo-Pennsylvanian settlers who came to the valley before the Boones and before the founding of Molatton Church disprove the idea of a unique Germanic preference for limestone-based soil. Anthony Lee, Benjamin Longworthy, and Owen Richard chose fine locations in the fertile northern valley. Conversely, the red shale soil of central and western Exeter Township did not prevent Germans from dominating settlement there, when development of that area began in the 1730s. These German homesteaders could have pressed on to limestone-based lands in distant valleys. But after all, though limestone soil may have been superior, Oley Valley farmers living on shale tended to prosper.

CLAIMING LAND

Having selected and occupied land, the securement of legal title to it became an important priority for Oley Valley settlers. To obtain ownership, settlers had to purchase either from the proprietary land office (Pennsylvania being the domain of William Penn's family) or from a wealthy land dealer.

The conditions stipulated for the purchase of land from the proprietors were not onerous, if the land office was operating. A downpayment of just half the purchase price was required to secure an official claim, which half-interest was henceforth a legal claim and one's transferable and heritable estate. Unfortunately, however, the land office was virtually inoperative from 1720 to 1733, years during which many migrants came to the Oley Valley in search of land. The reason for the hiatus was a protracted legal struggle between the children of the deceased William Penn by his first wife and those by his second wife as to who had the rights to Pennsylvania. Land office officials accepted payment for land claimed before 1720, but could not authorize the making of new claims.

One effect of the impasse was a more marked tendency toward squatting during

THE LAND

these years. The practice of homesteading without any legal title for a few years was very common throughout the colonial period. This can be seen by comparing the dates of land purchase by settlers to other documentary evidence of their presence in the valley (church records, road and township petitions, etc.). Squatting was at its most common and protracted between 1720 and 1733. Jacob DelaPlank, for one, passed that entire thirteen-year period on his Oley homestead before initiating its purchase.

The solution adopted by many settlers concerned to establish legal title, was to strike a bargain with a land dealer. Floating about the coffers of the wealthier denizens of Philadelphia and vicinity were large allotments of "First Purchase rights." In 1682 William Penn had desired to encourage Englishmen of substantial means to settle themselves in his province, or to recruit reliable yeomen to do so. He sold, cheaply, rights to claim given amounts of land, sight unseen, anywhere in Pennsylvania. These "plots" tended to be of a size that would have conferred extensive estates, one thousand or two thousand acres in individual purchases. Some First Purchase land was claimed and settled in the 1680s by the actual purchasers, in the Philadelphia area. More often, however, holdings of First Purchase rights encompassing thousands of unplotted acres remained unsurveyed for decades, traded or bequeathed through a variety of successive hands. As happened with so many aspects of Penn's plan for his province, the First Purchase program did not work out as he had envisioned. Many of the rights were bought up by well-placed speculators. But since in the 1720s prices for rights were still reasonable, and arrangements to extend payment of the purchase price over time could be arranged, many pioneers were afforded the opportunity for land ownership who would otherwise have been left out.

Between 1725 and 1732 thirty-two Oley Valley settlers were able to establish some measure of land ownership via First Purchase rights. Sometimes the settler approached the grandee holding the rights, as happened between Johannes Joder, Jr., and James Logan, the proprietary secretary, in 1732. Other times, the land dealer took the initiative, as when Chief Justice William Allen used rights to claim a fourteen-hundred-acre tract in the Schwarzwald vicinity in 1730. He found nine nascent "Palatine" homesteads established on this land and struck deals with all the settlers, often for purchase over time. The last two settler families to pay off Allen did so in 1763.

A few wealthy land speculators invested in large tracts of Oley Valley land, generally over four hundred acres, to hold for the long term, for eventual resale or as tenant farms. The last of these tracts was broken up and sold in pieces to local residents in 1769.

In Amity Township the process of land acquisition diverged somewhat from the above-described methods. William Penn's ten-thousand-acre grant of 1701 to a group of Delaware Valley Swedes represented an effort to mollify the Swedish community over unfair treatment by Penn's land officials. Only one of the seventeen beneficiaries actually settled there, Magnus Jonasson (or Mounce Jones), though with a handful of near relations he established the small Swedish settlement. The great majority of Swedes' Tract land passed through the hands of a dizzying succession of land dealers. Some of these were Philadelphians, but many were New England Yankees residing on Long Island and in east-central New Jersey. It was the interest of this latter group that led to the migration of New Jersey people, one of the four known large contingents of settlers. Some Yankee purchasers were probably parents or grandparents of migrants who had bought the land to provide for their progeny.

RELATIONS BETWEEN THE SETTLERS AND THE LENAPE INDIANS

The Oley Valley had been a place of human habitation long before the European settlers made their appearance in the early 1700s. The valley was within the domain of the Delaware or Lenape Indians, the "original people," an English phrase giving the meaning of their name. The number of the Indians living there in 1700 is unknown, but it is likely to have been quite small. The Lenape were a hunting-and-gathering people, organized in territorial bands averaging twenty-five to thirty adults and children. Each band ranged over one of the valleys (such as the Oley Valley) aligned along the tributary streams that fed the Schuylkill and Delaware rivers. Home was a village, the location of which would be moved a few miles every so often, as much-used resources such as firewood were depleted within a near radius. In the summer a plot of maize at the village would be planted, cultivated, and harvested; the rest of the diet consisted of small game, fish, shellfish, and wild plant life.[4]

Dr. Peter G. Bertolet, an 1850s Oley antiquarian and a pioneer in oral history, recorded the reminiscences of his great-grandmother Esther DeTurk Bertolet (1711-1798) as conveyed by his father Daniel. Among these was Esther's account of the affecting vista created by the Lenape in burning off large expanses of the lower two-thirds of the bowl-shaped northern valley to kill saplings so that the area would retain its attraction for game animals and birds. The latter preferred meadowlands to deep woods. The sight had apparently made quite an impression on the young child Esther. Peter Bertolet availed himself of a local physician's opportunity to interview many of the valley's elderly. According to the doctor, when pioneers began locating in the northern valley, around 1712, they found that the only forested areas within the limestone-based Oley Valley proper were its northern third and the lands lying close along the courses of the Manatawny and Monocacy creeks. The settlers, following the mode in early Pennsylvania to favor relatively low-lying, wet locations, chose to take up these wooded lands, leaving the natives their hunting ground for a decade or so. The accuracy of this account is borne out by the geographical sequence of settlement revealed in the records of the proprietary land office.

Another part of the valley that appears to have held some special significance for the Lenape was Molatton. The Swedes were evidently well-acquainted with this spot because it had been a meeting site for fur trading and negotiations between Swedes and Indians since the middle seventeenth century. In fact, the Lenape word *manatawny* translates as "where we drank" or "where we got drunk." Manatawny was the usual name applied to the Swedes' Tract and to the entire Oley Valley during the first two decades of settlement. The meaning of the word "Molatton" is unknown, though the "ton" could have stood for "town." Molatton continued to be the site of important meetings between local Lenape leaders and provincial officials through the first third of the eighteenth century.

The importance of their Oley home for the Lenape Indians is confirmed because a Lenape community continued to exist there, amidst the ever more numerous European homesteaders, for many decades longer than anywhere else in Berks County. The last Indian inhabitants did not depart the valley until the 1770s. Relations between the two peoples in the valley, though sometimes tense, were much better generally than elsewhere in the Thirteen Colonies, at least until 1754 (the outbreak of the French and Indian War). Many apocryphal anecdotes survive, testifying to a benevolent attitude toward the Lenape by the Swedes, Huguenots, and Quakers, and a reciprocal friendship felt by the Lenape. The above-mentioned Esther Bertolet was said by her grandson to have mastered the Lenape dialect as a child (about 1720) and to have formed several friendships with individual tribe members that she continued well into adulthood. A descendant of the Molatton Swedes named Holstein told the Philadelphia antiquarian John Fanning Watson in the early 1800s of his grandmother's recollections. Magdalena Hulings, born at Molatton around 1725, remembered that the Indians still lived in the vicinity during her girlhood, and that she had once "been carried some distance on a squaw's back."[5]

The only significant violence between Europeans and Indians in the area took place in the spring of 1728. The violence began when a small band of armed braves from outside the region, not Lenape, used threats to extort provisions at some valley farmsteads. The report of these encounters threw the settlers of the valley and adjoining areas into a panic. With impressive speed they gathered and barricaded themselves in a few of the more substantial homesteads. At Colebrookdale, to the east of Oley, a posse of settlers put the strangers to flight in a skirmish that wounded a few on both sides. A full-scale war pitting Indians against Europeans suddenly threatened when two hot-headed Anglo-Pennsylvanian pioneers at Cacoosing (up the Schuylkill some distance from the valley) slew an unsuspecting Lenape man and two women. Successful peace talks were quickly arranged, however, with the Cacoosing killers tried and hanged soon thereafter.

Study of early land records suggests that the local settlers and Indians reached a tacit accommodation around 1730 that reserved for the use and residence of the Lenape a small section of the northern valley. Charting the gradual march of land claims, one finds that an odd-shaped tract containing some eight hundred acres remained unclaimed until 1760. This land, fine valley-floor soil certainly superior to much land in Amity and Exeter townships settled by Europeans two decades earlier, lies just to the west of the modern intersection of Route 662 and the Oley Turnpike. It was this "reservation" that enabled a small band of Lenape to stay on in Oley in the midst of the growing white settlement. How this enclave managed to survive through a quarter century in the face of continued European arrivals probably will never be explained. Ethnohistorian Marshall J. Becker has identified a similar arrangement in the Ridley Creek vicinity of Chester County, where in 1703 the Okehocking band of Lenape was granted a tract of almost five hundred acres via the proprietary land office, which they then occupied until the early 1730s.[6] The Oley Lenape are said to have adopted European ways to some limited extent. Hunting in the old manner may not have been possible on their limited turf. Dr. Bertolet recounts that one sign of Lenape favor to a settler was an invitation to join the tribe on one of their hunting expeditions over the Blue Mountain (the front ridge of the Appalachians in this region).

The coming of the French and Indian War (1754-1763), the final one in the long series of Anglo-French imperial conflicts in North America but the first to bloody Penn's Quaker colony, spelled the end for the Oley Indians' precarious hold on a piece of their old domain. His elderly informants told Peter Bertolet that, one morning in the war years, the white inhabitants awakened to find that the tribe had disappeared.

The Lenape Indians of Oley would have had plenty of reason to decide at some point that a sudden departure was in order. In 1755 members of other tribes, allied to the French, began launching attacks on the Pennsylvania frontier. The targets included farmsteads along the base of the Blue Mountain in Berks County, where over the war years about a hundred settlers were massacred or carried off. A panic spread across the province, engendering in many Pennsylvanians a hostility to all Indian tribes. In Berks County even the leading officials, who seem to have been generally level-headed men, became so alarmed that at one point they considered imprisoning the innocent German Jesuit missionaries who worked out of Goshenhoppen. They thought the Catholic priests must be French spies and agitators. Considering the massacres of peaceful christianized groups of Indians (men, women, and children) perpetrated by Pennsylvania frontiersmen at Lancaster in 1763 and at Gnadenhütten in 1782, the Oley Indians' decision to leave was a prudent course of action. Oley legend has it that a few of the local Lenape men fought as French auxiliaries. At least three young valley residents (Samuel Joder, Benjamin Millard, and Moses Webb) served with Pennsylvania's provincial regulars.

In 1760 the vacant eight-hundred-acre sanctuary of the Oley Lenape was claimed by the Pennsylvania Land Company in London, then in the process of dissolution. This languishing British corporation, generally referred to by contemporaries as "the London Company," took up the abandoned tract in order to spend the residue of land rights it had purchased from William Penn in 1699. Within three years the land was all in settlers' hands.

But the saga of the Oley Indians was not over. A few tribe members returned following the cessation of hostilities, but with their enclave now farmed by German colonists, things could not be the same. Relations in the interim between the French and Indian War and the War of Independence were always tense. There was enough contact for one of Dr. Bertolet's great-aunts, born about 1749, to learn to speak the Lenape dialect well. But another of the antiquarian's patients, a Widow Schlutman born about 1768, told him that when she was a little girl and the Indians came to her father's house selling blankets, she was afraid of them. Bertolet, writing in 1860, locates four tribal habitation sites indicated to him by

THE LAND

contemporary farmers and still traceable then. These places were in the northwest corner of the upper valley, and along its eastern side, at the foot of the surrounding hills. The sites appeared to have been minor ones each occupied by one or two households. The settlers on whose properties these dwellings were located chose to keep the peace.

The Lenape returnees grew a few acres of crops and made baskets that they sold to their white neighbors for petty cash and provisions. The greater degree of economic dependence on the Europeans that the tribe now experienced grated on them. For their part the German and English residents were just then enjoying new heights of prosperity from the flowering of the Pennsylvania wheat export economy. According to Bertolet, the Indians drank much more than formerly, and some ugly incidents nearly occurred when they pressed baskets on reluctant purchasers. The last of the Oley Indians departed their traditional home during the War of Independence. At that time raids by hostile tribes allied to the British again made the safety of the remnant Lenape population precarious.

NOTES

[1] The account of colonial-period German-speaking immigration to Pennsylvania presented here is based largely on Marianne Sophia Wokeck, "The Flow and Composition of German Immigration to Philadelphia, 1727-1775," *Pennsylvania Magazine of History and Biography* 105 (1981): 249-78; and Wokeck, "A Tide of Alien Tongues: The Flow and Ebb of German Immigration to Pennsylvania, 1683-1776" (Ph.D. diss., Temple University, 1983).

[2] To this list might be added the names Griesemer and Reiff. Caspar Griesemer and Conrad Reiff wed Rebecca Aschmann and Maria Kühlwein, respectively, daughters in Oley "founding families" whose second generations lacked sons. By so doing, Griesemer and Reiff succeeded to the Aschmann and Kühlwein landholdings, and started lines that have long been numbered among Oley Township's most prominent families.

[3] See James T. Lemon, *The Best Poor Man's Country: A Geographical Account of Early Southeastern Pennsylvania* (Baltimore: The Johns Hopkins University Press, 1972), 63 and Fn. 69 (pp. 247-48), for references to late-nineteenth- and early-twentieth-century works positing a uniquely German affinity for limestone-based soil.

[4] The account of Lenape Indian life presented here is based on Marshall J. Becker, "Search for the Lenape Indians," *Archaeology* 35, no. 3 (May 1982): 10-19; Becker, "The Okehocking Band of Lenape: Cultural Continuities and Accommodations in Southeastern Pennsylvania," in *Strategies for Survival: American Indians in the Eastern United States*, ed. Frank W. Porter III (New York, Greenwood Press, 1986), 43-83; and Becker, "A Summary of Lenape Socio-Political Organization and Settlement Pattern at the Time of European Contact: The Evidence for Collecting Bands," *Journal of Middle Atlantic Archaeology* 4 (1988): 79-83.

[5] Israel Daniel Rupp, *History of the Counties of Berks and Lebanon* (Lancaster: G. Hills, 1844), 82.

[6] Becker, "The Okehocking Band of Lenape."

OLEY VALLEY BARN, NINETEENTH CENTURY, Exeter Township.
Located on the Daniel Boone Homestead, the structure is typical of the forebay barns that became common after the colonial period.
Photo by James Lewars.

Chapter 2

THE ECONOMY

AGRICULTURAL SYSTEM BASED ON WHEAT

By the end of the colonial period (1775), the Oley Valley had become a prosperous place by the standards of the Western world. Oley was singled out by observers in the period for its pronounced abundance, but southeastern Pennsylvania as a whole was considered a noteworthy economic success. This bounty was due to the production of huge quantities of wheat. Although the economic story of colonial Pennsylvania includes other factors, for instance, the well-known charcoal iron industry, wheat was the basis for Pennsylvania's dramatic economic growth and relatively high standard of living. As early as 1685, merchants in the nascent city of Philadelphia had recognized that wheat would be the key to prosperity for the region. They began organizing shipment of Pennsylvania farmers' surplus grain to the Caribbean the following year.[1]

The "wheat boom" began to build around 1730, accelerated in the late 1740s, and reached a peak in the late 1760s. This pace was maintained through the last few years before the Revolution. In 1770 wheat accounted for 69 percent of the value of the province's exports, with at least a third of the province's wheat crop sent abroad.[2] Bread made with flour from "Penn's Woods" fed people in New England fishing towns, Caribbean sugar plantations, the elegant townhouses and slum hovels of London, and Spanish villages. Pennsylvania had fertile soil, adequate rainfall and a temperate climate ideally suited to growing this crop. The rolling nature of the topography, combined with the many streams, provided abundant sites for gristmills that derived their power from falling water. Nowhere in Pennsylvania were these attributes more evident than in the Oley Valley.

Agricultural techniques did not change greatly during the colonial period. Most tools—the sickle, the scythe and so on—took the same forms they had for centuries past in Europe, whether or not the immigrant had ever used them in the homeland. Also seemingly immutable were most farmers' economic goals and the central role of wheat in the Pennsylvania agricultural system. Rye and other lesser grain crops, livestock, orchards, gardens, and flax patches ensured that the farmer's family ate and was clothed. The profits made from the sale of large wheat surpluses would enable the purchase and development of new homesteads, whether in Oley or in some distant place, so that the farmer's children might also live the life of the autonomous freeholder. Local economic life became increasingly complex as the years passed. Ever more artisans and tradespeople were present in the valley to provide useful services and goods conducive to a greater level of creature comfort for most residents. But

OLEY VALLEY FARMLANDS, 1994
The Oley Valley is still an area of working farms. This view, facing South, shows lush cornfields in October, 1994.
Photo by Jerry Orabona.

29

OLEY VALLEY HERITAGE

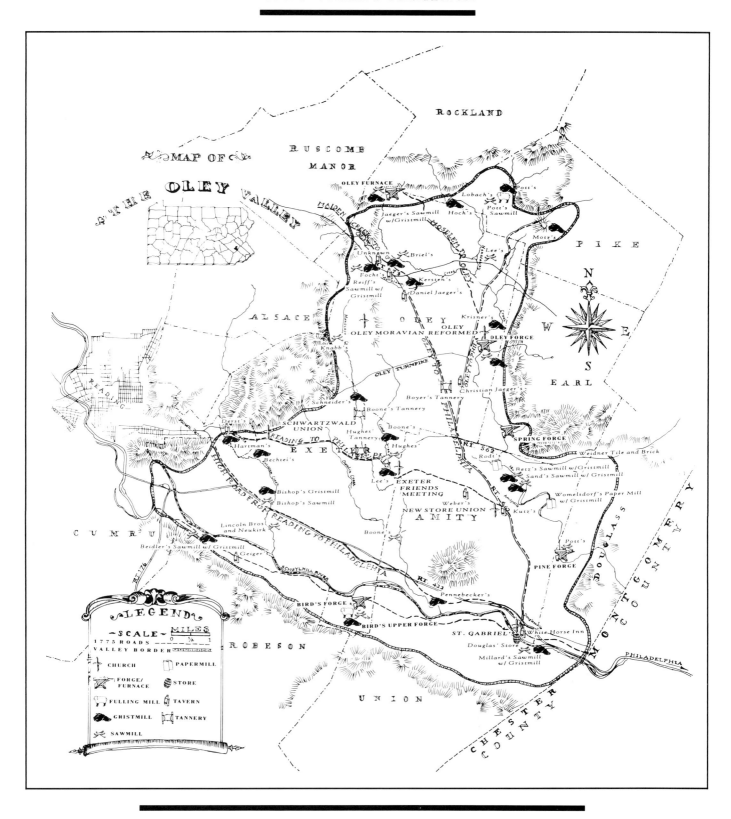

THE OLEY VALLEY SETTLEMENT, 1775
Roads, businesses, and the locations of religious congregations. The valley settlement's process of development is represented by stages (delineated for the years 1725 and 1750 as well as 1775) in the more detailed maps that are presented in Appendix 8. The latter maps, which chart all the properties in the valley in addition to settlement features such as roads and businesses, are accompanied by a brief narrative account of the settlement's development.
Map by Hope M. LeVan, from computerized cartography by Petra Zimmermann and the G. I. S. Laboratory, Kutztown University, Kutztown, Pennsylvania.

THE ECONOMY

the making of money for money's sake does not seem to have been a goal for more than a few people. Success meant the creation and perpetuation of a family legacy. This legacy was embodied in a well-developed and well-tended principal homestead capped by a two-story stone "mansion house" and in the thriving homesteads of one's offspring. For the farmers who made up the majority of the Oley Valley's inhabitants, wheat was the key to this success.

The southeastern Pennsylvania agricultural system consisted of growing wheat destined for the international market, while raising a variety of farm commodities for one's own subsistence and a limited local market. It is likely that this agricultural system worked as a major cultural influence. It induced European settlers to adopt and develop American farming methods. They often had to forsake the familiar commodities and practices that in Europe had provided their livelihood. For example, the production of wine was a major element in the agriculture of the Rhine Valley from whence so many of the German inhabitants had come. Jacob Weber, who settled in Amity Township around 1712, had his occupation in Germany referred to in a list of emigrants made in 1709 as that of "husbandman and vineyardist,"[3] as did many others on the list. If Weber and others tried to make wine in the Oley Valley, the experiment evidently failed; no documentary evidence of winemaking activity has survived. "The Germans who have emigrated to America mourn after the good things they have lost by doing so, especially the Württemberger and the Rhinelander who miss the noble juice of the grape,"[4] noted the somewhat jaundiced commentator Gottlieb Mittelberger in an account of Pennsylvania he published in 1756, after returning permanently to the homeland. The organist-schoolmaster had resided at Trappe, in New Providence Township about twelve miles southeast of the Oley Valley during the years 1750-1754.

Many British immigrants to Pennsylvania made a similar agricultural transition. Grain cultivation, especially that of wheat, was not widely practiced in the highland topographical region that extends the length of the western half of the island of Great Britain, including Wales. Most English-speaking families who settled in the Oley Valley had adopted the wheat-dominated Pennsylvania agricultural mode while living in the earlier-occupied region of the province closer to the Delaware River. Still, early Welsh-Pennsylvanian settlers, such as valley residents Ellis Hughes, David Harry, Owen Richard, and Thomas Ellis, had been raised amidst the hill country of North Wales. The agricultural environment of their childhood had been focused on livestock raising, not on the wheat that they and other Oley people proceeded to make the main target of their farming energies.

This dominant and pervasive wheat-dominated mode of agriculture probably facilitated communication among the different settler nationality groups. Farming methods, the state of each other's crops and herds, market prices, and the weather became common concerns. After a few years in the Oley Valley, the German, Welsh, Swedish, Swiss, and English farmers could speak a common agricultural language.

Estate inventories and other documents show that this mixed but wheat-dominated agricultural system was practiced by practically all of the farmers in the valley, whether they were German, English, or members of another national group, whether they lived in the especially fertile upper valley or in the lower valley, whether they were landowners or tenants, or whether they were full-time farmers or craftspeople who farmed on the side. This was true throughout the era, from the time the first settlers were able to raise a marketable surplus, to the onset of the Revolution. The different soils of the neighborhoods in the valley (limestone in the bowl-shaped "Oley Valley proper," red shale in the lower valley) appear to have had little or no impact on the emphasis in farming chosen by individual farmers. The effect of geology was just that farmers on the superior limestone soil tended to fare better.

Wheat took up the major share of the planted acreage on a farm (or "plantation," as any Pennsylvania farm generally was referred to in the discourse of the period) in any given year. Most grain crops resembled those of Nicolaus Foos, 1764, with twenty-two acres of wheat and eleven acres of rye; Abijah Sands, 1769, with sixteen acres of wheat, six acres of rye and one-and-a-half acres of spelt (a German cereal known to Anglo-Pennsylvanians as "German wheat"); and Samuel Joder, 1771, with seventeen acres of wheat and nine acres of rye, barley, and spelt. Overall, grain crops raised by full-time farmers ranged from twenty to thirty-five acres planted. The number of acres apparently was dependent on the size of the farm, the amount of cleared land on it, and the labor the farmer could muster.

The price of wheat made it an attractive commodity. This price was subject to market fluctuations, but throughout the period the men appraising estates assigned wheat a value a good deal higher than that of other grains. The grain growing in Nicolaus Foos's fields in 1764 was worth 15s. per acre for wheat, 10s. per acre for rye. The price of wheat moved upward over the colonial period, and the price margin of wheat increased over other grains. The representative sample below shows prices assigned to cleaned grain in estate inventories:

1743 Peter   Wheat: 2 s., 7 d. per bu.
     Ballie Rye: 2 s. per bu.
             Oats: 1 s., 4 d. per bu.
             (Wheat worth 29 percent more than rye)

1762 Samuel Wheat: 4 s., 3 d. per bu.
     Hoch   Rye: 3 s., 3 d. per bu.
             Oats: 2 s. per bu.
             (Wheat worth 28 percent more than rye)

1771 Abraham Wheat: 6 s. per bu.
     Peter   Rye: 3 s., 9 d. per bu.
             Oats: 2 s. per bu.
             (Wheat worth 60 percent more than rye)

The vitality of the wheat-and-flour trade was at a truly flourishing level during the late 1760s and early 1770s, the culmination of the colonial period.

Farmers did not just accept the going price at the nearest merchant flour mill. They sought the best price, consulting one another, millers (of course), Philadelphia newspapers, and the talk at inns or taverns in their neighborhood. In his will made in 1757, wealthy farmer Hans Mirtel Gerick directed that his son Jerg and his son-in-law Heinrich Kerst divide the grain then growing in Gerick's fields (some thirty acres of wheat and rye). Father Gerick charged Jerg with assisting Kerst in getting the latter's portion "to the best market."[5]

OLEY VALLEY HERITAGE

AGRICULTURAL IMPLEMENTS

The common agricultural experience shared by German speakers and English speakers is reflected in the lists of farming utensils found in estate inventories. These same tools were evidently to be found on every farmstead, indicating little difference in basic methods:

Axes

Grubbing hoes (a heavy sort of hoe used for digging out stumps and roots, especially when clearing land)

Plows (horsedrawn implements with a large bladelike moldboard at the front and two long handles, used to break and turn over the soil)

Harrows (horsedrawn implements usually with an open triangular shape and fitted below with vertical teeth, drawn over plowed land to further break it and smooth it)

Sickles (sharply curved blades with short handles, used to reap grain, held with one hand)

Rakes (used to gather the reaped grain stalks)

Cutting boxes (boxes with holes and blades mounted inside, used to cut the stalk near the grain kernel prior to threshing)

Riddles (large, basket-like coarse sieves used to clean threshed grain)

Scythes (long, gently curved blades with long handles, used to cut grass in haymaking, held with two hands)

Pitchforks

Dung forks

Dung hooks

Flax brakes

Garden or weeding hoes

Shovels and spades

Threshing flails were curiously rare items in inventories. These simple tools were wooden clubs coupled to wooden handles with which the farmers literally threshed kernels of grain apart from the straw and chaff. They may have been considered too low in value to be worth listing specifically.

Inventories suggest that established methods prevailed throughout the valley and that those methods changed little over the colonial period. Few innovations appeared in the lists of implements possessed, but when they did, these new farming tools appeared at an almost equal rate among Germans and English. The one most frequently found, in thirty-five of the ninety evidently complete farm inventories recorded in the Oley Valley during the colonial years, was a hand-powered mechanical contrivance variously referred to as a "fan to clean corn," "windmill to clean corn," or "winnowing mill." It was used to improve on or to supplement the traditional method of winnowing, or cleaning threshed grain, which was to toss the kernels in the air on a slightly breezy day and catch them in a riddle. The large, boxlike winnowing mill had an opening on the top and one on the side. Within were a crank-operated fan and some sieves, and beneath was a removable drawer. The threshed kernels went in at the top, and fell through the draft from the fan, through the sieves and into the drawer. The first "fan to clean corn" appeared in the 1725 inventory of miller Johann Heinrich Kersten.

Other innovations in farming tools included fitting a plow with a plowshare (the cutting head of the moldboard) made of iron instead of the usual wood, and fitting harrows with iron teeth in place of traditional wooden ones. Iron-toothed harrows appeared in eleven of the ninety colonial farm inventories, beginning with that of Yankee farmer John Warren, Jr., in 1734. Only two estates included iron-shared plows, those of Quaker tanner John Hughes (1764) and German farmer Benjamin Huffnagel (1773). The inventory of German blacksmith Samuel Oyster (1767), however, mentioned an iron share he apparently had recently produced for sale.

Winnowing mills, iron plowshares, and iron harrow teeth were employed by some members of various groups, but one other innovation, the scythe with an attached wooden cradle, seems to have been accepted only by Germans. The scythe with cradle was used to reap oats and barley. The wooden cradle behind the scythe blade allowed the small-kerneled stalks of these grains to fall gently into neat rows. Less barley or oats was lost than when a sickle was used. The first cradled scythe recorded in the valley appeared in the probate inventory of Johannes Bishop in 1754. By the 1770s the cradled scythe appeared in most estate inventories of German farmers, but it was absent from those of English farmers. Thus the farming methods followed by the two main divisions of inhabitants were similar but not completely identical.

THE AGRICULTURAL YEAR

Agricultural life has always been characterized by its seasonality. The rhythm of grain cultivation and harvest was perhaps the strongest contributing element in the seasonal pattern. Wheat, the chief commercial crop, and rye, probably the most important for the family's own sustenance, were winter crops, meaning that they were planted in the autumn and matured over the winter months. Buckwheat, oats, Indian corn, barley, and spelt were summer crops. The agricultural year on the colonial Oley Valley farm might be said to have begun with the plowing and sowing of the wheat fields in September. Plowing was described by the Swedish clergyman Israel Acrelius in a book he wrote in 1759, upon his return to Sweden, about life in the Delaware Valley region.

> The plowman . . . throws up the field into high "lands," plowing first on the one side and then on the other side of a "land," so that the earth is thrown up high. Immediately before the plow, a pair of oxen draw, or a pair of horses, which are guided by some little boy either leading or riding on them.[6]

The workhorse was overwhelmingly the Oley farmer's choice for draft animal, as opposed to the ox. Among ninety farm inventories, only that of Jacob DelaPlank from 1760 listed oxen, seven of them, though John Warren, Jr.'s (1734) showed two ox yokes and an ox chain. Farmers generally had from two to four draft horses.

When the work of the plow was done, its place behind the team was taken by

THE ECONOMY

the harrow. "A pair of horses before the harrow," wrote Acrelius,

> and a boy on the horse's back, smooths the field into fine and even pieces without any great trouble. Sometimes two harrows are fastened together after the same team.[7]

Many farmers owned two harrows. When the field had been harrowed, the sowers broadcast the seed on the field by hand.

The wheat harvest took place in early July. "The stalk is cut just about half its length, so that the stubble is quite high," noted Acrelius. Stalks of wheat were tied together in bundles called "sheaves." These were "short and small," according to the minister.[8] A dozen sheaves were stacked together to make a "shock." The shocks of wheat went from the field to the stackyard and eventually inside a barn or another building, slowly drying to a state appropriate for threshing.

The participants at harvest included all capable family members (male and female, adult and child), whatever servants the family had, and laborers hired for the occasion, if taking on extra help was judged useful and could be afforded. Neighboring families might aid each other, "trading works" as it was called in early America, though there are no explicit references to this practice in valley sources. Harvest was likely the single most concentrated expenditure of effort put out during a year by a farmer and his household. "One week at harvest" was the labor required from Benjamin Boone's "negro man Dirk" in Boone's 1762 will, in return for a lifetime habitation on Boone's tract.[9] A week was probably the usual duration of this all-important event. Harvest's coming in early July ensured that reaping was hot work, requiring liquid refreshment. Observed Acrelius,

> The heaviest consumption [of rum] is in harvest-time, when the laborers most frequently take a sup, and then immediately a drink of water, from which the body performs its work more easily.[10]

It may have been slightly besotted hired reapers that provoked the wrath of Benjamin Boone's brother Joseph in 1754. The latter had to apologize to his fellow Quaker worshipers at Exeter Meeting. The minutes of Exeter Monthly Meeting for August of that year tell what happened:

> Joseph Boone has of late been too rash in expressing himself passionately, using unsavory words to some reapers in his son's fields last harvest.[11]

Threshing the wheat, separation of the grain kernel from the straw and chaff, took place over the winter months. This could be done by having draft horses tread on the grain or by threshing with the traditional flail. "Winnowing" (i.e., cleaning the grain) followed threshing. An examination of colonial-period farm inventories finds that proportions of wheat crops "on the stalk" or "in the straw" decrease, and those of wheat "threshed" or "cleaned" increase, over the months January through March. Once cleaned the wheat was ready for sale, whether to a local merchant miller or to one down the river, perhaps borne down the rock-bottomed and generally shallow Schuylkill on boats taking advantage of the spring freshets. The busy gristmills of southeastern Pennsylvania ground wheat into flour almost year-round, however, so the farmer might hold his cleaned wheat in his granary until he judged the time, and the price, to be right. From sowing to packing for sale, a crop of wheat was an investment that required a year and a half to mature.

Rye was the other winter grain. The seasonal rhythm of its cultivation was similar to that of wheat, except that rye was sown in November instead of September. Both winter grains were harvested in early July. Rye was the chief source of valley people's bread. Estate inventories suggest that this was just as true for the English inhabitants as it was for the Germans. Like the produce of herds, orchards, and gardens, rye was sold locally, providing food for landless laborers and those crafts- and tradespeople who did not run full-scale farms. An inventory made of George Anders's store at New Store (now Amityville) in 1752 included rye bread, already baked, worth 18 s., and rye meal valued at over £6, sizable sums.

Rye consumption in the Oley Valley did not take place in liquid form, meaning whiskey, during the years before independence. Whiskey's future role was filled by rum. Quantities of rum appeared in many inventories, including the three from the estates of inn- or tavernkeepers. Hard cider and imported wine also were present in the tavern inventories, the latter in smaller quantities than rum or cider.

The summer grains included oats, Indian corn, buckwheat, barley, and spelt. The first two appear to have been grown on all valley farms, the former to feed horses, the latter to feed all livestock. The settlers consumed little if any Indian corn or maize themselves, except perhaps in the initial stage of settlement, though it had been a mainstay for the region's Lenape Indians. Oats were sown in early March and reaped in July after the wheat and rye. The cultivation and harvesting of Indian corn was different from that of the European-derived grains. Seed was planted in individual "hills" in late April or early May, the strongest blades of the corn plant cut off for fodder in September, and the ears harvested by hand in late October.

In contrast to oats and Indian corn, buckwheat, barley, and spelt were not universally planted crops. Small fields of buckwheat were grown on most farms, sown in late July on freshly plowed ground from which the wheat and rye had just been reaped. It was harvested in early October. Some of the buckwheat became meal for the eternally popular morning repast of pancakes, some was turned into feed for hogs and fowl. Exeter farmer and justice of the peace William Maugridge sent buckwheat flour to the table of his friend Benjamin Franklin in 1765. "Speaking of buckwheat cakes, our good friend Mr. Maugridge has sent some of the best of the flour that I ever saw and we had them hot,"[12] wrote Franklin's wife Deborah to her husband, absent as colonial agent in England. Barley and spelt were less frequently encountered. The Oley Valley's meager production of barley may have been sold to breweries in Reading or Philadelphia as malt. No inventories reported beer; according to Acrelius, it was a beverage of townspeople. The estates of Martin Schenkel (1738) and Johann Dietrich Jungmann (1747) included small quantities of hops, and that of Abraham Peter (1771) listed seven bushels of malt. Spelt was grown in occasional small quantities by both English and Germans.

CARELESS HUSBANDRY

Modern historians concur with observers in the period that grain cultivators throughout Pennsylvania in the early to middle eighteenth century abused the land by the European standards of the time.[13] This appears to have been as true of the Germans as it was of the English, though after the War of Independence (1775-1783) Pennsylvania Germans may have led other groups in adopting more careful methods. Direct evidence is scant, but there is no reason to suppose that Oley Valley farmers were any less wasteful than those in other regions of the province during the first decades of settlement. Farmers working Pennsylvania land in the early 1700s have been condemned for several agricultural sins. They forsook the traditional European system of crop rotation, instead planting grain repeatedly on the same ground until the yield diminished to a discouraging level. The field would then be left fallow for perhaps five or seven years, with livestock grazing on it, after which it would be returned to cultivation (albeit with a diminished return in size of crop from that of former years). Farmers could have sustained or rebuilt the fertility of their crop lands to some extent by spreading the manure produced by their herds over it. But, at least until late in the colonial period, most farmers did not construct buildings to house their animals and thereby create an area where concentrated manure could be collected.

These careless habits of early Pennsylvania farmers should not come as any great surprise. Labor was generally scarce and hence expensive, and the clearing of the land was an arduous task, so why not get as much grain as possible out of a field for a few years? Moreover, the tracts claimed by pioneers tended to be large, two or three hundred acres. So, it must have seemed that one could always clear a new field when an old one was exhausted. If anything, the remarkable fertility by European standards of the fresh, heretofore uncultivated Pennsylvania soil, red shale and limestone, encouraged the tendency to milk the land for all it was worth. Many settlers who followed the general Pennsylvania immigrant's economic path, becoming grain farmers in Pennsylvania, had not had firsthand experience in grain cultivation back in Europe. Such people had not practiced "proper methods" on their own farms in the homeland. As for putting up structures to house animals, the services of building craftsmen were much more expensive than in Europe, due to the comparative scarcity of these and other artisans.

There is evidence to suggest that, in the middle eighteenth century, Oley Valley farmers began to take a more stewardly attitude regarding the natural assets of their farms. In this period observers such as Pehr Kalm and Israel Acrelius reported that on plantations in the earlier-settled regions by the Delaware River, the land had been thoroughly ruined by exhaustive exploitation. Farmers in backcountry districts like the Oley Valley had the opportunity to take notice of such conditions. Those on plantations settled early could no doubt have remarked on the deteriorated condition of some of their land. Farmer Johannes Geldbach prescribed crop rotation in his 1758 will. Geldbach bequeathed his son Jacob the family's two-hundred-acre homestead in Oley Township and his daughter Magdalena his adjoining but little-developed two-hundred-and-seventy-acre tract in Amity, on which "there is now a small tenement and some meadow ground cleared."[14] Until Magdalena married a suitable man, Jacob was permitted to use the Amity land as his own, but he had to maintain its fences and was restricted to plant only wheat, and to do so only once in four years on any given piece of ground. Similarly, beginning with Henry Gibson in 1754, some farmers directed in their wills that executors should take care to see that the timber on their plantations should be used conservatively. The demand for firewood and for building and fencing lumber was gradually denuding plantation woodlands.

Documents do not shed as much light on the question of conservation or waste of farmland as might be wished. It is difficult to perceive when and to what extent valley farmers began to shelter livestock in buildings, or to gather and spread manure. Dung forks and dung hooks first appeared in estate inventories in 1736 and were thereafter universal features of farm inventories, though on many homesteads the use of these implements may have been restricted to manuring the garden. In 1746, however, the Lutheran minister Heinrich Melchior Muhlenberg related the tale of a blasphemous Oley Township farmer who rebuffed a pious man in search of a loan.

> The rich man pointed to his manure pile outside the door and said, "There is my God; he gives me wheat and everything I need."[15]

Evidently at least some farmers were making an effort to use livestock byproducts constructively. Whether many built structures to house livestock, and thus facilitate proper manuring, is questionable. Barns appear to have been common features of farmsteads, widespread in the valley by the end of the colonial period. But these buildings probably were used mainly to protect hay and harvested crops, and as shelter for milking. Observed Gottlieb Mittelberger in the early 1750s,

> Every plantation owner pastures his cattle, horses, and sheep on his own property, or lets them run about in the underbrush and has them brought in mornings and evenings in order to have the cows milked. Then he lets them go again the whole night through until morning. In this way the animals find their own food, and one doesn't have to feed them daily, as in Germany. And no cattle has to be stabled during the summers, except when cows are about to calve.[16]

Colonial-period barns were too small to house the fifteen to twenty cattle that were typical, let alone the five or six horses, fifteen or so sheep, and ten or so swine. Only five colonial documents that described individual farms referred explicitly to the presence of a stable, with the earliest of these from 1755.

HERDS, FLAX PATCHES, ORCHARDS, AND GARDENS

Like the cultivation of minor grains and orchards, the breeding and raising of livestock was an essential element in valley residents' subsistence, providing meat, dairy products, leather, wool, and the brute energy

THE ECONOMY

essential to raising grain crops. The herd owned by Benjamin Boone, appraised in 1762, is fairly representative of the complement of animals to be found on a full-scale farm:[17]

1 white mane and tail horse	£15	
A black horse with a bald face	£7	
A white mare	£12	
A little bay mare	£2	10s.
A grey mare	£4	
A black colt a year old	£4	
6 cows @ 50s. each	£15	
3 heifers and 1 steer, 2-year-olds	£6	30s. each
2 heifers and 2 bulls, yearlings	£3	15s. each
4 calves, 10s. each	£2	
13 sheep, 5s. each	£3	5s.
13 swine, 8s. each	£5	4s.

Like other aspects of farming, German and English farmers had no apparent difference in their approach toward livestock.

Horses were the most valuable of farm animals. Large, muscular draft horses, perhaps of the breed called the Conestoga horse, were owned in teams of two, three or four and supplied the farm's brute labor. A fine riding mare was a prized possession of well-established farmers, craftspeople, and tradespeople alike. The presence of this highly visible asset was often noted, with her saddle and bridle, at the head of an estate inventory. The presence of the mare proclaimed one as a person of substance; she often figured in a will as a prominent bequest. In Benjamin Boone's inventory the white mare worth £12 was likely that well-off yeoman's mount.

Although Oley Valley farmers may not have taken great pains to shelter their animals, they did keep them close to home. Predators such as wolves were a worry in the very early years, but the main concern in controlling livestock was probably to prevent damage to crops. The crooked rail fences that farmers erected were not built very high. The wood was more economically used to yoke and hobble animals so they could not cross the low barriers. The Swedish naturalist Pehr Kalm observed pigs fitted with "triangular wooden yokes" in all the parts of southeastern Pennsylvania through which he traveled in his long visit around 1750. He often saw fastened to a horse's neck,

> a piece of wood, which at the lower end had a tooth or hook which would catch in the fence and stop the horse just when it lifted its fore feet to leap over.... They were likewise kept in bounds by a piece of wood, one end of which was fastened to one of the fore feet, and the other to one of the hind feet. It forced them to walk pretty slowly, and at the same time made it impossible for them to leap over the fence.[18]

For a time horses were allowed a somewhat freer rein than other livestock. Seven estate inventories ranging chronologically from 1723 through 1743 referred to "mares and colts running in the woods," though the farmer's riding mare and his workhorses were denied this measure of liberty.

Poultry were seldom mentioned in valley estate inventories, though a complement was probably present on every full-scale farm. Eggs were necessary for baking. According to Mittelberger,

> Almost everyone raises pigs and poultry, especially turkeys. In this region chickens are not confined to coops or especially looked after during the night. But they sit summer and winter on trees near the houses. And every evening many trees are so weighted down with chickens that the boughs bend underneath them. Poultry is in no danger from beasts of prey, because every plantation owner has at least one very large dog roaming the estate.[19]

One aspect of agriculture to which farmers in the Oley Valley and in other parts of the province sought to bring improvement in the mid-eighteenth century was the feeding of their livestock. Pennsylvania farmers mowed hay on their meadows twice a year, generally in mid-to-late June and early-to-mid August. By the 1750s Oley agrarians began the European custom of irrigating meadows in order to make more and better hay, a practice followed both in Germany and in England. Pehr Kalm noted in 1749 that

> The summer in Pennsylvania is very hot, and the sun often burns the grass so much that it dries up entirely. The husbandmen are therefore very attentive to prevent this in their meadows.... They conduct the water as much as possible and necessary to the higher part of the meadow, and then make several narrow channels from the brook down into the plain, so that it is entirely watered by it.[20]

Sometimes farmers built races to take water to the meadows. These races were similar to those created to deliver water to power mills. Kalm noted that these races could run for over a mile. In decreeing that his sons Benjamin and Samuel divide his Exeter Township tract, Benjamin Boone specified in his will of 1762 "the whole to be equally divided both in quantity and quality between them, . . . the dam for . . . watering their meadow to be maintained at equal cost between them."[21]

In 1769 four owners of various portions of the thousand-acre Robeson-Lincoln tract in southern Exeter Township agreed on an elaborate arrangement whereby they would share the upkeep expense and the benefits of the tract's irrigation system. The latter had evidently been created by the Lincoln family at some point before the three brothers Mordecai, Thomas, and Abraham conveyed part of the tract to their brother-in-law William Tallman in 1757. The man-made water course diverted land from Antietam Creek and took it to a number of meadows. The four landowners devised a system in which any week between March 1st and October 16th was divided into twenty-one eight-hour periods. Mordecai Lincoln was entitled to the creek's flow during seven periods; Abraham Lincoln to seven; Michael Zeister to four; and Jacob Bechtel to three. During the cooler part of the year, meadows did not need race-conducted water, but a sawmill run by Abraham and Mordecai did. Milling lumber was largely a winter activity.

Farm families met much of their need for clothing and other cloth goods with wool from their flocks of sheep and linen from their crops of flax. Almost all farms raised sheep and flax. The conversion of raw wool and flax into yarn, ready to be

OLEY VALLEY HERITAGE

DAVID MILLER LOSING HIS HAND IN THE APPLE MILL
The horse-powered apple mill and the great cider press were still the standard equipment for cidermaking in the early nineteenth century, when the process was depicted by York folk artist Lewis Miller.
Courtesy, The Historical Society of York County, Pennsylvania.

woven into cloth, demanded a significant share of a farm's annual labor. Shearing took place in April, the pulling of the flax (by hand alone—hard work) in July. The latter had been sown in March. Flax had to be threshed, then allowed to rot somewhat, broken, swung, and hackled; wool had to be carded; both required spinning. In the colonial Oley Valley the weaving of the "homemade" textiles did not take place on the homestead that had produced the spun yarn. The only estate inventories that featured looms were those of weavers, though three (from 1725, 1769, and 1771) mentioned "yarn at the weaver's."

The inventory of George Anders's store shows that by 1752 imported textiles were a noticeable presence. Anders presented for sale at least twenty-six varieties of fabric, the value of his total supply of dry goods amounting to some £120, a very large sum. He also offered ready-made handkerchiefs, hats and caps, stockings, gloves, and garters, as well as ribbon, thread, lace, needles, buttons, and buckles.

Orchard tending was yet another secondary but essential element in farming for both market and subsistence. Contemporary travelers who visited Pennsylvania noted that most farmers cultivated only three kinds of fruit trees: apple, peach, and cherry. The first two were planted in orchards, but cherry trees were sited along lanes and fences. Like apples, peaches were converted into an alcoholic beverage (peach brandy), and were dried to be used year-round in making pies. In addition, peaches were fed to pigs. The only fruit specifically mentioned in Oley Valley documents of the period is the apple. Acrelius, writing about the broader Delaware Valley region, noted that

> Apple trees make the finest orchards, planted in straight rows with intervals of twelve or fifteen paces. . . . For apples not less than two or three acres are taken; some have five or six. The cultivation consists in grafting and pruning in the spring, and plowing in the ground every five or six years, when either maize [Indian corn] is planted, or rye or oats sowed, in the orchard.[22]

Johann David Schoepf added that

> When the trees begin to show age, a new orchard is set on fresh land, for it is not regarded as good practice to put young trees where the old ones stood.[23]

In 1770 the half of the tract settled by Benjamin Boone around 1730, which his family called "the old place," meaning his original homestead, included two orchards within its 163.5 acres. The estate of Walter Campbell, appraised in 1745, included a "nursery of young apple trees," as did that of Benjamin Longworthy (1765).

Most of the apples raised may have ended as hard cider, the chief beverage of the inhabitants. Every full-scale farm featured an apple orchard. But estate inventories suggest that the direct conversion of apples to cider was a service business pursued as a significant sideline by a few farmers, in a manner similar to those who processed their neighbors' timber on water-powered sawmills. "Apple mills" or "cider mills" were listed in only ten of the ninety farm inventories. Cidermaking yeoman Jacob DelaPlank

THE ECONOMY

had eleven hogsheads (large barrels) of cider on hand when he passed away in 1760, or about seven hundred gallons. Like others rendering a custom service, the cidermaker kept a percentage of what he processed for his neighbors, leaving him a large quantity of the drink that he could sell to local landless people or tavernkeepers, or send to the Reading or Philadelphia market.

The equipment necessary to make cider in quantity, a mill and a press, represented a sizable investment in the colonial period. Described by historian Thomas Jefferson Wertenbaker, a cider mill

> consisted of two solid cylinders fifteen inches in diameter and twenty inches long, cut from the trunk of a tree, notched to fit into each other, and set upright side by side in a stout wooden frame. A long pole or sweep, drawn by a horse, set the cylinders in motion, while a hopper fed in the apples.[24]

The mashed-apple substance, called "pomace," that came out of the mill was next put under the press. This was a huge instrument, as Samuel Heilman related in an 1899 account of a surviving specimen in Lebanon County.

> The beam of the press was a very heavy piece of oak timber, fourteen by eighteen inches thick and about thirty-six feet long, and the crib at the end of the press beam [was] filled with stones, half a ton or more in weight. The piece extending upwards from the crib was like a long screw, and its thread fitted into a screw-cut block fastened to the end of the long beam, and by turning the crib round and round, great pressure could be brought to bear on the bed at the other end on which the crushed apples as they came from the mill were built up in tiers.[25]

One such massive cider press from central Berks County is preserved by the Historic Preservation Trust of Berks County at its Jacob Keim House property in Pike Township.

Unlike cider mills, presses were not explicitly listed in estate inventories. Evidently the sheer size of a cider press made it one of a property's architectural assets, part of the real estate rather than the personal or "movable" estate. Ownership of both mill and press appears to have been standard practice for farmers who produced cider, however. The account kept of Magdalena Schenkel's administration of her late husband Martin's estate noted for the year 1746 the building of a cider press house and the purchase of an apple mill.

Some of the mildly alcoholic cider was converted by means of distilling apparatus into a potation of sterner character, apple brandy, also known as applejack. As noted above, whiskey does not appear to have found favor with valley residents during the colonial years. The distilling of brandy was pursued by some farmers on a semi-specialized basis similar to that for cidermaking. Copper stills were listed in nine estate inventories. Interestingly, in no instance did a still appear along with a cider mill, so that cidermaking and brandy distilling were apparently considered two discrete activities within the general sphere of agricultural processing. At the time of his death in 1771, still-owner Abraham Peter had six hogsheads of "sour cider" (probably about 400 gallons). It was necessary for the cider to be in a fermented state before brandy could be made. He also possessed one hogshead of "cider royal," a mixture of regular hard cider and applejack, as well as one barrel of "distilled liquor."

Valley people rounded out their diet with a variety of tubers, legumes, and salad vegetables grown in homestead gardens. A farm's garden, along with the poultry flock and dairy activities, would have fallen within the agricultural province of the women's sphere of activity. According to Acrelius, the people of southeastern Pennsylvania raised and consumed potatoes, sweet potatoes, cabbage (for the inevitable sauerkraut), beets, parsnips, onions, parsley, radishes, green beans, peas, red peppers, and lettuce. They raised herbs including wormwood, rue, sage, thyme, chamomile, and others. Many farmers practiced beekeeping, thereby procuring honey for sweetening.

ARTISANS AND MILLS: INTEGRAL TO AGRICULTURE

A prosperous farming community like the Oley Valley required the services of industrial proprietors, specialized artisans, tradespeople, and simple laborers as well as farmers. A traveler passing through the valley in the late colonial years (i.e., after around 1760) would have beheld a place

SMITHY ON THE DANIEL REIFF HOMESTEAD, Oley Township
The smithy was in the process of having its tile roof rehung when this view was taken.
Photo by Philip E. Pendleton.

OLEY VALLEY HERITAGE

SPOHN'S SMITHY, Oley Township
The construction date of this log-built smithy, which once stood at the intersection of Route 662 and Blacksmith Road, is unknown, but the structure's form is likely representative of many built before 1776.
Photo by Harry F. Stauffer. Courtesy, The Historical Society of the Cocalico Valley.

decidedly rural, but one humming with the activity of many industrial sites and craftshops.

In order to provide the necessities of life, not to mention whatever luxuries people thought they could afford, many varieties of nonfarming occupation were integral to eighteenth-century agricultural society. Blacksmiths hammered wrought iron into an endless variety of implements and building hardware. Coopers assembled the wooden barrels and kegs that were essential for flour and other commodities to be stored and shipped. Wheelwrights saw to it that wagons were available to carry the valley's products. Weavers wove fiber into cloth. Tailors made clothing and shoemakers (or "cordwainers") shoes and other leather goods. Carpenters, joiners, and turners created furniture and wooden buildings and building elements. These were perhaps the most numerous sorts of craftspeople. But there were many other less common

SMITHY ON THE MARTIN SCHENKEL HOMESTEAD, Oley Township
One among the Oley Valley's gradually but ever diminishing collection of small work buildings and outbuildings.
Photo by Kenneth LeVan.

types, such as masons, millwrights, gunsmiths, tilemakers, and hatters, whose volume of business was such that one person could serve a fairly large area. The makers of more luxurious items, such as silversmiths and clockmakers, had to be sought out in urban centers such as Reading, Germantown, and Philadelphia. There were also people in the valley who provided services who cannot properly be called artisans, such as storekeepers, who imported items not produced in the valley itself; wagoners, who hauled the imported and exported goods; and inn- and tavernkeepers, who ensured that their neighbors had some social outlet. Among the poorer people were day laborers who did jobs for those who needed and could afford this service, as well as indentured servants and slaves whose labor was bound to the command of the more affluent.

The labor of most craftspeople engaged in providing the specialized work and products necessary to sustain the agricultural economy was done in relatively simple workshops. But some crafts, namely the tanning of leather and the various types of custom milling, operated on a larger scale. Both mills and tanneries required flowing water, which had to be diverted from streams by means of dams and races. In custom work, the miller, tanner, or other artisan exacted a toll, or "custom," ranging from an eighth to a quarter of the product, paid in kind. This was a service business, in which the customer brought a commodity to the mill, had it processed, and then took it back to the farmstead for use or to the market for sale.

Tanning was a process of several consecutive stages in which animal hides were refined into leather. This entailed soaking the skins in several different chemical solutions. Sunken vats contained the solutions, which consisted of organic materials, principally different kinds of tree bark, dissolved in water. The solutions stripped and cleaned the hides. Successful tanning needed plenty of fresh water and a large space for the tanyard with its tanning vats. The Oley Valley was home to three tanneries in 1775.

Mills were complex machines powered by falling water. A mill, with its waterwheel and gearing, required elaborate construction and a high degree of tech-

THE ECONOMY

WHITE HORSE INN, Mid-Eighteenth Century, Amity Township
The original section, to the right, is a three-bay example of the double-cell type. A property of the Historic Preservation Trust of Berks County, which has restored the building to its eighteenth-century appearance. As a "tavern stand" or innkeeper's place of business (as opposed to this specific building), the White Horse was in operation by April 17, 1740. The *Pennsylvania Gazette* of that date printed an advertisement seeking to recruit soldiers for a British "expedition against the Spanish West Indies," listing "Marcus Huling's at Manatawny" as one of twenty enlistment locations in the province. The White Horse was referred to as a "thriving inn" in an advertisement of 1751, a year after Huling had conveyed the property to Philip Balthasar Craesman. Huling, a Swedish Indian trader who married fellow Swede and first valley settler Mounce Jones's daughter Margaret, had established his homestead in 1716, and three years later the property became the location of the first road junction in the Oley Valley, an eminently suitable place for a public house. It is unknown whether this building was constructed for Huling, Craesman, Samuel Cookson (owner 1757-1762), or storekeeper George Douglass (1762 onward).
Photo by Philip E. Pendleton.

SCHNEIDER MILL, Circa 1730-1760, Exeter Township
Photo by H. Winslow Fegley, circa 1900-1925. Courtesy, Schwenkfelder Library.

OLEY VALLEY HERITAGE

JUDAH BOONE MILL (Mill Tract Farm), Circa 1770, Exeter Township
The mill appears in the foreground of this view of the classic millseat arrangement in which the miller's house surveys the gristmill. The building at right is a small bank-sited horse stable for the mill's team, aligned with its gable end against the bank, and likely of the same circa 1770 vintage as house and mill.
Photo by Cervin Robinson, 1958. Courtesy, The Historic American Buildings Survey, Prints and Photographs Division, Library of Congress.

nical know-how on the part of the miller. There were four kinds of service mills found in the Oley Valley: gristmills, sawmills, fulling mills, and oil mills. The first two kinds were fairly numerous, while of the latter types, two fulling mills and one oil mill were enough to meet the valley's needs in 1775. Some millers operated complexes with several different mills situated on the same race, or on systems of races taking water from the same source stream.

Gristmills, in which pairs of large carved, circular stones with sharpened inward edges ground grain into meal or flour, were the most common sort of mill, and the most important. Twenty-one gristmills are known to have been operating in 1775. Not only was bread the staff of life, as was so throughout the Western world, but the gristmill's function was central to the wheat flour export business.

"Up-and-down" sawmills (more properly called "reciprocating" sawmills), numbering seventeen in 1775, were also vital. The abundant local timber was sawn into boards and staves necessary for furniture, roof structures, floors and room partitions, and barrels and kegs, including those in which the precious flour would be exported.

In a fulling mill, cloth was cleaned with water and fuller's earth (a particular sort of clay), and softened and thickened (fulled) by power-driven paddles or mallets. Flax seed was ground by stones in an oil mill to make linseed oil, an essential ingredient of paint. The oil mill Johannes Umensetter was running at present-day Spangsville in 1759 is the earliest documented example in the valley.

OPEN FOR BUSINESS

Daniel Womelsdorff on the Manatawny makes known, that if by chance a recent immigrant was formerly a woolen weaver, and does not want to miss a good opportunity, by applying to Daniel Womelsdorff, who has a fulling mill, situated among many neighbors, he will find a house and garden available, and he can take advantage of the opportunity.

—*Pennsylvanische Berichte*, January 16, 1743/44

Johannes Umensetter in Oley at Hans Joder's mill makes known, that he will buy flaxseed, and promises at all times to give as good a price, as anyone in the backcountry gives, he promises also to give cash money up front at all times. He will always give the price, that those in town give, except that he might deduct 7 or 8 pence for a carrying fee.

—*Pennsylvanische Berichte*, July 20, 1759

THE ECONOMY

EXPORT INDUSTRY: MERCHANT MILLS, PAPER MILLS, AND IRONWORKS

Besides the farms and the service craft businesses essential to an agrarian community, the Oley Valley was home to many industrial enterprises that processed raw materials into commodities that the operators then exported to distant places. These operations were of five types: merchant flour mills, merchant sawmills, paper mills, iron-making furnaces, bloomery forges, and iron-refining forges or "fineries." All of these industries were powered by falling water, in the same manner of raceway, waterwheel, and gearing as the water-powered service mills referred to above. Except for the iron-plate stoves and cookware cast at Oley Furnace, the products were not finished ones. Rather, they were all unfinished materials that had gone through one or two stages of processing. Therefore, this industrial activity cannot be considered full-fledged "manufacturing."

The first two of the above industries, merchant flour mills and merchant sawmills, differ from the customwork gristmills and sawmills described above only in that the merchant millers operated on a larger scale and concentrated on export commerce. Theirs were not custom businesses. These entrepreneurs, literally merchants as well as millers, bought farmers' wheat or lumber outright and milled and shipped it themselves to Philadelphia. There they sold it to city merchants, who most likely would send it abroad. Prices for commodities on the international market rose and fell then as they do today. The transmittal of information regarding prices was slow, however, being dependent on sailing ships, so the merchant milling business was speculative. By the late colonial years, the merchant flour mill had become the economic linchpin of the southeastern Pennsylvania countryside, with merchant millers buying a high proportion of the wheat crop. It is not clear how many of the twenty-one gristmills of 1775 were merchant mills and how many were custom mills.

OLEY FURNACE, Oley Township
The basic technology of the American charcoal-fired iron industry continued with relatively little change into the middle nineteenth century. This scene (as with that at Oley Forge) likely appeared much the same in 1760 and 1860. At the upper right a worker is visible, trundling a wheelbarrow full of raw material (iron ore, limestone, or charcoal) to be dumped into the furnace for smelting. Down the slope other figures can be seen about the entrance of the casting shed, where molten iron was cast into "pigs" (i.e., long bars of cast iron), stoveplates, and cookware in molds in the shed's floor.
Drawing by Francis Devlan, circa 1860. Courtesy, The Historical Society of Pennsylvania.

The export of lumber from the Pennsylvania countryside did not nearly approach the wheat business in importance, but it was significant. Large quantities of building lumber, coopers' ware, and wood of superior quality for furniture, such as black walnut, went from Pennsylvania to the British Isles and West Indies. The demand for lumber in growing Philadelphia, at that time largely a timber-frame town, not brick, constituted a lucrative trade for rural sawmills. In about 1732 Jonathan Robeson established what appears to have been a merchant sawmill in northern Robeson Township at present-day Gibraltar, with the name "Lebanon Sawmill."

Paper was another item much in demand in the province's capital. There were two papermills in 1775, both located in Amity Township, run by the Rodt and Womelsdorff families. These papermakers exported to the Philadelphia paper market, though now little is known about their business. Philadelphia printer and newspaper publisher Benjamin Franklin bought paper from Daniel Womelsdorff's papermill during the middle years of the century.

The most striking aspect of the Oley Valley's early industrial life is its role as a center of charcoal-fired iron production. Iron was yet another important export product for Penn's province, the chief iron-producing colony. Colonial ironmaking operations were of three sorts. A **furnace** was where most iron was made: that is, iron ore was smelted with charcoal and limestone to "draw out the iron." The iron produced thus, while still molten, was cast on the furnace floor into stove plates, cooking pots, or "pigs," loglike lumps of iron.

Cast iron from the furnace contained a great deal of carbon. This conferred a brittle quality that prevented its direct application for most purposes. It had to be taken (often sold) to a **finery forge**. Here the pig was beaten at very high temperatures with a huge water-power-driven hammer (called a "tilthammer") to expel the carbon. The resulting **wrought iron** was a fibrous, malleable material. Now blacksmiths could beat it into shape as nails, tools, horseshoes, hinges, and all sorts of hardware. Some ironmasters owned furnaces *and* fineries. Most of the forges that operated in the Oley Valley during the colonial years were finery forges.

The simplest ironmaking process was the **bloomery forge**. Ironworks of this type were present mainly in the early years of settlement. At a bloomery wrought iron was produced directly by heating the ironstone itself to a very high temperature and literally beating the impurities out of it with the heavy tilthammer. The whole process was more primitive than the furnace-and-finery system, and it lacked efficiency of scale. It seems unlikely that any large-scale ironmasters continued using this process beyond the early settlement years, though the Boone family members evidently ran a bloomery in Exeter Township for some years around 1800 (a late date for this sort of ironmaking operation). They processed iron ore that they had discovered on their land. Evidently a few colonial-era landowners did the same.

The valley's first ironworks, and the first in Pennsylvania, was Pine Forge, in Douglass Township, established as a bloomery forge by Thomas Rutter in 1715.[26] Pine Forge became a finery forge when Rutter built Colebrookdale Furnace in the neighboring community of that name in 1719. In 1738 Thomas Potts founded Spring Forge, in present-day Earl Township, with the financial participation of Philadelphia merchants Samuel Mickle and George Mifflin. The year

JOSEPH RUTTER HOUSE (Pine Forge Mansion), 1731, Enlarged Circa 1791, Douglass Township
The earliest, center section of this house is an example of the three-cell type. The fenestration (i.e., arrangement of doorways and windows) of that part of the building has been altered somewhat. The small section to the right is of unknown age, possibly a Colonial Revival-inspired addition from early in this century.
Photo by Philip E. Pendleton.

THE ECONOMY

1744 saw the establishment of Oley Forge by blacksmith Johannes Lesher with Oley miller Johannes Joder (Lesher's father-in-law) and Philadelphia investor John Ross as partners. In 1746 William Bird started a forge at present-day Birdsboro, and within four years he was running a pair of forges at this location. Bird, an Irishman, had worked his way up through the iron industry, beginning as a young indentured servant cutting wood for Pine Forge's charcoal in the 1720s. At his death in 1761 he was the wealthiest man in Berks County. The last of the five colonial-period ironworks to get off the ground was the first furnace for the valley itself. Dietrich Welker built Oley Furnace in 1759 with Oley innkeeper Peter Harpel and Benedict Swope, probably another Philadelphia capitalist, as his partners.

It takes nothing from the Oley Valley's prestige to note that the valley shared its importance as an iron industry center with the neighboring communities of Moselem, the Oley Hills, Colebrookdale, Pottsgrove, and Coventry to the north, east, and south. These adjoining localities together formed one great concentration of ironmaking activity.

Discovery of deposits of iron ore worth mining was a common occurrence in the colonial years. Antony Jaeger's 1767 tax assessment recorded the existence of a mine on his six-hundred-acre Oley property. Jaeger (a surname often anglicized as Hunter) probably had made a mutually advantageous contract with Oley Furnace or another furnace to have the ore dug out. Wealthy farmer Caspar Griesemer, on the other hand, taxed for a forge in 1768, probably ran his bloomery for a time to process iron ore from a deposit on his extensive property. Ore was extracted from the surface by men quarrying with pickaxes and other simple tools, obviating the need for the more complex technology necessary for tunneling into the earth to mine the ore.

"Iron plantations" are famous as the most elaborate industrial establishments of eighteenth-century America. Iron making and exporting was another speculative business. Some colonial ironmasters, such as William Bird and Johannes Lesher, achieved a financial success that put them on the same footing as the wealthier among their contemporary city merchants and southern planters. The ironworks, especially the furnaces, required dozens of workers, some of them skilled artisans. Most of these workers were somehow housed by the ironmaster. Thus, an ironworks generally created its own hamlet. There would be a farming operation to feed the workers, and typically a complex of service mills to meet the iron plantation's needs and bring in some added income. This existence of a self-contained community enabled some ironmasters to cast themselves in a paternalistic role not far removed from that envisioned by many southern planters.

OLEY FORGE, Oley Township
The waterwheel drove a tilthammer that forced impurities out of red-hot cast iron, refining the latter into wrought iron suitable for use by blacksmiths.
Drawing by Francis Devlan, circa 1860. Courtesy, The Historical Society of Pennsylvania.

GROWTH OF COMPLEXITY IN LOCAL ECONOMIC LIFE

The Oley Valley began as a frontier settlement where almost all the homesteads were struggling pioneer farms, one little different from the next. In 1775 the valley was a prosperous community of farmers,

OLEY VALLEY HERITAGE

BIRD HOUSE (Birdsborough Forge Mansion), Circa 1746-1751, Enlarged Circa 1770, Birdsboro
The original section, consisting of the three leftmost bays, was built by William Bird on a hall-parlor plan. The center-passage single-pile addition, with its symmetrical "Georgian" facade arrangement of five bays with entry at center, was constructed by William's son Mark Bird circa 1770, doubling the overall size of the house.
Photo by Philip E. Pendleton.

ironmasters, artisans, tradesmen, laborers, and their families, with complex economic relationships to one another and to the outer world.

Surviving tax assessment lists comprise an invaluable source for investigating the economic makeup of early American communities. Although assessors tended to attribute values for landowners estates that were artificially low, examination of land and probate records indicates that tax assessment lists are reliably representative in their comparison of landed taxpayers' wealth.

The abstracts of the 1731 Amity tax assessment and the 1767 Oley and Amity assessments, presented below, convey some sense of the growth of complexity and variety in economic life that took place in the valley over the colonial period. Social historians of recent years, in presenting their analyses of the socioeconomic structure of past communities, usually make use of graphs that chart the proportions of the wealth as it was distributed among the residents of the locality (as discerned from tax assessments and probate inventories). These "wealth cohorts" among the population by necessity are defined somewhat arbitrarily: usually the top 10 percent, the upper 30 percent, the middle 30 percent, and the bottom 30 percent. Such measurements have their uses, but no doubt the people of the historic communities so analyzed would not have found these graphs to be true to their perception of economic life and status in the society around them.

Modern analysts' perceptions regarding present-day society may be the basis of their division of past communities into top ten-percentile and upper, middle, and lower thirty-percentile cohorts. An inhabitant of the colonial-period Oley Valley would likely have made a hierarchical division of his or her neighbors into five classes based on a person's possession or lack of autonomy, and on the nature of the person's working life. At the top were those few wealthy people who operated farms or industrial establishments but who did not have to work with their own hands, probably represented in the 1767 tax assessment abstract below by just three households (those of Johannes Lesher, Conrad Reiff, and Antony Jaeger). The next class, the backbone of colonial Pennsylvania society, was that of the autonomous freeholder, the economically solvent farmer, artisan, or tradesperson who owned his or her homestead. Third was the class of the upwardly mobile person who had not attained the status of autonomous freeholder but who aspired to that status and showed promise of attaining it, generally young adults who were renting properties on which they farmed or pursued a craft or trade. The fourth class was that of laboring people, generally renters of small dwellings or spaces within better-off people's houses, who depended on freeholders for the opportunity to work and who had little prospect of upward advancement. The lowest class was that of the bound servant, constantly subject to direction by another. This was generally a temporary status for white indentured servants or apprentices, a permanent one for black slaves.

Between the class of the autonomous freeholder and that of the aspirant to that status might be said to lie the great division in society, for in a sense colonial

THE ECONOMY

Pennsylvanians appear also to have made a simpler socioeconomic classification into two groups: the autonomous and the nonautonomous. The goal for most was to be independent, to own one's freehold, and to be in a situation to provide for one's children.

A tax assessment list for Amity Township from 1731, when the valley settlement was just beginning to move out of its pioneer stage, indicates a relative economic equality and lack of differentiation in occupation among the inhabitants. This is the only tax assessment list for one of the three major valley townships to have survived from the Philadelphia County period (1700-1752). At this early date large expanses of land that would later fall within Exeter and Douglass townships were administered as parts of Amity. The roster indicated only tax values, without explanatory data, and named eighty-two taxpayers, including:[27]

- 6 men rated £21-35 (7 percent of taxpayers, 11 percent of households)
- 48 men rated £12-20 (59 percent of taxpayers, 86 percent of households)
- 2 "poor" men, not taxed (2 percent of taxpayers, 4 percent of households)
- 7 single freemen (i.e., men twenty-one or older but without wives or real estate) who are sons in local families (9 percent of taxpayers, 27 percent of freemen)
- 19 other single freemen (23 percent of taxpayers, 73 percent of freemen)

Of the forty-eight taxpayers rated £12-20, thirty-four were landowners with assessments ranging from £12 to £20, and fourteen were evidently tenants or squatters, rated £12 to £16. This lack of a strong division in value between owners and nonowners seems to indicate that even the homesteads of the owners were still at a somewhat rudimentary stage of development.

It is likely that all these taxpayers were engaged in farming, at least to meet their own needs. But craftspeople and tradespeople had made an appearance. For thirty-four of the forty landowners there is a fair amount of additional documentation. These thirty-four included an ironmaster, two millers, an innkeeper, a house carpenter, and a tanner. The seemingly high number of unmarried, landless men is puzzling. There was, if anything, a general shortage of labor in the colonies during the period. Perhaps many were workers at Pine Forge.

A 1767 tax list, compiled a generation later and about when the flour industry was reaching its zenith, paints a portrait of a place hardly recognizable as the same but for the persistence of family names. This document is rich with data, including real estate owned or rented, occupation, and acreage currently planted in grain, enabling detailed analysis of both Amity and Oley townships, the two townships whose then-settled areas are included in the study area in their entirety.[28]

The basis for the taxation of married householders was the likely income that the assessor deemed the taxpayer's productive assets to be capable of generating. (These assets included land, improvements, crops planted, livestock, and the facilities and equipment for a craft or trade.) Judging from a comparison of estate inventories to the tax record of 1767, however, with its figures on "corn planted" (i.e., grain), tax assessors underreported acres planted as well as the size of livestock herds, by about 40 percent. This undervaluation of properties was linked to the overtaxation of single freemen, who had to pay a poll tax; together these two tacit policies represented the prevailing practice in Pennsylvania. There appears to have been a pervasive sentiment in the thirteen colonies against adult men's remaining bachelors. The tax law of the province linked the tax rates for householders and single freemen, dictating that for every penny of tax raised on a pound of householders' taxable property, the poll tax levied on single freemen should be raised three shillings. A tax rate of three pence in the pound for householders, with a poll tax of nine shillings, was typical. (There were twelve pence in a shilling, and twenty shillings in a pound.) Local officials generally shifted an extralegally disproportionate share of the tax burden onto single freemen, charging them the full nine shillings, for example, while underreporting the property, such as acres planted or cattle, upon which the three-pence-in-a-pound would be due.[29]

On the 1767 assessment a full-scale farm, growing wheat for export, was generally listed with ten to twenty acres planted (representing approximately sixteen to thirty-three acres planted in reality). Judging from the acres-planted listings for nonfarmers, a household required about two to twelve acres (one to seven acres in the assessment record) planted for its own subsistence, depending on the number of mouths to feed and the quality of the soil.

The abstract of the 1767 tax assessment divides the two townships' inhabitants into eighteen groups, in order to show the variety of economic situations, occupations, and degrees of prosperity. The five social classes defined by degree of autonomy can be discerned, however.

The assessment of Oley and Amity townships notes the presence in 1767 of 189 households, 70 single freemen, and 41 servants and slaves. A rough estimate of the size of the population, assuming five people or so per household, indicates over a thousand people for these two townships. There were perhaps two thousand residents or somewhat fewer for the Oley Valley study area as a whole.

In 1767 the heads of households, workers, and servants of Oley and Amity included:

- 3 entrepreneurs with ratings of £60 or more, all in Oley Township, namely Johannes Lesher, ironmaster, £100; had 80 acres of grain listed (50 more than anyone else in the valley); owned gristmill, sawmill, several tenancies (including a tannery), two-thirds interest in Oley Forge
  Conrad Reiff, £94; had 20 acres of grain listed; owned gristmill, sawmill, and several tenant farms
  Antony Jaeger, £60; had 12 acres of grain listed; was mining iron; owned inn, gristmill, sawmill
  (1 percent of taxpayers, 2 percent of households)

- 26 farmers who owned their land, with ratings of £21-48, who had 10 acres or more of grain listed, and whose farms were old, well-established ones, all but three on the floor of the more fertile northern valley; three also owned sawmills; included one widow

(10 percent of taxpayers, 14 percent of households)

3 crafts- or tradespeople who were also farmers, with ratings of £23-34; each had 15 acres listed on an old farm on the northern valley floor; included a miller, a blacksmith, and a doctor; the doctor was a renter; two owned their homesteads; the miller was a widow
(1 percent of taxpayers, 2 percent of households)

3 craftspeople or tradespeople, with ratings of £23-30; all owned their homesteads; included a storekeeper, an innkeeper, and a blacksmith
(1 percent of taxpayers, 2 percent of households)

34 farmers who owned their land, with ratings of £8-20, who were in the second rank because of various factors: newer, not-so-established farmsteads, land of secondary quality, lack of labor, or a less commercially-oriented attitude (with less acreage planted in crops); one owned a sawmill; included a widow
(13 percent of taxpayers, 18 percent of households)

9 craftspeople or tradespeople who were also full-scale farmers, with ratings of £8-20; had 8 or more acres listed; included two millers, three blacksmiths, two weavers, an innkeeper, and a shoemaker; five owned, four rented
(3 percent of taxpayers, 5 percent of households)

5 craftspeople or tradespeople with ratings of £8-20; an ironmaster, a storekeeper, three millers; two owned, three rented
(2 percent of taxpayers, 3 percent of households)

12 tenant farmers, with ratings of £1-9
(5 percent of taxpayers, 6 percent of taxpayers)

10 farmers who owned their land, with ratings of £2-7; nine were working recently created farmsteads, one was a widow with only six acres listed as planted (evidently running a scaled-down operation)
(4 percent of taxpayers, 5 percent of households)

4 craftspeople or tradespeople who were also full-scale farmers, with ratings of £2-7; included two weavers, an innkeeper, and a millwright; two owned, two rented
(2 percent of taxpayers, 2 percent of households)

13 craftspeople and tradespeople, with ratings of £2-7, whose ownership of their homestead or practice of a more lucrative craft or trade set them off from their poorer colleagues; ten owned, three rented; five had ten or more acres listed as planted; included two innkeepers, three blacksmiths, three shoemakers, a mason, a weaver, a tanner, a joiner, and a saddler
(5 percent of taxpayers, 7 percent of households)

30 craftspeople and tradespeople, with ratings of £1-2, only one of whom owned his home; included five shoemakers, five tailors, three wheelwrights, three blacksmiths, three weavers, three coopers, a forge hammerman, a cabinetmaker, a carpenter, a hatter, a tinker, an innkeeper, a doctor, and a schoolmaster
(12 percent of taxpayers, 16 percent of households)

32 laborers, with ratings of "poor"—£2, none of whom owned his home; the seven rated at £2 may have been skilled ironworkers; two were rated as "poor"
(12 percent of taxpayers, 17 percent of households)

31 single freemen who were sons in local families
(12 percent of taxpayers, 44 percent of freemen)

39 other single freemen, evidently laborers
(15 percent of taxpayers, 56 percent of freemen)

31 indentured servants

10 slaves

5 households of elderly people living separately in "retirement," with ratings of £1-7; included one widow
(2 percent of taxpayers, 3 percent of households)

According to the 1767 assessment, the German speakers and English speakers of Oley and Amity were distributed in a roughly proportionate manner among the various occupational groupings (excluding that of the slaves, entirely African-American), 78 percent of the heads of household overall being German and 22 percent English (including 4 percent Swedes). The exceptions to this even economic balance between the nationalities were the three first-mentioned entrepreneurs and the twelve tenant farmers, who were all Germans. The only other men in the valley of the same economic standing as Lesher, Reiff, and Jaeger, namely ironmasters Mark Bird (£105), Thomas May (£65), and John Old (£64), were all English (half-Swedish in Bird's case), however.

The picture presented in the 1767 tax list is far different from that of 1731. By 1767 there was a higher degree of occupational specialization and far greater variation in the distribution of the valley's wealth among its population. In 1731 forty of the fifty-six Amity heads of household (71 percent) had been landowners. In 1767 only one hundred and three Oley and Amity heads of household (54 percent) owned their land, and some eighty-six (46 percent) rented. A survey of the assessments of the valley landowners in the townships that fall partly into the study area suggest that the population of those areas of the valley had a similar economic composition. Southeastern Pennsylvania had matured, curtailing homesteading opportunities in the region for children coming of age and for the still-arriving immigrants. Between 1750 and 1767, those coming from Europe had tended to be younger and of less means

THE ECONOMY

than formerly. This trend represented a source of labor for those farmers who could make the investment and desired to participate more aggressively in the booming wheat export trade.

Some were certainly doing so. Johannes Lesher of Oley Forge was leading the way. He was listed for eighty acres of planted grain, representing one hundred and thirty or so acres planted in reality, out of his valley floor holdings of one thousand acres. Other ironmasters, who like Lesher had workers to feed, were listed for twenty acres. Besides Lesher, fifty-six Oley and Amity heads of household (30 percent) were listed with fifteen acres or more, yielding large amounts of wheat to sell at mill or market. (Wheat comprised the bulk of what was planted over subsistence needs.) Forty-three (23 percent) participated in the wheat trade on a lesser basis, listed for eight to fourteen acres planted. They still had a surplus to sell. Twenty-five heads of household (13 percent) were assessed for only one to seven acres in grain, more or less satisfying their own needs. Such people, however, were in an enviable position compared to the sixty-four households (34 percent) and the single freemen who had to purchase meal or bread from fellow residents.

Farming was unquestionably the backbone of the local economy, and the basis of most wealth, as ironmaster Lesher appears to have appreciated. Most better-off crafts- and tradespeople in Oley and Amity were involved in farming for market as well, thirteen (65 percent) of the twenty rated at £8-34. Only fifteen (31 percent) of the forty-nine craftsmen and tradesmen who did not farm (except in some cases to grow their own food) owned their homes. A mere two (6 percent) of the thirty-five taxpayers rated above £20 were nonfarmers.

Craftspeople had their skills, but in the late colonial period these alone evidently could not generate a substantial income for most, compared to that possible from farming. A tax assessment of £1 on paper represented a hard, pinched existence in real life. Samuel Dewees, a collier at Berkshire Furnace in western Berks County, had to place all his seven children as indentured servants at young ages just to ensure their subsistence. His son Samuel went to Oley Valley farmer Richard Lewis at age five.

MEANS OF EXCHANGE AND CREDIT

The method by which the eighteenth-century people of the Oley Valley (and elsewhere in the thirteen colonies) exchanged goods and services was somewhat different from that of modern America. Coin and paper currency (in circulation in Pennsylvania from 1723 onward) were somewhat scarce. At the same time, though this may at first seem odd, the value of all commodities and labor was measured in money terms. This practice allowed exchange to have a much more fluid nature than was possible in a more primitive barter system. The system of money exchange without cash operated by means of credit extended between people doing business. Most people involved in business kept account books in which they recorded all the transactions in which they were involved. Hence basic skills in reading, writing, and arithmetic were considered essential.

A man might well do regular business with hundreds of people in the valley, nearby communities, and Philadelphia and Germantown. A person's credit network thus could become quite elaborate. The long-lived funereal colloquialism "final reckoning" originated in the importance on someone's death of ascertaining the extent of the departed's solvency or insolvency. This was a process that often kept the heirs in a state of considerable anxiety until its completion.

The extension of credit took four forms that, in the interest of simplicity, might be said to have varied according to magnitude and term. "Book debt," represented by an entry made in the creditor's ledger in lieu of payment for a good or service, whether this creditor was a storekeeper, carpenter, farmer, or whatever, was expected to be made good within a year. If the customer wanted to extend the time of payment for a small debt, the creditor generally agreed to accept his "note," a small-scale obligation not subject to interest. A "bond" was a long-term, interest-bearing agreement not necessarily requiring collateral, that might be made regarding a small debt. A "mortgage" was a bond for a large amount of money, secured to the creditor by agreement to transfer, if necessary, a specified major asset of the debtor, usually real estate.[30]

Day-to-day transactions were paid off in kind and in cash, but mostly by means of the former. Ironmaster William Bird kept an account ledger for his store at Pine Forge. For the years 1741-1744 Amity farmer Jonas Jones, typical of Bird's local customers, purchased a variety of items. These included cloth, thread, buttons, pins, paper, sugar, molasses, rum, small quantities of bar iron, and "schooling their children by my schoolmaster."[31] Jones and family paid from time to time, with butter, eggs, mutton, reaping in Bird's fields by Jones's sons as well as by the farmer himself, hauling loads of iron, maid and nurse work by Jones's daughter Margaret, cutting wood for the ironworks' charcoal by the sons, grave digging, "making a trough," and by a small cash payment at a reckoning in 1745.

Credit was undoubtedly the great lubricant of the eighteenth-century economy, as it is today. In that day, though, credit was extended or not extended, and foreclosed if need be, on a much more personal basis. Local and distant exchange operated largely by means of a credit system. Borrowing money to make improvements for higher productivity was normal procedure. Such improvements might include purchase of a homestead, building a house or barn, planting an orchard, buying livestock or more land, or improving one's craft workshop, mill, or ironworks. In families of substantial means, money was often given to children as credit to help them get started with their farm, craft, or other business. These loans would then be figured into the reckoning and disposition of the father's estate when he died.

The taking out of a mortgage was a common practice. Before 1775 some 170 mortgages on Oley Valley properties were recorded in the books of county recorders of deeds and those of the General Loan Office of Pennsylvania. (This latter was a program run by the provincial government from 1723 to 1756 to encourage economic growth by infusing the economy with paper money.) People lending money included the wealthier inhabitants of the valley itself, similarly placed individuals in neighboring localities, and many wealthy Philadelphians. Mortgages on distant rural properties were a popular investment among executors of city estates with funds to invest while children matured. Only four foreclosures took place in the valley during the colonial period, one in 1740, two in 1766, and one in 1770.

CASH SETTLEMENT REQUESTED

As George DeBenneville has lived in Oley until now, and lent both to those who had no money and those who could pay readily, and has now come to live about 2 miles outside Germantown, and it requires much time and trouble to visit his debtors, and he might come at the wrong time when they do not have it, so he asks all those who are owing to him and can pay, that they should do so between now and next April, and he will thank them.
—*Pennsylvanische Berichte*, September 17, 1757

The undersigned hereby make known publicly that all those who are owing for over a year, should come immediately and pay their debts; and those who do not have the money, should still come and give bond for what they owe; otherwise they are resolved to proceed at law with them.
  JOHN BOONE and JAMES BOONE, tanners in Exeter Township, in Berks County
—*Pennsylvanische Berichte*, October 23, 1761

SERVANTS AND SLAVES

In 1767, as seen in the tax assessment for that year, bound workers were augmenting the Oley Valley's supply of labor to a noticeable extent. These bound servants, who included white indentured servants and black slaves, presented an alternative for those proprietors who could afford them. Indentured servants were people who made a contract (an "indenture") putting themselves into a temporary state of bondage to another person in return for sustenance and one or more benefits to be delivered before, during, or at the end of their term of servitude. If under age, a person could be bound to someone's service by his or her parents. In Europe this was a centuries-old custom, a practice by which many future craftspeople were apprenticed and many children of poor families at least housed, fed, and given a small stake with which to essay adulthood. In the migration of northwestern Europeans to the thirteen colonies, indentured servitude evolved into a standard mechanism enabling poorer immigrants to obtain passage to the New World. During his or her period of bondage, the servant could learn the "custom of the country," as regarded farming or another means of livelihood, and other aspects of life, so that servitude functioned to integrate immigrants into Pennsylvania society. At the completion of his or her term, a servant received something to ease the passage to life as a free citizen, such as clothing, tools, a cow, or a small sum of money.

Alongside the institution of indentured servitude providing basic manual labor, there persisted another arrangement evidently of lesser magnitude in the valley, the traditional system of craft apprenticeship. Several wills specified the putting out of a son to learn a craft or trade of his choice, though others bequeathing the craftsman's tools or equipment imply that crafts tended to be handed down within the family. An indenture for apprenticeship, dated 1778 but no doubt similar to those made in the colonial years, was made for Johannes Hill, Jr., son to an Oley Township farmer, to "learn the trade, mystery or occupation of a tanner or currier" from elderly Exeter Quaker tanner James Boone. Young Johannes was to live with and serve Boone for three years, and to have the necessary instruction from him or from his son Moses. Johannes was to be fed, housed, clothed, and provided with laundering. "And the said apprentice may take the liberty (without making the same good again) of keeping all the Holy Days (so called), commonly kept by most Protestants, to wit, New-Year, Easter, Ascension, Whitsuntide, and Christmas, that is five days per annum."[32] Despite Boone's Quakerly disapproval of religious festivals, he provided Hill with the opportunity to trek across the valley to spend these holiday times with his family, an opportunity many young indentured servants, far separated from their kinsfolk, could not share.

Indentured servants probably did not become common in the valley until at least 1750, when the composition of German immigration into Pennsylvania took a decided turn toward younger and poorer people. Valley people began bringing Irish servants to their homes from the Philadelphia wharves by the 1740s. These may have for a brief time outnumbered German servants, but their ranks were evidently soon eclipsed by the latter. Slaves were also a presence throughout the colonial period, though because their purchase was expensive, there were never many.

A dearth of available labor was a problem in the early decades. Benjamin Longworthy and James Richard, unmarried men who owned tracts large enough for good-sized farms, were identified in documents as "laborers" instead of "yeomen" (i.e., freeholding farmers) in 1739 and 1741 respectively. Without children of their own they had no work force with which to farm. Family labor was essential at that point. On the other hand, Longworthy's and Richard's work on others' farms was no slight to their dignity as freeholders; they were probably garnering very good wages by European standards of the time. The colonies were plagued by an overall shortage of labor, so that wages were high.

As immigration of poor Irishmen and Germans rose in the 1740s, the taking of indentured servants began to be a more readily available option for people seeking laborers. But this was an investment that only those already wealthy, or those whose need for workers was imperative, could afford. A list of immigrant servants whose indentures were recorded before Philadelphia officials (a legally required process) from 1745-1746 named just five Oley Valley men as purchasers of eleven servants' terms. Servant indentures were freely transferable; the initial holder was the merchant or ship's captain to whom the servant owed the fee for his passage across the Atlantic. At wharfside this business person marketed the terms of the servants, who were inspected on shipboard by prospective purchasers.

One of the five Oley purchasers of 1745-1746 was Conrad Reiff, a farmer

THE ECONOMY

whose nine-hundred-acre plantation dwarfed almost all those of his contemporaries. Reiff bought the time of one servant. The other purchasers were all men involved in the valley's nascent refining and manufacturing industries, who had pressing needs for workers: ironmasters Johannes Lesher and William Bird, miller Johannes Joder, and tilemaker Jerg Adam Weidner. The two ironmasters bought five and three servants respectively, and the other two men one servant each. All terms were to run four years, except two that were for five years. All the servants were men, presumably single. All were Irish save the one chosen by Weidner, Jacob Tigle, who was perhaps an experienced German kiln tender. Fellow Irishman Bird had entered the Pennsylvania iron industry by the same route as these men, some twenty years earlier. The price to purchase a man's term of servitude ran from £15 to £21, or about £4 per annum. All were to receive "customary dues," nature unspecified. These were probably just food and drink and one simple suit of clothes while bound, and another suit and a tool when freed. Tigle managed to hold out for a two-year-old heifer in addition.

The tendency for better-off valley residents to buy the time of imported servants had picked up considerably by the years 1771-1773, when a similar list from the Philadelphia mayor's office recorded the acquisition of sixty-one servants, more than three times the annual rate of 1745-1746. The composition of servants had changed considerably—all were Germans, for one thing, though several Irish servants' indentures were sold to people from other localities.

Perhaps more striking, twenty-six of the servants constituted seven full if small (and probably young) family households of father, mother, and children, each family taken in service as a whole by the purchasing master. Ironmaster Mark Bird, then the county's wealthiest citizen, acquired four of these families with the stated intention of employing the fathers as woodcutters, promising them that they would "be found a log house to live in and a garden free of rent."[33] The mothers and children were no doubt to make themselves useful about Bird's ironworks and its hamlet of Birdsborough in a myriad of ways. Ironmasters Johannes Lesher and John Old, and well-off miller Johannes Bishop invested in the other families. Unlike Bird and Old, who settled for five- or seven-year indentures for the entire families, canny businessmen Lesher and Bishop had the indentures for the solitary children (both boys) in their servant families made out separately from those for their parents. Lesher required thirteen years from young Martin Effert, Bishop fifteen years from David Muller. The pairs of parents were to serve for five years and six years, respectively.

Also among the 1771-1773 servants were five married couples without children, one acquired by well-off Exeter Township farmer Abraham Levan (son of Isaac Levan), the others by ironmasters Lesher and Bird, and two evident brother-sister pairs, one pair going to miller Bishop, the other to his prosperous farmer neighbor Adam Altstadt. The remaining nineteen single servants, eighteen men and one woman, went to Bird, Lesher, Altstadt, and fifteen other well-off farmers, innkeepers, millers, and tanners. Therefore, the holding of servants remained concentrated among a small group, especially ironmasters.

The term of servitude for the single males varied from two years, nine months, to seven years, two months. The money paid the merchants selling the indentures ranged from about £5 to £7 per year of service, so that given a general upward movement in prices, the money value of servitude appears to have been about the same as in 1745-1746. The two lowest annually valued and longest-termed indentures for single male immigrants, for seven or more years at just £3 or £4 per annum, carried the provision that the servant was to be "taught to read in the Bible and write a legible hand,"[34] (as were the young sons in families indentured to Lesher and Bishop), suggesting that these lone immigrants were quite young. The sole single female in the group, Magdalena Weber, taken by Mark Bird, was also to be taught to read (though writing was not specified), and had her time of servitude valued very low, just £15 for twelve years. She was no doubt also quite young.

The 1767 tax assessment list for Oley and Amity townships, a few years earlier, recorded the presence of thirty-one indentured servants and ten slaves held by thirty-one heads of households. Not surprisingly, most of the people holding bound servants were relatively wealthy. Twenty (65 percent) of the thirty-one were rated at £20 or more, a status possessed by only forty-one (22 percent) of the two townships' households. As for the other masters, four were middling farmers (rated £16-18) and two were elderly men whose low assessments (£1 and £3) obscure the fact that they had turned their productive assets over to their children and retired. The final five were young men, without households full of well-grown children to assist them, for whom the bond servants represented ambitious investments. The tax assessments of these men ranged from £4 to £9. Among them was Johannes Fritz (£9), a blacksmith and tenant farmer listed for twenty-five acres planted in grain, one of the two townships' seven largest reported crops.

The tax list tells us the age of the black slaves in both townships, and that of the white servants in Oley, though it neglects to mention their sex. The twenty-one Oley servants were a youthful group. Most of them, twelve (57 percent) of the twenty-one, were between nineteen and twenty-one. Two (10 percent) were what we would call "teenagers" (though adolescence was an unheard-of cultural concept in 1767), sixteen and fourteen. A surprising five (24 percent) were only ten to twelve years old. The anomaly among the township's servants was a pair in Friedrich Meinert's household, a fifty year old and a six year old.

The practice of paying for passage across the Atlantic with indentures for servitude shattered many families, at least temporarily. Many immigrant families bound one or more of the family members to service in order to pay the passage charge. This phenomenon was likely responsible for the presence of some young servants, though the very young ones could just as easily have been poor people's children, like Samuel Dewees. Beginning in 1749, servants and former servants in the Oley Valley placed advertisements in the *Pennsylvanische Berichte*, a German-language newspaper printed in Germantown, seeking news of family members from whom they had become separated through servitude (as well as ones they knew had preceded them to Pennsylvania). For instance, in 1750 Margareta Hoffsess, a servant to Antony Jaeger, sought the whereabouts of her daughter Maria. In the same year Peter

Weller, who after nine years in America was "with Philip Beyer" of Amity, wanted news of his sisters Anna and Eva Maria, who had come on ship with him.

By the late colonial period, conditions were difficult for male servants. Of course, there always had been some masters who expected their investment in what might otherwise have been the best years of someone's life to be a good bargain, so that the work demanded tended to be plenty and arduous. Mittelberger, residing not far from Oley during the servant-dominated peak of German immigration, 1750-1754, observed his fellow countrymen's labors.

> Occupations vary, but work is strenuous in this new land; and many who have just come into the country at an advanced age must labor hard for their bread until they die. I will not even speak of the young people. Most jobs involve cutting timber, felling oak trees, and leveling, or as one says there, clearing, great tracts of forest, roots and all. Such forest land, having been cleared in this way, is then laid out in fields and meadows. . . . Our Europeans who have been purchased must work hard all the time. For new fields are constantly being laid out; and thus they learn from experience that oak tree stumps are just as hard in America as they are in Germany.[35]

By the 1760s, the opportunities open to a servant completing his term were becoming increasingly constricted. It took capital to buy a farm, set up as a tenant farmer, start in a craft, or migrate to the frontier, and wages for simple laborers had begun to decline. The situation of female servants was even more precarious. Young Katarina Krebs, an unmarried servant at Johannes Lesher's Oley Forge, stood trial for infanticide in 1767. Her predicament, that of a woman whose prospects for marriage and hence almost any kind of life would have been ruined by illegitimate motherhood in that era, had evidently driven her to desperation. The coroner gave as his opinion that the child had been strangled, though Katarina insisted the baby had been stillborn. She had managed to keep the pregnancy a secret. All that is known of this case's outcome is the endorsement on the back of the indictment paper, "Judgment suspended."[36]

Like Oley's white servants, the ten black slaves of Amity and Oley in 1767 were young. The majority of these slaves were a good deal younger than most servants. One was twenty-one, five were thirteen to fifteen, one was nine, and one was a "child." Nine years old, of course, was considered old enough to help with most work on a farm. The exceptions were ironmaster Johannes Lesher's two slaves, aged about forty. These were probably skilled ironworkers; William Bird's heir Mark had eight slaves working at his ironworks in Robeson and Union townships. There do not appear to have been any slave families in Amity or Oley in 1767. Other than Lesher, Conrad Reiff was the only slaveowner with two blacks, his both fourteen years old.

One wonders just how and where the slaveholders of the Oley Valley acquired these black youngsters. As far as their motives in purchasing slaves were concerned, the blacks evidently represented a secure, predictable source of labor. White indentured servants did not. It was too easy for them to run away and melt into the general population. The *Pennsylvanische Berichte*, *Pennsylvania Gazette*, and other regional newspapers printed numerous advertisements in which Oley Valley men offered rewards for runaway servants. The majority of servants worked out their terms without attempting escape, and most fugitives were ultimately apprehended. Mittelberger believed that

> No one in this country can run away from a master who has treated him harshly and get far. For there are regulations and laws that ensure that runaways are certainly and quickly recaptured. Those who arrest or return a fugitive get a good reward. For every day that someone who runs away is absent from his master he must as a punishment do service an extra week, for every week an extra month, and for every month a half year. But if the master does not want to take back the recaptured runaway, he is entitled to sell him to someone else for the period of as many years as he would still have had to serve.[37]

Still, antiquarian Peter Bertolet's elderly informants told him in the 1850s that flight by servants had been a chronic problem in colonial days.

In 1758, tilemaker Jerg Adam Weidner gave notice that his tilemaker-servant Johann Heinrich Unckelbach had taken leave of his own accord. Weidner, seen as new master to immigrant Jacob Tigle in 1746, had a frustrating time getting and keeping help. He put advertisements in the *Berichte* in 1743, 1749, 1750, and 1752 seeking tile-and-brickmakers and limeburners to work at his kiln. In 1767 he was listed as master to two slaves, but no white servants. It was more difficult for blacks to "disappear" into the Pennsylvania countryside.

How many valley farmers or craftspeople would have scrupled at buying a fellow human being, condemned to bondage for all his life, is impossible to tell. Abolitionism was a powerful force only among Quakers then, rooted in their belief that "the Light" (a Divine presence) existed within every person. No valley Quaker is listed as owning a slave in 1767, and for several years previously some local Friends had been quietly speaking to neighbors about the wrongness of slavery. As regards the valley's inhabitants at large, however, they were imbued with a European tradition of many centuries that saw all people as permanently placed in one particular social condition or another. Some of these social classifications were characterized by a lack of personal liberty. Many German immigrants to Pennsylvania, for example, had had to pay fees to their rulers to gain manumission from a state of feudal bondage in order to emigrate. To many people, American slavery was just the bottom-ranked regulated social status in their new homeland.

Some Oley Valley blacks unfortunately faced insensitivity from their owners, and in one case, savage cruelty. Of course, a master's heavy hand was not an unknown phenomenon to white servants, as Samuel Dewees relates in his memoirs. As a boy in the 1760s, Dewees was bound by his poor parents to the service of Richard Lewis, a Quaker farmer. Lewis, a poor excuse for a Friend, beat young Dewees frequently, despite the efforts of other Lewis family members and neighbors to intervene. Doctor Bertolet reports that ironmaster Lesher was reputed to have

THE ECONOMY

been a harsh taskmaster to his slaves.

Murder was the charge brought against Elisabetha Bishop after the death of her slave Louisa in 1772. The court testimony made a seemingly incontrovertible case that Bishop had killed Louisa by repeated and savage beatings and other physical abuse that took place over some time, but she was acquitted. Evidently the jury would not convict a white person for the murder of a black person. This testimony is preserved in transcripts that make difficult reading due to Bishop's evident sadism.

On some homesteads slaves fared better than on others. There were masters who manifested a paternalistic attitude by providing their slaves with opportunities for Christian religious experience. In 1741 the Reverend Gabriel Falck, the Swedish pastor of Molatton Church, baptized Elizabeth (four years old), Abigail (three years), and Dinah (seven months), the children of John and Jane Cudgeon, "black people and servants to Philip John, who promised to bring them up in the Christian faith."[38] Another Molatton parishioner had Heinrich Melchior Muhlenberg "deliver an exhortation to her numerous domestics, both negroes and white people."[39]

Proceedings of the Berks County Orphans Court from 1765, regarding the will of Benjamin Longworthy, throw some light on local attitudes toward black people and slavery. The elderly farmer was possessed of a black woman named Violet, and her three children, when he died that year. Longworthy was one of Oley's most longstanding residents in 1765, having settled by 1720 on land taken up and given to him by his father John, a farmer in Radnor, Chester County. Benjamin was born into a Quaker family, but was less than a fervent Friend himself. In 1752 Exeter Meeting officially expelled him from membership for marrying a non-Quaker, Maria Meinert, nonattendance at meeting, and "disorderly practices,"[40] precise nature unknown.

Benjamin's plantation had apparently gone unfarmed by him for decades, probably until he married Meinert, widow of a nearby neighbor. It is not known whether Longworthy's acquisition of Violet occurred before the marriage, perhaps to provide a bachelor with some domestic help, or afterward, to render the bride's resumption of wifely duties more palatable. Maria Meinert was a daughter of early settler Jacob Weber. Her husband Friedrich died in 1752, leaving her with three of their seven children still to raise. Her remarriage to Longworthy did not yield any new offspring.

After his death, some of Longworthy's Quaker neighbors charged that, in the elderly farmer's final few days, his wife Maria had taken advantage of his weakened, distraught mind to persuade him to replace his standing will with one more to her financial advantage. She had talked him out of his longstanding plan to free Violet's children (two sons and a daughter), and into the making of a new will. Evidently, neither old nor new will freed Violet. The new will retained the inheritance by Longworthy's devout Quaker nephews Moses and Joseph Roberts of the Longworthy farm, while reserving to the widow tenure of the house and its homestead appurtenances. The new will's real bonus for Maria was the right to sell Violet's three children. Violet was to remain a slave in Maria's supervision and care. Longworthy allowed "My old negro Violet" some belongings to call her own, "her bed and [bed]clothes, her spinning wheel, some flax she hath, and some few household goods that goes in her name."[41] The preceding will, drafted by Longworthy two months before his death, had been "thrown into the fire."[42] This destroyed testament would have set the young slaves free at age twenty-seven, entrusting them meanwhile to the care of the Roberts brothers.

The local Friends who made the situation of Longworthy's slaves their concern were William Boone, Mordecai Ellis, and Samuel Lee. They evidently had been working for years to bring their old meeting fellow to see the light, regarding the right of his African charges to their freedom. In May 1765 success was in view; Longworthy confessed to Boone that "He did not think his negroes as they were flesh and blood should be slaves."[43]

The three Exeter Quakers proved to the Berks justices' satisfaction that Maria had persuaded her failing husband to dictate the new will while "not of sound mind," rendering that document invalid. It was said that both Maria and her brother Jacob Weber, named with neighbor Jacob Geldbach as executors, intended to turn Longworthy's estate to their advantage.

As events unfolded, Moses Roberts took up ownership and residence at the Longworthy place. In 1768 he became a Quaker minister at Exeter Meeting. Maria Meinert Longworthy went to live with her son Friedrich Meinert at his rented farm. The slaves must have gone free, but there is no record of their subsequent experience.

PHILADELPHIA NEWSPAPER ADVERTISEMENTS FOR RUNAWAY SERVANTS FROM THE OLEY VALLEY

Runaway from Thomas Rutter at the ironworks in the county of Philadelphia, a servant man, named William Newberry, aged about twenty years. He is a West-Country man, and talks like one; of a brown complexion, his hair cut off, wearing a brown cap under his hat. He is remarkable, having lost his forefinger of his left hand. He has on very ordinary habit and leather breeches. Whoever secures him, and gives notice to his said master, or to John Rutter of Philadelphia, smith, shall have two pistoles as a reward.
—*American Weekly Mercury*, June 8, 1721

Run away, on the 4th of July past, from Samuel Tamplan, hammerman at Spring Forge, near Oley Township, in Philadelphia County, an Irish servant man, named James Murfy, about 20 years of age; he is a well-set thick fellow, of middle size and pretty fresh complexion, somewhat marked with the smallpox, and black hair lately cut off; he is slow of speech and smooth tongued, talks both Irish and English pretty well. Had on when he went away, a light colored kersey coat, a fine shirt, a yellowish colored silk handkerchief, a new castor hat, a linen cap, a pair of check linen trousers with brass buttons, a pair of thread stockings, new strong shoes and a pair of large brass buckles, somewhat carved or figured at the corners. He pretends to be something of a hammerman, but knows very little of it.

N.B. (Nota Bene) The said servant stole his indentures, which it is supposed he makes use of for a pass.

Whoever takes up and secures the said servant so that his master may have him again, shall have four pounds reward and reasonable charges,

    Paid by me, SAMUEL TAMPLAN
—*American Weekly Mercury*, July 28, 1743

RUN away the 5th of this instant from John Yoder, of Oley Township, Philadelphia County, two Irish servant men; the one named Daniel Donahew, about 40 years of age, of middling size, long thin visage, much pockmarked, has a large scar on his left cheek, and another on his neck, black hair, if not cut off, by trade a miller. Had on when he went away, a felt hat, homespun shirt, a light brown linsey jacket, with brass buttons, tow trousers, yarn stockings, and half worn shoes. The other named Thomas Lynch, about 20 years of age, well set, much frecked in his face, black hair, if not cut off. Had on when he went away, a chestnut colored linsey jacket, a fine hat, an ozenbrig shirt, tow trousers and new shoes. They took some other clothes with them, and perhaps may change those described above. Whoever takes up and brings the said servants to their master, or secures them in any gaol, so that he may have them again, shall have THREE PISTOLES reward for each, and reasonable charges, paid by
    JOHN YODER
—*Pennsylvania Gazette*, July 9, 1747

RUN away on the 13th inst. from William Bird, and James Keemer, of Amity Township, Philadelphia County, the 4 following men, viz.

William Burchell, an Englishman, about 30 years of age, a tall slender fellow, of a swarthy complexion, has short black hair; had a bundle of clothes, and it is not known what he may have on.

George Brooks, an Englishman, about 25 years of age, a short well-set fellow, of a swarthy complexion. Had on, a check shirt, and a striped flannel jacket, his other clothes not known.

Patrick Wall, an Irishman, a slender fellow, with a large nose, and very much freckled. Had on, a brownish coat, with a small velvet cape, he having a bundle, it is not known what he may have on.

Joseph Moore, an Irishman, a little short fellow, has short red hair, his right foot a little lame; who stole away from a servant man in the house, some Dutch writings, and a broad-cloth coat, lined with red, and yellow buttons, a scarlet jacket, with horse-hair buttons, 2 fine shirts, and a check ditto. Whoever secures the said men, so as they may be had again, or puts them in any gaol, shall have thirty shillings reward for each, paid by William Bird, and James Keemer.

The 3 first mentioned men, came lately into the country, and have stolen (which of them unknown) the following goods, viz. a brown jacket, a pair of trousers, and eighteen shillings in money, some brass buckles, and a fine shirt. It is supposed they will use the clothes, in order to make their escape.
—*Pennsylvania Gazette*, July 18, 1751

RUN away on the 8th inst. from William Bird, of Robeson Township, Lancaster County, an Irish servant man, named Patrick Wall, about 21 years of age, 5 feet 8 inches high, has a long sharp nose, thin faced, very much freckled, short brown hair, and has much of the brogue. He is a plasterer by trade, but pretends to be a sailor. Had on when he went away, a dirty colored cloth coat, old blue striped breeches, old blue stockings, half-worn shoes, with rusty iron buckles, and an old felt hat; is one of the four that run away last July, and was advertised in the weekly papers. He was lately brought home from New York, and it is supposed he will make that away again, in expectation to meet his companions, that were not taken. Whoever takes up and secures said servant, so as his master may have him again, shall have three pounds reward, and reasonable charges, paid by
    WILLIAM BIRD

N.B. He being bare of clothes, it is supposed he will steal others, as he did before, and change his name, in order to make his escape.
—*Pennsylvania Gazette*, September 12, 1751

Run away the 25th of this last December, from John Harrison, of Union Township, Berks County, near Bird's ironworks, a servant lad, named John or Johannes Manskul, about 19 years of age, of middle stature, and pretty round faced, his cheeks red, and marked with the smallpox. Had on and took with him when he went away, a good felt hat, a red silk handkerchief, a blue-gray jacket, and an old flannel or linsey one under it, a good new cloth one of a dark ash color, home made, the button holes worked with white worsted, a good pair of leather breeches, and old stockings, the upper parts speckled, and newly footed with a brown color, his shoes almost new, tied with strings. Whoever secures said servant, so that his master may have him again, shall have twenty shillings reward, and reasonable charges, paid by
    JOHN HARRISON
—*Pennsylvania Gazette*, December 31, 1754

Nicolaus Jaeger in Oley in Berks County makes known, that on October 20th a German servant named Christoph von Ernst ran away from him. He is 40 years old, short of stature, has black grayish hair, had on a blue shirt and a leather one over it, black short breeches, blue and white stockings, and a kid shirt, marked H. S. Whoever takes up the said servant and brings him, shall have forty shillings plus justified expenses from
    NICOLAUS JAEGER
—*Pennsylvanische Berichte*, November 6, 1761

CONCLUSION

The Oley Valley is well-known today for its collection of surviving colonial-period houses. These extant buildings might be considered an index of the economic success of their original owners and of the valley settlement at large. For those eighteenth-century houses that stand in America today, a small fraction of those built, have withstood a process of natural selection. In general, the survivors are here because of a superior durability, substantial character, and attractiveness that appealed to intervening generations as well as to our own. Among southeast-

THE ECONOMY

ern Pennsylvania houses built before 1776, two-story stone houses have tended to outlast their one-story and log-constructed mates. One result of the Oley Valley's economic success appears to have been the construction of a high proportion of two-story stone houses in comparison to other places in the province.

The prosperity of the farmers and other proprietors was rooted in their mastery of the southeastern Pennsylvania agricultural system of wheat cultivation for export coupled with general subsistence farming, as well as in the fertility of the earth of the valley. This agricultural system, an American development, benefited English-speaking and German-speaking settlers alike, and underlay the generally good relations among the nationalities that characterized the community life of the valley settlement.

NOTES

[1] Barry Levy, *Quakers and the American Family: British Settlement in the Delaware Valley* (Oxford: Oxford University Press, 1988), 14, 125-26.

[2] James T. Lemon, *The Best Poor Man's Country: A Geographical Study of Early Southeastern Pennsylvania* (Baltimore: The Johns Hopkins Press, 1972), 181.

[3] E. B. O'Callaghan, ed., *Documents Relative to the Colonial History of the State of New York*, vol. 5 (Albany: 1855), 52.

[4] Gottlieb Mittelberger, *Journey to Pennsylvania*, translated and edited by Oscar Handlin and John Clive (Cambridge, Mass.: Harvard University Press, 1960), 55.

[5] Will of Hans Martel Gerick, 1757, Berks County Wills, vol. 1, 44, Office of the Berks County Register of Wills, Berks County Courthouse, Reading, Pennsylvania.

[6] Israel Acrelius, *A History of New Sweden*, translated and edited by William M. Reynolds, vol. 11 of *Memoirs of the Historical Society of Pennsylvania*, 147.

[7] Ibid., 148.

[8] Ibid., 149.

[9] Will of Benjamin Boone, 1762, Berks County Wills, vol. 1, 124.

[10] Acrelius, *History of New Sweden*, 161.

[11] Exeter Monthly Meeting Men's Minutes, August 29, 1754, Friends Historical Library, Swarthmore College, Swarthmore, Pennsylvania.

[12] J. Bennett Nolan, "Ben Franklin's Mortgage on the Daniel Boone Farm," *Historical Review of Berks County* 10, no. 4 (July 1945), 115.

[13] Lemon, *Best Poor Man's Country*, 150, 169-80.

[14] Will of John Gelback, 1758, Berks County Wills, vol. 1, 51.

[15] *The Journals of Henry Melchior Muhlenberg*, edited by Theodore G. Tappert and John W. Doberstein (Philadelphia: The Evangelical Lutheran Ministerium of Pennsylvania and Adjacent States, 1945), vol. 1, 138.

[16] Mittelberger, *Journey to Pennsylvania*, 51-52.

[17] Inventory of Benjamin Boone, 1762, Probate Files, Office of the Berks County Register of Wills.

[18] Pehr Kalm, *Peter Kalm's Travels in North America*, edited by Adolph B. Benson (New York: Dover Publications, Inc., 1987; reprint of 1937 edition), 115.

[19] Mittelberger, *Journey to Pennsylvania*, 48-49.

[20] Kalm, *Travels in North America*, 162.

[21] Will of Benjamin Boone, 1762, Berks County Wills, vol. 1, 124.

[22] Acrelius, *History of New Sweden*, 152.

[23] Johann David Schoepf, *Travels in the Confederation 1783-1784*, translated and edited by Alfred J. Morrison (New York: Bergman Publishers, 1968; reprint of 1911 edition), 131.

[24] Thomas Jefferson Wertenbaker, *The Founding of American Civilization: The Middle Colonies* (New York: Charles Scribner's Sons, 1938), 278.

[25] Quoted in Amos Long, Jr., *The Pennsylvania German Family Farm*, Publications of the Pennsylvania German Society 6 (1972), 177.

[26] An erroneous reference to Pine Forge's later neighbor Pool Forge as having been Pennsylvania's first ironworks has been perpetuated via numerous studies of the charcoal iron industry. Pool Forge was located approximately two miles down Manatawny Creek from Pine Forge (and outside the study area researched for this work). It was built in 1725 by a partnership in which the Rutter family combined with five Philadelphia investors. The confusion regarding the respective dates of the Pine and Pool forges likely arose due to the relative similarity of the names, and perhaps to Pine Forge's not having been known by that name until around 1730. Earlier it was referred to simply as "Rutter's Forge" or "the Forge at Manatawny." The longstanding historical error was first identified by Linda McCurdy, in "The Potts Family Iron Industry in the Schuylkill Valley" (Ph.D. dissertation, The Pennsylvania State University, 1974), 45.

[27] Amity Township Tax List, 1731, Archives, Historical Society of Berks County, Reading, Pennsylvania.

[28] Berks County Tax and Exoneration Lists, 1767, Record Group 28 (Treasury Department—Office of the State Treasurer), Pennsylvania State Archives, Harrisburg, Pennsylvania.

[29] Mary M. Schweitzer, *Custom and Contract: Household, Government, and the Economy in Colonial Pennsylvania* (New York: Columbia University Press, 1987), 84-85, 240.

[30] This description of the prevalent forms of credit in colonial Pennsylvania is based on the discussion in Schweitzer, *Custom and Contract*, 142-45.

[31] William Bird Store Ledger, 1741-1744, Forges and Furnaces Collection, Manuscript Division, Historical Society of Pennsylvania, Philadelphia, Pennsylvania.

[32] Indenture of apprenticeship of John Hill, Jr., to James Boone, May 1, 1778, Boone Family Collection, Archives, Historical Society of Berks County.

[33] "Record of Indentures of Individuals Bound Out as Apprentices, Servants, Etc., October 3, 1771, to October 5, 1773," Pennsylvania German Society *Proceedings* 16 (1907), 43.

[34] Ibid., 323.

[35] Mittelberger, *Journey to Pennsylvania*, 20.

[36] Depositions in the case of Catharine Krebs, Berks County Oyer and Terminer Records, Record Group 33 (Supreme Court—Eastern Division), Pennsylvania State Archives.

[37] Mittelberger, *Journey to Pennsylvania*, 19-20.

[38] Churchbook of Saint Gabriel's Church, Saint Gabriel's Protestant Episcopal Church, Douglassville, Pennsylvania.

[39] *The Journals of Muhlenberg*, vol. 1, 210.

[40] Exeter Monthly Meeting Men's Minutes, July 30, 1752.

[41] Will (disallowed) of Benjamin Longworthy, 1765, Probate Files, Berks County.

[42] Minutes of hearing on the will of Benjamin Longworthy, 1765, Probate Files, Berks County.

[43] Ibid.

Chapter 3
THE ARCHITECTURAL LANDSCAPE

MORDECAI LINCOLN HOUSE, 1733, Exeter Township
A bank-sited example of the double-cell type.
Photo by Philip E. Pendleton.

The surviving colonial-period vernacular architecture of the Oley Valley is the primary source that permits the most intimate, evocative investigation into the daily experience of the people of that era. The term "vernacular architecture" refers to the traditional architecture of a given people, place, and time, as opposed to architecture founded on academic principle and cosmopolitan fashion, and derives from the concept of regional cultural tradition as developed by linguists.

Architecture represented investment. People needed structures for shelter and to provide spaces for work and for storage. Families put a large portion of their wealth into buildings. The more commodious and soundly constructed a building was, the better executed would be the work or the greater and safer the storage that would take place there. This was equally as true for houses as it was for barns or workshops. A family's house provided the space for much of a homestead's work and the safekeeping of produce and food, as well as being the setting for a family's sleeping, cooking and eating, fellowship, and entertaining. Much of the preparation of foodstuffs took place in the house. Some dairy work might be done in the cellar, the house's area of cold storage. The house garret (attic) was also an important storage space, providing a dry environment for the farmstead's grain crop. In addition a substantial house might have a smoke chamber (*Rauchkammer*) for smoking meat in the garret. This chamber adjoined the chimneystack, permitting admission of the necessary smoke. A large first-floor room, where cooking and informal gathering generally took place, very likely also would be the setting of handcraft manufacturing, whether done by the family itself or by visiting craftspeople such as shoemakers.

Architecture could represent another sort of investment for valley inhabitants, a social one. People use their ownership of material objects to communicate social status and aspirations. Architecture, the largest in scale and hence most visible of manmade objects, holds a paramount role in this function of artifacts. The elegance of a well-off colonist's cut-stone house facade or his parlor's nicely carved woodwork proclaimed to the passerby or guest that this was a man of substance. His (or, for that matter, her) pride in owning such a house reassured the owner himself that his life had been and was continuing a well-lived one. The modest rented cabin of a poor man conveyed his economic and social standing just as effectively.

OLEY VALLEY HERITAGE

CONSTRUCTION

One factor that molds the character of an area's vernacular architecture is the range of natural resources available to serve as building materials. Oley Valley people constructed buildings in four ways: log construction, timber frame, stone masonry, and brick masonry. Almost any given type of building, whether a Georgian house, a gristmill, or a stable, might be constructed in whatever material suited the prospective owner's preference and budget.

Perhaps the most commonly used of these methods was log construction. In Amity Township in 1799, fifty-three of the one hundred and four houses were built of log, and forty-five of the eighty barns. In 1775, twenty-four years earlier and before the post-Revolutionary wave of new building, the proportion that was log was probably somewhat higher. In general, the trend in the region over the eighteenth and early nineteenth centuries was away from log and toward stone construction. The more expensive latter form was desired for its image of permanence and its association in the still powerful European tradition, inherited by Pennsylvanians, with higher social status and material well-being.

The stereotypical view of log buildings as necessarily flimsy and coarse should be discarded, however. In the log house construction that appears to have predominated in the valley, walls were built of broad, hand-hewn logs locked together at the corners with carefully cut notching, the spaces between the logs chinked with mud, straw, and small wooden slats or rocks, the walls finished with plaster on the interior, and the whole set on a stone-masonry foundation. In hewing a log, a felling axe and a broadaxe were used to shape the timber to be roughly rectangular. The logs in many log-built outbuildings probably were left "round," that is, unhewn. The logs in the valley's corner-notched log buildings were joined by means of simple "V notches" and were built up on the exterior walls in courses to create a boxlike structure. The gable ends of the roof structure were covered with vertical boards.

This mode of construction would make a perfectly sound and comfortable dwelling by standards of the period. Many such log houses built in the 1700s were occupied well into the 1800s. The construction of a substantial log house was not a casual undertaking that any prospective homeowner could do with the aid of a comrade or two. The paid services of skilled professional carpenters were required.

Two variations on log construction were practiced in the Oley Valley, to at least a limited extent, though no examples are known to have survived. One was corner-post log construction, in which the logs were tenoned into vertical posts at the corners of the building, instead of being joined to those in the connecting walls

JACOB KAUFFMANN HOUSE, 1766, Oley Township
Detail of the attic, showing the smoke chamber.
Photo by G. Edwin Brumbaugh, circa 1931.
Courtesy, The Winterthur Library: Joseph Downs Collection of Manuscripts and Printed Ephemera.

THE ARCHITECTURAL LANDSCAPE

BERTOLET-HERBEIN HOUSE, Circa 1720-1750, Oley Township
A log-built example of the stove-room house type, in its original setting. The house has been moved to the Daniel Boone Homestead State Historic Site in Exeter Township.
Photo by Cervin Robinson, 1958. Courtesy, The Historic American Buildings Survey, Prints and Photographs Division, Library of Congress.

by notches. A one-and-a-half-story building at the Oley Moravian mission homestead, long gone but drawn by Francis Daniel Devlan around 1860, was an example of corner-post log construction. Devlan's friend Peter Bertolet identified this structure as the small Moravian schoolhouse built sometime in the middle years of the eighteenth century, but it is also possible that this was the original Moravian church or meetinghouse of 1742.

The other log building technique was that of plank or sawn-log construction. In this variant, builders employed logs that were sawn at a sawmill into straight-edged planks typically three or more inches deep and about a foot broad, and then planed smooth by hand. The very narrow spaces between the planks were caulked with oakum, instead of being chinked with mud and straw like ordinary corner-notched buildings. The corner joints of plank structures generally employed dovetail or half-dovetail notches for a particularly secure fit. Amity blacksmith and innholder Jacob Weber noted that his house was built "of sawn log"[1] in a notice he placed, advertising the property, in the *Pennsylvanische Berichte* in 1755. An "innholder" was the possessor of a license to keep an inn or tav-

BERTOLET-HERBEIN HOUSE, Circa 1720-1750, Oley Township
An example of V-type log corner notching, evidently the predominant technique in the colonial-period Oley Valley settlement. This house has been moved to the Daniel Boone Homestead State Historic Site in Exeter Township.
Photo by Philip E. Pendleton.

57

OLEY VALLEY HERITAGE

BAKEHOUSE-SMOKEHOUSE, COLONIAL-PERIOD LOG HOUSE AND NINETEENTH-CENTURY STONE HOUSE ON THE BERTOLET-HERBEIN HOMESTEAD, Oley Township
The same geometrical arrangement between log house and bakehouse persists at the two buildings' present location, the Daniel Boone Homestead State Historic Site, Exeter Township.
Photo by Harry F. Stauffer, 1965. Courtesy, The Historical Society of the Cocalico Valley.

ern, and not necessarily an innkeeper himself. A landowner who held a license often rented out the tavern stand, (i.e., the location of a tavern).

In recent years, scholars have put many speculative words to paper regarding the European origins of American log construction and the process by which this method came to take a preeminent role in the history of New World vernacular building. The discussion has focused on the absence of log construction from the early modern vernacular repertoire of the British Isles, and on the question as to whether the Finns and Swedes of New Sweden, or the early German-speaking immigrants from the Alps and other mountainous regions to the east, were the prime movers in bringing and adapting the particular forms (of corner notching and so on) that came to prevail.[2] Although none of the participants' arguments appear unassailable, it should be noted that both Swiss people and Delaware Valley Swedes were present in the Oley Valley.

Post-and-beam timber-frame construction was a method of building with wood less frequently employed in the colonial Oley Valley. In this form of work the building's structure or frame was composed of wooden members (sills, plates, posts, girts, joists, rafters, and purlins) secured together by mortise-and-tenon joints. Timber-frame construction had two main variations that appeared in the thirteen colonies. That favored by Pennsylvania Germans was half-timbering (*Fachwerk*), in which the building's skeleton of timbers was visible on its exterior and in fact composed an element in its external decoration. The wall space between the timbers was filled in with stone or brick masonry, or in the picturesque manner still seen in surviving buildings in the Rhineland, with plasterlike daub applied to wattle (woven sticks). At least two (now vanished) *Fachwerk* buildings, the Kühlwein House (Oley Township, 1724) and the Moravian Boarding School (Oley Township, 1748), were constructed by local Germans. It is likely that many buildings put up by the German settlers in the valley in the first half of the eighteenth century were half-timbered. The gradual collapse of the Moravian Boarding School building over the middle decades of the twentieth century was a tragic loss to the Oley Valley's architectural heritage.

The other basic form of timber-frame work was that in which the post-and-beam structure was clad in walls of clapboard or weatherboard. This method is associated by historians most strongly with the Chesapeake, New England, and New Netherlands (i.e., the Hudson Valley, western Long Island, and northern New Jersey) regions, though it was also practiced in southeastern Pennsylvania, especially in the city of Philadelphia. As Amity Township was home to many people of New England Yankee and Netherlandic heritage whose families had come there early in the eighteenth century, it is possible that some of the three frame houses and ten frame barns reported in 1799 from that township were built in this manner in the colonial years.

Stone masonry gives the valley landscape its distinctive architectural look. Stone construction, of course, had its own subcategories, depending on the character of the stone used and the manner in which it was laid. An elegant and expensive form, seen on many late-colonial

58

THE ARCHITECTURAL LANDSCAPE

valley houses but always restricted to the principal facade, was that of cut or finished stone, also known as "coursed ashlar." In this method stone was cut in precisely rectangular blocks of uniform height, which were laid in straight courses. Builders might have to bring appropriate stone from a distance, adding to the expense.

Other stone construction fell into the broad category of fieldstone or rough stone masonry. The relative regularity of a facade's constituent stones was the trademark of cut stone work; in rough stone masonry this regularity was absent. Stone from the homestead or nearby was used, which had an effect on the character of the stonework. If adequately large stones were readily available, as frequently happened in the Oley Valley, they could be laid in rough courses. If only small stones were available, the stone would be laid as random, uncoursed rubble.

All modes of stone construction employed in the Oley Valley necessarily shared one technique, the use of large, rectangular corner stones or quoins, to lock the structure together. Composing a sturdy corner of the building's "box," quoins were set one atop another, alternating between the wall directions in which they were oriented. Quoin stones were sometimes chosen, for decorative effect, of a distinctive and uniform color that contrasted with that of most of the stones in the building.

One necessary matter with which builders constructing masonry buildings had to deal was how to properly bridge the window and door openings to support the wall structure. Simple lintels of wood or stone could be used for the construction of such relieving arches, and most often were. A stylish touch was conferred to some houses of Georgian Palladian design by using the straight or jack arch, made of cut stone. This element from the Georgian architectural vocabulary was a segmental lintel embodying the three-part symmetry so often expressed in Georgian design, with a wedge-shaped keystone flanked by horizontal blocks. Popular with German-speaking builders desiring to add a decorative touch was the segmental arch composed of bricks (with the head or end of each brick visible).

Regardless of the particular sort of stone construction employed, limestone was generally available, especially in the upper valley, to be burned in order to procure lime with which to make mortar. Master tile- and brickmaker Jerg Adam Weidner advertised in the *Pennsylvanische Berichte*, seeking to employ lime-burners, in 1750 and 1752.

Weidner's operation was making bricks by 1749, at which date he announced that he was the proprietor of both "a tileworks and a kiln in good running order."[3] Jerg Adam's father Adam Weidner had begun making tiles, and possibly

JOSEPH BOONE HOUSE, 1765, Amity Township
An example of cut stone masonry.
Photo by Philip E. Pendleton.

JOHANNES BISHOP HOUSE (Bishop Hall), Circa 1774, Exeter Township
Detail showing jack arch lintels spanning vertical sash windows, cut stone masonry and the Georgian-style decorative woodwork of the cornice.
Photo by Philip E. Pendleton.

59

OLEY VALLEY HERITAGE

bricks as well, at his homestead in northeastern Oley Township around 1727. Jerg Adam took over the kiln business around 1740, and soon moved the operation to a property just outside the northeastern corner of Amity (in present-day Earl Township) that he purchased in 1741. In notices published in 1752 and 1760, Jerg Adam Weidner explicitly sought to employ brickmakers as well as tilemakers. In addition to the Weidners' ongoing production at a central location, bricks presumably also could have been manufactured at a given construction site, so long as a deposit of appropriate clay was present.

Brick masonry was seldom employed in the valley to build the essential structure of a building during the colonial years, however. Instead, it was limited to the construction of segmental fenestration arches, chimney structures, bake-ovens, and vaulted cellar-roofs. The presence of small relic deposits of square, relatively flat bricks at some valley settlement sites, and the presence of such bricks in situ in the spring cave on the Schenkel Homestead and in the cellar of the Jacob Kauffmann House, both in Oley, show that such bricks were used sometimes for flooring in kitchens and cellars. The only known example of a completely brick-built house is the original section of the Robert Stapleton House, built around 1730-1735 in Oley Township.

The materials used in construction varied, but there were certain methods of structural engineering to which practically all colonial-period Oley Valley vernacular buildings adhered. Buildings in general may be thought of as structural

MARTIN SCHENKEL HOUSE, 1766, Oley Township
Three views of the vault-ceiled spring cave adjoining the cellar. In View A, within the cave, the stairs lead to the open air next to the gable end of the house. Behind the arched opening at left-center is another subterranean room, its floor covered entirely by several feet of water, communicating with the barrel-vaulted half of the Schenkel House cellar by means of a short, stone-built stairway. View B looks out from the spring cave to the adjacent, circular walled pond. View C looks across the pond at the spring cave and the house. Above the foundation, it appears that the house may have been altered considerably during the nineteenth century.
Photos by Kenneth LeVan.

THE ARCHITECTURAL LANDSCAPE

MAUGRIDGE-DETURK HOUSE (Daniel Boone Homestead), Cellar Circa 1730, Exeter Township
Detail of the cellar. To construct a house's foundation so as to incorporate an existing spring was a common practice in rural Pennsylvania during the colonial period. The stone arch visible in the photo had supported the hearth of the original house on the site, a structure of one-room plan erected circa 1730 by Squire Boone (father of the Kentucky pioneer Daniel Boone, born at this site in 1734). Circa 1770-1775, Johannes DeTurk raised the walls and ceiling of the cellar in replacing the structure built by Boone.
Photographer unknown, circa 1960. Courtesy, Jane Levan.

JOHANNES HOCH, JR., HOUSE-MILL (Peter's Mill), 1761, Oley Township
Detail of brick segmental arch over a window.
Photo by Kenneth LeVan.

systems designed to remain standing. Buildings may accommodate or facilitate any number of functions, but this is the essential one. The key consideration in a building's structural design is the ability of any given component part of the whole to withstand the pressure wrought by the force of gravity acting on those parts situated above it.

The basic construction materials employed to build the outer walls of valley buildings, thick logs, stout timbers or stone, were equal to the general task. Exterior walls, especially those of stone, generally were built diminishing in width from foundation to summit, by a step at each floor level, in order to ease the load. Joists, timbers anchored in the lateral (or eaves) exterior walls, spanned the depth of the building to carry the floor boards. Still, the weight of the floors, and that of all the human activity and possessions that moved or stood on them, tended toward the interior of the house, particularly in broad double-pile (i.e., two-room-deep) buildings. To compensate for this centripetal force, at each floor level building craftspeople used a large beam anchored in the end walls. This beam, called a summer or summer beam, ran the length of the building and carried the floor joists. The summer beam itself required some support at or near the center of the house. In Pennsylvania German houses with massive, centrally-positioned chimneys, this support would be provided by running the summer beam through the masonry chimney stack. In some large double-pile structures, an internal masonry-bearing wall, that also served as a partition wall, helped carry the summer beam. In other buildings, sturdy vertical posts fulfilled this function. Anglo-Pennsylvanian builders generally morticed the joists into the summer beam, so that both timbers were on the same level. Pennsylvania German builders usually had the joists rest atop the summer beam.

The summer beam and joists supporting the second floor of a two-story, stone-constructed house were often positioned projecting through the exterior walls to fulfill an additional architectural function, one external to the building. This was the support of a pent roof, a shed-roofed structure encircling the building, the purpose of which was evidently to shelter the first-story masonry from the effects of wet weather. Pents were used both in England and the Rhine Valley in the period. Although now missing from most Oley Valley houses that originally had one, a pent's former presence is suggested by a belt of rubble stonework surmounted by a drip course, a line of narrow, projecting stones placed to protect the joint between the pent roof and the wall, and by the ends of the wooden beams, now flush with the exterior wall surface. Two-story log houses were occasionally constructed in Pennsylvania with pent roofs for the benefit of the chinking, though no examples are known from the valley. Some valley houses built after mid-century boasted pent eaves across both gable ends. These were pent structures at eaves level, generally joined with a relatively broad eaves overhang of roof beyond the house's lateral walls, to provide greater protection for the walls.

In the colonial period, Oley Valley carpenters could almost have their pick of mature hardwood trees from previously uncut forest. The result was the use of

single large timbers for such sizable wooden building elements as summer beams and plates (the timbers that ran atop the lateral exterior walls and carried the rafter feet), thereby conferring additional strength to the structure. Summer beams were often particularly imposing timbers; in larger buildings these beams were often a foot or more square in cross section. Oak, tulip poplar, and chestnut were the favored woods.

The partition of a house's interior space into smaller spaces necessitated the construction of additional, internal walls. In a particularly large house, one partition wall running the full depth of the building might be a masonry-bearing wall, that is, one that helped bear the load of the structure. But most partition walls were constructed either of vertical boards, or of plaster over studs and lath. Plaster was concocted from lime, mud, sand, straw, and animal hair. During the late colonial years, ceiling surfaces in the more substantial houses were often finished with plaster, at least on the first floor, though this practice was more common among Anglo-Pennsylvanians than among Germans. In the words of architectural historian Edward A. Chappell, Pennsylvania Germans tended toward "open expression of the construction methods"[4] in their approach to a house's finish. With

JACOB KAUFFMANN HOUSE, 1766, Oley Township
View looking from the level-ceiled half of the cellar through the passage into the barrel-vaulted section.
Photo by G. Edwin Brumbaugh, circa 1931.
Courtesy, The Winterthur Library: Joseph Downs Collection of Manuscripts and Printed Ephemera.

JACOB KAUFFMANN HOUSE, 1766, Oley Township
View within the cellar barrel vault.
Photo by G. Edwin Brumbaugh, circa 1931.
Courtesy, The Winterthur Library: Joseph Downs Collection of Manuscripts and Printed Ephemera.

THE ARCHITECTURAL LANDSCAPE

regard to ceilings, this preference meant leaving the summer beams, the joists, and the underside of the flooring exposed.

For building foundations, stone construction was practically universal in the Oley Valley. In addition to marshaling adequate strength to support the upper stories and roof of a house, thick cellar walls provided an appropriate space for the storage of food and drink, resistant to the southeastern Pennsylvania climate's sudden swings in temperature. An excavated cellar might extend beneath the entirety of a house's first floor, or be only partial in plan. At the Johannes Lesher House, Jacob Kauffmann House, and Martin Schenkel House, all built by German-speaking inhabitants in Oley Township, the cellar is divided between a barrel-vaulted chamber and a room ceiled (like most house cellar spaces) by the first-floor structure. German settlers also built vaulted root cellars as structures separate from houses. A method of further insulation for level-ceiled cellar spaces, favored by German inhabitants, was to pack the spaces between first-floor joists with clay, straw, and nuts, and seal this infill with plaster.

Crowning the architectural edifice was the roof structure, a system within the complex system of the overall building to which master builders devoted particular care. A building's walls might be constructed of log, timber frame, stone, or brick, but its roof structure was necessarily an example of mortised-and-tenoned timber framing. Following traditional European practice, roof structures built in the Oley Valley during the colonial period tended to be constructed of relatively numerous and heavy timbers. These timbers added considerably to the load that had to be borne by the lower structure of the building. This was especially true of the roof frames on buildings belonging to the German-speaking members of the community.

Two basic types of roof structure commonly were employed in the valley. One structure consisted simply of common rafters. The other structure relied primarily on the eminently sturdy strut-supported roof (in German, a *liegender Dachstuhl*), a truncated-principal-rafter-and-collar structure that had originated in the German-speaking area of Europe. An apparently less common, but also heavily framed, post-supported roof (in German,

ROOT CELLAR ON THE JACOB KEIM HOMESTEAD, Pike Township
Photo by Kenneth LeVan.

JACOB KAUFFMANN HOUSE, 1766, Oley Township
Strut-supported roof frame.
Photo by Cervin Robinson, 1958. Courtesy, The Historic American Buildings Survey, Prints and Photographs Division, Library of Congress.

63

a *stehender Dachstuhl*), was used by Germans on small buildings in Oley, two of which survive (the Keim and DeTurk ancillary houses). In the latter system, vertical posts, arranged in pairs, supported particularly stout through purlins that in turn carried the common rafters.

A common rafter is a timber that runs sloping from roof peak down to eaves, directly supporting the roof covering. Rafters are arranged in pairs, one rafter for each slope. The rafters might be footed in joists for the garret floor or in plate timbers, and are fastened together with a mortise-and-tenon carpenter's joint at the peak. One timber has the mortise (i.e., the receiving excision), the other the tenon (i.e., the projection). A treenail (wooden peg), hammered through the two timbers, secures the joint. Each pair of rafters is usually connected and reinforced by a collar beam, a horizontal timber positioned perhaps half or three-quarters of the distance from floor to peak. A through purlin is a horizontal timber, that runs through the roof structure against the sloping side, parallel to the roof ridge and situated about halfway from eaves to peak, on which common rafters rest. A principal rafter is a large sturdy timber, built to carry (with its fellows) all the rest of the roof structure elements. Only a few pairs of principal rafters would be employed in a roof structure of that type, as opposed to several times as many common rafters in a roof frame composed solely of the latter.

The strut-supported roof system might be said to represent a double roof structure. The roof covering is carried by a common-rafter structure that is in turn borne by a heavy principal-rafter structure. The principal rafters are truncated, that is, cut off about halfway from floor to peak, with each pair of principal rafters connected by a collar beam. A through purlin runs directly beneath each roof slope, supported by the principal rafters. The purlin carries the lighter and much more numerous common rafters. Architectural historians have recorded several variants of the strut-supported roof system. Most often, for each pair of principal rafters there is a pair of common rafters directly above, with the common rafters also connected by a collar beam. The resulting paired collars are immedi-

JOHANNES LESHER HOUSE (Oley Forge Mansion), Circa 1750-1755, Oley Township Isometric projection of the strut-supported roof structure. In the variant of the strut-supported system embodied in the Lesher House, the rafters are footed on a top plate, which rides the ends of the attic floor joists, which are carried in turn by the plate proper.
Drawing by Hope M. LeVan, from field measurements by Kenneth LeVan and Hope M. LeVan.

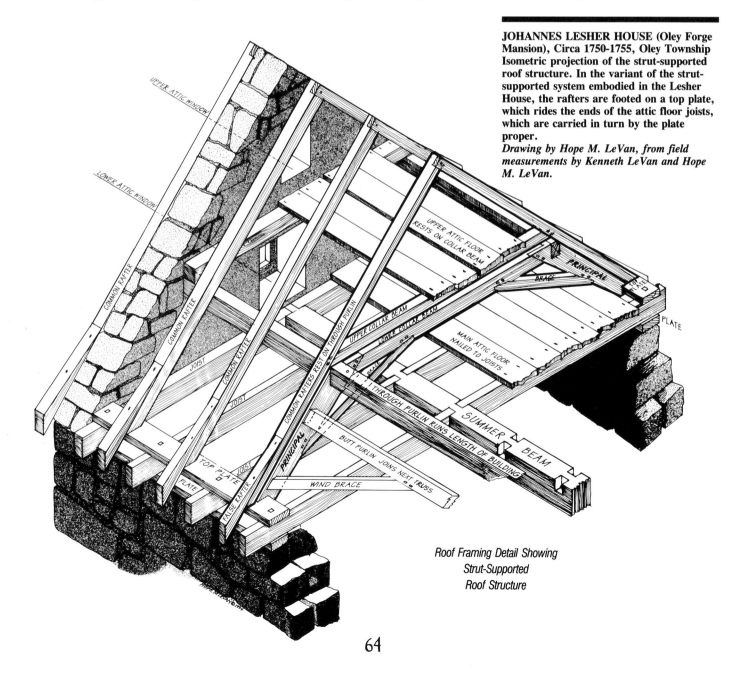

Roof Framing Detail Showing Strut-Supported Roof Structure

THE ARCHITECTURAL LANDSCAPE

ately suggestive of the doubled roof structure. Sturdy braces reinforce the basic truss of truncated principal rafter and collar. Others situated along the roof slope strengthen the structure's resistance against wind pressure, while further securing the purlins to the principal rafters. These latter wind braces are sometimes assisted by (and joined to) butt purlins, shorter purlins that run from one pair of principal rafters to the next. The surviving Oley Valley examples of the complex and sturdy strut-supported roof structure are impressive representations of the eighteenth-century vernacular builder's art.

A final, and very German, touch applied to many roof structures by German-speaking builders was the "kick," an outward flare to the roof at the eaves. The kick confers a slight bell cast to the roof as viewed from a gable-end perspective. The builder's intent is thought to have been to give some further protection to the building's walls by deflecting the rain, as with the pent roof and pent eaves. To create the kick a builder attached a "false rafter" timber, typically two feet or so in length, to the upper surface of each true rafter at the latter's lower end, so that the false rafter overlapped and extended outward.

"The barns are often roofed with thatch, and the houses with tiles, fabricated in the neighborhood,"[5] observed John Penn in 1788, in the vicinity of Pottsgrove (now Pottstown), just to the southeast of the Oley Valley. A builder's choice regarding roof structure appears not to have been a random decision, nor one based on simple adherence to architectural tradition. Instead, the choice was directly related to the sort of roof covering the owner had chosen for the building interior's shelter. The choice of roof covering in turn represented considerations regarding function and expense. Clay tile was the most fire-resistant, thatch made of rye straw the least expensive. Wooden shingles were relatively durable and moderate in price. The application of thatch to a roof required the use of far fewer expensive nails, wrought individually on a blacksmith's hearth, than did wooden shingle.

The preferences of the cultural groups among the settlers exerted significant influence on the choice of roof covering. Both English-speakers and German-speakers generally used thatch on barns and agricultural outbuildings. A former Oley Valley thatcher told writer Alliene DeChant in 1953 that he had thatched roofs as late as 1900.[6]

ABRAHAM BERTOLET HOUSE, 1736, Oley Township
An example of the chambered hall house type. The one-story wings to either side of the main block are additions, both made subsequent to the colonial period, after the role of this building had evolved from the homestead's principal dwelling to the part-dwelling, part-work space one of an ancillary house. The roof is still covered entirely with clay tiles.
Photo by Kenneth LeVan.

In roofing houses, however, the two cultural groups tended to differ. German-speaking families were in general more recently arrived from Europe, and their connection with their European heritage was stronger than that of their Anglo-Pennsylvanian counterparts. Germans preferred to employ the traditional clay tiles on large houses (also known and used in England), as well as on the somewhat more fire-prone bakehouses and smokehouses. The tiles, however, were heavy, and in large houses the weight required the construction of a heavy roof structure, such as that based on the strut-supported roof structure, for support. The post-supported roof structure, also sturdily framed, was used to support tiles on

OLEY VALLEY HERITAGE

GEORGE BOONE, SR., HOUSE, 1733,
Exeter Township
The original arrangement of front stoop, flanking benches and door hood.
Photo by Eleanor Raymond, circa 1930. From Eleanor Raymond, **Early Domestic Architecture of Pennsylvania, 1930.**

some small buildings. The use of the strut-supported system in the Abraham Bertolet House, a small dwelling built in Oley Township in 1736, implies that this was the predominant system for tile-roofed houses in the early years (before about 1750). In a substantial house the distinctively steep roof pitch, conferred by the strut-supported structure, enabled German farmers to create a two-level garret for ample grain storage. The tiles lessened the danger of fire that might originate in the smoke chamber (*Rauchkammer*), often built in a house's garret.

Today's weekend traveler, embarked on a tour of the valley, might remark that surviving clay tile roofs are restricted to small buildings. At some time evidently the local supply of tiles became finite, probably around the passing of Oley Valley tilemaker Jerg Adam Weidner in 1781. After that time, as tiles were broken, commonly because of encounters with tree limbs or branches felled in windstorms, and the number became inadequate to roof a house properly, the shrinking complement of tiles on a given homestead (eighteenth-century artifacts all) was moved to cover smaller buildings.

Inhabitants of English-speaking heritage favored the readily available hand-split wooden shingle to roof houses, a mode of covering virtually unknown in the British Isles, where thatch, stone flag, stone tile, and clay tile held sway. Roof structures consisting only of common rafters and their collars were adequate to carry this relatively light covering. With their long, tapering rafters, such frames can be striking exemplars of the builder's craft in their own way, when spanning the broad garrets of double-pile houses.

Germans also frequently roofed small houses with wooden shingles, supported by common-rafter roof structures, but struck a note of cultural separateness by doing so with the distinctive double-beveled or side-lapped shingle. The double-beveled shingle probably was brought to Pennsylvania from the Swiss area of the Rhine Valley, which was better forested than the region farther north. The Bertolet-Herbein House, built in Oley Township about 1720-1750 and thus roughly contemporary with the Abraham Bertolet House, was built with a common-rafter roof. Thus the common-rafter system probably was employed in German houses in the valley as early as was the strut-supported roof system.

Both kinds of shingles, the single-beveled type used by Anglo-Pennsylvanians and the German double-beveled shingle, are long, narrow, thin boards. When laid on the roof in company with its fellows, most of a shingle is not visible because the shingles above are overlapping it. Single-beveled "English" shingles taper only over their long dimension, to permit this overlap, while double-beveled German shingles taper both in that manner and sidewise, with a second bevel along one long side. Thus, double-beveled shingles are laid with overlapping occurring from the side as well as from above. Covering a roof with shingles the German way was noticeably more intensive in its expenditure of labor and materials than the English way, but it evidently resulted in a roof that lasted a good deal longer and was more watertight.

A building's exterior walls were pierced by the fenestration (a handy term, in that it incorporates windows, doors, vents, and other openings). On valley houses built before 1750 or so, windows tended to be few and small. The number and size of windows on the typical house increased as the years passed, and window construction changed. At the opening of the eighteenth century, and hence the beginning of European settlement in the Oley Valley, casement windows were predominant. The simple swinging shutter might be glazed (i.e., containing glass) or merely wooden. No intact casement window has survived in a valley building designed solely as a dwelling house. A pintel (the short vertical, bar-shaped piece of hardware, on a pair of which the casement window turned) is in place at a window opening in the Hans Mirtel Gerick House (Exeter, built 1741), however. The wide rectangular shape of the window openings in the Mounce Jones House (Amity, 1716) suggests that that building originally had the casement type. The window openings of somewhat later valley English-speakers' dwellings, such as the Joseph Rutter House (Douglass, 1731), George Boone, Sr., House (Exeter, 1733), and Mordecai Lincoln House (Exeter, 1733), appear to have been built to accommodate the familiar vertical sash window, as do those of valley Germans' houses from the 1750s onward. Thus German people in the valley probably continued the use of casement windows for a period after this type had been forsaken by their English-speaking neighbors.

A third type of window used in the valley, identified with relatively early use in houses by Pennsylvania Germans, was horizontal sash, in which the moving piece slid sideways to open. The Bertolet-Herbein House (Oley Township, about 1720-1750) and the Wilhelm Pott House (Pike, about 1735-1740, no longer standing) both bore evidence that they had been fitted with windows of this type. A window of this kind is still in situ in a nondwelling building, in the around-1775 section of the Schneider Mill (Exeter).

Many colonial-period houses in southeastern Pennsylvania were fitted with a stoop, a small porch adjoining the principal entry, and no doubt many in the Oley Valley displayed this feature. Gottlieb Mittelberger, resident in the hamlet named Trappe (located about twelve miles southeast of the Oley Valley) during the early 1750s, noted that

> All houses have two benches on each side, set up about four feet straight out in front of the door. Resting on two columns . . . is a roof like that of a garden pavilion. . . . Every evening when the weather is fine people sit on the benches.[7]

The elaborate dwelling of Oley Forge ironmaster Johannes Lesher originally boasted full-width balconies across both front and rear facades. These balconies were similar to those often seen on refined residences and public buildings of German Palladian design in Europe, as well as on a few elite houses in the Philadelphia vicinity. Many substantial Pennsylvania German houses in the Oley Valley had a small balcony on the rear facade, the precise function of this feature unknown.

VERNACULAR HOUSE TYPES

The colonial inhabitants of the Oley Valley built houses in several different types. The term "house type" means a sort of house defined by its plan, the configuration of the house, and the spaces within it. A given house type embodied a particular way of living in a house, with the different rooms in the plan the settings for certain activities or functions. The amount of resources that a family could put into the creation of its house was, of course, a limitation on the house's size, so that the number of options a family had about house type was necessarily somewhat circumscribed. There was a world of difference between the way the various rooms were used (and no doubt life in general was lived) in a house type with two rooms versus one with eight or more rooms plus two hallways. No two houses were exactly the same, but early American people adhered to a few familiar types. Many house types were rooted in architectural tradition that was an aspect of folk culture, so that people of a certain national or regional background tended to build certain types. The number of different house types built in the Oley Valley was in part a reflection of the variety of nationalities represented there.

The full range of house types built in the valley is not known. Present knowledge indicates that the surviving colonial buildings, of which the valley's modern residents are so justifiably proud, do not represent the full domestic architectural spectrum that was present in the period. In particular, it is largely the impressive homes built by the better-off residents that have survived from pre-Revolutionary days. There are only a few examples of tenant houses and the homes of other people of modest circumstances. This dearth of evidence presents a particularly difficult obstacle to discussion of the architecture of the early period of settlement, before 1750 or so.

The first dwelling on a given homestead, during the settlement's early decades, was usually a rudimentary abode, assembled immediately upon the arriving pioneer's having made a tentative selection of land to claim. In many cases this was probably just a tent, perhaps pitched over a dugout. Doctor Bertolet, the 1850s Oley antiquarian, noted a Boone family member's recounting that the patriarch George Boone, Sr., had built a "log cabin without floor"[8] for his first dwelling in 1718. Such simple houses, probably consisting of only a single room, would shelter a family during the first few backbreaking years of establishing a farmstead. Creating fields took precedence over building a permanent house.

Only a few substantial houses in the Oley Valley are reliably dated to the first half of the eighteenth century. Scholars of the vernacular architecture of early southeastern Pennsylvania suspect that, during the first few decades of the eighteenth century, the region's architectural landscape was characterized by a wide diversity. This corresponded to the equally diverse backgrounds of the area's settlers, who had come from so many different areas in northwestern Europe. A small region of Germany or England might have a distinctive architectural tradition. The first generation of permanent houses in the Oley Valley, which was a community of settlers as wide-ranging in variety of backgrounds as any in the Mid-Atlantic region, may have included domestic architecture of highly diverse description.

The known house types built in the valley before 1776 can be classed in six groups: (1) one-room plans, (2) a two-room plan possibly derived from urban housing of the period, (3) types rooted in English tradition, (4) those derived from German tradition, (5) the double-pile center-passage plan that embodied Palladian or "Georgian" architecture in colonial America, and (6) types that represent Palladian-influenced modifications of vernacular plans. The house types are illustrated by isometric projection drawings of Oley Valley examples. Each drawing represents a reconstruction of the building's evident original form. The level of detail has been restricted to enhance clarity, and the houses have been rendered in a uniform scale to facilitate comparison. Although the drawings are based on field measurement, the tendency for a historic building to have been altered somewhat over time has necessitated the speculative positioning of some features. For these isometric projection drawings, see Appendix 6.

Houses with one-room plans could be of one story or two in height. Dwellings composed of one first-floor room are called "halls" by vernacular-architecture students, the English word "hall" in its medieval sense meaning the domestic space in which cooking and the other work of daily household living were done. In such a one-room house, not only all the work but all the living, including giving birth and dying, went on in the hall and a low, ill-lit loft. Privacy as moderns define it was unknown. One-room houses probably composed a great share, perhaps a majority, of Oley Valley houses during the first half of the 1700s. They were no doubt the usual sort of residence occupied by poorer people (e.g., those rated with taxable wealth worth just £1 or £2 on the 1767 tax list) throughout the colonial period. This once-predominant house type is an almost invisible element in the surviving landscape. Some extant houses built in two or more stages started as one-room houses a single story in height. Examples of these include the ancillary buildings (i.e., multipurpose auxiliary structures generally incorporating additional dwelling space) at the Leinbach-Knabb and Gregory-Weidner homesteads, both in Oley Township. The original section of the Gregory-Weidner ancillary was built of log, probably sometime in the first third of the eighteenth century, that of the one at the Leinbach-Knabb Homestead of stone, around 1735.

If a person wanted to build a house comprising two full rooms, then a "chambered hall" (i.e., a hall with a full-story room [chamber] over it) was a logical choice. The Abraham Bertolet House in Oley Township, built in 1736, is an example. Like the single-room hall, the chambered hall was a modest dwelling type not peculiar to any particular nationality group among the settlers. Given the somewhat spartan conditions of material life prevailing at the still early date of 1736, Abraham Bertolet's stone house with its refined woodwork was probably considered a respectable home.

A house type with evident city roots was the "double-cell house," also known as the "Penn-plan house." (Such names for house types were not used by contemporaries; they have been coined by scholars to facilitate discussion.) The double-cell house was a structure only one room wide, but two rooms deep. Picture a single early Philadelphia row house taken out of line, away from its mates, and set down in a rural environment. The double-cell house was predominantly an early house type in the valley, like the chambered hall (which was also a common urban house type). The double-cell house may seem an unlikely choice of plan for the early Pennsylvania countryside. The probable explanation is that the stonemasons brought out to the Oley Valley from Philadelphia in the early eighteenth century were well practiced in building this type. To the wealthier residents who were employing these craftsmen, this was a house of appropriate size and familiar plan. Double-cell houses were built in one-story and two-story versions, as in contemporary towns and cities.

The original section of the Mordecai Lincoln House in Exeter, built 1733, is a bank-sited, one-and-a-half-story rendition that had its kitchen in the cellar and had finished living space in the garret, as was common in Philadelphia. (The term "half-story" refers to a building in which the exterior walls rise a few feet above the level of the garret floor, thereby creating a "knee wall." In a one-story or two-story building the garret floor and the top surface of the exterior wall are at roughly the same level.) Around 1760, Mordecai Lincoln, Jr., doubled the size of the Lincoln House with an addition similar in plan to the earlier half.

Houses of the double-cell type, being of modest size, were very commonly added to; the plan is also a typical form taken by additions to houses in the eighteenth and early nineteenth centuries. The west wing of the Johannes Joder, Sr., House, Oley Township, added in 1741, is an early example of a double-cell addition. Some double-cell houses were built on a larger scale with three bays (i.e., window or door openings) in the facade instead of the more common two bays. The original section of the White Horse Inn in Amity, built sometime in the middle years of the eighteenth century, is one such two-story house.

ANGLO-PENNSYLVANIAN HOUSE TYPES

The "hall-parlor house," also a two-room plan, was the most common Oley Valley house type derived from the English folk-architectural tradition. In Pennsylvania, the hall-parlor house was built in one story or two, though only two-story examples survive in the Oley Valley. The single-pile (i.e., one room deep) hall-parlor had a general composition similar to that of the double-cell. These two house types differed, however, in the roof's orientation to the shape of the house, the typical position of fireplaces and external doors, the relative proportions of the rooms, and often the location of the kitchen. In the double-cell house, the two rooms were usually of equal size, while in the hall-parlor, the hall was almost invariably somewhat larger than the parlor.

The hall of the hall-parlor remained the less formal space where cooking and

HOUSE ON THE GREGORY-WEIDNER HOMESTEAD, Circa 1719-1730, Oley Township
The original log-built section, to the left, is representative of the hall or single-cell house type. The building was enlarged to serve as an ancillary house by the early nineteenth century.
Photo by H. Winslow Fegley, circa 1900-1925. Courtesy, Schwenkfelder Library.

other household work was performed. The ground-floor parlor was generally the master bedroom as well as the sitting room for entertaining esteemed guests. The cooking hearth was located in the hall. A larger hall-parlor had an additional heating fireplace in the parlor, often a corner fireplace, but a smaller one might not. Space was still at a premium in this plan, which typically served as a home for substantial English-speaking residents of the valley in the colonial period. The house on the Samuel Whitacre Homestead (Amity, around 1739) is a small "stone-ender" log-built hall-parlor house. The original sections of the Thomas Lee House (Oley Township, around 1740-1745), the Bird House or Birdsborough Forge Mansion (Birdsboro, around 1746-1751), and the Maugridge-DeTurk House (Exeter, around 1752-1755), are relatively large stone-constructed examples of the type.

The Mounce Jones House in Amity, a hall-parlor house, is the oldest known standing house of the Oley Valley, built 1716. Nearby stands the Jonas Yocom House (Douglass, 1723), a chambered-hall house later greatly enlarged. Both houses are built of stone, a mode of construction the log-building Delaware Valley Swedes adopted only after the mass immigration of English and Welsh Quakers to Pennsylvania in the early 1680s. Thus, they are illustrative of the Swedes' rapid acculturation to the developing Anglo-Pennsylvanian culture. The "ancient Swedes" who settled at Molatton evidently soon forsook any traditional, distinctively Swedish house types they may have built in the settlement's early years. The parlor of the Mounce Jones House was constructed with a corner fireplace. Such fireplaces, which radiate heat in a manner superior to those built flush with a wall, have been thought by some architectural historians to represent a Swedish contribution to American vernacular architecture.[9] It is now recognized, however, that the corner fireplace was also an element in the vernacular architecture of England, and many colonial-period examples have been found in Anglo-Pennsylvanian houses distant from areas of Swedish settlement. Swedish corner fireplaces, with Delaware Valley examples known from archaeological investigation, incorporated large ovens in the traditional Swedish manner. The cor-

ner fireplace in the Jones House does not.

Some well-off English people built larger houses. Two early examples, which must have represented imposing mansions by the local standards of the 1730s, are the oldest, central section of the Joseph Rutter House at Pine Forge (Douglass, 1731) and the George Boone, Sr., House (Exeter, 1733). The two-story, stone-built Rutter House was constructed on a plan known as a "three-cell house," which essentially extended the length of the single-pile hall-parlor plan by an additional room. The Rutter House is the only one of this house type known

HOUSE ON THE SAMUEL WHITACRE HOMESTEAD, Circa 1739, Amity Township
An example of the hall-parlor house type, the house is a "stone ender" log house, i.e., the end wall incorporating the single chimney is built entirely of stone.
Photo by Philip E. Pendleton.

THOMAS LEE HOUSE, Circa 1740-1745, Enlarged in the Nineteenth Century, Oley Township
The earliest, center section of this house is a specimen of the hall-parlor type.
Photo by Philip E. Pendleton.

OLEY VALLEY HERITAGE

GEORGE BOONE, SR., HOUSE, 1733, Enlarged Circa 1750-1770, Exeter Township
In its original form, the house had a two-story front section of hall-parlor plan with a one-story outshut, i.e., a lean-to structure to the rear. George Boone, Sr.'s son James raised the outshut to two-story height.
Photo by Philip E. Pendleton.

THE STOVE-ROOM HOUSE: A PENNSYLVANIA GERMAN HOUSE TYPE

German settlers built a house type markedly different from those built on English precedents. This type, the "stove-room house," derives its name from its *Stube*, or "stove-room," which made it Pennsylvania German and differentiated it from Anglo-American houses built on a two or three-room floor plan. It has also been known to American scholars as the "Continental house." It was sometimes built in the valley in a small two-room version, but most surviving local examples feature a three-room plan. (A four-room subtype also was built in some areas of German settlement in the region, but no such houses are known to have been built in Oley.) The first-floor rooms constituting this plan were the *Küche* or kitchen, *Stube* or stove room, and, in the three-room version, the *Kammer* or chamber. The Pennsylvania German words for the three rooms were *Kich*, *Schtupp*, and *Kammer*.

to have been built in the Oley Valley, though others have been found in areas of English-speaking settlement in southeastern Pennsylvania.

George Boone, Sr., met his desire for a spacious dwelling by erecting a stone house that incorporated an original one-story "outshut" or lean-to structure to the rear, creating a rank of two or three first-floor rooms behind a basic, two-story hall-parlor plan. The spaces within the outshut were probably small service rooms. This tactic for creating a somewhat larger house was common in England and New England, but the rarity of surviving examples in Pennsylvania suggests that the form was less often employed in the Quaker colony. Later in the colonial years, George, Sr.'s son James Boone raised the outshut to two full stories to provide additional space, thereby making a two-story double-pile (i.e., two-room-deep) house in a traditional and very English mode.

A type of larger Anglo-Pennsylvanian house of which there are several surviving examples in the valley is the "double-parlor house," often called the "Quaker-plan house." This plan featured three rooms in a double-pile structure. All local specimens are two stories in height. About half the ground-floor space in one of these nearly square houses was taken up by a spacious hall. The other two rooms were parlors, each in a corner and usually boasting a corner fireplace. The Joseph Boone House, built in Amity in 1765, is an elegant rendition of this house type. It is important to note that this house type, designed and constructed on principles derived from English architectural tradition, was not built in England. Whereas George Boone, Sr., built an English house in 1733, his son Joseph built an Anglo-Pennsylvanian (i.e., an American) house in 1765. The Abraham Lincoln House, built in Exeter around 1770, is a somewhat plainer, perhaps more generally representative example of the double-parlor type.

ABRAHAM LINCOLN HOUSE, Circa 1770, Exeter Township
A house of the double-parlor type, with a small kitchen wing that probably represents an early addition.
Photo by Philip E. Pendleton.

THE ARCHITECTURAL LANDSCAPE

The distinctive feature of this type of house, and one that did much to determine the house's form, was its reliance on the five-plate jamb stove, a German method for heating living space. The house's chimney stack was in an off-center position. The kitchen was a large room that ran the depth of the house at one end, and one entered the house through it. The kitchen was on one side of the chimney stack, with the stove-room on the other. A small opening through the stack, about knee-high, enabled the shoveling of hot coals from the kitchen hearth into the back of a five-plate stove that was positioned against the other aperture. The stove was essentially a great iron box, with one side, or "plate," absent. Many iron plates, from which such stoves were assembled, were cast at Berks County furnaces. While much work besides cooking evidently took place in the kitchen, as in the English hall, the stove-room was the room for family gathering, eating, entertaining of visitors, and the display of prized possessions. Thus, it was the family's sitting and dining room. Built-in benches against the corner usually provided seating on two sides of the dining table, while just above was often a small alcove or niche in the wall for a Bible and other religious books, to facilitate family devotions. The chamber generally played the role of ground-floor master bedroom.

The stove-room house type was built in the valley in one-and-a-half and two-story versions, and varied widely in square footage, suggesting the importance that this configuration of spaces held for Pennsylvania German householders. The Bertolet-Herbein House (Oley Township, now moved to Daniel Boone Homestead State Historic Site in Exeter) is the only surviving log one-and-a-half-story stove-room house in the valley, built around 1720-1750. This building exemplifies what may well have been the typical dwelling of the comfortably situated Pennsylvania German farmer of the period. At least four more log one-and-a-half-story houses of this type survived on valley farmsteads long enough to be drawn or photographed by antiquarians. A common pattern in the upper Oley Valley appears to have been for a substantial German-speaking inhabitant of the second generation to replace a log one-and-a-half-story stove-room house with a two-story stone rendition of the same type

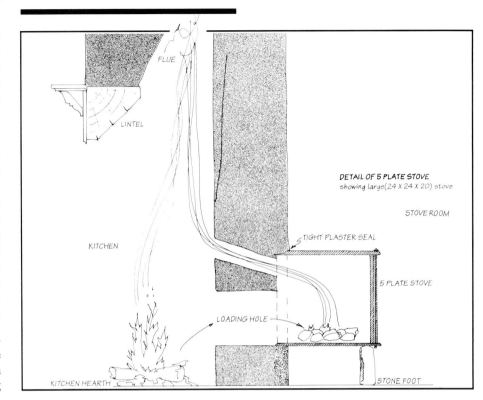

REPRESENTATIVE PENNSYLVANIA GERMAN JAMB STOVE ARRANGEMENTS, IN CROSS SECTION
Above is the more typical stove, composed entirely of iron plates. Below is the tile-topped form that evidence suggests was originally in place on the first floor of the Johannes Lesher House. Tile stoves were relatively common in Germany. Stove top plates with apertures designed for use with tiles are known to have been produced at Pennsylvania iron furnaces. Outside of the Moravian communal settlements, however, tile-topped stoves were probably restricted to the dwellings of a relative few of the province's better-off German-speaking inhabitants.
Drawing by Hope M. LeVan.

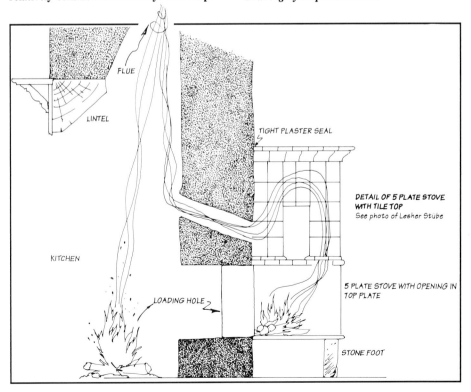

71

OLEY VALLEY HERITAGE

HANS MIRTEL GERICK HOUSE, 1741, Exeter Township
A large, relatively early example of the stove-room type, with a rare surviving half-hipped roof. The porch and external stairway are modern, as are two of the gable-end windows.
Photo by Philip E. Pendleton.

HANS MIRTEL GERICK HOUSE, 1741, Exeter Township
A rear view showing cellar windows and the stream flowing from the spring in the cellar.
Photo by H. Winslow Fegley, circa 1900-1925. Courtesy, Schwenkfelder Library.

during the third quarter of the eighteenth century. Many such two-story stone houses survive. Such an architectural gesture proclaimed a family's intention to sink roots. In this respect, the upper valley (with its especially fertile soil) differed strikingly from the lower valley. There a somewhat higher rate of transience among settler families, many of whom were English-speaking, resulted in the creation of fewer stone-built colonial-period "architectural monuments."

The Bertolet-Herbein House and the spacious two-story Hans Mirtel Gerick House (Exeter, 1741), both early specimens of the stove-room house, feature a sparse, asymmetrical fenestration that confers a medieval feeling. The Gerick House's atmosphere of profound antiquity is enhanced by its "half-hipped" roof structure. The roof reflects a form endemic in the Germany of 1700 and is the only surviving eighteenth-century one in the valley. The form possibly was common in the early Pennsylvania German settlements. This mode of resolving the end of a roof ridge also is known as a "clipped gable," or "jerkin head" (for its resemblance to a medieval hooded cowl garment). The German term for such a roof is *Walmdach*.

The medieval Germanic impression conveyed by the Bertolet and Gerick houses' traditional features masks their type's nature as one only recently developed in the Rhine Valley at the period of emigration to Pennsylvania. The stove-room house was not an exclusively American type as its three-room-plan counterpart, the Anglo-Pennsylvanian double-parlor house, appears to have been. But the stove-room house, which has become synonymous with traditional Pennsylvania German domestic architecture, was a progressive form when it was transferred by the immigrants to the Pennsylvania landscape.

It is interesting that the only valley Englishmen known to have had houses built for their families in the German-derived stove-room house mode were Robert Stapleton of Oley Township, around 1740-1745, and John Sands of Amity in 1759, whose wives were German (both named Katarina). Evidently the women participated in decisions regarding the nature of the domestic architecture in which they were to work and dwell. In the Stapleton House, the creation of a two-story, three-room stove-room house plan for the second, German Mrs. Stapleton appears to have been accomplished by building a stone kitchen addition to the brick double-cell house Stapleton had built around 1730-1735, during his first marriage to an Englishwoman. Reversing this mixed-marital architectural equation, Pennsylvania German resident Herman Umsted built a house of Anglo-Pennsylvanian double-parlor type in northern Robeson Township around 1770. Perhaps his wife Ann's Vanderslice family was of anglicized Dutch background.

Unlike the greatly outnumbered Delaware Valley Swedes, who appear to have

THE ARCHITECTURAL LANDSCAPE

abandoned their Swedish architectural traditions, colonial-period Pennsylvania Germans in the Oley Valley and elsewhere developed and maintained a distinctive architectural tradition. There is more to domestic architecture than house types, and this tradition was also expressed in construction techniques and architectural decoration. In general, Pennsylvania German builders exhibited a stronger tendency to follow traditional European methods and forms than did Anglo-Pennsylvanians. Perhaps they sought thereby to show their sense of their difference and thus to claim a degree of apartness.

Examples of stove-room houses surviving from the third quarter of the eighteenth century have facades that exhibit a balanced, ordered look, as well as interiors better lit by more windows. These buildings include the Jacob Keim House (Pike, 1753), the Abraham Levan House (Oley Township, around 1753, said to have been constructed by the same builders as the Keim House), the original section of the Cornelius DeHart House (Amity, around 1760), and the Jacob Kauffmann House (Oley Township, 1766). Balance, symmetry, and order were trademarks of the domestic architecture built in the late colonial period by Americans of means, including the Oley Valley's more substantial farmers and tradesmen. The emphasis on a balanced, orderly facade, which could manifest itself in individual specimens of any house type, was one effect of the importation of Palladian or Renaissance architectural principles to America.

PALLADIAN-INFLUENCED HOUSE TYPES

The classical architectural ideal rediscovered by the Italian architect Andrea Palladio (1508-1580) was disseminated throughout the Western world during the seventeenth and eighteenth centuries. In the British seaboard colonies of North America, Palladian architectural principles were embodied in the center-passage double-pile house, commonly known today by the physically undescriptive name of "the Georgian house." The center-passage double-pile house represented a truly international type, and one of academic architectural parentage. It might be built using vernacular construction methods or fitted with vernacular features, such as the pent roof in southeastern Pennsylvania, but its floorplan of center passage flanked by two rooms on either side made it essentially the same house in whatever region of Europe or the American colonies it stood.

The large size of this type of house tended to make it the preserve of a privileged few, though some Pennsylvania innkeepers built it in log because it so well suited their need for space. The Nicolaus Herner Tavern in Exeter (in recent years, the "Black Angus Pub" on Route 422) is a well-disguised surviving log ex-

JACOB KAUFFMANN HOUSE, 1766, Oley Township
A view of the house's east gable end, showing the steep pitch of the strut-supported roof and the small doorway for the upper garret, enabling the hoisting of grain. The tall window of the lower garret level was probably also originally a door.
Photo by Robert C. Bucher, 1959. Courtesy, Robert C. Bucher.

JACOB KAUFFMANN HOUSE, 1766, Oley Township
A rear view showing the closed second-story balcony doorway.
Photo by Cervin Robinson, 1958. Courtesy, The Historic American Buildings Survey, Prints and Photographs Division, Library of Congress.

73

OLEY VALLEY HERITAGE

JOHANNES BISHOP HOUSE (Bishop Hall), Circa 1774, Exeter Township
Detail of the front entry, an outstanding Oley Valley example of the Georgian-style decorative woodwork of the period. The fanlight surmounting the doorway was just entering the vocabulary of fashionable architecture in the colonies when the house was built.
Photo by Philip E. Pendleton.

ample, probably dating to the early 1780s. The wealthy Oley Valley ironmaster and his wife who built a house of this sort, similar to those they had enjoyed visiting in Germantown or Philadelphia, were creating a domestic monument the symbolism of which their urban hosts would comprehend and appreciate. The center-passage double-pile house held equal attraction for status-conscious English and German Pennsylvanians.

The center passage or hallway with an open flight of stairs, a diagnostic trait of this house type, represented a dramatic departure from folk-architectural practice. The winding stairway situated in a corner of a room, and usually enclosed (or "boxed"), was the standard means of access between floor levels in Pennsylvania English and German vernacular houses. With eight rooms, and perhaps an original kitchen ell as well, the center-passage double-pile type was a large house. The numerous rooms, accompanied by the two passages and their stairway, made possible a specialization in room function and a potential for privacy heretofore unknown in the valley. A rather central aspect of the transformation wrought by the Palladian plan, in the way

JACOB KAUFFMANN HOUSE, 1766, Oley Township
Detail of a built-in corner cupboard located in the large room on the second floor (the space over the first-floor stove room), another example of the Georgian woodwork associated with Palladian-influenced architecture in eighteenth-century America.
Photo by Cervin Robinson, 1958. Courtesy, The Historic American Buildings Survey, Prints and Photographs Division, Library of Congress.

a substantial house functioned, was the introduction of a more pronounced separation between the formal spaces of a house, such as the parlor, and those devoted to domestic or service activities, including cooking. In at least two rather elegant Palladian-influenced dwellings, the Johannes Jaeger or John Hunter Inn

THE ARCHITECTURAL LANDSCAPE

JACOB KEIM HOUSE, 1753, Pike Township
Detail of the enclosed winder staircase.
Photo by Kenneth LeVan.

JACOB KAUFFMANN HOUSE, 1766, Oley Township
Detail of the second-floor landing. In the relatively spacious Kauffmann House, the pre-Palladian stairway arrangement consists of two ninety-degree-turn enclosed staircases.
Photo by Cervin Robinson, 1958. Courtesy, The Historic American Buildings Survey, Prints and Photographs Division, Library of Congress.

(Oley Township, 1768) and the Johannes Bishop House (Exeter, around 1774), the cooking hearth was banished to a separate kitchen building. The Palladian impact on Pennsylvania's vernacular architecture may have had a role in the development of the summer kitchen building as a widespread element in the region's nineteenth-century architecture.

In colonial-period Pennsylvania houses of other than Palladian-derived design a person entered directly into a room, and

JOHANNES JAEGER (JOHN HUNTER) INN, 1768, Oley Township
Representative of the center-passage double-pile type that embodied Georgian Palladian house plan in colonial America. The symmetrical five-bay facade with principal entry at center was a rarely varied trait of the type.
Photo by Donald A. Shelley.

JOHANNES JAEGER (JOHN HUNTER) INN, 1768, Oley Township
Two details of the open stairway. The panelled wainscot and spandrel (i.e., side wall of the staircase), as well as the lighter, more attenuated Queen Anne styling of the stair rail, newel post and balusters, represented a stylistic advance from the plain plaster finish and the somewhat simpler, heavier William and Mary woodwork of the Lesher House stairway of about fifteen years earlier. In either case, such a stairway was immediately visible to the visitor entering a fashionable, Palladian-influenced dwelling, and tended to serve as an especially imposing visual focus for the house's interior.
Photos by Kenneth LeVan.

JOHANNES LESHER HOUSE (Oley Forge Mansion), Circa 1750-1755, Oley Township
Detail of the open stairway.
Photo by Kenneth LeVan.

THE ARCHITECTURAL LANDSCAPE

GEORGE DOUGLASS HOUSE, 1763,
Amity Township
An example of the center-passage double-pile type. The three-bay, two-story section to the right was added in 1834. The dormers were an element in the house's original construction, but the corner entry at left represents an alteration. As of 1994, this property of the Historic Preservation Trust of Berks County awaited restoration.
Photographer unknown, early twentieth century. Courtesy, Christopher Witmer.

thenceforth went from room to room. With the appearance of the center passage there was now intervening space between the entrance and any room, as well as between rooms. This room specialization and potential for privacy enabled a new measure of exclusivity in local social relations. The wealthy owner of a center-passage double-pile house could more easily channel visiting clients' movements within the house than had been possible in the intimate setting of a double-parlor house or stove-room house, admitting people only to the spaces he or she chose.

The center-passage double-pile house was brought relatively late to the Oley Valley (and the rest of rural Pennsylvania). It appeared in the third quarter of the eighteenth century, a few generations after its appearance in the seaboard cities of the colonies. Valley examples include the 1763 house of prominent Amity storekeeper George Douglass, and the house of innkeeper Johannes Jaeger, built in 1768.

One of the most intriguing houses of the Oley Valley is the baronial residence constructed by the proud ironmaster Johannes Lesher at Oley Forge around 1750-1755. The plan of this center-passage double-pile house had a distinctively German twist. The house has imposing facades on both the front and the rear, each with a full balcony when first built, as often seen on fashionable houses of the period in German-speaking Europe. Both facades surveyed the lane serving the ironworks, which curved around the house.

The front facade of the Lesher House has but four openings per floor, instead of the five symptomatic of the center-passage double-pile type, and the rear but three. The off-center location of the doors, and of the stair passage within, also atypical, reflects an asymmetrical division of space in the floorplan. To one side of the passage, in the smaller spatial division, are two very Anglo-Pennsylvanian parlors with corner fireplaces, as might be seen in any center-passage double-pile house of the region. Across the passage is a characteristically Pennsylvania German arrangement of kitchen and stove-room for jamb stove, with the necessary hearth and chimney stack projecting from the gable-end wall. The house's floorplan and the feel of the rooms confer something of a "split personality," with one side of the passage English and one side German. It has been suggested by some scholars, however, that Lesher's house may not have been an elegant attempt to reconcile vernacular Pennsylvania German and fashionable English Palladian architectural practices. Perhaps it was an expression of a distinctively German Palladian architecture. The forge's mansion is all the more impressive for its fortress-like foundation and situation. Lesher had this site blasted out of the rock outcrop overlooking the forge.

Another variation of German Palladian plan was represented by the great half-timbered Moravian Boarding School building, constructed in Oley Township in 1748 but no longer standing. In this two-story, center-passage double-pile structure with the usual four rooms and passage for each floor, four fireplaces located in the side walls of the hallway, one for each side of each floor, serviced stoves in rooms to either side. The two chimneys, flanking the passage, arched over the second floor hallway to unite in one great stack in the garret. Such an arrangement can still be seen at the house "Schifferstadt" in Frederick, Maryland, along with the only known in situ five-

OLEY VALLEY HERITAGE

JOHANNES LESHER HOUSE (Oley Forge Mansion), Circa 1750-1755, Oley Township
An example of one German Palladian variation of the center-passage double-pile plan. A number of architectural elements of the Lesher House were similar to, or virtual facsimiles of, elements in the Germantown country mansion of John Wister, a wealthy Pennsylvania German merchant of Philadelphia. For example, the ground dimensions of the two houses are identical, and both boasted (as originally built) second-story front balconies, though only Lesher's extended the full width of the facade. The house is thus representative both of Oley's close connections with Germantown, which functioned almost as a sort of cultural capital for the more easterly Pennsylvania German settlements, and of wealthy ironmaster Lesher's emulation of the province's English-speaking elite. Wister's house was renamed "Grumblethorpe" in the early nineteenth century.
Photo by Kenneth LeVan.

JOHANNES LESHER HOUSE (Oley Forge Mansion), Circa 1750-1755, Oley Township
Detail of the corner fireplace in the second-floor southwest chamber.
Photo by Kenneth LeVan.

JOHANNES LESHER HOUSE (Oley Forge Mansion), Circa 1750-1755, Oley Township
Detail of the stove apertures as viewed from the stove room.
Photo by Kenneth LeVan.

THE ARCHITECTURAL LANDSCAPE

JOHANNES LESHER HOUSE (Oley Forge Mansion), Circa 1750-1755, Oley Township Detail of the stove room, showing the aperture to the kitchen hearth against which the jamb stove was set. As perhaps befitted an ironmaster, the break in the chair rail suggests that the five-plate iron box of Lesher's tile-topped stove was an uncommonly large one.
Photo by Kenneth LeVan.

JOHANNES LESHER HOUSE (Oley Forge Mansion), Circa 1750-1755, Oley Township Detail of the kitchen hearth, showing the aperture for feeding the stove that was located in the stove room, the latter room visible through the doorway to the right. Also visible are the return, i.e., the smaller hole above the feeding aperture through which the smoke returned from the stove to the chimney, and the smoke channel, an indentation in the back wall of the hearth starting about four feet above the floor that facilitated the drawing of smoke up the chimney. Smoke channels have been found in some colonial-period Pennsylvania German houses in combination with evidence of the former presence of a raised hearth, a masonry platform two feet or so deep and rising to about knee height. The raised hearth was a standard architectural feature for the kitchen in substantial houses in the German-speaking portion of Europe during the early modern period; it is possible that a raised hearth was originally in place in the Lesher House.
Photo by Kenneth LeVan.

plate jamb stove. An additional end chimney served a large walk-in cooking fireplace on the first floor of the boarding school.[10]

The stair passage was introduced to the architectural repertoire of southeastern Pennsylvania as an element in the academically derived center-passage double-pile house. Builders began to adapt this stylish feature to older house types in the late colonial years, creating new vernacular types in the process. These new house plans were harbingers of a shared regional vernacular tradition in which types were not necessarily expressions of separate ethnic traditions. The introduction of six-plate and ten-plate stoves that could connect to gable-end chimneys via pipes meant that the Pennsylvania German attachment to stove-generated warmth could be accommodated in a house type other than the stove-room house. Some English residents also adopted the practice of heating their homes with pipe-fitted stoves. These im-

OLEY VALLEY HERITAGE

MOSES ROBERTS HOUSE, 1769, Oley Township
The original section, consisting of the two leftmost bays, is an unadorned rendition of the side-passage double-pile type, built for a Quaker minister.
Photo by Philip E. Pendleton.

BERTOLET-HERBEIN HOUSE, Circa 1720-1750, Oley Township
A ten-plate stove, made at Oley Furnace, in place, though its installation represented a minor alteration to the house. Vertical-board partitions, similar to that visible in the background, were constructed in many colonial-period Oley Valley houses.
Photo by Cervin Robinson, 1958. Courtesy, The Historic American Buildings Survey, Prints and Photographs Division, Library of Congress.

THE ARCHITECTURAL LANDSCAPE

JOHANNES BISHOP HOUSE (Bishop Hall), Circa 1774, Exeter Township
This example of the side-passage double-pile type is one of the most elegant structures built in the Oley Valley during the colonial years, though its three-bay facade is standard for the type.
Photo by Kenneth LeVan.

plements, called "flue stoves," "pipe stoves," or "English stoves," began to appear in the probate inventories of Oley Valley Englishmen in 1762, and in those of Germans in 1770.

The story of Palladian-influenced transformation of the region's vernacular architecture belongs largely to the years following 1775, but the trend was underway at the end of the colonial period. Houses of plans representing earlier types revised to incorporate stair passages began to appear in the Oley Valley soon after the first local center-passage double-pile houses. The original section of the Moses Roberts House, erected in Oley Township in 1769, is a "side-passage double-pile house," essentially a double-cell house with a stair passage to one side. Like its double-cell cousin of a generation earlier, the Mordecai Lincoln House, the Moses Roberts House is a banked structure with its kitchen in the cellar. The Johannes Bishop House, a large and refined Exeter example built around 1774, possesses the three-bay fenestration usually seen on the side-passage double-pile house. This house type, often with its kitchen located in a smaller wing or ell, would become one of the most common southeastern Pennsylvania types of the late eighteenth and early nineteenth centuries, both in towns and in the countryside.

The original section of the oft-enlarged Judah Boone House, built in Exeter

JUDAH BOONE HOUSE (Mill Tract Farm), Circa 1770, Exeter Township
Detail of the parlor in the house's original section, its refined finish incorporating baseboard, paneled wall and cupboards, and molded mantelpiece, cornice, and chair rail. The room is another example of the decorative woodwork found in dwellings representing the upper end of the valley's architectural spectrum.
Photo by Cervin Robinson, 1958. Courtesy, The Historic American Buildings Survey, Prints and Photographs Division, Library of Congress.

around 1770, is a "side-passage single-pile house," more or less a chambered hall with a stair passage. It may seem odd that someone would build a small house in this configuration, with a stair passage, when with just a little more expenditure he might have had a two-story hall-parlor house. But the question of what the homeowner needed or thought he needed is always a complex one. The passage was not only a space to contain a stairway; it was an entryway, the existence of which conferred a greater measure of privacy for the house's rooms. Presumably, young

81

OLEY VALLEY HERITAGE

JUDAH BOONE HOUSE (Mill Tract Farm), Circa 1770, Enlarged Circa 1780-1785 and in the Nineteenth Century, Exeter Township
The original section, consisting of the entry bay and the two bays to its left, was built as an example of the side-passage single-pile type. The addition to the right of a decade or so later in effect remade Boone's dwelling into a house of center-passage single-pile type.
Photo by Cervin Robinson, 1958. Courtesy, The Historic American Buildings Survey, Prints and Photographs Division, Library of Congress.

merchant miller Judah Boone had a reason why he wanted to segregate his ground-floor parlor from the house's entry. The original kitchen was in the cellar. After a decade or so, Boone enlarged the structure with a room-over-room addition opposite the passage from the original first-floor parlor and second-floor chamber, plus a separate kitchen building to the rear.

In making his addition in the early 1780s, miller Boone in effect realized yet another Palladian-influenced vernacular house type, one that was to become common in the region, the "center-passage single-pile house." Essentially a hall-parlor house modified by the insertion of a center passage and the equalization of the floor space in the flanking rooms, the center-passage single-pile house featured Georgian symmetry in facade and plan, though it was only one room deep. The only known colonial-period example from the valley is the later section of the Bird

JACOB KEIM HOUSE, 1753, Pike Township
Detail of the kitchen, showing the doorway for the enclosed winder staircase towards the rear, as well as the great walk-in cooking fireplace found in unaltered large examples of the stove-room house type.
Photo by Kenneth LeVan.

THE ARCHITECTURAL LANDSCAPE

ABRAHAM BERTOLET HOUSE, 1736, Oley Township
Detail of the second-floor chamber, its relatively plain plaster finish representative of that in many colonial-period Oley Valley houses.
Photo by Kenneth LeVan.

House or Birdsborough Forge Mansion, added by Mark Bird around 1770.

In the years after 1775, Palladian-influenced modification of traditional house types took a course other than that of adding the stair passage. Pennsylvania Germans built houses with the traditional three-room plan of the stove-room type, but with chimneys at the gable ends instead, and with facade fenestration showing four evenly spaced openings. This house type incorporated the flue stove as a factor in its design. It is known as the "four-over-four" (a name derived from the type's usual pattern of fenestration) or "Pennsylvania farmhouse" type. The use of the latter term gives some idea of its nineteenth-century popularity. The large additions to the colonial-period Johannes DeTurk House (Oley Township, enlarged 1844) and to the Cornelius DeHart House (Amity) are among numerous valley examples of the four-over-four type.

THE DOMESTIC MATERIAL ENVIRONMENT

The people of the colonial Oley Valley shaped their domestic living environment by their choice of house type. But the house was just the outer shell of this environment. People made use of other material objects in daily living: furniture, cooking utensils, and so on. Farmer and turner Johannes Keim evoked the look and feel of the domestic material world of 1747 when in his will he summed up the estate he was leaving behind. He included "all the movables in the house and out the door, brass, pewter, iron, wooden and earthen things."[11]

As time passed and the valley community became ever more developed, most people could invest in a greater number of useful items and creature comforts, as well as build larger and more substantial houses. Among the dry goods (of which there was a large and varied assortment), kitchenware, tools, hardware, spices, staple groceries, ammunition, and other supplies at George Anders's store in 1752 were such luxury items as "sundry new books," "one dozen painted snuff boxes," and "eleven gilt pocket books."[12]

An example of the general, gradual improvement in living standards during the colonial years shows in the estates left by Swedish settler Peter Jones (died 1739) and his son Peter Jones (died 1773). Father and son lived on essentially the same property. Peter II added fifty acres purchased from a neighbor to the two-hundred-acre plantation Peter I had received from his father, the pioneer Mounce Jones (or Magnus Jonasson in strict Swedish parlance). Both men died prematurely,

JACOB KEIM HOUSE, 1753, Pike Township
Detail of the decorative kitchen fireplace mantel.
Photo by Kenneth LeVan.

OLEY VALLEY HERITAGE

JOHANNES HOCH, JR., HOUSE-MILL (Peter's Mill), 1761, Enlarged 1850, Oley Township
The original house section consists of the two rightmost bays. The gristmill section, which had been rebuilt at least once, collapsed after suffering severe storm damage in the 1950s. The first mill section had been the earliest part of the overall building, starting life circa 1742 as a freestanding one-and-a-half-story structure, constructed for miller Derick Hilt. The outline of the first mill's steep-pitched roof is visible on the gable-end wall of the house section, as well as a small, shuttered window that looked out over the roof of the first mill.
Photo by Philip E. Pendleton.

Peter I at age forty-six, Peter II probably a few years older. So both estate inventories were those of men in their prime who had not yet disposed of most of their belongings to grown children. Tax lists suggest that both were men of average economic status for the valley's landowning farmers.

The inventory of the elder Peter Jones, who was a weaver and a farmer, portrayed an environment of few possessions and sparse comfort. Its significant items included two feather beds, a chaff bed, a chest, a table and four chairs, two looms, and two spinning wheels. The inventory did not explicitly mention bedsteads, but it is possible that bedsteads accompanied the feather beds. The domestic material world enjoyed by his son held far more amenities. In his 1772 will, Peter II directed that his wife, while a widow, should have use of "the front room in my new dwelling house,"[13] perhaps a stone-constructed double-cell, double-parlor, or side-passage double-pile house. In this new house were a house clock worth £5 10s. (a large sum), a desk, a "black walnut noble table," a "black walnut case of drawers," four beds and bedsteads, two more tables, sixteen chairs, three chests, three spinning wheels, and a tea kettle, tea pot and teaware.[14] An expensive standing clock, like a riding mare, was a possession imbued with special significance—its presence seems to have certified one's claim to consideration as a substantial, freeholding yeoman.

HOUSE-MILLS AND ANCILLARY HOUSES

Some homesteads of Oley Valley Germans featured buildings that contained discrete spaces for dwelling, work, and storage. These structures were of two kinds: the house-mill and the ancillary house. These cannot properly be called house types; rather they were whole other building forms that incorporated dwelling areas laid out following various house plans of the period. Much work, of course, went on in any Pennsylvania German house. But in these two kinds of buildings, a large section of the structure was explicitly and solely devoted to work.

In the house-mill, a house and a gristmill were sheltered under one roof. The house-mill was the traditional mode of dwelling for millers in northwestern Europe, predominant in both England and Germany, though only German-bred millers appear to have employed it in America. The house-mill epitomized the dwelling in which work and other aspects of living mingled. The noise and vibration of the machinery, as well as the swirling grain dust, would seem to have made living in a dwelling attached to an operating gristmill uncomfortable, noisy, and literally unsettling. A gristmill might run twenty-four hours a day during particularly busy periods. The proximity of his living quarters to the mill machinery was an advantage to the miller, though, who would want to know instantly if an element of the mill began to misfunction.

The house and mill sections might be constructed concurrently, as appears to have been the case at the Johannes Pott House-Mill, erected in Pike Township around 1760. Or, as evidently happened at the nearby Johannes Hoch, Jr., House-Mill in Oley Township in 1761, the house section could be an addition to an extant gristmill. A house-mill might or might not serve as the miller's principal residence, a status that could change in response to needs and resources. Elisabetha Womelsdorf's will of 1772 referred to "the dwelling house where I now live" and "the lodging room belonging to the gristmill and paper mill" (the latter with two beds and its own kitchenware) as separate structures.[15] At both the Pott and Hoch house-mill sites, only the house section survives.

The house-mill was a direct continuation of a European architectural tradition, and one evidently forsaken from the first by some Pennsylvania German millers. A sort of combination dwelling-work building that represented an American reworking of German tradition, which was adopted by some Oley Valley Germans, was the Pennsylvania German ancillary house. It was customary for a farmhouse in the homeland to be accompanied by one or more adjacent small structures. These might include a granary or storehouse (*Speicher*), a washhouse (*Wäsch-*

THE ARCHITECTURAL LANDSCAPE

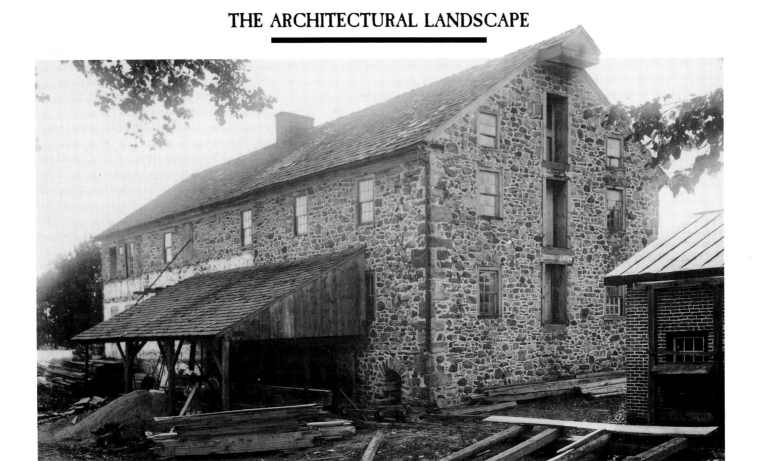

erei), or a small house (*Stoeckli*) for aging parents who had relinquished active direction of the farm. The retirement cottage or "grandfather house" tradition was particularly strong in Canton Bern, Switzerland, a region from whence came many immigrants to Pennsylvania, including several Oley Valley families. These small, single-function, European ancillaries occupied positions practically in the shadow of the principal house. On the Pennsylvania German farmstead two or more of these functions, with the additional possibilities of summer kitchen, craft workshop and springhouse, would often be housed in one ancillary structure.

The colonial-period ancillary houses of the Oley Valley provided housing for retired farmers and their wives. Following German custom, many elderly couples chose to withdraw to live on their own to some degree, for example David and Katarina Weiser. In their 1772 deed for the Oley Township homestead, made to their son Christian, the Weisers ensured to themselves the right "of dwelling in the small new house with a garden to themselves."[16] David and Katarina presumably lived until their respective deaths in 1786 and 1787 in this building. With their

JOHANNES HOCH, JR., HOUSE-MILL (Peter's Mill), 1761, Enlarged 1850, Oley Township
Front and rear views, taken when the complete structure, i.e., both the house section and the later edition of the mill section, was still standing. In the frontal view, the house section is obscured by the adjoining sawmill and its shed. The two-story stone gristmill replaced its smaller predecessor sometime in the early-to-mid nineteenth century, perhaps in 1850, the date of the addition to the house section. *Photos by H. Winslow Fegley, circa 1900-1925. Courtesy, Schwenkfelder Library.*

OLEY VALLEY HERITAGE

SAMUEL HOCH III HOMESTEAD, Oley Township
A full view of the farmstead, showing the eighteenth-century house of ancillary type at left. Of the other buildings, only the barn survives. The larger house is a brick rendition of the four-over-four or Pennsylvania farmhouse type, of similar mid-nineteenth-century date to the barn.
Photographer unknown, circa 1955. Courtesy, Jane Levan.

departure the dwelling space was no doubt made use of by children or servants. Some ancillary houses were evidently occupied just by the widow following her husband's death, rather than by both husband and wife as a retired couple. In his 1757 will, Hans Mirtel Gerick bequeathed to his wife Katarina the right of residence in "the house near my present dwelling house called the wash house."[17] When Gerick's English neighbor William Boone appraised the estate, he referred to cleaned wheat stored in "the milk house loft."[18] It is likely that these two references were made to one multipurpose structure, that one floor in the Gerick ancillary house may have been employed both for laundering and dairy work, while its garret served as a granary.

HOUSE ON THE SAMUEL HOCH III HOMESTEAD, Circa 1750-1780, Oley Township
This house on the ancillary pattern is today a ruin located approximately three-quarters of a mile north of Bieber's Mill. It may have been the first dwelling on this homestead, which by 1754 was occupied by Heinrich Neukirch, tenant to owner Samuel Hoch, Sr., and in 1780 became the residence of the latter's grandson Samuel Hoch III. The visible gable end was originally pierced by doorways on both first-story and attic levels, as at the Johannes DeTurk Ancillary House.
Photo by Charles H. Dornbusch, 1941. Courtesy, The Historic American Buildings Survey, Prints and Photographs Division, Library of Congress.

THE ARCHITECTURAL LANDSCAPE

The living apartments in ancillary houses were generally every bit as nicely finished as the interiors of the houses they accompanied. They might be laid out on a one-room plan or on a two- or three-room stove-room house plan. The little-altered ancillary house at the Lotz Farm in Amity, built 1762 on the stove-room house plan, features an elegant mantelpiece over its first-floor kitchen hearth, a chimney cupboard in the stove-room with decorative German-style strap hinges, and a beaded summer beam.

An ancillary's house space was segregated from its work space. These were bank-sited buildings, with the dwelling on the first (or upper) floor, the work area in the cellar, and separate doors to the

HANS MIRTEL GERICK TENANT HOUSE, 1741, Exeter Township
Built in the same year as the main house, probably by the same building craftsmen, at Gerick's tenancy a mile or so to the southeast of the main homestead. This recently renovated and much-enlarged structure was originally constructed as a one-and-a-half-story stone-masonry example of the stove-room type.
Photo by Philip E. Pendleton.

DAVID WEISER HOMESTEAD, Oley Township
A classic arrangement of main house and ancillary house, the ancillary house built circa 1770 to right, the late-nineteenth-century main house to left. The main house probably occupies the site of an earlier one, possibly incorporating an earlier foundation.
Photo by Philip E. Pendleton.

OLEY VALLEY HERITAGE

exterior for each floor. There was usually no stairway for internal access between the living and work levels. The cellar generally had a cooking hearth and a lined channel in the floor in which flowed water from a spring. This level of the ancillary might be employed as washhouse or springhouse, and be the site of dairy or butchering activity.

The valley's surviving Pennsylvania German ancillary houses from the late colonial years have frequently been taken to be "settler cabins" built in the 1720s or 1730s. This has been true even for the one-room-plan ancillary house at the DeTurk Farm in Oley Township (settled by 1712), with its incised doorway lintel inscription "Johan DeTirck—1767—Debora DeTircken." A gable-end cut-stone facade, and doors and shutters with painted flower and bird motifs conferred a self-consciously quaint feeling to this elegant little building. The elder DeTurks were evidently proud to take up residence there. The garret of this ancillary house served as a granary; on the facade were a garret door and pulley with protective hood, features reminiscent of a gristmill. The stove-room-type ancillary house at the Kauffmann Farm in Oley Township, often attributed as an early principal dwelling dating from the 1730s, was more likely built a half-century or so later. To

JOHANNES DETURK ANCILLARY HOUSE, 1767, Oley Township
Restored by the Historic Preservation Trust of Berks County, and administered by the Trust under a long-term lease.
Photo by Charles H. Dornbusch, 1941.
Courtesy, The Historic American Buildings Survey, Prints and Photographs Division, Library of Congress.

JOHANNES DETURK ANCILLARY HOUSE, 1767, Oley Township
Details of a decorated window shutter, now in the collection of the State Museum of Pennsylvania, with a rose on the upper panel and a tulip on the lower. The seemingly intentional picturesque character of this little "grandfather house" is epitomized in the decorative treatment of a mundane architectural element.
Photographer unknown. Courtesy, The State Museum of Pennsylvania, Pennsylvania Historical and Museum Commission.

 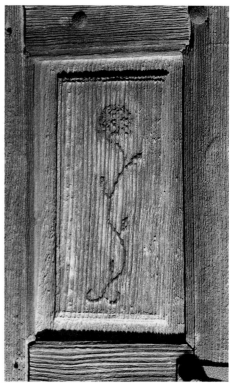

THE ARCHITECTURAL LANDSCAPE

JOHANNES DETURK ANCILLARY HOUSE, 1767, Oley Township
A rear view.
Photo by Charles H. Dornbusch, 1941.
Courtesy, The Historic American Buildings Survey, Prints and Photographs Division, Library of Congress.

JACOB KEIM HOMESTEAD, 1753, Pike Township
Another classic arrangement of main house and ancillary house. The main house was built in 1753, and the ancillary, evidently originally Keim's turner's workshop, at or near the same time; the two rightmost bays on the main house represent a later addition. This well-preserved homestead is a property of the Historic Preservation Trust of Berks County.
Photo by Philip E. Pendleton.

confuse interpretation, there were small early houses that survived to function in the role of ancillary houses, such as the 1736 Abraham Bertolet House. One-room, story-and-a-half houses from the first half of the eighteenth century were enlarged to serve as ancillaries at the Leinbach-Knabb and Gregory-Weidner homesteads.

The ancillary house at the Jacob Keim Homestead in Pike, a stove-room-plan example, represents one exception to the employment of the first (or upper) floor primarily as a retirement apartment. This multifunctional building was evidently built at or near the same time (around 1753) as the main house, and its first floor

ANCILLARY HOUSE ON THE LEINBACH-KNABB HOMESTEAD (Settler Farm Cabin), Circa 1735, Enlarged Circa 1810, Oley Township
This tile-roofed building was originally a story-and-a-half house of one-room plan, consisting of the lower part of the central third of the present structure. It was enlarged and fitted with a ten-plate stove to serve as the retirement quarters of Maria Elisabetha Knabb, widow of Peter Knabb (who had died in 1799).
Photo by Robert C. Bucher, 1962. Courtesy, Robert C. Bucher.

THE ARCHITECTURAL LANDSCAPE

JACOB KEIM HOUSE, 1753, Pike Township
The rear of the house, showing the second-story balcony.
Photo by H. Winslow Fegley, circa 1900-1925. Courtesy, Schwenkfelder Library.

JACOB KEIM ANCILLARY HOUSE, Circa 1753, Pike Township
Unlike the center chimney, the bell housing seen in this view was not an original feature. It has since been removed, and the building reroofed with clay tiles.
Photo by Robert C. Bucher, 1962. Courtesy, Robert C. Bucher.

JACOB KEIM HOUSE, 1753, Pike Township
Detail of the second-story balcony door, constructed of board and batten but with the front surfaces of the two boards painstakingly scored so as to present the appearance of a chevron-style door composed of several small boards.
Photo by Kenneth LeVan.

OLEY VALLEY HERITAGE

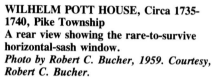

WILHELM POTT HOUSE, Circa 1735-1740, Pike Township
A rear view showing the rare-to-survive horizontal-sash window.
Photo by Robert C. Bucher, 1959. Courtesy, Robert C. Bucher.

WILHELM POTT HOUSE, Circa 1735-1740, Pike Township
A log-built house with a small enclosed chamber against the first-floor center hearth similar to that in the Jacob Keim Ancillary House, likely a kiln for drying wood. Pott, like his near neighbor Keim, was a woodworker, specifically a joiner. He also ran a sawmill and a fulling mill. This structure may have been built as an ancillary house; it had a cooking hearth and spring in the cellar, but had no direct source of warmth other than the evident kiln for the large room on the first floor. The house, its log structure clad in weatherboard when this view was taken, collapsed in the 1960s.
Photo by Robert C. Bucher, 1959. Courtesy, Robert C. Bucher.

stove-room appears to have been designed as a workshop. Jacob Keim was a turner, a craftsman who used a lathe powered by a large manually driven wheel to shape chair and table legs, balusters, and other woodwork. Iron and wooden fittings on the wall of the stove-room workshop evidently represent surviving elements of the lathe apparatus. This room also features a stove alcove, with the jamb stove aperture in the side of the adjoining kitchen's cooking hearth instead of in its rear, so as to be out of the turner's work area. Four windows, an unusually high number for a room of the stove-room workshop's size, provided light for work. An original, enclosed chamber, adjoining the chimney stack and occupying the jamb stove's usual position, probably was built as a drying kiln for wood to be used by the turner. A similar chamber occupied a space on the first floor of the nearby Wilhelm Pott House (around 1735-1740). Pott was also a woodworker, a joiner (furniture maker). The Keim ancillary cellar has a spring channel for cold storage, as well as an additional walk-in fireplace, and may have been used as springhouse and washhouse.

Much remains to be learned about the history of the Pennsylvania-German ancillary house. Although the form grew out of the European "grandfather house" and ancillary structure tradition, it appears that some of these buildings constructed in the late colonial years may have represented an adaptation of the form to primary residential purposes (as opposed to auxiliary). Those primary purposes would have included a tenant farmhouse or a beginning house on a new homestead.

JACOB KEIM ANCILLARY HOUSE, Circa 1753, Pike Township
Detail of the first-floor workshop room, its windows providing abundant daylight relative to the standards of the period.
Photo by Kenneth LeVan.

THE ARCHITECTURAL LANDSCAPE

The ancillary house built by Jerg Lotz in 1762 was evidently his primary dwelling. Lotz had purchased the Amity Township property around 1746; its previous occupants had been a rapidly changing succession of Anglo-Pennsylvanian settlers. After 1762 Lotz and his family apparently inhabited both the house purchased from John Campbell (form unknown but probably a modest affair) and the ancillary house. The first (or upper) floor of the latter served as master bedroom and as a Pennsylvania German architectural expression, complete with five-plate jamb stove. Lotz's germanizing of a previously Anglo-Pennsylvanian homestead is similar in a sense to Robert Stapleton's expansion of his double-cell house to create a stove-room house around 1740-1745, as well as Johannes DeTurk, Jr.'s conversion of William Maugridge's English hall-parlor house (the main house on the "Daniel Boone Homestead") into a stove-room house around 1770-1775. DeTurk extended an addition from the kitchen-hearth end of his house, and then made a stove aperture through the hearth's wall.

When farmer and cidermaker Lotz died in 1766, the contents of the cellar of the ancillary house included three-and-a-half barrels and six hogsheads (i.e., large barrels) of cider. The inventory of Lotz's movable estate also noted an apple mill. The evident design of the cellar for cider storage is another instance of specialization of work function in ancillary houses. Besides featuring an enclosed spring, as was common in ancillary houses, the cellar has two fireplaces, and an exterior doorway and an interior doorway (between the two rooms) that are each three-feet, ten-inches wide. The doorways were probably constructed of such breadth to enable the moving of large, cider-filled barrels.

JERG LOTZ ANCILLARY HOUSE, 1762, Amity Township
The grade against the visible lateral elevation of the building has been raised considerably in recent years. Originally, there was level access to the broad cellar doorway, through which large barrels of cider were rolled for storage.
Photo by Philip E. Pendleton.

ANCILLARY HOUSE ON THE JOHANNES SCHNEIDER HOMESTEAD, Oley Township
This tile-roofed building, probably of relatively early date but no longer standing, was the scene of the notorious Susanna Cox infanticide of 1809.
Photo by H. Winslow Fegley, circa 1900-1925. Courtesy, Schwenkfelder Library.

OLEY VALLEY HERITAGE

BANK BARN ON THE DEBENNEVILLE-KNABB HOMESTEAD, Circa 1750-1775, Oley Township
The dormers and gable-end windows represent alterations.
Photo by Philip E. Pendleton.

BARNS AND OUTBUILDINGS

There were, of course, many other sorts of buildings besides houses built in the valley during the colonial period. A farmer might construct several outbuildings to provide workspace, storage, and animal shelter. Chief among these was a barn, in which the farmer might milk dairy cows, store hay and grain, thresh the latter, and stable the most prized cattle or horses. The two earliest documentary references to barns in the valley both appeared in 1729, in an estate inventory and in an advertisement of a plantation for sale. A 1783 Oley Township tax list shows that by that year barn ownership was nearly universal among farmers, at least in that wealthiest of the valley's townships. The presence of a barn was reported for seventy-two of the seventy-six properties larger than twenty-five acres. By 1775 it is likely that barns were present on most farmsteads in the valley at large.

Just what sort of building was meant by "barn" in the colonial years is a more complicated matter. It was emphatically *not* the large bank barn that dominates the valley landscape today. The earliest dated local specimen of such a building was built in 1782. Colonial-period barns probably varied a good deal in size, though none were on the scale of the barns built between the Revolution and the Civil War. Valid generalization is hampered somewhat in that there is less than a handful of surviving barns that appear likely to have been built before 1776.

As early as 1744 the heirs of Martin Schenkel built a stone barn that cost them £78. This now vanished building was evidently a substantial one, perhaps of similar scale as the small stone bank barn at the DeBenneville-Knabb Homestead in Oley Township. In 1744, £78 was a large sum of money and a large share of the family's available funds. At his death in 1738, Schenkel, who had settled by 1719 and owned a 256-acre farm on rich northern Oley Valley limestone land, left an estate with a total value of £383 (£120 real estate, £263 personal estate). His heirs also built a stone springhouse in 1740 for £24.

The Schenkel family's stone barn was apparently situated near the upper end of the spectrum for Oley barns during the period. A 1799 tax list from Amity Township reported that at that late date forty-five (56 percent) of Amity's eighty barns were built of log, while ten (13 percent) were of frame construction, and twenty-five built of stone (31 percent).

Based on the limited available evidence, the barns of the colonial-period Oley settlement were probably built on three basic plans. One of these, with English and Rhine Valley variants, was the ground-level barn, or *Grundscheier* ("ground barn"). There is no record of an example of this single-floor-level type of barn having been built in the valley during the colonial years, though a large one dated 1791 survives in Oley Township. Because the ground-level barn was prevalent in both England and the Palatinate, and because the type was built in other early Pennsylvania settlements, it is likely that barns of this sort were used in the Oley Valley before 1776.

Another form of barn based closely on European antecedents was the "Switzer" or "Swiss" barn. Its Swiss origins and adaptation in early Pennsylvania have been recently (and authoritatively) docu-

THE ARCHITECTURAL LANDSCAPE

mented by Robert Ensminger.[19] A photograph of a now-vanished, apparently early log-built specimen of this type was taken, around 1915, near the hamlet of Basket. (Basket was located where Oley, Alsace, and Ruscomb Manor townships meet and is on the edge of the study area researched in detail for this work.) Perhaps the chief diagnostic trait of the bank-sited Swiss barn type is the forebay, a cantilevered projection of the upper floor along the down-bank lateral elevation of the barn. Stables were located on the basement level, the threshing floor (where grain was threshed), mows for hay storage, and granary space on the upper or ground-floor level. Trap doors piercing the floor of the forebay were used to pass down feed for livestock. Animals also could shelter themselves from the elements beneath the forebay. The stable area in the small colonial-period Swiss barn was probably generally used for milking and to house a few prized or pregnant animals.

Two surviving valley barns, likely to date to the colonial period, represent a third barn type, one evidently not directly related to a European prototype. These are the aforementioned DeBenneville-Knabb Barn, and the log-on-stone example at the Leinbach-Knabb Homestead in Oley Township. The form is that of a bank-sited barn lacking a forebay. The existence of later, larger barns of like design in other southeastern Pennsylvania settlements, and because a similar form developed in the Lake District of northern England, led to speculation that an English-derived bank barn tradition also played a role in early Pennsylvania's barn architecture.[20] The DeBenneville-Knabb and Leinbach-Knabb barns, built by Germans, however, may represent evidence that the forebayless form of Pennsylvania bank barn developed because farmers and builders observed the barns built for their Swiss immigrant neighbors. Perhaps non-Swiss settlers borrowed selectively from the Swiss barn form. They used the general concepts of bank siting, positioning

of hay storage and threshing floor on the upper level, and stabling on the lower level, but forsook that of the forebay. Many early Anglo-Pennsylvanian bank barns in Chester County and other Quaker settlements also were constructed without forebays.

The small colonial-period barns did not have the space or the design for nearly as

SWITZER BARN ON AN UNIDENTIFIED FARMSTEAD, Oley Township Vicinity
This small barn of the Switzer type, built of V-notched logs, is said to have been built in 1747. Featured in a newspaper article of 1915, it stood in the vicinity of a hamlet called Basket, where Oley, Alsace, and Ruscombmanor townships meet.
Photographer unknown. Courtesy, Robert F. Ensminger.

BANK BARN ON THE LEINBACH-KNABB HOMESTEAD, Circa 1735-1765, Oley Township
The log-built upper story is clad in weatherboard.
Photo by Harry F. Stauffer, 1963. Courtesy, The Historical Society of the Cocalico Valley.

many different activities or nearly as much stabling or storage as their nineteenth-century descendants. Some homesteads lacked barns altogether, since a barn's various functions could be done by other outbuildings. Smaller stables sheltered livestock on some farms, beginning by 1755.

A survey of estate inventories found wheat, rye, and "corn" (at the time a general term for grain) stored "in the house" (four instances), "in the loft" (probably a house's garret), "in the granary," and "in the crib," as well as "in the barn" (three instances). Johannes Schneider (died 1743) kept wheat both in his barn and in his house. The deceased persons whose inventories have references to grain storage in house or loft were all Germans. The roomy garret (attic) formed by the high-pitched strut-supported roof frame of a substantial Pennsylvania German house was customarily employed by its owner as a granary. In a large house the garret often had two floor levels. It is in early inventories of English-speakers that the references to crib and granary occur. Charles Bell (English, died around 1725) had "corn in the crib,"[21] and Peter Jones (Swedish, died 1739) had "wheat in the granary."[22] In the building traditions of the British Isles and Sweden, farmsteads tended to have many small buildings with specialized functions, rather than concentrating many functions in a large barn.

The colonial farms of the Oley Valley may not have had the elaborate array of outbuildings typical of a Pennsylvania German farm of the late nineteenth century, many examples of which can still (for the moment) be seen in the region. By the 1770s, however, the typical farmstead, whether owned by English or German, was probably composed of several structures. In 1772 Johannes Bishop's homestead had at least a house, a separate "kitchen adjoining the house,"[23] a springhouse, a barn, and a stable. References to springhouses in period documents can be confusing: the term could denote a small structure such as that at Bishop's, or an ancillary house with a spring in the cellar.

A variety of auxiliary structures could be found on valley farmsteads. Extant outbuildings at the well-preserved Daniel Reiff Homestead (known locally as the Moxon Farm), in Oley Township, include a smithy, a bakehouse, a smokehouse, and a pig stable. These structures are thought likely to have been built in the early 1770s, when the homestead was established, though the tendency to use traditional construction techniques for outbuildings long after their discontinuation in houses makes outbuildings hard to date. The small buildings on farmsteads have tended to suffer a higher replace-

BAKEHOUSE-SMOKEHOUSE ON THE DANIEL REIFF HOMESTEAD (Moxon Farm), Oley Township
This homestead was first occupied by Reiff, grandson to pioneer Philip Kühlwein, circa 1770, and this as well as others of the many tile-roofed outbuildings likely date to its early years.
Photo by Philip E. Pendleton.

THE ARCHITECTURAL LANDSCAPE

ment rate than the large ones.

Abijah Sands, Jr.'s estate inventory of 1773 referred to a wagon house; Christian Rothermel's of 1769 to a still house; Hans Mirtel Gerick's of 1757 to a milk house (a term probably synonymous with that of "springhouse," an appropriately cool location for dairy goods); and Daniel Womelsdorf's of 1759 to a smith shop. Most farmers and other homestead proprietors did the simpler of their own smithy and carpentry work. In 1755, in an advertisement he ran regarding his homestead, Jacob Weber noted the presence of a root cellar, an excavated, stone-lined cave designed for food storage that probably incorporated a vaulted ceiling. In 1746, Widow Magdalena Schenkel had a cider press house built at the Schenkel farmstead. The inventory of Herman Dehaven's estate made in 1761 listed "hay in the barrack."[24] A hay barrack was a device designed to shelter hay from the wet, consisting of four corner posts and a roof that could be slid up or down to an appropriate height.

THE LARGER FARMSTEAD

The individual farm buildings existed within the setting of the farmstead. Benjamin Longworthy's contested will of 1765 left to his wife Maria "the house and office houses [outbuildings] that are belonging to the house I now live in, together with a square containing four acres wherein shall be enclosed the said houses and garden and some apple trees." Longworthy also directed that his nephews (heirs to the larger farm) should provide Maria with "any wood she needs for fence and repairs."[25] A common form of fence in the region was the stake-and-rider fence, also called a "worm" or "zigzag" fence, such as the one Moravian artist Nicholas Garrison depicted in his 1757 drawing of the Oley Moravian mission. Roughhewn post-and-rail fences and picket fences probably were built also, the latter to enclose home lots and gardens. It is likely that none of Longworthy's four-acre home lot was wasted. Although the vegetable garden may have been laid out in an orderly manner, the rest of the farmstead probably would have taken on a

rather ramshackle appearance to modern eyes. There would not have been any carefully tended lawn to set off the house or other structures. Wherever there was not a building, there was a space that had a particular function. John Yocom's 1757 estate inventory included "corn in the stackyard,"[26] the latter an area of the farmyard where grain was stored between cutting and threshing.

Beyond the home lot's fence lay the farm's arable fields, improved pastures, and woodland. The process of clearing the land continued throughout the colonial years. A visitor at the close of the period still would have found the valley an uncrowded patchwork, with a considerable amount of uncleared forest, save for those sections of the upper valley where, prior to European settlement, it had been the custom of the local Indians to burn off the saplings and brush for hunting. The survival of extensive forested areas was beneficial because of the inhabitants' need for firewood and lumber.

In 1770 a large tract of fine valley bottom land in northern Oley Township, originally taken up by early settler Johann Arnoldt Huffnagel, comprised 120 acres of arable land, 30 acres of meadow, and 380 acres of woodland. This was a large proportion of woodland considering that the Huffnagels had been in residence since at least 1717. By 1770 the Huffnagel tract had been divided into four large properties and a seven-acre house lot, the latter situated on the High Road from Maiden

PIG STABLE ON THE DANIEL REIFF HOMESTEAD (Moxon Farm), Oley Township
Photo by Robert C. Bucher, 1963. Courtesy, Robert C. Bucher.

Creek to Oley. These five homesteads contained five houses, three barns, four orchards, and a mill seat with gristmill and sawmill. The visitor would have seen few acres actually in crops. On the 1767 tax list, the three Huffnagel tract farmsteads apart from the mill seat were assessed for a total of 20 acres planted in grain out of their 110 acres of arable land. These 20 acres probably represented 30 to 40 acres in reality, due to the tax assessors' custom of making artificially low assessments of crops and herds.

In the same year (1770), the situation was somewhat different on the Exeter Township tract settled by Benjamin Boone around 1730. Here there was a total of 145 acres of arable land, 56 acres of meadow, and just 126 acres of woods. Benjamin Boone and his sons were rooted in a Quaker culture that extolled hard work and the taming of the land for husbandry. They may have pursued a more energetic clearing and development of their realm than did the Huffnagels, resulting in the larger extent of arable land and improved meadow cleared in a decade or so shorter expanse of time. An alternative explanation for the difference might be that the higher quality of the limestone soil of Oley Township enabled the Huffnagels to meet their needs and desires while clearing fewer acres.

In either case, the Huffnagel and Boone tracts were similar in that the process of clearing and development was ongoing at the close of the colonial period. When Benjamin Boone made his will in 1762, the tract was already divided into two plantations, which he called "the old place" and "the new place."[27] In 1770, the old place had been settled for some forty years and consisted of 100 acres of arable land, 26 acres of meadow, and 37.5 acres of woodland. On it were a house, a barn, and two orchards. The new place, evidently a tenancy in 1762, comprised 45 acres of arable land, 30 acres of meadow, and 88.5 acres of woodland, with three houses, two barns, and two orchards in 1770. The proportions of arable and wooded land on the new place were roughly the reverse of what they were on the old place. Samuel Boone, the new place's inheritor, had evidently started yet another farmstead and was letting part of his property as a tenancy. One of the three houses was probably the modest habitation of old Benjamin Boone's "negro man Dirk." Boone had bequeathed to him "freedom from work" and two acres on the new place on which to live during Dirk's lifetime.

MILL BUILDINGS

Industries other than agriculture required specialized architecture. Unfortunately, there are no standing survivors of any of the valley ironworks' forge or furnace or related buildings, nor any known tannery buildings, fulling mills, or oil mills. Of the many gristmills that dotted the landscape in colonial times, four at least partially intact examples survive. However, in two of these latter cases, the Hoch House-Mill in Oley Township and the Pott House-Mill in Pike Township, only the house-sections survive. The Schneider Mill and the Judah Boone Mill are intact gristmill buildings. Most gristmill sites in the valley continued to function as mills through the Civil War period (1861-1865), but meanwhile were rebuilt thoroughly in response to changes in technology and business practice.

The Schneider Mill in Exeter Township was built originally sometime in the middle years of the eighteenth century as a small custom-business mill run by that prosperous farming family in part to meet their own needs. About the close of the colonial era, the mill was enlarged, and the previously external water wheel enclosed, when Daniel Schneider, a third-generation family member, opted to pursue milling as his full-time occupation. Daniel may have operated the business as a merchant mill. The mill building is a bank-sited, one-story example exhibiting such German vernacular architectural traits as strut-supported roof framing in the original section, a horizontal-sash window in the later section, and a roof kick in both parts.

The Judah Boone Mill, in Exeter, is also a bank-sited mill building of one story, but one of more spacious dimensions. It was constructed about 1770, probably to house a merchant-milling business from the start. The Boone Mill has been much altered over the years, obscuring the nature of its original appearance.

Both the Schneider and Boone mills have the characteristic gable-end doors on three levels, the uppermost entry to enable delivery of grain via hoist to the garret. The simplicity of the colonial-period mill building veiled the complexity of the architectural and engineering arrangement within (which is not intact at either surviving Oley Valley mill building). The hurst frame, the great, eminently sturdy wooden structure bearing the millstones and machinery, stood free of the building structure that contained it. The first floor was split between two or three levels. The highest, in mill buildings with internal wheels, was that over the wheel pit. The main first-floor level adjoined the exterior entry and served as the principal platform for human movement within the building. The stone floor was the lowest of the first-floor levels, where the sets of millstones were arranged atop the hurst frame. There were at least two sets of stones in each rural mill building of the period. One was a set of buhr stones, necessarily imported from particular quarries in France, for the milling of fine wheat flour. Also present would be a set of locally obtained stones for grinding other grain. The basement of the mill building also was divided into two or three spaces: the main basement floor, the gear pit for the hurst frame and its machinery, and, again in mill buildings with internal water wheels, the wheel pit.

No reciprocating or "up-and-down" sawmills survive from the colonial period. The Bertolet Sawmill is an early-nineteenth-century example whose form conveys an idea of the appearance and operation of its eighteenth-century forebears. Waterpower propelled the up-and-down movement of a vertically mounted saw blade. (The Bertolet Sawmill has been moved from Oley Township to the Daniel Boone Homestead historic site in Exeter and has recently been restored to running order.)

The remains of the headrace and tailrace, the walled ditches that conducted the waterflow necessary for power to and from the mill, respectively, are clearly visible at the Schneider, Boone, and Pott mills. The creation of a millseat (i.e., a property on which was situated a mill and the waterworks necessary for its operation) represented a major undertaking. As at an ironworks, construction of a dam on a natural watercourse was required to divert the water into the headrace. An additional dam was usually built on the headrace immediately above the mill to create a millpond and thereby to ensure a source of waterpower for periods of lesser natural flow. Many millers operated more than one type of mill at a millseat, located in adjacent buildings on the millrace.

The smithy building at the Daniel Reiff Homestead in Oley Township, constructed of stone, appears to date to the late eighteenth century, possibly to the early 1770s when the homestead was started. The log-built smithy known as Spohn's, that stood until recent years in Oley Township on the corner of Route 662 and Blacksmith Road, a mile and a half north of the village of Yellow House, also may have been an eighteenth-century building. The same is true of the ruined smithy at the Schenkel Homestead (also in Oley Township).

CONCLUSION

Considering life in America before the War of Independence, historians of earlier generations generally celebrated the newness of American civilization. They considered the colonists from Europe to

THE ARCHITECTURAL LANDSCAPE

have wrought a virtual reinvention of their culture in the New World. Over the past three decades or so, historians and other scholars of the past have undertaken a much-needed revision of this skewed vision of our early cultural history. They have emphasized the continuity between European and colonial American lifeways, depicting early Americans as concerned (in some accounts, even anxious) to duplicate the patterns of life they had known in their homelands, and as naturally doing so during their daily rounds.[28]

The colonial-period vernacular architecture created by European settlers in the Oley Valley, and in other early American communities, suggests a balance between views emphasizing tradition-bound Europeanness and unique Americanness. The many elements of the evolving Pennsylvania architectural tradition, especially the techniques of construction, were deeply rooted in European folk practice, or in academic architecture as it had developed since the European Renaissance. But responses to American conditions, and contact between settlers of varying European regional origins, had engendered combinations of old and new architectural elements. By the middle of the eighteenth century, architecture constructed in the Oley Valley was in almost all instances, considering a building as a whole, notably different from anything in Europe.

REAL ESTATE

To be *sold*: a tract of very good land, containing about two hundred acres, 60 acres clear, 6 of it good meadow, with a young orchard of 300 bearing trees, and a good house and barn; situate on the River Schuylkill, on Chester County side, about a mile above Thomas Millard's Mill. Enquire of *Thomas Rees* at the said plantation, and know further.
—*Pennsylvania Gazette*, February 19, 1729/30

For sale: a plantation near Oley, about four miles from the Schuylkill, 40 miles from Philadelphia, containing 100 acres of good land. 30 acres are clear, and well fenced, 15 acres are planted with wheat and other grain, 4 acres are meadow. There are two dwelling houses; one was just recently built. There is a good orchard, good well water, and other amenities. Moreover, it is amidst lands long since taken up; the neighbors are mostly German.

Whoever is inclined to buy, can apply to Peter Robeson at the Indian King Inn, or at the place itself. JOHN HARRY
—*Pennsylvanische Berichte*, January 16, 1743/44

Hans Mirtel Gerick, in Exeter Township in the so-called Schwarzwald three miles from Justice Boone, makes known, that he wants to rent out a plantation for four years from October 3. There are 40 acres cleared, there are 9 acres meadow, and 2 acres orchard. Whoever has the desire, can inspect it and become further informed.
—*Pennsylvanische Berichte*, March 16, 1749/50

To be sold by William Bird, late of Robeson Township, Lancaster County, the following plantations, and tracts of land, with the improvements and buildings thereunto belonging, viz., one thousand acres of land, well timbered and watered, together with two forges, in good repair, coal house, houses for forgemen, and a commodious stone house, two stories high, a cellar the whole length of the house, not above 100 acres of wood cut off the premises. Also the plantation and sawmill where Francis Hughes formerly lived, adjoining the river Schuylkill, containing 212 acres of land, a dwelling house, a large square log barn, a good bearing orchard, 40 acres of corn land, within fence, and 25 acres of meadow, 8 of which is well watered, and the remaining part may be watered, by making a small drain from the sawmill race, etc. Also the plantation where Victor Nealy formerly lived, adjoining to the said forge, containing 200 acres of land, 40 acres of which is cleared, a dwelling house, and a young bearing orchard, etc. Also 150 acres of land, where John Surrey now lives, with a small improvement thereon, and a plantation in the township of Amity, and county of Philadelphia, containing 200 acres of very good land. The plantation is commodiously situated on Cocalico road, and joins on the river Schuylkill, there is on it a good gristmill, a dwelling house, which has been a tavern there several years past, barn and stables, a good bearing orchard, 10 acres of meadow, and 80 acres of corn land cleared, and the remaining part well timbered, now in the tenure of Rees Williams; the said plantation and mill is now rented for thirty pounds per annum. And also the half part of 500 acres of land, situated in Amity Township, and county of Philadelphia, in partnership with John Potts, Esq.; has good improvements, a dwelling house, and out houses, a good spring, about 100 acres of corn land and meadow cleared, within fence, with two fine streams, which run through said plantation. For title and terms of sale, apply to James Keemer, in Amity Township, at the sign of the White Horse, and know further, or to the subscriber at Mount Pleasant.

N.B. All persons indebted to the above William Bird, are desired to make speedy payment; and those that have any demands against him, to bring in their accounts, that they may be settled, he intending to leave this province, in a short time.
—*Pennsylvania Gazette*, April 12, 1750

Philip Balthasar Craesman in Amity Township, 42 miles from Philadelphia, 14 miles from Reading Town, makes known, that he wants to sell his plantation, which lies on the road by the Swedes. There is an inn, the White Horse, a thriving place, where Marcus Huling formerly resided. There are 140 acres of good land, with a good orchard, good meadow, and other useful amenities. Whoever is inclined, may apply.
—*Pennsylvanische Berichte*, September 16, 1751

To be sold by the subscriber, living in Union Township, Berks County, a plantation and tract of land, containing 228 acres, whereon there is a good stone house, good log barn, stables and other out houses, seventy acres of land cleared, a good thriving young orchard of 200 apple trees, standing in a fruitful place, and bearing well, the whole being fresh good land, well watered, and good timber. Any person inclining to purchase the same, may know the terms of sale, by applying to John Godfrey, living on the premises.

Likewise a likely young Negro boy to be disposed of by the said subscriber. N.B. He was born in the country, and understands most sorts of country business, and is about 16 years old.
—*Pennsylvania Gazette*, April 10, 1755

Jacob Weber in Amity Township, 10 miles from Reading on the Tulpehocken Road, wants to sell his plantation. It has 170 acres. 70 acres are clear, 6 acres could be watered and made into good meadow. There is thereon a two-story house of sawn log, and a good barn and stable. It has been for four years an inn, has a smith shop and smithware, has a good orchard and a good root cellar. There is also his horses and wagon, plow, harrow, cow and houseware.
—*Pennsylvanische Berichte*, July 1, 1755

Johannes Lesher in Oley makes known, that he has a good plantation there to rent. Thereon there is a good orchard and meadow, and it would be a comfortable place to keep store or pursue some other public occupation. He wants to lease it for a good period. Likewise he makes known, that if there is a capable schoolmaster anywhere, who can teach English and German, he shall have a good wage, and he can apply to the aforesaid
JOHANNES LESHER
—*Pennsylvanische Berichte*, November 23, 1759

To be *sold* by *public vendue*, on the 16th of November next, at 12 o'clock at noon, at the house of *Thomas Dewees*, tavernkeeper, in Potts Grove,
A valuable *plantation*, containing five hundred acres and upwards, situated in Douglass Township, in Berks County, between Manatawny and Schuylkill, within four miles of Potts Grove, sixteen miles from Reading town, and forty from Philadelphia, adjoining the lands of John Potts, Esq., Marcus Huling, and Jonas Yocom. There is about 140 acres of the land cleared, of which there is 25 acres good meadow, and as much more may be made; the plow land is counted extraordinary good for all sorts of grain, and the uncleared land well timbered. About 10 acres of the meadow may be watered with little trouble, as a stream of water runs through a part of said land. There is two small log houses, and a large frame barn, on said premises, also a good apple orchard of 250 trees, which seldom fail to bear plentifully. The said land contains 274 perches on both sides of the great Manatawny road that leads from Philadelphia to Reading, and the same front on the river Schuylkill. It would suit very well to divide into two or three plantations, and will be sold either altogether or in parcels, as will best suit the purchasers.

[The plantation] belongs to the estate of Thomas Potts, of Colebrookdale, late deceased. The title is indisputable; and the terms will be made known at the time of sale, by
THOMAS RUTTER and WILLIAM DEWEES, executors
—*Pennsylvania Chronicle*, October 28, 1767

JOHANNES JAEGER (JOHN HUNTER) INN, 1768, Oley Township
Rear and gable-end view showing kitchen wing and bakeoven at left.
Photo by Kenneth LeVan.

NOTES

[1] *Pennsylvanische Berichte*, July 1, 1755.

[2] Key works regarding the origins of early American log construction include Harold R. Shurtleff, *The Log Cabin Myth: A Study of the Early Dwellings of the English Colonists in North America* (Cambridge, Mass.: Harvard University Press, 1939); Fred B. Kniffen and Henry Glassie, "Building in Wood in the Eastern United States: A Time-Place Perspective," in *Common Places: Readings in American Vernacular Architecture*, edited by Dell Upton and John Michael Vlach (Athens, Ga.: The University of Georgia Press, 1986), 159-81, reprinted from *Geographical Review* 56 (1966), 40-66; Warren E. Roberts, "Some Comments on Log Construction in Scandinavia and the United States," in *Viewpoints on Folklife: Looking at the Overlooked* (Ann Arbor, Mich.: UMI Research Press, 1988), 273-88, reprinted from *Folklore Today: A Festschrift for Richard Dorson*, edited by Linda Degh, Felix Oinas, and Henry Glassie (Bloomington, Ind.: Indiana University Press, 1976), 437-50; Terry G. Jordan, *American Log Buildings* (Chapel Hill, N.C. The University of North Carolina Press, 1985); Donald A. Hutslar, *The Architecture of Migration: Log Construction in the Ohio Country, 1750-1850* (Athens, Ohio: Ohio University Press, 1986); Terry G. Jordan and Matti Kaups, *The American Backwoods Frontier: An Ethnic and Ecological Interpretation* (Baltimore: The Johns Hopkins University Press, 1989); and Patricia Irvin Cooper, "Some Misconceptions in American Log-Building Studies," *Material Culture* 23, No. 2 (Summer 1991), 43-61.

[3] *Pennsylvanische Berichte*, November 1, 1749.

[4] Edward A. Chappell, "Acculturation in the Shenandoah Valley: Rhenish Houses of the Massanutten Settlement," in *Common Places: Readings in American Vernacular Architecture*, edited by Dell Upton and John Michael Vlach (Athens, Ga.: University of Georgia Press, 1986), 32.

[5] J. Bennett Nolan, ed., *Early Narratives of Berks County* (Reading: Historical Society of Berks County, 1927), 125.

[6] Alliene Saeger DeChant, *Down Oley Way* (Kutztown: published privately, 1953), 34. A detailed discussion of thatching techniques practiced in southeastern Pennsylvania is available in Robert C. Bucher and Alan G. Keyser, "Thatching in Pennsylvania," *Der Reggeboge* 16, no. 1 (1982): 1-23.

[7] Gottlieb Mittelberger, *Journey to Pennsylvania*, translated and edited by Oscar Handlin and John Clive (Cambridge, Mass.: Harvard University Press, 1960), 91.

[8] Peter G. Bertolet, *Fragments of the Past: Historical Sketches of Oley and Vicinity* (Oley: The Women's Club of Oley Valley, 1980), 60.

[9] Thomas Tileston Waterman propounded the theory of solely Swedish origins for the corner fireplace in *The Dwellings of Colonial America* (Chapel Hill, N.C.: The University of North Carolina Press, 1950), 123 and 126-29.

[10] Daniel Miller, "The Early Moravian Settlements in Berks County," *Transactions of the Historical Society of Berks County*, vol. 2 (1905-1909): 320-21.

[11] Will of John Keim, 1747, Berks County Wills, vol. 1, 8.

[12] Estate inventory of George Andrews, 1752, Probate Files, Office of the Philadelphia County Register of Wills.

[13] Will of Peter Jones, 1772, Berks County Wills, vol. 2, 121.

[14] Estate inventory of Peter Jones, 1773, Probate Files, Office of the Berks County Register of Wills.

[15] Will of Elizabeth Womelsdorf, 1772, Probate Files, Berks County.

[16] Deed from David Weiser to Christian Weiser, 1772, Berks County Deeds, vol. B1, 239.

[17] Will of Hans Mirtel Gerick, 1757, Berks County Wills, vol. 1, 44.

[18] Estate inventory of Hans Martin Gerick, 1757, Probate Files, Berks County.

[19] Robert F. Ensminger, *The Pennsylvania Barn: Its Origin, Evolution, and Distribution in North America* (Baltimore: The Johns Hopkins University Press, 1992).

[20] Ibid., 10, 89, 108-09, 128-29. The originator of the theory that the English Lake District bank barn played a role in the development of the Pennsylvania bank barn was Henry Glassie, in *Pattern in the Material Folk Culture of the Eastern United States* (Philadelphia: University of Pennsylvania Press, 1968), 62.

[21] Estate inventory of Charles Bell, n.d. (circa 1725), Probate Files, Philadelphia County.

[22] Estate inventory of Peter Jones, 1739, Probate Files, Philadelphia County.

[23] Depositions in the Case of Elizabeth Bishop, Berks County Oyer and Terminer Records, Record Group 33 (Supreme Court—Eastern Division), Pennsylvania State Archives.

[24] Estate inventory of Herman Dehaven, 1761, Probate Files, Berks County.

[25] Will (disallowed) of Benjamin Longworthy, 1765, Probate Files, Berks County.

[26] Estate inventory of John Yocom, 1757, Probate Files, Berks County.

[27] Will of Benjamin Boone, 1762, Berks County Wills, vol. 1, 124.

[28] Frederick Jackson Turner represented the view of early American society as exceptional, or essentially discontinuous from that of Europe. Turner, developing his well-known "Frontier Thesis" in the 1893 address, "The Significance of the Frontier in American History," proposed that for centuries the abundance of inexpensive frontier land worked a liberating transformation on the mentality of Europeans who came to America. *Annual Report of the American Historical Association for the Year 1893*, 197-227. A more recent leading exponent of American exceptionalism is Daniel J. Boorstin, in *The Americans: The Colonial Experience* (New York: Random House, 1958).

Noteworthy studies emphasizing the continuity of European cultural patterns in the lives of colonial-period Americans include Thomas Jefferson Wertenbaker, *The Founding of American Civilization: The Middle Colonies* (New York: Charles Scribner's Sons, 1938); Henry Glassie, *Pattern in the Material Folk Culture of the Eastern United States* (Philadelphia: University of Pennsylvania Press, 1968); James Deetz, *In Small Things Forgotten: The Archaeology of Early American Life* (Garden City, N.Y.: Anchor Press, 1977); David Grayson Allen, *In English Ways: The Movement of Societies and the Transferral of English Local Law and Custom to Massachusetts Bay in the Seventeenth Century* (Chapel Hill, N.C.: The University of North Carolina Press, 1981); and Bernard Bailyn, *The Peopling of British North America: An Introduction* (New York: Alfred A. Knopf, 1986). Most ambitious and insistent (and controversial) in the delineation of a pervasive and lasting influence of European culture on early American culture is David Hackett Fischer's *Albion's Seed: Four British Folkways in America* (Oxford: Oxford University Press, 1989).

Chapter 4

SOUL

From the oldest grave at the Molatton Churchyard:

The front of the headstone:

**HERE
LYETH YE
BODY OF
ANDREW
ROBESON
WHO DIED
FEBY. 19th
1719/20
AGED 66
YEARS**

The back of the headstone:

**Removed from noise & care
This silent place I chose
When death should end my years
To take a sweet repose
Here in a peaceful place
My ashes must remain
My Savior shall me keep
And raise me up again**

The footstone (the side facing the headstone):

A R

REMEMBER DEATH

CHURCHYARD OF SALEM UNITED CHURCH OF CHRIST (Formerly Oley Reformed Church), Oley Township
The present church building, shown here, was constructed in 1821 under the direction of noted builder and woodworker Gottlieb Drexel. The original stone church building of circa 1755 was taken down long ago.
Photo by Philip E. Pendleton.

GRAVE OF ANDREW ROBESON, Headstone
Photo by Philip E. Pendleton.

The markers at the Andrew Robeson grave at Saint Gabriel's Protestant Episcopal Church in Amity Township, originally known as Molatton Church, make it a virtual meeting place between Protestant religious attitudes of the seventeenth and eighteenth centuries. The footstone contains the traditional admonition to be ever mindful of the yawning chasm of eternity. The back of Robeson's headstone starkly contrasts, however, with the hopeful sentiment regarding Robeson's place in the heavenly home. The tombstone arrangement and decoration, unusually elaborate for the early Oley Valley, was in keeping with the socioeconomic status of Andrew Robeson. In 1714 Robeson stepped down from the post of chief justice of the Supreme Court of Pennsylvania and moved to the Oley Val-

GRAVE OF ANDREW ROBESON, Front of Footstone
Photo by Philip E. Pendleton.

GRAVE OF ANDREW ROBESON, Rear of Headstone
Photo by Philip E. Pendleton.

ley, evidently intent on becoming a major booster of the nascent settlement. Robeson, a Scotsman, and his wife Mary, a Delaware Valley Swede, were members of the Swedish Lutheran congregation at Wicacoa (Gloria Dei or Old Swedes' Church, Philadelphia) and thus connected with the Swedes who settled at Molatton. Robeson took up over two thousand acres of land along the Schuylkill, and in 1719, he had one of the first two high roads of Oley Valley put through to his homestead at his sole request. (Successful petitions usually bore many names.)

Andrew Robeson died in the latter year, however. The gravestones are of the same green stone and are arranged, decorated, and inscribed in the same style as many stones at Gloria Dei, including that of Robeson's wife Mary (died 1716). This similarity implies that Robeson's gravestones were carved in Philadelphia and brought up the Schuylkill to Molatton, no doubt at considerable expense. Robeson's daughter Mary became the second wife of Mordecai Lincoln (great-great-grandfather of President Abraham Lincoln by Mordecai's first wife Hannah Saltar) around 1727. The Lincolns took over Andrew Robeson's homestead, and in 1733 built a house that still stands.

The religious life of the colonial Oley Valley forms one of the more intriguing aspects of its history. Spiritual tumult was particularly prevalent among the German-speaking people of the valley, who embraced several different churches and sects as the years passed. As one looks into the Oley Valley's early history via the surviving primary documents, it is startling to see how appallingly bad a reputation for moral and spiritual life the valley had with clergymen of the time. Wrote the German Reformed minister Bartholomew Rieger in 1755, "Notwithstanding it was one of the earliest settled, well-to-do, and best farming regions, [it] has always been the haunt of the wildest and most unruly people and sects."[1] To the leading Lutheran minister Heinrich Melchior Muhlenberg, the Oley Valley of 1747 was

> a place where practically all the inhabitants are scoffers and blasphemers. It is a place like Sodom and Gomorrah and I have preached there several times for the sake of a Lot or two who live there, but the wanton sinners only scoffed and jeered me. They were willing to accept my teaching if I could prove it with signs and wonders. . . . Life there [is] lucrative and lascivious.[2]

The more devout among readers should not become too forlorn, nor the jaded irreligious too mirthful. It was not lack of religion that inspired these writers' remarks, but rather lack of a religion of which they could approve. The men who made these assessments of the people of Oley Valley were ministers born and educated in Germany. Each believed his particular Protestant confession to be the one true faith. To clergymen Rieger and Muhlenberg, the religious freedom established in Pennsylvania was unsettling and threatening, not to mention dangerous to the colonists' souls. A minister accustomed to deferential treatment in Germany was very likely to be greeted in Pennsylvania by some sectarian who would thumb his nose at him.

The unconventionality of spiritual life among Oley Valley Germans in the early 1700s was just an extreme example of conditions that prevailed throughout the German-settled area of the province. This matter must be examined in the context of German immigration into colonial Pennsylvania. A small, intermittent stream of German arrivals, including a variety of visionary religious radicals, came during the earliest phase of the migration, from 1683 to 1727, to flee persecution and avail themselves of the religious freedom proffered by William Penn. It is little wonder, then, that loyal Lutheran Justus Falckner could report from Germantown in 1701 that the European population of Pennsylvania was

> divided into almost innumerable sects, which preeminently may be called sects and hordes, [such] as Quakers, Anabaptists, Naturalists, Rationalists, Independents, Sabbatarians and many others, especially secret insinuating sects, whom one does not know what to make of, but who, nevertheless, are all united in these beautiful principles, if it pleases the Gods: Do away with all good order, and live for yourself as it pleases you![3]

The adherents of the two more conventional German Protestant churches, the Lutheran and the Reformed (or Calvinist), did not become a significant element in the Pennsylvania story until 1727. That is when the massive, mainly economically motivated second wave of German immigration began. German church people were present in the colony before 1727. Many were refugees from French invasion or oppression by rulers of Roman Catholic or differing Protestant persuasions. They were a scattered minority, however, who found it difficult to organize themselves or to attract the concern of ecclesiastical authorities back in Germany. In fact, when German Reformed adherents in Pennsylvania obtained a permanent relationship with a supervisory body in Europe, in 1731, it was with the *Dutch* Reformed Church in Holland. When the Dutch Reformed leaders had asked the directors of the German Reformed Church in the Palatinate about their intentions regarding their spiritual offspring in Pennsylvania, they had been informed that the Palatine church could not spare the resources necessary to guide the Pennsylvanians.

In the absence of accustomed church leadership, many church people who came to Pennsylvania in the decades before 1740 joined with the sectarians or the more radical religious experimenters. These persuasions provided alternatives for communal spiritual expression, and their adherents tended to be assiduous proselytizers. Firsthand accounts of early Pennsylvania depict the province as a veritable spiritual battleground, swarming with regiments of contentious believers, as sectarians and visionaries tried to convert one another as well as to convert the orphaned church people. When churches and ministers did come to Pennsylvania, most sectarians were not pleased. To sectarians these were reminders and possible portents of oppression.

Religion, the spiritual impulse in people, was thriving in early Pennsylvania and in the Oley Valley in particular. People's spiritual lives colored or impinged on all their other spheres of feeling and activity. This was no less true for all the mentions of moral transgressions in court records, Quaker meeting minutes, or other sources from the period.

The comments of church ministers that comprise such a major share of the available documentary evidence should be weighed carefully. When Lutheran and Reformed divines arrived in the province, and they did so relatively late, they faced a rather intractable situation, and one difficult for them to comprehend. As oppressed as their churches might recently have been in parts of Europe, approval of religious toleration did not come easily to them.

GRAVE OF ANDREW ROBESON, Overall View, Churchyard of Saint Gabriel's Protestant Episcopal Church, Amity Township
Photo by Philip E. Pendleton.

Despite the shrill disunity only too apparent to observers, many, perhaps most, among the more spiritually minded of the German settlers of early-eighteenth-century Pennsylvania shared an underlying set of ideas and attitudes about religion and the proper way of life. These ideas and attitudes were known as "pietism." Pietism was a widespread movement among German Protestants of the seventeenth and eighteenth centuries aimed at revitalizing what was considered a corrupt, overly scholastic Protestant Christianity. Pietists believed that conversion and spiritual regeneration were intrinsic elements of the true Christian life. The reborn person's life would be one of piety, hence the term. Pietists believed that one should strive to live in as unworldly a manner as practicable. While pietism formed a spectrum across churches and sects, most German pietists remained within the Lutheran and Reformed churches, and conflicts in those organizations between "pietists" and "orthodox" (nonpietists) could sometimes be bitter. In Pennsylvania, outside the anti-pietist church authorities' geographical sphere of concern, pietism would emerge as a dominant element in Pennsylvania German Protestantism before the end of the colonial period. An analogous and related movement was that of the Methodists within the Church of England during the middle eighteenth century, before they broke away to form their own church.

THE NEW BORN

The dominant religious gathering among the Oley Valley's German settlers up to the 1730s was a radical sect called the New Born. This band of believers was responsible for the abysmally low level of esteem in which colonial Lutheran and Reformed clergymen held the valley. Ministers concurred that New Born beliefs were more dangerous to people's souls and to the social order than those of any other sect in Pennsylvania.

The charismatic founder of the New Born was a "poor day-laborer and helper,"[4] from Lambsheim in the Palatinate, named Matthias Baumann. In 1701 Baumann was suddenly taken terribly ill. He went into a delirium lasting days during which, by his account, God summoned him to heaven. God informed Baumann that the end of the world was nigh, and God was sending Baumann forth to proclaim God's truth to the people.

The "truth," as God had revealed it to Baumann, was that all church and sect life as it was known—clergy, sacrament, ritual, catechism, scripture, prayer, communal worship—was an abomination before God and a waste of time. The only way to salvation was through a traumatic experience of spiritual death and rebirth, which incorporated an actual interview with the heavenly Being. Those who underwent this wrenching transformation emerged saved and, from then on, forever free of and incapable of sin. The only true sin, after all, was original sin, which Baumann interpreted as "death to God in spirit."

In the year following his metamorphosis Baumann's preaching moved several of his relatives and neighbors to embrace his theology, but Baumann's logic failed to persuade the Lambsheim authorities. The town court tried the former Reformed worshiper in 1702 for "pietism" and banished him. Orthodox church and state authorities such as those in Lambsheim considered the pietist movement threatening. Pietism, whether in or out of the established churches, might undermine the political and social order by revolutionizing the established churches. Hence their employment of the name "pietist" when describing the terrifying Baumann and his followers.

In 1706 the town of Lambsheim also convicted nine of Baumann's followers on a pietism charge, including Philip Kühlwein, brother of Baumann's wife Katarina. The court compelled the nine men to clean the town ditches, a noisome task.

Philip Kühlwein, Baumann's brother-in-law, left Lambsheim in 1709. He joined the exodus of thirteen thousand people from the Rhine Valley to England that took place that year, inspired by Queen Anne's promise of protection for impoverished Protestants. Some of these people eventually settled in Pennsylvania, but most in New York and some in other corners of the British realm. This mass movement of Germans formed an exceptional event in the years preceding the great, continuous migration that began in 1727. Besides Kühlwein, the participants included Jean LeDee, whose daughter Maria wed Kühlwein; Johannes Joder, a widower who married LeDee's other daughter Anna Rosina; and Isaac DeTurk and Jacob Weber with their families, all future Oley Valley settlers. LeDee and DeTurk were from Eppstein and Frankenthal, towns a few miles from Lambsheim. Before the end of 1709 Kühlwein, LeDee, and DeTurk had selected land in Oley. They were the first German-speaking settlers in the valley (though DeTurk, having landed in New York, did not move his family to Oley until at least 1712). In 1714 the master himself, Matthias Baumann, arrived in Oley from Germany.

It is likely that the German-speaking settlement created in the northern Oley Valley in the 1710s was a virtual New Born colony. Perhaps most early-arriving, soon-intermarried families settling in that section were adherents of New Bornism. Some may have converted to "Baumannism" in Germany, others en route to America, some soon after coming to Pennsylvania. This hypothesis of a "New Born settlement" is difficult to prove, however, as the only positively identified New Born members were Baumann himself, Kühlwein, Joder, Maria DeTurk (wife of Isaac), and Martin Schenkel. Strong circumstantial evidence helps identify several others, though. Also, many contemporaries of the New Born commented that the New Born were very numerous in the valley. All the marriages of children and the many friendships (revealed in wills and other documents) make the German-speaking, northern Oley Valley group of early settler families an identifiable cadre. One has to wonder whether these relationships would have been possible between New Born and non-New Born families, considering the contentious demeanor that seems to have accompanied New Born convictions.

Baumann and company spared no effort to convey their divine message to the "unregenerate" of Pennsylvania, at least during the prophet's lifetime (he died in 1727). The visionary from Lambsheim set out his beliefs in a tract, *A Call to the Unregenerate*, written in Oley in 1723. Baumann posited what was at times an almost disarmingly simple logic.

> There are but two kinds of people in the world: sinners, as we are

born, and righteous, as we are reborn. . . . There is but one sin, which Adam committed. He died unto God in spirit. And this is what all persons get from Adam: they have died unto God. This they could learn . . . when they approach God in prayer. Then the world overwhelms them so that they cannot keep to God as long as one Lord's Prayer lasts without other thoughts entering. . . . I know, for I began the Lord's Prayer three or four times and could not bring it to God without other thoughts popping into my head. . . . If God does not first show Himself to man, and come to him, man cannot love Him. . . . If someone were to write me that I should love him, and if I had never in my whole life seen him, I would . . . reply that he should first come to see me so that I could get to know him, otherwise it would be impossible to love him. . . .

You must discover that you lack God in your heart and you must call upon the unknown God that He shall make Himself manifest within you so you can come to love Him. . . . Man must be ever dying until he comes with Christ to the Cross, dying to his first nature. Just as Christ felt pain outwardly in his flesh, so [you] must feel it in [your] mind. . . . You will think that God does not want you, that you are finished and must perish! . . . You will say that never in your whole life have you ever had greater pain than now. This is the time when life and death contend. If man then remains constant and thinks that even if he be lost he still will not forsake God, presently, God will hear him anew and take up his abode in him. . . .

With the body we cannot sin before God, only before people and other creatures; this the judge can correct. Adam did not do evil with the body. He performed spiritual sin; he died to God. And Christ announced a spiritual righteousness and warned us against spiritual sin. . . . God dwells in a Christian [i.e., a New Born], therefore he can sin no more. . . . God teaches him what he is to do outwardly. . . .

God has made him a person who lives according to His law and keeps it. . . . As Adam was before the fall, so have I been made.[5]

Insisting "that they had only been sent by God to confound men,"[6] Baumann made many trips to other parts of the province, accompanied by some of his followers. A favorite destination for such excursions was the market at Philadelphia, where "their disputations . . . were often heard with astonishment, [and] where also Baumann once offered, in order to prove that his doctrine was from God, to walk across the Delaware River."[7] Although the reaction of the Philadelphia audience to this proposal is unknown, it may have been similar to that of Conrad Beissel, the rival mystic who gathered the Seventh Day Baptists in the Cocalico Valley of Lancaster County, organizing the Ephrata Cloister in 1733. The chroniclers of the cloister community wrote in 1786 that the New Born had come to instruct Beissel, "when Baumann commenced about the new birth. The Superintendent [Beissel] gave him little satisfaction, telling him to smell of his own filth, and then consider whether this belonged to the new birth; whereupon they [the New Born] called him a crafty spirit full of subtlety, and departed."[8]

An important element in the New Born mission to "confound men" was the disruption of other groups' religious services. As late as 1753, with Baumann dead twenty-six years and the sect thought to be approaching extinction, Heinrich Melchior Muhlenberg could not conduct the funeral service for devout Oley Valley Lutheran Philip Beyer without an inspired interruption.

An obstinate old man, who called himself Newborn, stood outside, . . . and began to preach to several people of his persuasion with noisy blustering which was intended to disturb me. But . . . because few people were willing to . . . listen to him, . . . he ran home in a fit of temper. . . . This was the basis of his authority: One night, many years ago, he saw a light in his room. He claimed that this light revealed to him that he was a child of God, that the magistracy, the ministry, the Bible, sacraments, churches, schools, etc. are of the devil, that all men must be like him, etc. This would certainly not be a good thing, however, for he gets drunk occasionally and beats his poor wife.[9]

A unique statement of New Born belief was made by one of Baumann's followers in a letter written by Maria DeTurk to relatives in Germany. She referred to the spiritual tumult, trauma, and "wonders" that she experienced in her process of "new birth."

Oley, May 14, 1718
Brothers, sisters, relatives and friends:

I greet you all cordially. I have received your letter, from which I learn what you wish; but to answer which is [not] a small matter. I will make my situation known to you—tell you how it is with me. I am now in a better state than I had been in Germany. Here God made me free from sin. I cannot sin any more, for which I now and shall ever praise God. I clave unto Him, and thus He drew me nigh and has taken His abode in me. If you desire to enjoy the new birth with me, withdraw your mind and thoughts from all worldly things—seek God only—continue to pray, sigh day and night, that God would regenerate you. If you prove sincere, you will experience wonders. Men boast of being Christians who know not what the new birth is. The new birth is the new [corner] stone, which no one knows, only he that receives it.

To emigrate to Pennsylvania is vain, if you are sinners. Who knows whether you will arrive safely? Most persons have to endure sickness—many die. In Pennsylvania there is unrest, too, as well as in Germany. If it is not by reason of war, there is something else which is disagreeable.

Men will never find rest in this world, go whither they will. With God only is there rest. If you see rest elsewhere, you will still be restless—thus it is in America. But if one is free from sin, he may go abroad, or remain in Germany, then he has the most precious treasure with him; he is contented where he is—is delighted with his treasure anywhere in the world.

Preachers and their hearers, all of them, are no Christians, they are sinners. Christ has come to abolish sin. He, then, that is not free from sin, for him Christ has not yet come into the world. All the preachers in the world that have not been made free from sin, and yet can sin, are false teachers, be they pious or impious. Naught but Christ is of any avail in His kingdom. He that hath not Christ is none of His; for where Christ is there is freedom from sin.

I again greet you all cordially. Think of what I have written, lay it to heart; it will be more precious to you than all else in the world.
Maria DeTurck
Whose maiden name was Maria DeHaroken.[10]

A discussion of the New Born must tangle with the question of the "outward deeds" of people who believed themselves incapable of sin. Detractors of the New Born alleged that many of Baumann's followers misinterpreted his proclamation of sinlessness as a license for extensive and varied immoral behavior. The Moravian bishop August Gottlieb Spangenberg locked horns with the New Born while preaching in Oley in 1737. He wrote that the New Born "claim that if a man is reborn then everything which he does is good and right, for he cannot sin any more; indeed, they consider obvious acts of the flesh as good," in keeping with this belief.[11] According to the Ephrata chroniclers of 1786, Matthias Baumann himself was "said otherwise to have been an upright man, and not to have loved the world inordinately; but Kühlenwein, Jotter [Joder], and other followers of his were insatiable in their love of the world."[12] The New Born always will be shrouded in mystery, in this intriguing respect as in others.

New Born beliefs certainly were troubling to Lutheran and Reformed clerics, but the New Born themselves were not unstable cranks. Matthias Baumann, Johannes Joder, and Martin Schenkel held enough respect in the discriminating eyes of the Philadelphia County Court to be ordered to serve on road surveying juries, an important responsibility. Joder and Kühlwein became particularly substantial farmers, garnering Oley Valley estates of 761 acres and 770 acres at the time of their respective deaths (1741 and 1736). Such freeholds put them on a footing with men like George Boone, Sr., Andrew Robeson, Mounce Jones, and Anthony Lee as founders of valley "first families."

The 1753 attempt to disrupt Philip Beyer's obsequies was the latest known direct reference to New Born activity. Whatever source from which it sprang, the New Born sect was essentially one generation's religion. Baumann's adherents did not succeed in transmitting their faith in the new birth to their children, in any lasting way, though they do seem to have bequeathed a tenacious heritage of anticlerical attitudes. As late as the 1850s, the antiquarian Dr. Bertolet noticed that a surprising number of Oley Township families, in comparison to other communities, were not affiliated with religious congregations.[13]

An apocryphal account by Lutheran church organist and schoolmaster Gottlieb Mittelberger, about actual Oley inhabitants who evidently were or had been New Born adherents, shows that Oley was still saddled with a reputation for irreligion in 1754. Mittelberger returned to Germany in that year, and two years later he published his account of life in Pennsylvania.

I cannot pass over yet another example of the wicked life some people lead in this free country. Two very rich planters living in the township of Oley, both very well known to me, one named Arnoldt Huffnagel [a settler in Oley by 1717], the other Conrad Reiff [son-in-law and heir to Philip Kühlwein], were both archenemies of the clergy, scoffing at them and at the Divine Word. They often met to pour ridicule and insults upon the preachers and the assembled congregation, laughing at and denying Heaven and future bliss as well as damnation in Hell. In 1753 these two scoffers met again, according to their evil habit, and began to talk of Heaven and Hell.

Arnoldt Huffnagel said to Conrad Reiff, "Brother, how much will you give me for my place in Heaven?"

The other replied, "I'll give you just as much as you'll give me for my place in Hell."

Huffnagel spoke again, "If you will give me so and so many sheep for my place in Heaven, you may have it."

Reiff replied, "I'll give them to you, if you will give me so and so many sheep for my place in Hell."

So the two scoffers struck their bargain, joking blasphemously about Heaven and Hell. When Huffnagel, who had been so ready to get rid of his place in Heaven, wanted to go down to his cellar the next day, he suddenly dropped dead. Reiff, for his part, was suddenly attacked in his field by a flight of golden eagles who sought to kill him. And this would have happened without fail had he not piteously cried for help, so that neighbors came to his assistance. From that time on, he would not trust himself out of his house. He fell victim to a wasting disease and died in sin, unrepentant and unshriven. These two examples had a visible effect on other scoffers, similarly inclined. For God will not let himself be scoffed at.[14]

Although Mittelberger appears to have misinterpreted New Born attitudes, there is one striking aspect to his admonitory tale—Johann Arnoldt Huffnagel did die in 1753, and somewhat suddenly, judging by the fact that he died intestate (without leaving a will). Conrad Reiff, however, punished by Mittelberger with an untimely death, lived to pass away in 1777, at a ripe old age.

Baumann, Kühlwein, and Joder were all dead by 1742. The sect literally died out (though the Moravians later liked to claim that they had "defeated" it). There may have been other leaders beside Baumann, but he was the only preacher with the power to keep the nascent sect expanding, and he died early (1727). As early as 1730 a somewhat relieved Johann Philipp Boehm could report, "The blasphemous sect, which calls itself the 'Newborn,' has almost been silenced, for its author, named Matthias Baumann, has been removed by God. A few of his adherents can still be found. . . . But these men have no longer a large following."[15]

OTHER GERMAN SECTARIAN GROUPS

By the mid-1730s a few other German-derived religious groups had taken places in the Oley Valley alongside the weakening New Born sect. Some of these groups' members may have been fallen-away New Born or their children; others were more recently arrived settlers. Each of the two Pennsylvania wings of the German Baptist Brethren (or "Dunkers") had a few adherents. The leaders of both wings visited the valley and preached from time to time in the 1720s and 1730s. Conrad Beissel of Ephrata, Matthias Baumann's old antagonist, made a number of converts to his mystical, sabbatarian (i.e., believing in Saturday worship) faction in the early 1730s. Some of these went to Ephrata to enter Beissel's cloistered community. A small congregation aligned with Peter Becker's less radical Germantown-based Brethren persuasion was formed in the northern Oley Valley by 1732. It never grew large, but persisted, and numbered about a dozen households in 1770 (many of these living in the hills adjoining the valley). The eighteenth-century meetinghouse built by this gathering is in Pricetown, outside the study area researched in detail for this work.

At some point in the eighteenth century, a small Mennonite congregation was established in the valley. The only definitely identified member was Lazarus Weidner, who in 1780 was a preacher in this group. But several colonial Oley Valley families are said to have had Mennonite backgrounds in Europe.

EARLY GERMAN REFORMED AND LUTHERAN ACTIVITY

The late 1720s and early 1730s saw the inception of Reformed and Lutheran church activity in the valley. These efforts met with noticeable interest, as the major post-1727 migration of German church people was beginning to have local impact. Jerg Michael Weiss, whose brief presence (1727-1730) temporarily doubled the number of Reformed ministers in the province, visited Oley in 1729. He tangled with the New Born, inspiring him to write a polemic against them. Pennsylvania's sole German Lutheran cleric, Johann Caspar Stoever, stopped at Oley at least five times over the years 1731-1734. Both men preached and baptized children, including some Lenape Indians on the part of Weiss.

By 1736 there were enough German Reformed faithful in the valley to justify the founding of a congregation. Local German Lutherans could worship with Swedish Lutherans and Anglicans at Molatton Church. This first gathering in the Oley Valley of either of the two German churches took a couple of decades to get beyond an initial stop-and-start stage, mainly due to interference from people of other persuasions. In early 1736 a group of Reformed people met and agreed to work together to establish a church in Oley. They asked Johann Philipp Boehm, the province's lone Reformed minister, to ride up from his home in Whitpain Township, Philadelphia County, and to hold a service. Boehm did so, and a few months later the minister led a meeting in Oley in which the people officially established a congregation, electing four elders and two deacons. Boehm pledged to execute the pastoral duties, visiting twice a year. At each of the 1736 services, he administered the Lord's Supper to about forty communicants. This was an impressive number for a nascent frontier congregation, considering that Boehm, like other regular ministers in Pennsylvania, was fairly strict as to whom he allowed to take communion. Participants had to prove of-

SCHNEIDER FAMILY CEMETERY
The gravestones of immigrant patriarch and matriarch Johannes and Katarina Schneider stand at the center of the family plot, surrounded by the burial markers of their numerous progeny.
Photo by Philip E. Pendleton.

OLEY VALLEY HERITAGE

TOMBSTONES OF JOHANNES AND KATARINA SCHNEIDER, Schneider Family Cemetery
Photo by Philip E. Pendleton.

ficial church membership (back in Germany) and undergo an examination by the pastor regarding their spiritual condition. As for a church building for Oley Reformed Church, there was none. In 1739 Boehm noted in regard to Oley that "Services are held with great inconvenience in houses and barns."¹⁶

Just twice a year was a frustratingly low frequency of proper church services for congregation members. This was normal, though, for Boehm's and Stoever's many scattered flocks. Throughout the colonial period, almost all local churches were required to share a pastor's Sunday attention with other congregations. Most services were held without benefit of a minister's leadership, consisting of prayer, song, and a reading by an elder, deacon, or schoolmaster.

When Boehm returned to Oley in the spring of 1737, he scorned to hold worship. Oley Church had decided to accept the services of one of the unauthorized, often itinerant Reformed and Lutheran clergymen who inhabited the Pennsylvania countryside. These men, who varied widely in motives and qualifications, preached, presided at worship services, and conducted weddings and baptisms that the official ministers were reluctant to recognize. The independent minister was a conspicuous element in rural Pennsylvania church life. So was the resultant quarreling, between the more willful congregants and those more cautious, that hampered the growth of stable congregational life.

A few of the unofficial clergymen were scoundrels, ministers defrocked in Germany for moral transgressions, or failed divinity students. Their general method of procedure was to go to a backcountry district, conveniently distant from the abode of a regular minister, and enlist a group of neighboring congregations to provide a living (i.e., financial support in return for ministerial services). When they were found out or got into an embarrassing scrape, they moved on. Most unordained clerics, however, were probably well-intentioned. They typically began their ministerial careers as schoolmasters who had been importuned to take on the pastorly role by their home congregations. People were desperate for want of spiritual guidance. Procuring properly sanctioned marital and baptismal rites involved hard work. Boehm himself, a former schoolmaster in Germany, had been but a farmer during the first four years (1725-1729) that he officiated and administered sacraments as a minister. He had been ordained in New York in 1729 by ministers of the Dutch Reformed Church.

The would-be minister who entered the Oley Reformed church in 1737 was a headstrong nineteen-year-old named Johann Heinrich Goetschy. This young man had been studying for the ministry in 1735 when his father decided to move the family from Canton Zurich, Switzerland, to Pennsylvania. The elder Goetschy was himself a Reformed minister who was to join Boehm, but died the day after the ship docked at Philadelphia. Young Johann Heinrich began behaving as if he were already a fully ordained Reformed cleric, working at several congregations. Some conservative members of the Oley Church, who could not scruple to accept Goetschy's services in the face of Boehm's opposition, withdrew from the congregation.

In 1739 young Goetschy had a change of heart, and ceased his unauthorized work. His contrition accepted by Dutch Reformed ministers, he returned to his studies, eventually to be ordained in New York. Boehm persuaded the Oley Church consistory to join with those of other Pennsylvania Reformed congregations in

SOUL

SCHNEIDER FAMILY CEMETERY, Johannes Schneider Homestead, Oley Township
Located up a gently rising slope in the typical manner, so as to overlook the homestead itself, in a field about two hundred yards to the rear of the farmhouse. The scarcity of churches and churchyards during the early period may explain the ubiquity of isolated family burial plots in Pennsylvania German settlements such as Oley. The practice was not generally followed by Anglo-Pennsylvanian settlers. A special effort was made by local citizens in the early 1990s to restore this outstanding example. Many others are desolate ruins.
Photo by Philip E. Pendleton.

pledging a regular contribution for ministers' salaries. For Oley this was to be £10 plus twenty bushels of oats per annum. Boehm noted that the congregation consisted "mostly of poor people, who cannot help themselves at all."[17] Evidently the Reformed faithful of Oley, a relatively wealthy locality, were largely recent settlers with homesteads not yet well established.

The 1739 reassertion of regular church order for the Oley Reformed Church turned out to be short-lived. In the words of turn-of-the-century church historian William J. Hinke, "After that Oley [Church] disappears from view for a number of years."[18] New and more powerful disruptions from outside had come for the congregation, this time from the Moravians.

THE MORAVIANS

The Moravian Church, properly named Unitas Fratrum or the United Brethren, is perhaps the oldest of Protestant churches. It was founded in 1457 in the central European kingdom of Bohemia (located as of 1994 within the Czech Republic). Many people of Germanic cultural heritage lived in Bohemia and the neighboring province of Moravia, and it was largely from among these German-speaking people that the United Brethren were drawn. In 1722, in the face of vigorous persecution by their Roman Catholic rulers, the Hapsburgs of Austria, the Moravians accepted the offer of Count Nicolaus Ludwig von Zinzendorf to take refuge on his huge German estate.

The young count, an ardent pietist to whom the simplicity and commitment of the Moravian religion appealed, provided the Moravians with a protected enclave in which to realize their vision of the proper Christian life. The Moravians' dependence on Zinzendorf meant that they had, in large measure, to accept the devout and imaginative nobleman's vision of their future, however. According to the count, the Unitas Fratrum was not a distinct church in its own right; it was just a particular approach to pietistic Christian living and evangelism. At Herrnhut, their name for the settlement they erected on the Zinzendorf barony, the Moravians developed their communal "choir" system. Choirs of church members, grouped according to their age and situation in life (married couples, bachelors, single women, widows, children, etc.), lived and worked together in the Moravian community.

A period account of how the Moravians came to Oley was entered in the Oley Moravian church register around 1758.

In the year 1736, Heinrich Antes [a Reformed lay pietist evangelist who became a Moravian] came to Oley and preached there with blessing. He found an entrance there and several were touched by the truth. The people expressed a great desire to hear his sermons, for which reason he visited this place faithfully. There were at that time all kinds of spirits in Oley, of which the New Born were the dominant party. Dear Antes was not equal to them. He waited, therefore, for the time when the Lord himself would check them, which took place in the following manner: In the year 1736, our dear and reverend brother [August Gottlieb] Spangenberg [a close associate of Zinzendorf] had come to Georgia and from there had traveled to Pennsylvania, which he reached in that year. He stayed for a little while at Skippack [a rural

Montgomery County community about twenty miles southeast of Oley], where he heard of the work of the dear brother, Heinrich Antes. He then resolved to visit Oley and came there in the year 1737. . . .

He [Spangenberg] is the first [Moravian] brother, who came to Oley and there he gave such testimony regarding the meritorious death of Christ, with such a demonstration of the Spirit, that the power of darkness received a severe blow. His first sermon was delivered in the house of Jonathan Herbein and the second in the house of Abraham Bertolet. He attacked the Newborn in his discourse from the words of I John 1:7-9. Through this address the spirit of the Newborn was so broken, that it could not gain strength again and is daily becoming weaker.[19]

Zinzendorf had dispatched Spangenberg to reconnoiter the state of religion in Pennsylvania's German-speaking community. Spangenberg held conclaves of devout settlers, who were concerned about this same subject, at his base in Skippack. Regular pilgrims to these meetings included Oley men Wilhelm Pott, Franz Ritter, and Jean Bertolet. Returning to Herrnhut in 1739, Spangenberg convinced Count Zinzendorf that conditions in Pennsylvania presented an opportunity for settlement, and a duty to do the Lord's work, that could not be ignored.

The count's immediate response to Spangenberg's report was the initiation of a program of missionary activity in Pennsylvania. The first Moravian appointed specifically to do missionary work in Pennsylvania was Andreas Eschenbach, and the place chosen to be the focus of his initial effort was Oley. Eschenbach arrived in Oley in October 1740. A former shoemaker and a lay preacher, Eschenbach was described as an eloquent, forceful speaker despite his lack of theological training. Eschenbach took up residence in Oley, probably as much for the rewards for good preaching promised by the spiritual restlessness endemic there as for the valley's relatively central location. The selection of Oley as the site at which to commence the great labors is one of several clues implying that the Moravian leadership expected the valley to be particularly fertile ground on which to proselytize.

OLEY MORAVIAN MISSION, Oley Moravian Boarding School (1748) At Left, Oley Township
The gambrel-roofed boarding school building was constructed of half-timbered frame on a German Palladian variation of center-passage double-pile plan. The double-pitched gambrel roof, a frequent element in German Palladian architecture, in effect provided an entire additional floor of living space (probably inhabited in this building by the boarding students). Note the people haying in the left foreground.
Drawing by Nicholas Garrison, 1757.
Courtesy, Moravian Archives, Bethlehem, Pennsylvania.

JOHANNES DETURK HOUSE, Circa 1740, Enlarged 1844, Scene of Zinzendorf's Third Synod, 1742, Oley Township
The original section is to the left. DeTurk's new two-story stone house would have been one of the larger and more substantial dwellings in the valley at the time of Zinzendorf's gathering, and thus a suitable site to host the many attendants. The 1844 addition, to the right, was constructed on a four-over-four or "Pennsylvania farmhouse" plan. Further extensive renovations were carried out in 1877. In one of these alterations, as happened in many colonial-period valley houses of the stove-room type at some point during the nineteenth century, the central chimney stack of the original section was removed. *Photo by H. Winslow Fegley, circa 1900-1925. Courtesy, Schwenkfelder Library.*

Eschenbach lodged at first with Jean Bertolet, later with Johannes Leinbach. In the following April the party of Moravian settlers came to Pennsylvania whose task was to begin building a major community (Bethlehem). Two women prominent in the movement, Sophia Molther and Anna Nitschmann, detached themselves from that group and joined Eschenbach at Oley. The Moravians were remarkably egalitarian, by the standards of the day, in their encouragement of women to develop and use their talents. This was certainly so in the missionary and teaching fields. Anna Elisabetha Leinbach (wife to Johannes) testified in her memoir that it was through Molther's "righteousness and trustworthiness she could accept into her heart the sinner's friend."[20]

Great initial success rewarded the efforts of these three missionaries, as recorded in the church register.

> In the year 1741 the until now smoldering ashes broke fully forth and began to burn mightily. Eschenbach preached during the year with power and conviction. The entire township was in a state of excitement. One saw the people in crowds on their way to hear the Gospel.[21]

Count Zinzendorf journeyed to Penn's province himself in 1741. Once disembarked, the charismatic, headstrong Zinzendorf devoted himself to a quixotic campaign to unite all Pennsylvania German Protestants in one ecumenical fellowship. This "synod movement," so called for the conventions of German religious leaders held during the count's sojourn, achieved little. Zinzendorf called for a search for "the common ground" and for forbearance of one another's particular beliefs. But mutual distrust and dislike seemed the only common ground the various sectarians could find. The Lutheran and Reformed church groups sent no delegations.

Count Zinzendorf visited Oley within a few weeks of his arrival in Philadelphia in December 1741. He preached at Jean Bertolet's homestead on the day after Christmas. The third synod met in Oley at the homestead of Johannes DeTurk (son of New Born member Maria DeTurk), February 10-12, 1742. On that occasion the founding of a nondenominational "Oley Church" was proclaimed. Eschenbach, ordained a minister at the synod, was made the pastor. Johannes Leinbach, Jonathan Herbein, and Franz Ritter were appointed elders. Among the Oley worshipers at this time was just one full-status member of the Unitas Fratrum itself, the synod's host DeTurk, who had been accepted into fellowship the preceding spring.

This Oley synod almost sounded the death knell for the ecumenical cause, as it ended amidst a storm of recrimination. Suspicions were voiced that the real intention of Zinzendorf and company was to bring all Pennsylvania Germans gradually into the Moravian fold.

The onset of Moravian activity in the

OLEY VALLEY HERITAGE

HOUSE ON THE STAUBER-LEINBACH HOMESTEAD, Circa 1715-1730, Oley Township
In this modest dwelling of the stove-room type, evidently of the two-room variant, Johannes and Anna Elisabetha Leinbach entertained a stream of Moravian missionaries and leaders during the years 1736-1741, including Count Zinzendorf and his daughter Benigna. Proprietor of the homestead, 1713-1723, had been Jacob Stauber, the restless promoter of German settlement who wed Sarah Boone in 1715, and introduced the Boone family to the Oley Valley.
Photo by H. Winslow Fegley, circa 1900-1925. Courtesy, Schwenkfelder Library.

valley apparently brought disruptive shocks to the fragile Oley Reformed Church. Some members aligned themselves with the Moravian-led congregation. Others, such as 1739 elders Heinrich Werner and Isaac Levan, kept their distance. The Oley Reformed gathering more or less came apart for the time being. It is not known how many Oley people listed in 1741-1742 as belonging to the Moravian-led nondenominational congregation had been members of Oley Reformed in the 1730s. The Leinbach family, however, which would be a prominent one in the affairs of the Oley Moravian Church, had been attached to Oley Reformed. Johannes Leinbach had been a Reformed Church organist and a devout adherent of that faith back in Hochstadt, Germany. One of his sons, Johannes, Jr., had his first three children baptized by young Goetschy during the latter's Oley pastorship. The matriarch of the Leinbach clan, Anna Elisabetha, had been "awakened" while still in Europe, and hence had reason to follow Heinrich Antes away from the strict nonpietist pastor Boehm and toward the Moravians.

The history of the nondenominational, Moravian-led congregation at Oley was brief, ending in schism. Eschenbach's ordination evidently went to his head; he proceeded unwittingly to subvert a promising start through inflexibility and arrogance. At the synod Moravian leaders had recommended that the congregation begin by building a church. Eschenbach envisioned a two-story brick structure incorporating a pastor's residence, perhaps something approaching the graceful German Palladian-style buildings to be built at Bethlehem itself. His charges looked into their pocketbooks, then went out and felled the trees for a small one-story log-built church, which, if rather prosaic, was more the mode in contemporary rural Pennsylvania. Eschenbach angrily refused the gift of this edifice; his enduring wrath ultimately resulted in his dismissal.

In a sternly worded (and sardonic) missive sent to Moravian leaders in 1742, former church elder Jonathan Herbein gave his version of events. An early settler of the upper Oley Valley (by 1720), Herbein was probably a former New Born. Most family names among the 1741-1742 and 1744 rosters of the Moravian-led Oley Church were those of prosperous families that had settled in the northern valley early on. It is likely that former New Born people were in quest for a stable but simple, non-ritualistic communal religious life in the wake of the deaths of Baumann and Kühlwein. Jonathan Herbein was hardly alone in suspecting that the real intent of the missionary effort was to make everyone into good Moravians. The Moravians made many organizational decisions (including the appropriateness of marriage matches) by casting lots; they believed that this resulted in an expression of Divine intent. According to Herbein, around the time of

CORNER POST LOG BUILDING, Oley Moravian Mission, Circa 1742-1760, Oley Township
This structure was identified by Peter G. Bertolet as the small schoolhouse built at the Oley Moravian Church settlement.
Drawing by Francis Devlan, circa 1860. Courtesy, The Historical Society of Pennsylvania.

the Oley synod and the creation of the congregation,

> Eschenbach came to us and spoke of beautiful institutions, including the education of the children and the preaching of the Gospel according to the pure custom of the Apostles, i.e., without any sectarianism, freely and without charge. And since there was nothing objectionable in these representations, we consented. He, however, demanded a call [a contract between pastor and congregation] from us, which was granted and signed by some.
>
> But when the Count came, there was at once talk of a congregation: he wanted at once to make elders and also helpers and servants, which was done. Then he gave directions how a meetinghouse should be built, about which a quarrel arose. One party wanted it simple, the other wanted it grand and stately, which as of old, at Babel, caused a confusion for which I unfortunately had to bear the blame. Because it was I who had made the proposition for a plain building and most of the people sided with me.
>
> Upon which the Count told me, "You should recognize that you have sinned against the Savior in this case." But my conscience did not accuse me, because it was evident to me that in this matter there was a desire for external show before hearts were inwardly converted or renewed.
>
> This was not without a special revelation of God [referring to the casting of lots]. For meanwhile the adherents of the Count claimed that the Savior had assured them that there should be a congregation in Oley. When, by means of the lot, the plans had been made, they demanded of us that we should hold conferences three times a week, in order to reveal our thoughts to one another, to act unitedly and to consider how best souls could be won and brought in, for which we were

OLEY VALLEY HERITAGE

OLEY MORAVIAN BOARDING SCHOOL, 1748, Oley Township
The gambrel roof had been taken down circa 1840. Following the slow demise of the Moravian congregation in the late eighteenth century, the building was employed by the DeTurk family as a tenant farmhouse.
Photographer unknown, early twentieth century. From Thomas Jefferson Wertenbaker, The Founding of American Civilization: The Middle Colonies, *1938.*

OLEY MORAVIAN BOARDING SCHOOL, 1748, Oley Township
A view of the gable end of this now-departed structure, when in ruins.
Photo by Harry F. Stauffer, 1955. Courtesy The Historical Society of the Cocalico Valley.

thought to have sufficient ability. Regarding this I got into a dispute and I said that I could not consent to it. For it seemed too simple and trivial to secure all the necessary ability to convert souls through an easily controlled lot.

The Count represented to us that such mistrust was only [to be expected] at the beginning. He acted very friendly, came to us, embraced and kissed us, and said: "I must love my brethren." Through this means he desired to set everything right. But there were more difficulties to be met. They thought by their cunning and love, together with flattery, they might cast their ropes around our necks. They wanted to ordain us by the laying on of hands in order to better convey to us their magical powers, since we were expected to partake with them of the Holy Supper. This I declined and told them I would not come. Eschenbach said that I was such a suspicious brother that I should tell him what was the matter with me.

I answered: "You promised us that we should neither be dependent on Herrnhut, or the Moravian brethren, but should be a congregation of Christ. Why then be ordained by men? Rather we should implore and await from the Savior, that he give us wisdom and ability." And thus it remained until the next Conference. . . .

Franz Ritter [Herbein's fellow elder from Oley] finally asked what the word "to forbear" meant, that they should interpret it to him. The sly Count, because he knew what questions were likely to follow, asked: "Who is it that speaks?" The answer came, "Franz Ritter." Whereupon the ardent Count broke forth in a storm: "You men from Oley, you do not belong to the congregation and have nothing to do with our conference."

Then Franz Ritter arose and spoke his mind, and putting his hand on the door, said, "Then continue in your self-righteousness," and left. On account of this the fire burnt more vehemently until finally he [the Count] began: "You men of Oley are hypocrites and liars, one should have debarred you from the first conference, but you ran after me, made apologies, and kissed me." At which I arose and said: "This is an apparent untruth, for he came to us and kissed us, and now impeaches us. We are not liars, but truth-loving souls." However, since no arguments [by the Oley people] were credited, and Ludwig [Zinzendorf] spoke only in vehemence, I said: "Here is only strife. It does not matter whether one belongs to a large congregation, for the Savior says that where two or three are gathered in His name there will He be in the midst of them." I opened the door and went away, wishing them much good.[22]

Eschenbach departed in late 1742, but irreparable damage was already done to relations between the Moravian Church and a large portion of the Oley congregation. A roster of the original members of 1742 listed thirty-four married adults. In 1744 there were only seventeen. Perhaps there was some consolation for the Moravian leadership because all the people who stayed eventually became full members in the Unitas Fratrum. After the imbroglio over the church building, the congregation functioned as a Moravian one, with no nondenominational pretensions.

Oley Moravian Church existed as a congregation of full standing with resident pastor until 1765, when the Moravian leadership decided that its anemic nature did not justify the continued stationing of a minister there. The occasional conversion or movement of a Moravian family into the valley had augmented the congregation a little, but an adult membership of about thirty-five in 1761 was the largest size recorded. The Moravians continued to serve Oley monthly, with a visiting minister leading worship for the shrinking flock, until at least 1784.

The composition and role of the Moravian establishment at Oley were changed repeatedly from 1742 to 1765, evidently reflecting vacillation by the leadership in Bethlehem. Ten different pastors served at Oley after Eschenbach, with the occasional hiatus of a few months. Moravian historian J. Taylor Hamilton states that many of them were of a distinctly second-rate cast as preachers.[23] Generally there were both a minister and a schoolmaster living there, with one or both accompanied by wives who shared the pastoral and educational duties. At times a second minister also was stationed there, because Oley was then serving as a station from which to proselytize in neighboring districts, due to the valley's central location. Two general conferences of missionaries were held there. Many itinerant Moravian ministers stopped to preach at Oley, gathering large crowds. Listening to good preaching, whether one's own denomination or not, seems to have been a popular form of entertainment in rural colonial Pennsylvania.

From 1748 to 1751 and from 1755 to 1761, the Moravians conducted a substantial boarding school at Oley, at one point (1756) educating fifty-three boarding students from over a large region. To house the boarding school, an impressive half-timbered structure was built in 1748, noticeably larger than any contemporary local house. The Moravians taught school to Oley children with few interruptions from 1743 to 1770, at first employing a small schoolhouse.

What success the Moravians had among people in Oley helped undermine their congregation there. Those souls who came to have a deeply felt commitment to the Moravian Church tended to move to Bethlehem or to other Moravian settlements in order to live the full, communal Moravian life. The widowed, seventy-five-year-old matriarch of the Leinbach family, Anna Elisabetha, retired to Bethlehem in 1755. Her sons Heinrich, Friedrich, and Johannes II, continued in Oley until the last resident Moravian pastor was called to leave in 1765. Then Johannes and Friedrich migrated with their families to Moravian settlements in North Carolina and Maryland respectively. Of the nine children of Johannes and Friedrich who had been born by 1743 and survived childhood, four went to Bethlehem to live in the community by 1760, before their fathers' exodus from Oley, at ages ranging from seventeen to twenty. The Moravian historian J. Taylor Hamilton found, in detailed research into the Oley Moravian records, that by 1758 sixteen men and twenty-three women from Oley had relocated to Moravian communities, most to Bethlehem, a few to the Salem, North Carolina vicinity.[24] These movements of Oley faithful to Bethlehem deprived the Oley congregation of the vital human energy that might have attracted more converts. A quarter of a century of missionary activity in Oley amounted in effect to an extended raid that picked up some members, rather than a cohesive effort to build a congregation.

Maria Barbara Leinbach, the younger of Johannes and Anna Elisabetha's daughters, won renown as a Moravian missionary, working among the Indians at Gnadenhütten, Pennsylvania, and among black slaves in the Virgin Islands. Her many adventures even included being taken captive by a band of pirates. (Another young Oley convert, Jerg Jungmann, also became a missionary to the Indians.) In this passage from Maria Barbara's memoir, she tells of her awakening and of her decision to live in Bethlehem. The elder Leinbachs apparently sought to protect their children from the influence of the New Born.

> I was born September 11, 1722, at Hochstadt in the Wetterau district, where my father was schoolmaster and organist. As a child of a half a year, I departed with my parents to Pennsylvania in the year 1723. They settled at Oley [that same year]. They brought me up in the Reformed religion. My father was a pious and God-fearing man, who made me cling, according to the best of his knowledge, to all that was good. We lived very retired and cut off from the world. My father held home devotions with us children and trained us in singing and prayer. In 1741 [sic] the brethren Spangenberg and Antes visited my parents. Through these brethren we became acquainted with the Brethren's Congregation at Bethlehem. Brother Antes preached in our home of the readiness of the Savior to forgive all sins, at which occasion I came to think about myself and felt my lost condition, but I thought: Is it possible that Jesus can love men so much and can forgive all their sins? Then he will be able to forgive my sins also. Whereupon I also received the assurance of forgiveness in my heart. About that time the sainted Count von Zinzendorf with his daughter Benigna and Sister Molther came to visit us. During this visit I became well acquainted with them, because the sainted Count took a special interest in me and asked me whether I had a desire to reside at Bethlehem. At this question I felt at once in my heart that they were the people to whom I belonged. But I asked him only for permission to visit them, to which he gladly consented. As a result I made a visit to Bethlehem with my mother. At that time I received permission to stay there. Together with my mother I was received into the congregation in December 1742.[25]

GEORGE DEBENNEVILLE

Some historians suspect that the presence of Dr. George DeBenneville in Oley during the years 1743-1757 played a part in the frustration of Moravian hopes for a vital congregation. A charismatic visionary and an eloquent preacher, DeBenneville might have shifted the focus of religious feeling from the less inspired Moravian ministers to himself. There could be something to this, but if so, DeBenneville was in no way responsible for the initial fall of interest in the Moravians that transpired in 1742. DeBenneville was permitted the use of the Moravians' log meetinghouse until 1745, when it was decided, after much soul-searching by the Moravians, that his testimony was in undeniable conflict with Moravian theology.

DeBenneville (1703-1793) was an advocate of universalism, the belief that all mankind will be "saved," that no soul is condemned to eternal damnation. In 1740 while sojourning in the town of Mons (in present-day Belgium) he collapsed with a traumatic sudden illness and went into a trance lasting two days. During this loss of consciousness, DeBenneville walked in heaven and hell. He learned from angels that all men would attain salvation, though many would atone for their sins in purgatory. If DeBenneville's spiritual experiences and convictions have a familiar ring to them, his message is distinguished from that of Matthias Baumann by DeBenneville's implication that all men would have to account for their conduct in this life.

DeBenneville had been born in London, the son of aristocratic French Protestant refugees. It is not clear when he acquired his medical education, as he was serving as a midshipman in the Royal Navy around 1721 when he had his initial religious awakening. Expelled from his church (presumably Presbyterian), he never again espoused any particular denomination. Through the 1720s and 1730s, he traveled widely in Germany and the Low Countries, preaching. He also may have acquired a university education in this period. DeBenneville was reputedly fluent in several languages.

In 1741, his Mons trance behind him, DeBenneville naturally concluded that he belonged in Pennsylvania. He settled in Germantown, for two years practicing medicine and managing the apothecary shop owned by the printer and newspaper publisher Christoph Sauer. There he struck up a friendship with the spiritually inclined Jean Bertolet, on whose recommendation DeBenneville moved to Oley in 1743. In the Oley Valley he practiced medicine, taught school, resumed preaching, and successfully wooed his friend Bertolet's daughter Esther. They wed in 1745.

DeBenneville was quite popular as a religious orator, attracting large crowds in Oley as well as on frequent preaching trips about the region. He traveled to provide the sick with his healing skills as well. The Goshenhoppen diarist David Schulze recorded a visit by DeBenneville in 1750 to bleed two of Schulze's neighbors. Schulze also noted DeBenneville's preaching in Goshenhoppen on three occasions between May 1756 and July 1757. (The diary, as it survives, has large gaps.) Little is known about the precise content of DeBenneville's preaching. Presumably he told the story of his heavenly journey many times.

In 1757, following the death of his father-in-law Bertolet, DeBenneville moved his family to the Germantown vicinity. There he could enjoy a more cosmopolitan environment, complete with the fellowship of other learned men. He continued his preaching trips until very late in life, however, often visiting the Oley Valley.

LUTHERAN AND GERMAN REFORMED CONGREGATIONS

One certain legacy of Moravian activities was the effort by disturbed European sponsors to put the Lutheran and German Reformed churches on a sounder footing in Pennsylvania. In the aftermath of the failed synod movement, the Moravian leaders determined that they would carry on with a program to minister to the spiritual needs of the forlorn Lutheran and Reformed church people. The Moravian Church sent out dozens of Moravian-ordained "Lutheran" and "Reformed" ministers. Moravian leaders insisted that their only intention was to enable church people to have a stable and fulfilled spiritual life.

The regularly ordained Lutheran and Reformed ministers on the battleground put up a determined and vituperative opposition to the Moravians, charging that the real goal of the latter was to make church people into Moravians. But this handful of certified Lutheran and Reformed clergymen could not be everywhere at once. The specter of an impending collapse of their dozens of church congregations with thousands of members into Moravian fellowship was finally adequate incitement for church authorities in Europe to recruit more and better ministers to send into Penn's Woods. At the time of Zinzendorf's arrival in Pennsylvania in 1741, there were two regular Lutheran ministers in the province and three German Reformed. In 1750 there were eleven Lutheran and nine Reformed.

In the midst of the spiritual commotion that was endemic to the Oley Valley in the middle eighteenth century, some scattered church people sought to worship in a semblance of the manner they had known in Germany. To do so required herculean effort, as Heinrich Melchior Muhlenberg related in his 1753 account of the life and passing of Philip Beyer. Beyer had come to America in 1731, and settled in the valley by 1735.

> In the month of May the aged father [Beyer] of a large family, which lives ten miles from the New Hanover church, died. He rejoiced when I and my colleagues came to this province [Muhlenberg arrived in 1742], for it gave him an opportunity to hear God's word. He attended services regularly, usually had his children instructed and confirmed, and was a diligent reader, at home, in the Bible, Arndt's *True Christianity* [a seminal, standard pietist devotional text, written in 1605], and other edifying books. His conduct was honorable, and he was able to speak edifyingly of divine truths in social gatherings. In his last years, he was unable, on account of age and weakness, to make the difficult journey to the New Hanover church. He accordingly attended some of the meetings which were held in his immediate neighborhood.
>
> He lived in a region inhabited by people who hold all kinds of curious opinions, despise preachers, churches, and sacraments without discrimination, and pride themselves in their own righteousness. Since evil communications corrupt good manners, and since this man probably had too much commerce in his last years with such people, he began to scruple at all sorts of indifferent trivialities in our religion and to consider the Evangelical [Lutheran] preachers, who receive charitable offerings from their parishioners for their bodily necessities, as servants of their own bellies, etc. . . .
>
> I visited several times when I had opportunity to preach in his neighborhood and I admonished him to have an earnest concern for his soul, etc. The Lord finally cast him upon a sick bed and reminded him, through His Spirit, of the truths which he had often read and heard in former times. In this way he was given an opportunity to reconsider. Inasmuch as he had on various occasions said harsh and uncharitable things against me, he was reluctant to call me when he was sick. . . . He requested that I be told after his death that, as a poor worm, he had sought and found grace in the blood and death of Jesus.[26]

From the mid-1740s through the mid-1750s, the dust kicked up in the spiritual agitations of the preceding decades began to settle. The rate of German-speaking migration to Pennsylvania was high during the period, and some new settlers, as well as people seeking work as laborers, were still coming to the Oley Valley. The new arrivals were predominantly church people. Most German inhabitants of the valley participated in the creation of three Reformed and two Lutheran congregations distributed among the valley's neighborhoods during the years around 1744-1754. All the Reformed gatherings were apparently offshoots of the dormant Oley Reformed Church of the 1730s.

One of the five flocks founded within the valley itself by 1754, a new "Oley Reformed," stood off by itself at Oley Forge (now Spangsville); the other four were paired in two Lutheran-Reformed "union congregations." One of these was located in the Schwarzwald vicinity (at present-day Jacksonwald); the other at New Store (Amityville).

Church people who lived a significant distance from these three valley locations attended congregations situated not far outside the valley. Lutheran families at the northern end of the valley made a long, steep climb to worship at Rockland Church and Oley Hill Church, both founded about 1747 and situated amidst the hills to the north and northeast respectively. Some German Lutherans living on the Schuylkill opted to attend Anglican rites at Saint Gabriel's Church (founded as Swedish Lutheran Molatton Church about 1719, converted to an Anglican congregation and renamed in 1753). A few church people, resident in western Oley Township, went to the Zion union congregation, located in the hills of Alsace Township, after it was founded in the early 1770s.

The union congregation was a common arrangement in Pennsylvania German communities, lasting long after the close of the colonial period. The last elements of the union compact were not terminated by Saint Paul's Lutheran and Saint Paul's United Church of Christ, of Amityville (formerly the New Store Union Church), until 1975. Lutheran and Reformed neighbors would pool their resources and erect one church building for shared use. The ideal was to have Lutheran and Reformed ministers hold services on alternate Sundays. In practice, since for most rural congregations a pastor's visit came only once every few weeks, perhaps not even once a month, the question of the two faiths' stepping on each other's toes was rarely an issue. Reformed ministers often wed Lutheran couples or baptized Lutheran babies, and vice-versa. Churchgoers of the one persuasion often helped fill an audience for a preacher from the opposite one, and marriages linking the two were widespread. In the nineteenth century, when resources had grown and ministers become common, a second church building would be built, permitting separate services. This union practice has left a distinct imprint on the landscape of the Pennsylvania German country, where paired churches standing on a knoll or ridge often dominate the vista.

The first of the valley church congregations to be established was the Schwarzwald union congregation, in the west end of the valley, in about 1744 (the date inscribed on the still extant communion tankard).[27] A church was soon built, probably of log, instead of continuing the old practice of holding worship in a house or barn. Muhlenberg, who arrived in 1742, wrote in later years that he had been present at the dedication of the Schwarzwald Church in his "first years" in Pennsylvania. Two of the five Oley Reformed Church elders of 1739, Isaac Levan and Heinrich Werner, lived near the Schwarzwald Church location. It is likely that they were instrumental in organizing the Reformed congregation there. As the Schwarzwald vicinity of Exeter Township is a neighborhood *within* the large area contemporaries called "Oley," it is very likely that the "Oley" congregation mentioned in the 1747 minutes of the Reformed Church Coetus is in reality Schwarzwald Reformed. (The church in question was "not yet ripe enough . . . for true and regular ministers."[28])

The new Oley Reformed (at Oley Forge) and the New Store union church were both established around 1753-1754. German Lutherans in the Amity Township area had for some three decades worshiped with Molatton Church (now Saint Gabriel's Protestant Episcopal). Other members of this interdenominational congregation were adherents of the Church of Sweden and of the Church of England. These three churches were close enough in matters of doctrine to rule out significant conflict. Those visiting ministers who possessed the adequate language skills would deliver sermons in two or even three languages. In 1753, however, the English-speaking Swedish and British majority decided to make a definite alignment of Molatton Church to the Church of England. Most of the Germans opted to withdraw and to form their own church at New Store, with the cooperation of local German Reformed people.[29] The exceptions were a group of German families who lived along the banks of the Schuylkill River, who would sooner worship as Anglicans than make the more arduous journey to New Store. Hence at Saint Gabriel's churchyard one can see German-inscribed tombstones from the late 1700s and early 1800s mingled with English ones.

Both the Oley and New Store congregations built churches at the outset, Oley's of stone, New Store's probably of log. That all the congregations formed in the 1740s and 1750s immediately constructed church buildings surely reflected the increased prosperity of the maturing valley settlement. The New Store faithful built their church on land belonging to Nicolaus Beyer, the son of the lately deceased Lutheran Philip Beyer. Ironically, the

COLONIAL-PERIOD GRAVESTONE,
Churchyard of Salem United Church of Christ, Oley Township
Photo by Philip E. Pendleton.

service rendered the German church denomination by Nicolaus Beyer merely realized a provision decreed by the tract's original settler, a Welshman named David Harry, that one acre of that one hundred acres should be forever reserved "for the use of the Church of England." The earliest reference to this grant of a churchground by Harry appears in the indenture for a mortgage he took on in 1736. In that year the one hundred acres in question (at present-day Amityville) became the location of the junction of the new High Road from Tulpehocken to Philadelphia with the High Road from Oley to Philadelphia, and thereby a desirable site for a church.

None of these Oley Valley German Reformed or Lutheran church congregations had an easy path to follow in becoming a proper constituent element in the official church organization of each denomination in Pennsylvania. The supervisory entities, both formed in 1748, were the Reformed Coetus and the Lutheran Ministerium, boards consisting of all the ordained, authorized clergymen of each persuasion. The persistent, if slowly improving shortage of approved ministers in the province remained a real hindrance to stable congregational life for the duration of the colonial period. A congregation regularly would petition its church's regional governing body for pastoral service by a properly ordained cleric. The board in question would demur for the time being, replying that more ministers would have to arrive in the province from Germany before any service could be given the congregation, or that the ministers would need time to learn more about the congregation's condition. The forlorn, almost desperate country congregation would employ one of the irregular "parsons" for a time. In retribution for such disorder, the governing board would flatly deny future applications for service, and so on.

To blame were the unconcerned church authorities in Europe, as well as the many clergymen in Germany who showed greater interest in securing comfortable livings than in emigrating to what they thought was a howling wilderness. Dedicated individuals like Muhlenberg, willing to undertake the move, were exceptional.

The experience of the Oley Reformed Church in its quest to receive regular ministerial service was representative. "Johannes Lesher, from Oley, together with Caspar Griesemer, appeared, being praiseworthily concerned for the increase of the Reformed Church in that district," recorded coetal secretary Bartholomew Rieger in 1755.

> These people now humbly desire to be subject to our coetal institutions, to be served in the future by no other than a minister approved and sent by the coetus; it being further noted that they had almost completed a stone church.... The committee on Johannes Lesher's request . . . suggested to the Rev. Coetus to direct five or six ministers in turn to conduct divine service there once a month until further arrangements could be made.[30]

Perhaps the substantial stone church was a gesture designed to entice the ministers out of some lingering antipathy toward the wild spirits of the Oley Valley. If so, it evidently failed to move the coetus to carry through with the above measure. There is no documentation of any such pastoral visits, and a year later Oley Reformed's enlistment of the wrong sort of pastor had alienated the coetus.

> The people at Oley, now as well as before, rather prefer to enter into the kingdom of heaven by the broad way. They have again chosen as their minister a man tainted with all kinds of vices, a demagogue, because they hate seriously to relinquish the sins of the world to follow Christ. Alas, the grief![31]

Not one of the five German church congregations in the valley enjoyed even an interval of regular service from a properly ordained minister before 1776. Historian Charles Glatfelter has painstakingly compiled the evidence of ministers who served or visited these colonial Lutheran or Reformed congregations, including the irregular clergymen. Restricting discussion to the years after 1740, Glatfelter found that, among officially approved ministers, the Lutheran Muhlenberg occasionally visited New Store and Schwarzwald, with some visits to New Store by his assistants Johann Helfrich Schaum and Johann Ludwig Voigt. The leading Reformed minister Michael Schlatter passed through the Oley Valley just once, in 1746, on his initial inspection tour of the colony. He was the only ordained Reformed minister known to have done so from 1740 through 1775.[32]

The presence of irregular ministers was more frequent and generally much more prolonged. There were six known to have been active in the valley during 1741-1775, including two ordained ministers not in good standing with their church organizations. One of the more colorful was Daniel Schumacher, who officiated as pastor to the Schwarzwald Lutherans from 1754 to 1758. Schumacher had evidently forsaken a wife in Nova Scotia. A heavy drinker with a complex personality, he was called a scholar by some, an adulterer by Muhlenberg. Schumacher possessed the soul of an artist, however, and produced a large and noteworthy amount of *fraktur*, decorative calligraphy. He elaborately decorated many documents, such as baptismal certificates and New Year's wishes, with ornate script executed in ink and colorful watercolors.

Many of the unordained ministers were originally Pennsylvania schoolmasters who had been pressed by neighbors to graduate themselves from leading worship to conferring the sacraments and had grown accustomed to the clergyman's life. It was standard practice for schoolteachers, where available, to officiate at pastorless church services, since they possessed learning superior to that of their neighbors. Philip Jacob Michael, an irregular who served all three valley Reformed congregations, may have been one of these. Michael won such respect from the ordained Reformed clerics of the province that in 1764 they united in asking their European overseers to authorize Michael's ordination. The latter's preaching, devotion to the holy work, upholding of Reformed doctrine, personal conduct, and cooperative attitude toward the Reformed Church Coetus were all objects of admiration to his would-be colleagues. These men of the cloth were no fools, either. They buttressed their support of Michael with the assertion that "we may thus be strengthened, by bringing under our control the [twelve] congregations which he is serving. . . . We would not put our pen to this were we not convinced that it would be of advantage to us, and of greater profit to his congregations."[33] But the shortsighted European church authorities refused. No great matter, perhaps; Michael did not ask again, and as far as is known, none of his followers ever complained.

THE CHURCH OF SWEDEN AND THE CHURCH OF ENGLAND

Religious life seems to have been a somewhat simpler, less contentious matter for the English-speaking people of the Oley Valley than it was for their German-speaking neighbors. For one thing, only three denominations are known to have been active among the Swedish and British settlers: the Church of Sweden, the Church of England, and the Society of Friends. In fact, the Swedish and English churches cooperated to such an extent in the greater Delaware Valley, and were similar enough in doctrine, that the two could almost be considered a single denomination.

The absence of the Presbyterian Church from the Oley Valley's colonial history is a mystery. The band of New Englanders, Scots, and Netherlanders, who migrated to the lower valley from central New Jersey in the 1710s and 1720s, could be expected to have had a Calvinist religious background. The general arrangement that these three cultural groups had adopted, in many of the New Jersey communities in which they were neighbors, was to pool their resources and all worship as Presbyterians. Having arrived in the Amity Township area, however, these people chose to join with local Swedish, English, Welsh, and German people and worship at Molatton Church. The latter, also known as Saint Gabriel's from at least 1753 on, was officially an outparish of the Swedish Lutheran (Church of Sweden) congregation at Wicacoa (properly named Gloria Dei Church) until that year. Wicacoa was an early Swedish settlement that, as Philadelphia grew, rapidly became just a neighborhood within that city. The frequent presence of Anglican and German Lutheran ministers in the pulpit, though, as well as the mixed body of parishioners, made Molatton virtually an interdenominational congregation.

GRAVESTONE OF TWO SONS OF WILLIAM BIRD, Churchyard of Saint Gabriel's Protestant Episcopal Church, Amity Township
The gravestone of two young children, leaning against the large table stone that marks the burial place of their wealthy and prestigious ironmaster father (died 1761).
Photo by Philip E. Pendleton.

The Molatton community held the first European worship service in Berks County. Andreas Sandel, pastor of Wicacoa, recorded in his diary for August 12, 1708, that "I went together with some Swedes to Manatawny, where I conducted a sermon and examination with the people."[34] (The use of "Manatawny" as an early place name referred to the southeastern part of the Oley Valley, through which runs Manatawny Creek.) Sandel returned in 1710.

> The 29th of October I went with several Swedes to Manatawny to preach, and on the 30th I arrived there. The 31st I preached a Swedish sermon in the morning, and an English one in the afternoon, and baptised one English child.[35]

Sandel probably visited a few more times before his return to Sweden in 1719. Thus in 1710 the sometimes fragile but ultimately enduring cooperation between Molatton Church parishioners of divergent national backgrounds had begun. Their cooperation embodied the role of the whole colonial Oley Valley as a place for communication and for the mingling of diverse peoples.

In about 1719, Mounce and Ingabo Jones donated a plot to serve as a churchground for Molatton. The impressive tombstone of Andrew Robeson, for the oldest known burial in the Saint Gabriel's graveyard, bears the date 1720. The churchyard is by the junction where the High Road from Oley to Philadelphia and Andrew Robeson's High Road joined and continued toward Philadelphia as the King's High Road. This intersection, a logical site for the locality's church, was created in 1719. The securing of the churchground preceded the erection of the first known church building by eighteen years.

The setting aside of a churchground emboldened the Molatton people to request from the ministers of their congregation at Wicacoa that they be accorded the favor of a resident pastor. They were contributing financially to the support of Wicacoa, but receiving little attention in return. At a parish meeting in 1720, a group of Wicacoa members from Molatton "with tears besought"[36] the lately arrived assistant pastor, Samuel Hesselius, to live with them. He agreed to do so. Unfortunately, life on the frontier evidently did not agree with the young clergyman, though he married Brigitta Lycon, daughter of local pioneer Anders Lycon, within a few months of moving there. The minister complained that the number of worshippers at Molatton, and at Neshaminy and Matzong, his two charges farther down the Schuylkill River, was too low to justify his remaining at the post. In 1722 he left to take up the pastorship of the Swedish church at Christina (now Wilmington, Delaware), a relative return to civilization.

With the departure of Hesselius, Molatton returned to the status of a decidedly secondary concern for the Delaware Valley's Church of Sweden ministerial contingent. Jonas Lidman, pastor at Wicacoa, went up three times a year. In 1730, however, in a characteristic lapse of attention, Lidman's superiors back in Sweden allowed him to resign his pastorship and go home without appointing a successor. One sympathetic clergyman, Alexander Howie, pastor at the Perkiomen and Whitemarsh Anglican parishes, reported in 1732 that

> At the earnest solicitations of a Swedish congregation about thirty

miles back in the country I have undertaken to read prayers and preach among them once in two months in the middle of the week. . . . The Swedes are a people that should be encouraged, for upon all occasions they have discovered their good will and friendship to the Church of England in these parts.[37]

In 1733 a new pastor for Wicacoa arrived from Sweden, Gabriel Falck. This cleric resumed the custom of regular trips up the river to Molatton, and in 1735 the country parish was honored to receive Falck as its second resident pastor. The circumstances under which Falck came to make the move could have made this seem a mixed blessing. The minister was deposed from the Wicacoa pastorship by his parishioners after losing a libel suit brought against him by one of his vestrymen. Molatton apparently was pleased to have Falck; the settlers built a church of log in 1737. The minister remained at Molatton nine years. Then an elderly man, he too returned to Sweden, no doubt desirous of a peaceful retirement, as his last years at Molatton were marred by noisy disputes with the Moravians.

Among Count Zinzendorf's party when the Moravian leader came to Pennsylvania in 1741 was Paul Daniel Brycelius, a young and ardent Swedish Moravian. In 1743 the Moravians ordained Brycelius a minister. As part of their program to provide assistance to Pennsylvania's underserved church people, they assigned to him the many scattered Swedish Lutheran parishes of the greater Delaware Valley. Muhlenberg (a leading anti-Moravian) recounted an episode of conflict between church minister and Moravian that gives some idea of the depth of feeling attending the general issue of Moravian missionary work among church people.

A Swedish preacher by the name of Falck, who appeared to mean well but had poor judgment, settled there for a time. This man preached in Swedish and English during my time. The Zinzendorfers were still roving around rather thickly and they sent there a Swedish student named Brycelius, who attracted a little group of all four nationalities [Swedes, English, Scots, and Germans]. He went into the church without the knowledge or consent of Mr. Falck and was going to preach. The old man heard about it and went to the church earlier. The people assembled and finally, when young Mr. Brycelius came into the church, the old man went up to him and said, "You are coming into the sheepfold as a thief and a murderer," and with great authority struck him hard on the mouth. . . . The members of the congregation leaped in and separated them. Old Falck did not remain in the place continuously, nor was he able to bring about harmony; consequently the Zinzendorfers got a foothold there. . . .

In the second year after my arrival [1744] some of the Swedes who had become disgusted with the Herrnhuters requested me to come up and preach an English sermon. I did this and they asked me to come up occasionally, whenever convenient, and preach during the week. But when the newly arrived Swedish preacher in Philadelphia, Magister Naesman, heard of this, he journeyed up here and told his brethren that they should not have anything to do with me since I was a Hallensian [i.e., pietist: The University of Halle was the center for German Lutheran pietism.] He promised to come occasionally himself. . . . Mr. Naesman, however, failed to go, Mr. Falck [had gone] back to Europe, and I had no time, so the door was wide open for the Zinzendorfers. . . . And now [1748], though they have had this field to themselves for several years, I still cannot see that they have accomplished anything good, for the Germans thereabouts have become more frivolous and epicurean than before. The Swedes still retained the customs of their old country, on every great festival engaging in idle revelries such as gorging, drinking, dancing, and the like. Such was the case also with the rest, with the exception of a wealthy, respectable Irishman [ironmaster William Bird] whom they had converted to *communio bonorum* to the extent that he sent two of his children to the Zinzendorfer school in New Hanover. . . . To this extent had the field been cultivated when the Zinzendorfers let it lie and went away.[38]

During the late 1740s, in the face of a dwindling degree of receptiveness among Pennsylvania church people, the Moravians wound down the missionary program. It was discontinued altogether in late 1748.

In the spring of 1748, with Molatton Church again shepherdless, the community suffered a particularly virulent onslaught of a disease the colonists called "pleurisy." This ailment struck people living along the rivers of the Delaware Valley region, especially the Swedes. The latter were concentrated in early-settled areas along waterways, but also appear to have had some hereditary susceptibility. The disease, which has never been identified in terms of modern medicine, may have been tuberculosis. In the same year, the Swedish settlement at Raccoon (now Swedesboro), New Jersey, also had a very bad outbreak of pleurisy. Muhlenberg described the epidemic's impact on Molatton:

A young Swede came to me and lamented with tears in his eyes that the pleurisy was raging among them and they had no preacher to give them consolation. The poor young people were growing up in ignorance and blindness; would I please come at least once and preach and exhort the people to repentance? Two weeks later this young man died and I had to bury him [and] also an Englishman. After the funeral sermon a number of men got together, particularly the above-mentioned Irishman [William Bird], an Englishman from New Hanover, another awakened Englishman [William Maugridge] who had been an officer in the Episcopal church in Philadelphia and moved to this place, and also several elderly Swedes. They entreated me with tears [and] finally they prevailed upon me to promise something *ad interim*.

I began in this month [March 1748], and preached once every two weeks during the week, and once every two weeks on Sunday afternoons. This place is twelve miles away over a good road, but only ten miles if one rides over a terribly rough stony mountain and crosses a stream. [Muhlenberg was coming from his house and church in the present-day village of Trappe, in Montgomery County. German miles were somewhat longer than English miles in this period.] When I had finished divine service in New Hanover on a Sunday about twelve o'clock noon, I would quickly mount my horse and with all possible speed ride through the sun's greatest heat in order to get there by two or three o'clock. First I preached an English sermon and then delivered a brief exhortation in German. . . . The Swedes and the Irish [evidently lumped with the Scots and the Ulster Scots or "Scotch-Irish" by Muhlenberg] understood English as well as their mother tongues. . . . On the weekdays, . . . I began to give catechetical instruction to both young and old. The ignorance that is to be found among both young and old is almost incredible, but still they are very attentive and very much frightened on account of the many sudden deaths which have occurred in their midst.[39]

Muhlenberg continued as visiting pastor until May 1752, though staying away the winter months.

I feel very definitely that added to my other work it is ruining my health. . . . If I had an assistant, . . . it would be easier for me to go to the aid of these abandoned little groups. But it is too burdensome for me alone and impossible to keep up.[40]

It is likely that Muhlenberg arranged with the Swedish church ministers for a successor to be provided. The German Lutheran leader always made the maintenance of a sound connection with his Swedish Lutheran and Anglican counterparts a high priority, despite the scorn of the more orthodox among them for his pietist outlook. Ever since the Molatton people had welcomed old Gabriel Falck in his disgrace in 1735, and so for a spell had had no need of Wicacoa, the central parish and its outparish had been estranged. In 1752 this rift was healed to the extent that a young assistant pastor from Wicacoa, John Abraham Lidenius, came up to Molatton to live as resident pastor.

Just like Samuel Hesselius three decades before, Lidenius within a few months wooed and wed a young Swedish parishioner named Brigitta. This one was daughter to a tailor named Anders Reinberg. On April 23, 1753, Molatton Church organized itself as a parish in its own right, named Saint Gabriel's. Furthermore, the new vestry of seven Swedes and seven Englishmen resolved

> that the canons of the Church of England be provided and got, that thus we may the better keep good order within ourselves and be conformable to our brethren, not only distinguishing ourselves from dissenters who are always jealous of their establishments, but also as dutiful Christian subjects setting forth our glorious profession in a true and devout light before God and men.[41]

It seems safe to assume that Lidenius encouraged this course of action. One result was the departure of many of the German Lutherans who were customary worshipers at Molatton, who then participated in founding the New Store Church.

Just what the Saint Gabriel's vestry undertook at this time, to make active its new allegiance to the Church of England, is unknown. Lidenius continued to officiate at Molatton until 1755. Like Samuel Hesselius, Lidenius quickly tired of life in a backwater. He no doubt observed the high proportion of Britons among the worshipers and was well aware of how far removed Molatton was from the heartland of the Delaware Valley Swedes. The circumstances of the final break between the young minister and Saint Gabriel's is not clear, though his pressing the congregation to become an Anglican one would imply a distaste for serving there. His charges were probably glad to see Lidenius go. A drunkard with a tendency to run up bad debts, he became an embarrassment to the Church of Sweden. His bride Brigitta's family, the Reinbergs, told the Swedish minister, Carl Magnus Wrangel, who visited Molatton in 1762, "much about this their son-in-law, who was indiscreet while he dwelt here among them. The man [Anders Reinberg] was afflicted with strong consumption, and said he had contracted it because of sorrow over his daughter's unhappy marriage with Lidenius."[42] Perhaps this "consumption" was the legacy of a non-fatal encounter with pleurisy. Unhappy Brigitta died young, in 1764, cause unknown.

Following Lidenius's departure, the Molatton people again besought Muhlenberg to act as their pastor. Muhlenberg responded by visiting occasionally for a couple of years. Then, for brief consecutive periods during the years 1757-1758, he arranged for his fellow Lutheran ministers Johann Christoph Hartwick and Bernard Michael Hausihl to officiate from time to time. In 1760, after a period of irregular service, the dormant embrace of the Church of England came to life with a somewhat dramatic flourish. Wrangel, provost (directing minister) of the Swedish churches in the Delaware Valley, while visiting a couple years later, recorded from a participant an account of what transpired. His informant was the elderly Swede Jonas Jones, son of the original pioneer Mounce Jones.

> This man is the last surviving trustee or title-holder of Manatawny Church, and had the deed thereof in his possession. I asked him how and in what fashion it came to be that they united themselves with the English and requested a minister from the [Anglican missionary] Society in London; then he explained the whole context to me in the following way. Several households of English in Reading town had for a long time sought to persuade them to unite with them in applying to the Society in London for assistance with a minister; but so long as they could have the pleasure of Pastor Muhlenberg's visits they did not want to consent to that. But by and by they took the following course to bring them into this design, namely, the last time the above-named Mr. Pastor preached among them, one from Reading was present and after the worship service stood up and addressed the peo-

ple: whereas they could not wait for a long time until Mr. Muhlenberg could serve them, it would be most just that the congregation united itself with them in Reading in order to apply to the Society in London for a minister, and so on. As this now happened in Pastor Muhlenberg's presence, the people believed that he knew about it and that this man, who assumed such great authority, had discussed the matter with him and consequently he had consented to it. Then immediately a document was hastily read to them, which they signed, in which they requested a minister from the Society. But they repented afterwards, when they heard that Mr. Pastor Muhlenberg knew nothing about all this. He, on the other hand, believed that this was a conspiracy between the congregation and this man from Reading; consequently from that day he left them and preached there no more. Thus they were pulled from both sides. Furthermore, those in Reading had requested from this Jones the deed to the church's land, which however he did not release, inasmuch as he had not subscribed to the above-named document. Since that time they have awaited a reply from the Society for almost two years, which first arrived this spring, with the promise to send them a minister. He asked me for a judgment, how he ought to conduct himself in case such a one arrived from England. I instructed him then, that if a minister arrived the congregation should in no manner oppose him, but only reserve the right for the Lutherans to use the church whenever any minister visited them.[43]

A definite sense of separateness between Swedish Lutherans and Anglicans was expressed here. It would appear that the cooperative relationship between the Church of Sweden and the Church of England in the Delaware Valley region, and the eventual absorption of the Swedish parishes into the Episcopal Church, did not proceed as effortlessly as some historians of religion believe. As for Muhlenberg, he bore no grudge against Molatton. He tried unsuccessfully in 1760 to arrange for a Lutheran minister to act as interim pastor until the Anglican missionary should come, in fact, and his journals of later years contain fond mentions of Saint Gabriel's. He preached to the Molatton people at least one more time, in 1767:

> We reached the New Store, where I was to preach. Since Swedes and Englishmen to whom I once ministered . . . live thereabouts, a large number of Germans, Swedes, and Englishmen had assembled. . . . Accordingly I was obliged to preach first in German and then in English.[44]

Wrangel noted that Muhlenberg was so well thought of at Molatton that "All the English here call themselves Lutherans and hold a great affection for the said Pastor."[45]

The reward for Molatton's patience was Alexander Murray, an earnest Scotsman of Methodist inclinations who served Molatton and Reading until he returned to Britain in 1778, forced to leave Berks County because of his unconcealed loyalty to Britain. Arriving in late 1762, Murray chose to live in the somewhat more cosmopolitan environment of Reading, where he enjoyed discussing theology and literature with his well-read neighbor James Read, chief clerk of the Berks County courts. The pastor conducted worship at Molatton every third Sunday, however, a comparatively frequent rate of service by local standards. In 1771 Saint Gabriel's honored their pastor with a repair and enlargement of the log church.

The matter of the pastor's finances several times threatened this healthy relationship between minister and congregants, as often happened at churches in Pennsylvania, citadel of religious freedom. There was no state-church establishment to compel citizens to provide clergymen's wherewithal. Many German ministers, regular and irregular, ran their own farms to provide necessities and make a little extra money. In 1765 Murray's Molatton and Reading parishioners were paying him £75 per annum, supplemented by a missionary society stipend of £47 (a total of £122). This was a sum "too scanty,"[46] according to a petition addressed by Murray's flock to the Society in that year asking a higher missionary's salary for the minister. A year earlier, Murray had reported that a year's room and board for his horse and himself in Reading was costing him about £100. He was "poorly entertained and accommodated for that money."[47] Murray did not blame his charges for the low recompense, affirming that this was "as much as can be expected from their yet small numbers and abilities."[48] Murray's pay was comparable to what other Anglican and Presbyterian ministers were then receiving, and nearly twice the salary typical for German Reformed ministers.

At one point, in 1768, Murray threatened that he might leave his mission to try his luck as a minister elsewhere in the colonies. All ended happily, however, for before the year was out, the young parson wed Nancy Morgan, the daughter of wealthy Philadelphians. Before the Revolution, Murray was able to build an elegant house on a 216-acre farm on Reading's outskirts. He also invested in two nearby three-acre lots with rental houses, as well as 625 acres of wilderness in frontier Northumberland County.

Parson Murray was not mercenary. It was the general practice of the time for ministers of the Church of England and other churches to be sure to take care with their worldly estates. Murray had a fine relationship with his parishioners. When he and his wife were forced out of their house in 1777 for their loyalist convictions, shelter and protection was proffered and accepted in one Molatton family's home until the couple's departure for England the following year. The Saint Gabriel's vestry testified about Murray's good character to the revolutionary government. Without such a witness the authorities would not allow the parson to sell his estate.

Twelve years later, in 1790, homesickness for Pennsylvania led Murray to return to America as a minister in the new Protestant Episcopal Church of the United States. He resided in Philadelphia, regularly traveling to Molatton, where he resumed his duties as Saint Gabriel's pastor. His homecoming was shortlived, though, as he died in the yellow fever epidemic of 1793. The epitaph on Murray's tombstone in the Christ Church graveyard, Philadelphia, bore witness to his character as a "truly honest man."[49]

MUHLENBERG'S JOURNALS: THE HEARTS OF THE PEOPLE

There survive in the journals of Heinrich Melchior Muhlenberg vivid accounts of the spiritual lives of some Molatton Church members. Once one gets beyond Muhlenberg's rancorous jibes at Quakers and Moravians, one gains some appreciation of religion's importance to the Molatton people. Most of them lived labor-crammed lives, circumscribed tightly by close family bonds, the difficulties of transportation and communication, and their own relative ignorance.

May 1748: After the sermon a young Englishwoman, named Susannah Hopkins, came forward and desired Holy Baptism. Her parents had died early and had failed to have her baptized, although they had been members of the English church. She was nineteen years old, able to read English, had read the New Testament diligently, had learned the little catechism in the English *Book of Common Prayer*. . . . I baptized her. . . . Even those who ordinarily had stony hearts, wept aloud and prayed with us as well as they were able. An old Swedish couple who had been born in this country said that they now had a vivid idea of what it must have been like in the early days of Christianity![50]

June 1748: Two grown daughters of an English Quaker came forward after the sermon and desired Holy Baptism. The father's first wife had been a Swedish woman of our religion, and these two daughters were theirs. They could not get the father's consent, . . . however, so they waited until they had attained their majority according to the laws of the land.[51]

September 1748: I was obliged to prepare several adult persons for Holy Baptism in the Swedish-English congregation. An Englishwoman who has a Swedish husband [Ruth Jones, nee Henton, wife of Peter Jones] had manifested a desire for Holy Baptism. . . . Her mother is a Quaker, still living, who allowed her to grow up in ignorance. She leads a Christian life, as far as I have learned from informed neighbors. The second person was her sister [Hannah Henton], an adult maiden. . . . The third was an unmarried man [William Hopkins, brother to Susannah Hopkins above] about twenty-eight years old. He lives among the Quakers and has to suffer many a trial at their hands. He is able to read, has an excellent understanding, uses the Bible diligently, and also desires to borrow edifying books from me. . . . The fourth person was an Englishwoman [Amy Allison] whose husband is leading a dissolute life. She said that since she was destitute in the world she would seek an abiding comfort in her Redeemer. . . . I asked them among other things whether they had any ulterior purpose or worldly motives in being baptized, but they replied that they had no other motives than the command and promises of Jesus Christ. Nor did they have any worldly interest in it; rather they would suffer derision and contempt on account of it, which, considering local conditions, we can readily believe.[52]

November 1748: I had an edifying conversation with a genteel English widow. Her husband had been upright, kind, hospitable to all men, and benevolent towards the poor. He died nine months previously without benefit of Holy Baptism. The Zinzendorfers had wooed him assiduously and had succeeded in winning him up to the point of *communio bonorum*. But when they could not budge him any further and gain possession of his wealth, they showed no further interest in his baptism. The woman also had not been baptized because her parents . . . adhered to the English Anabaptists [Baptists]. The woman said that she had come to every one of my services and on each occasion had been awakened. . . . Since her widowhood, the faithful Savior . . . had led her to repentance.
. . . Much as she had been afraid when God made her a widow, with not only a number of small children, but a large, extensive household to care for all alone, she nevertheless found it greatly lightened because she saw evidences of a special, gracious providence even in the smallest affairs. . . . She asked me to deliver an exhortation in English to her numerous domestics, both Negroes and white people. . . . She received Holy Baptism amid many tears and heartfelt emotions. She, too, will not fail to meet scoffing and derision.[53]

THE SOCIETY OF FRIENDS

The one religious group with a significant presence in the Oley Valley that enjoyed stability and order throughout the colonial period was that of the Society of Friends. Quakerism (Friends being best known to their countrymen by that name) had been born in Britain, and remained a vital if small denomination in the homeland. By the eighteenth century, however, William Penn's "Quaker colony" had become the Society's spiritual homeland. Unlike the various churches in the province, the Quakers did not strain to be loyal subjects to remote denominational organizations. Their religious life did not require the ministrations of clergymen ordained in Europe.

Quakerism had originated in the civil-war-ravaged England of the 1650s as a radical, visionary sect. It was one of many such sects that emerged in the Cromwellian era. A comparison of the Quakers of 1660 to the New Born of 1710 would not be completely unwarranted, certainly not as regards perceptions of Friends and New Born in the eyes of the authorities. Any group of believers who denied the efficacy of priests and sacraments frightened rulers and churchmen, in England as in Lambsheim. The Society of Friends underwent vigorous persecution. But while fellow visionary English sects disintegrated, the Society endured and ultimately thrived.

Quakers believed that a Divine presence, which they called the "Light," resided within every person. An individual's salvation was a voluntary act in which that man or woman embraced the Light within him- or herself, and reconciled his or her life to its presence. The concept of the Light was a radical idea that informed every aspect of Quaker belief and practice.

Any religion must address the question whether the devout believer can live "in the world" or must strive to live in a spiritual realm as far removed as possible from worldly influence. The survival and

SOUL

EXETER FRIENDS MEETING HOUSE, 1759, Exeter Township
Photo by Cervin Robinson, 1958. Courtesy, The Historic American Buildings Survey, Prints and Photographs Division, Library of Congress.

success of Quakerism in the late seventeenth century may perhaps be attributed to the Quaker vision of a devout, moral way of life firmly anchored in a warm, loving, religiously oriented family and community environment. Friends emphasized patient nurturing and strong religious and moral guidance for children. In addition they extolled hard work and careful economic management in order to sustain an affectionate, supportive family and build a foundation for the next generation to carry on in the Quaker way. One was to participate energetically in the economic world so as to provide well for one's family, while living in a godly manner (honestly and simply) to testify to "the truth" before all people. Quakers accepted their place in the world while shorter-lived English sects had rejected the world absolutely.

William Penn's acquisition of Pennsylvania, called "the best poor man's country" in the eighteenth century for its oft-fulfilled economic promise, seemed to ensure the future of the Society of Friends. But the sect paid a price for the vitality it enjoyed. Members' commitment to Quaker principles, to moral uprightness and to plainness in lifeways, softened. The routine admission of the children of Quakers to membership in the Society ("birthright membership") threatened to make the sect gradually more an inherited cultural identity than a religion. The economic prosperity that Quakers enjoyed in Pennsylvania seemed to encourage worldliness. By the second quarter of the eighteenth century, the once vigilant discipline that Quaker meetings had exercised over their members' personal behavior had been relaxed to a wider latitude in personal conduct. Through most of the colonial period, Quakers exercised a greatly disproportionate degree of political power in Penn's colony, controlling the provincial assembly and most county-level offices. Quaker officials, whether speakers of the house or local justices, often had to compromise strict Quaker principles in order to continue to bring a strong measure of Friends' guidance to public affairs in Pennsylvania.

Oley or Exeter Meeting was the Quaker congregation of Oley Valley. The name became Exeter in 1741 when the township was created. Many of Exeter Meeting's constituents—farmers, tradespeople, and craftspeople—were among the more prosperous citizens of the valley. Local governmental leadership was concentrated in the hands of Exeter Meeting members through the early 1760s, centering on the family of Justice George Boone, Jr. (hereinafter called simply George Boone). George Boone was active in the temporal affairs of Exeter Meeting, while his wife Deborah was a leader in its spiritual life. The lives of this husband and wife are evocative of the tension between worldliness and spirituality that existed among Quakers at Exeter and elsewhere before the sect's internal reform movement of the late 1750s. The fact that George Boone remained a member in good standing of the Society is evidence of the degree to which the more spiritual of Friends were willing to tolerate the laxity of the more worldly for the sake of the Quaker community.

There is little documentary evidence regarding the life of George Boone's wife Deborah, though after Deborah's death in 1759, at age sixty-seven, Exeter Friends wrote a memorial account of her life. This was an honor reserved for a few "weighty Friends," as ministers, elders, and other foremost congregants were known. Among Quakers any person, man or woman, might be a minister, though his or her suitability had to be acknowledged by the meeting elders. Since Quakers recognized no sacraments, the minister's role was limited to preaching, and lending spiritual aid on an individual basis. Her memorialist related that in 1713 Deborah was

> married to George Boone; a few years after which she appeared in a public testimony, wherein she frequently communicated to her Friends the experience she had of the mercies and goodness of God to her. . . . Though her appearances as a minister were but short and seldom, . . . they were generally received in love. She several times accompanied Friends in the service of visiting families, in which she appeared to be remarkably favored.[54]

For his part George Boone possessed an aggressive, entrepreneurial temperament. He was the eldest of nine siblings (seven brothers and two sisters) whom George Boone, Sr., and Mary Boone raised in Devonshire in the southwest of England. After coming to Pennsylvania and wedding Deborah in 1713, he claimed a four-hundred-acre tract in the Oley Valley in 1718, and by 1725 built one of the first three gristmills in the valley. George, Jr., was the most ambitious member of an ambitious family. George, Sr., and Mary followed their three eldest children to Pennsylvania in 1717. From 1718 to 1734 they took up additional lands totaling over two thousand acres in the Monocacy Creek watershed, which they distributed among the seven youngest Boone siblings.

The Boone family's interest had been drawn to the promising lands of the Oley Valley when Sarah, second eldest, married Jacob Stauber, an entrepreneurially inclined Swiss immigrant. Stauber was one of the earliest settlers (1713) of the northern valley. He left Oley in 1723 following Sarah's premature death, and was subsequently an influential developer of German-settled communities in northwestern New Jersey and the Shenandoah Valley of Virginia. Brother Joseph Boone built and operated a sawmill, and James and John ran what was perhaps the valley's first tanyard in partnership.

George Boone turned his attention to affairs of church and state as well as those of business. Local Friends had begun worshipping together around 1721. Boone was appointed Oley Meeting's recorder of births and burials in 1723, a post he occupied for the ensuing twenty-seven years. In 1726 he and Deborah donated an acre of their plantation on which to build a log meetinghouse for Oley Meeting. In 1728 George Boone was commissioned as the first justice of the peace in the valley. The post of justice was the most powerful office in local government. In addition justices were entitled to charge fees for the issuance of marriage licenses and the certification of deeds, and Boone's talents as a scrivener brought yet additional income. He drafted many local wills as well as many of the deeds he certified.

The primary source of George Boone's wherewithal, however, was his gristmill. At one point in the year 1728 (a comparatively early date), he claimed to have a thousand bushels of wheat and flour in hand. The mill served as a foundation on which Boone built wide-ranging and successful interests, though he may have weathered a lean initial decade or so while the local settlement economy gathered steam. Between 1735 and 1750, he claimed or bought over eight thousand acres of land outside of the Oley Valley, much of which he subsequently sold. He also acquired the Lebanon Sawmill, a merchant sawmill built in northern Robeson Township (in the lower Oley Valley) by Jonathan Robeson.

George Boone's expansive approach to business often strained his financial resources to the limit. He also walked a tightrope regarding his status as a member of the Society of Friends. He initiated new investments without having fully paid the purchase price of assets already in hand. Such high-handed procedures (especially by eighteenth-century standards) were in direct violation of Quaker strictures about the conduct of business. Failure to execute debt as rapidly as possible was a sin in Quaker eyes, just as much as was dishonesty. Willingness to risk overextending oneself was severely frowned on.

George Boone's willingness to diverge from Quaker precepts appeared in other areas of behavior. The depth of his adherence to the peace principle is definitely put in question by the plea for help he rushed to Governor Gordon during the Oley Valley war scare of 1728:

> Our condition at present looks with a bad vizard [i.e., visage], for undoubtedly the Indians will fall down upon us very suddenly, and our inhabitants are generally fled, there remains about twenty men with me to guard my mill, where I have about one thousand bushels of wheat and flour; and we are resolved to defend ourselves to the last extremity, and not to quit our habitation if we can have any succor from you.[55]

Boone slipped in his worldly Friend's tightrope walk in 1749, at age fifty-nine. He was accused by some fellow Quakers from Philadelphia of bribery. The matter was never officially brought before any government official. At first Exeter Monthly Meeting tried to put the disciplinary responsibility in the lap of Philadelphia Quarterly Meeting. The Exeter Monthly Meeting claimed the case of the justice "seems an affair too difficult for this meeting to go through with,"[56] but the Philadelphia body demurred. Upon reconsideration, Exeter Monthly Meeting investigated and found

> the persons who charged him with bribery to be of mean credit, and he himself also positively denies it; so that this meeting drops that affair.[57]

There is no explicit evidence that George Boone suffered a tacit disgrace following this episode. But the governor failed to renew Boone's commission as justice of the peace in 1749, when he did so for Philadelphia County's other jus-

EXETER FRIENDS MEETING HOUSE, 1759, Exeter Township
Detail of the interior.
Photo by Cervin Robinson, 1958. Courtesy, The Historic American Buildings Survey, Prints and Photographs Division, Library of Congress.

tices, including fellow Exeter member Anthony Lee. A few months after the meeting's deliberations, Boone also stepped down from the post of recorder of births and burials at Exeter Meeting.

The recording duty had been George's most direct connection with the life of the meeting as a community, other than that his wife Deborah was a minister. Not being one of the most devout, he had never been a weighty Friend. Boone's notation in his fine hand, over the passage of twenty-seven years, of the demographic events affecting the meeting's families, had symbolized his status as its wealthiest and most influential constituent, as its patron. By piloting the Boone clan from Abington and Gwynedd to the Oley Valley, and by donating the land for the meetinghouse and burial ground, he had virtually created Exeter Meeting.

In the eyes of his fellow Exeter worshipers, Boone had additional problems. In the same session in April 1750, in which the monthly meeting decided to dispense with the bribery question, the Friends present agreed that they would have to take the justice to task for "his sometimes being too free with strong drink, and overstaying his time in company." In accord with Friends' practice, a contrite George Boone came to the following monthly meeting and made a statement "to clear Truth and satisfy Friends":

> My business for many years hath been much from home, and of consequence in diverse sorts of company, where oft times I have tarried too long, and have drunk more than was needful or commendable, and have been under trouble for the same when no man reprehended me for it. But [I] do design for the future by and with the help of Divine Assistance to be more careful.[58]

George Boone's profound affection for his wife can be seen in his will of 1753, which dictated the specifics of his sons' maintenance of their mother Deborah. He included the provision that she be allowed to reside in "the best room in the old house where she has had her residence the chiefest part of the time since it pleased God to couple us together."[59] She was also to have her riding horse, enabling her to continue the Friendly work of attending the quarterly meeting, visiting families, and testifying to the Truth before distant meetings.

Exeter Meeting was a stable religious gathering throughout the colonial period, in the sense that once organized, its continued existence was never in question.

But its history in that era did not pass without some tumult. Beginning in 1756, the Society of Friends went through a catharsis that amounted to a purge of its less devout and committed members, and a rededication of Friends to the original spirit of Quakerism. This purification of the Society affected Exeter as it did every Pennsylvania meeting; a number of members at Exeter were expelled from the fold.

The thoroughgoing reform of the Society of Friends was remarkable for it seemed to begin as the impulse of one man, an English Quaker named Samuel Fothergill, and proceeded to transform the entire sect. The enthusiasm with which weighty Friends received and took up Fothergill's call to reform suggests that others had come to similar conclusions about the Society's future. With the work of reform underway in England, Fothergill came to Pennsylvania in 1754 and found the brethren there in what he considered a sorry state.

> Their fathers came into the country in its infancy, and bought large tracts of land for a trifle; their sons found large estates come into their possession, and a profession of religion which was partly national [i.e., a matter of cultural environment], which descended like the patrimony from their fathers, and cost as little. They settled in ease and affluence, and whilst they made the barren wilderness as a fruitful field, suffered the plantation of God to be as a field uncultivated, and a desert.[60]

By 1756 Fothergill, after having visited most of the meetings within its jurisdiction, had convinced the weighty Friends of Philadelphia Yearly Meeting that a drastic cleansing action was necessary. In July 1756 Exeter Monthly Meeting received its first copy of the new, far more detailed "queries" about the state of the meeting, as well as a copy of "the Rules of our Discipline."[61] The latter were new guidelines determined by the yearly meeting.

The quest undertaken by the Society of Friends to regain its original purity and spiritual energy had three main aspects: the tightening of communal discipline of offenses against moral conduct or plain lifeways, a movement away from the automatic admission of Quaker children to membership in the Society, and a more rigid insistence that Friends marry only Friends. The creation of the true Quaker family environment in which children's early lives would be immersed in Friendly love and principle was held to be the key to the future of their souls as well as that of the Society. Quakers who wed other than their fellow Quakers were to be summarily expelled, or as Friends put it, "disowned." In effect the Society's broad leadership was willing that if need be the future of Quakerism would be that of a small and exclusive perfectionist sect. The new, more rigorous Friends' discipline must have taken great emotional stamina to put into practice in a small rural community where the person involved might be an old friend, a child one had bounced on one's knee, or one's relation.

Modern eyes perusing colonial-period meeting minutes might interpret Quaker disciplinary activity as interference in people's personal lives. In reality, though, communal discipline was a central element in Friendly conviction and practice. Quakers believed that they must bear testimony to God's "Truth" in all ways at all times, while accepting that anyone could easily and temporarily lose his or her way. When a person converted to Quakerism, as happened from time to time in the Oley Valley, the meeting noted that he or she "requested to be taken under the care of Friends." When "received," "after a due consideration," it was for "as long as his life and conversation [i.e., general comportment] answers his profession."[62] Disciplinary procedure was a unique form of moral suasion in which weighty Friends "eldered" or discussed the offender's wrongdoing with him (or her) at length. They attempted to open the person's heart, discover the facts in the case, and bring the person to see the error of his or her ways. The question of disownment from the Society was treated in the most deliberate manner, and the weighty Friends of a meeting undertook all disciplinary actions in unanimity. If this "sense of the meeting" could not be obtained, which rarely happened, the matter was referred to the quarterly meeting for advisement.

The weighty Friends of Exeter Meeting appear to have concurred with the yearly meeting's reforming impulse, responding with a heightened watchfulness and a commitment to hold straying members to a higher standard of contrition. In the ten years prior to July 1756, there had arisen nineteen disciplinary cases among Exeter Friends, which had resulted in eight disownments (or 42 percent). In the ensuing decade, there arose twenty-seven cases, with twenty-one disownments (78 percent). The French and Indian War had some effect in enlarging the later group of offenders, in that four men were dealt with for violations of the peace testimony.

Weighty Friends also began to hold members to account for misconduct that would not have been deemed worthy of notice before. A soon pardoned but significant offense was Sheriff William Boone's "having suffered oaths to be administered by his authority,"[63] brought up in April 1757, a practically unavoidable official duty of which William's father Justice George Boone must have been guilty many times. One gradual effect of the reform was to impel Quakers to leave the political arena, a setting in which a measure of sinful compromise with the world appeared to be inevitable. Good Friend William Boone declined to run in the ensuing October election for a sheriff's usual third consecutive one-year term.

Friends took a sterner attitude toward sexual misconduct. Six Exeter Quakers were disowned for fornication (in these instances, not accompanied by the often related offense of improper marriage) in the years 1756-1766. Only one such transgression had been brought to the meeting's notice in all the years from 1721 to 1756, and the sorrowful perpetrator had been pardoned.

One disciplinary case that must have started a ripple of comment through the broader valley community was that of Sarah Webb, a granddaughter of George Boone, Sr. She was first dealt with in 1757 for "keeping company with one not of our Society, and leaving her father's house,"[64] at which time she condemned her misconduct to Friends' satisfaction. True love appears to have ultimately triumphed, though, as in 1760 the meeting disowned Sarah for marrying Philip Jacob Michael, "a hireling minister of the Calvin Church."[65] Michael, though not recognized by the official German Reformed coetus, was the influential pastor of several German Reformed congregations in the Berks County area.

Perhaps the weightiest Friend in Exeter Meeting in the middle eighteenth century was Ellis Hughes, a Welsh-born farmer, sawmill owner, and minister. Hughes's years as a particularly active and influential member stretched from 1731, when he was drawn to settle his family in the Oley Valley by "a strong draft of love attending his mind," through to his death in 1764 at age seventy-six. During Hughes's ministry, he saw his son Edward repent in 1749 for marrying a non-Quaker woman and suffered the pain of seeing his son William disowned from meeting membership in 1754, after three disciplinary episodes due to William's proclivity to excessive drink. As the meeting's most prominent minister, Ellis Hughes must have participated in the disciplinary deliberations regarding his son.

Buoyed by the love of his wife Jane, however, who was herself an elder of the meeting, Ellis Hughes was said by his memorialist to be a man "naturally of a very cheerful disposition." He embodied the Quaker ideal of charity, commitment, and effort.

He was always one of the number who went on the visit to Friends' families; which weighty work he undertook in much diffidence of himself and fear of a forward spirit. [This work,] he used to say, "He thought must be a good one, since it occasioned greater nearness, and was a renewal of love, both among visitors and visited." And by accounts received, it was so in a good degree.

In meetings for worship he was a good example in silent patient waiting upon the Lord, and when raised to bear a public testimony, it was with that power and authority, which accompanies a true gospel minister, and hath made lasting impressions upon some minds. Though he was of an exceeding tender disposition, yet being a lover of good order in the church, and well knowing the dangerous tendency of undue liberty, he both by precept and example, endeavored to promote the former and discourage the latter; in which he gave repeated proofs, that the near connections of natural kindred did not bias his judgment.

His deportment being meek and loving, and his conversation familiar and instructively cheerful, gained him the esteem of most who knew him, of different ranks and religious persuasions. He was a nursing father in the church, and particularly so to diverse whom the Lord had visited that were under affliction, whether of body or mind; nor was his charity in this respect confined to the members of our society.

He was an affectionate husband, a tender parent, a kind master; and having by the blessing of divine providence on his honest industry, obtained a competency of the necessaries of life, was very hospitable, entertaining both Friends and others freely and kindly, not with ostentation or for applause, but for the promotion of piety and virtue, and the good of mankind. . . .

The day he was taken ill of his last sickness, at the funeral of one of his sons [John], which was the last meeting he was at, he was remarkably favored in his public testimony to a large gathering of people. [Eleven days later he followed John to the Exeter Meeting burial ground,] accompanied by a large number of his friends and neighbors.[66]

QUAKER MEETING DOCUMENTS

WHEREAS Samuel Boone, son of Samuel Boone deceased, having by birth a right to, and hath made profession of, the Truth as held by us the people called Quakers; but for want of giving due heed to the dictates thereof in himself, hath so far deviated from the ancient and well known rules of our discipline as to be guilty of that Unchristian practice of shooting for a wager, quarreling and fighting, and using vile and unbecoming expressions: all which Friends have tenderly treated with him for, in order to bring him to a true sense of his misconduct therein; which labor of love seems not to have the desired effect on him. Therefore, for the clearing of Truth and the professors thereof, we find a necessity of testifying against him and his said actions; and do hereby disown the said Samuel Boone to be a member of our Society, until that by his more circumspect walking we may be convinced of a true reformation wrought in him; which, that we may happily witness, is our sincere desire for him.

SIGNED in and on behalf of Exeter Monthly Meeting held the 25th day of the 4th month 1765 by

Benjamin Lightfoot, Clerk

WHEREAS Thomas Lee, son of Anthony Lee of Oley in the county of Philadelphia in the province of Pennsylvania, and Eleanor Ellis, daughter of Thomas Ellis of the same place, having declared their intentions of marriage with each other before several monthly meetings of the people called Quakers at Gwynedd in the county aforesaid (according to the good order used amongst them) and nothing appearing to obstruct their proceedings: were approved of by the said meetings: NOW these are to certify to all whom it may concern that for the full accomplishing of their said intentions this 18th day of the 3rd month in the year of our Lord 1736, they the said Thomas Lee and Eleanor Ellis appeared in a public meeting of the said people in Oley aforesaid and the said Thomas Lee, taking the said Eleanor Ellis by the hand, did in solemn manner openly declare that he took her to be his wife, promising through the Lord's assistance to be unto her a faithful and loving husband until death should separate them, and then and there in the said assembly the said Eleanor Ellis did likewise declare that she took the said Thomas Lee to be her husband, in like manner promising to be unto him a faithful and loving wife till death should separate them: and moreover the said Thomas Lee and Eleanor Ellis, she according to custom assuming the name of her husband, as a further confirmation thereof did there and then to these presents set their hands, and we whose hands are here under written being amongst others present, at the solemnization of the said marriage and subscription in manner aforesaid, witness whereunto, have also to these presents set our hands the day and year above written.

Thomas Lee   Eleanor Lee   38 other signatures

CONCLUSION

Setting aside the respective histories of the New Born and the Moravians in Oley, sectarian groups that ultimately failed to sink roots locally, the development of congregational life among the various Oley Valley denominations during the colonial period might be perceived simply as mirroring the overall evolution of an undeveloped pioneer community into one of prosperity and socioeconomic complexity. As the valley filled with settled homesteads, industrial establishments were built, township governments founded and expanded, population grew, and the material environment offered greater security and comfort for most people, so the various local Lutheran, German Reformed, and Anglican flocks gradually if painfully realized greater stability, and their congregants became more nearly fulfilled as worshipers.

There is an additional dimension to the colonial-period history of religion in the valley, however. The story is again one of cultural elements brought from Europe, then reshaped by American conditions. In regard to this aspect of life, conditions were perhaps particularly adverse. The relative absence of ministers in Pennsylvania, and the lack of the buttress against "irreligious" (or at least dissenting) influences that had been maintained in Europe by the state establishment of a given church, led many to join with alternative groups of believers, or perhaps to take up a more solitary religious life. There was a newfound freedom to choose how and with whom one would worship. Even the Society of Friends experienced the effect of the American environment, as the elders sensed a softening of devotion and conviction because of American prosperity, and then organized a reaffirmation of Friendly principles that represented a virtual purge of the less devout.

ELLIS-LEE HOUSE, Exeter, 1752
This Quaker homestead was built in several stages, beginning with the central, two-story, hall-parlor section in 1752. When its original owner, Morris Ellis, moved to the Shenandoah Valley of Virginia in 1769, it was sold to the Lee family.
Photo by Kenneth LeVan.

NOTES

1. William J. Hinke, ed., *Minutes and Letters of the Coetus of the German Reformed Congregations in Pennsylvania 1747-1792* (Philadelphia: Reformed Church Publication Board, 1903), 125.

2. *The Journals of Henry Melchior Muhlenberg*, edited by Theodore G. Tappert and John W. Doberstein (Philadelphia: The Evangelical Lutheran Ministerium of Pennsylvania and Adjacent States, 1945), vol. 1, 146.

3. Julius Friedrich Sachse, *Justus Falckner* (published privately, 1903), 41.

4. John Joseph Stoudt, ed., "Matthias Baumann: The New Born," *Historical Review of Berks County* 43, no. 4 (Fall 1978): 136.

5. Ibid., 136, 137, 138, 142, 144.

6. From *Chronicon Ephratense* (1786), reprinted in M. A. Gruber, ed., "The Newborn," *The Penn Germania*, vol. 13 (1912): 360.

7. Ibid.

8. Ibid.; Julius Friedrich Sachse, *The German Sectarians of Pennsylvania 1708-1742* (published privately, 1899), 73.

9. *Journals of Muhlenberg*, vol. 1, 358.

10. From I. Daniel Rupp, "Die Neugeborene," reprinted in Gruber, ed., "The Newborn," 363-64.

11. Donald F. Durnbaugh, *The Brethren in Colonial America* (Elgin, Illinois: The Brethren Press, 1967), 281.

12. *Chronicon Ephratense*, reprinted in Gruber, ed., "The Newborn," 361.

13. Peter G. Bertolet, *Fragments of the Past: Historical Sketches of Oley and Vicinity* (Oley: The Women's Club of Oley Valley, 1980), 106.

14. Gottlieb Mittelberger, *Journey to Pennsylvania*, translated and edited by Oscar Handlin and John Clive (Cambridge, Mass.: Harvard University Press, 1960), 84-85.

15. William J. Hinke, ed., *Life and Letters of the Rev. John Philip Boehm* (Philadelphia: Publication and Sunday School Board of the Reformed Church in the United States, 1916), 202.

16. Ibid., 280.

17. *Minutes and Letters of the Coetus of the German Reformed Congregations in Pennsylvania*, 16.

18. *Life and Letters of Boehm*, 74.

19. From the Churchbook of the Oley Moravian Church, in P.C. Croll, *Annals of the Oley Valley in Berks County, Pa.* (Reading: Reading Eagle Press, 1926), 116.

20. Memoir of Anna Elisabeth (Kleiss) Leinbach, transcribed by Laurel Miller and translated by Paul Sukop von Marko, from the Report of the Congregation of Bethlehem, 1766, Moravian Archives, Bethlehem, Pennsylvania.

21. Croll, *Annals of Oley Valley*, 15.

22. Ibid., 118.

23. J. Taylor Hamilton, "The Moravian Work at Oley, Berks County, Penna.," *Transactions of the Moravian Historical Society* 13 (1944): 14.

24. Ibid., 18.

25. Memoir of Maria Barbara Nitschmann, nee Leinbach, addition to the Report of the Congregation of Bethlehem, 1810, translated by William J. Hinke, in collections of Evangelical and Reformed Historical Society, Archives of the United Church of Christ, Philip Schaff Library, Lancaster Theological Seminary, Lancaster, Pennsylvania.

26. *Journals of Muhlenberg*, vol. 1, 357.

27. Charles H. Glatfelter, *Pastors and Congregations*, vol. 1 of *Pastors and People: German Lutheran and Reformed Churches in the Pennsylvania Field*, Publications of the Pennsylvania German Society 13 (1980): 257.

28. *Minutes and Letters of the Coetus of the German Reformed Congregations in Pennsylvania*, 37.

29. Glatfelter, *Pastors and People*, vol. 1, 237.

30. *Minutes and Letters of the Coetus of the German Reformed Congregations in Pennsylvania*, 124-26.

31. Ibid., 144.

32. Glatfelter, *Pastors and People*, vol. 1, 252-53.

33. Ibid., 211.

34. Journal of Andreas Sandel's Visits to Manatawny, 1704-1710, translated by Richard H. Hulan, from "Swedish Settlement at Manatawny," manuscript compiled by Peter S. Craig, not published.

35. Ibid.

36. Israel Acrelius, *A History of New Sweden* (1758), translated and edited by William M. Reynolds, republished as *Memoirs of the Historical Society of Pennsylvania*, vol. 11 (1874), 227.

37. Alexander Howie to the Society for the Propagation of the Gospel in Foreign Parts, July 28, 1732, Papers of the Society for the Propagation of the Gospel (Church of England), Series B (facsimiles of records in the British Public Records Office), Manuscript Division, Library of Congress, Washington, D.C.

38. *Journals of Muhlenberg*, vol. 1, 186.

39. Ibid., 185-87.

40. Ibid., 222, 246.

41. Churchbook of Saint Gabriel's Church, Saint Gabriel's Protestant Episcopal Church, Douglassville, Pennsylvania.

42. Journal of Provost Carl Magnus Wrangel's Visits to Manatawny, 1762-1763, translated by Richard H. Hulan, not published.

43. Ibid.

44. *Journals of Muhlenberg*, vol. 2, 326.

45. Journal of Wrangel's Visits to Manatawny.

46. William Stevens Perry, ed., *Historical Collections Relating to the American Colonial Church* (published privately, 1871), vol. 2, 388.

47. Ibid., 357.

48. Alexander Murray to the Society for the Propagation of the Gospel, June 25, 1765, Papers of the Society for the Propagation of the Gospel, Library of Congress.

49. J. Bennett Nolan, *Early Narratives of Berks County* (Reading: Historical Society of Berks County, 1927), 34.

50. *Journals of Muhlenberg*, vol. 1, 196.

51. Ibid., 197.

52. Ibid., 203.

53. Ibid., 210.

54. Exeter Monthly Meeting Men's Minutes, July 31, 1760, Friends Historical Library, Swarthmore College, Swarthmore, Pennsylvania.

55. *Pennsylvania Archives*, First Series, vol. 1: 217-18.

56. Exeter Monthly Meeting Men's Minutes, February 26, 1749-1750.

57. Ibid., April 28, 1750.

58. Ibid., April 28, 1750, and May 26, 1750.

59. Will of George Boone, Berks County Wills, vol. 1, 6. Office of the Berks County Register of Wills, Berks County Courthouse, Reading, Pennsylvania.

60. Jack D. Marietta, *The Reformation of American Quakerism, 1748-1783* (Philadelphia: University of Pennsylvania Press, 1984), 40-41.

61. Exeter Monthly Meeting Men's Minutes, July 29, 1756.

62. Ibid., September 26, 1747, and January 31, 1747-1748.

63. Ibid., April 28, 1757.

64. Exeter Monthly Meeting Women's Minutes, April 28, 1757, and April 27, 1758.

65. Ibid., June 17, 1760.

66. Exeter Monthly Meeting Men's Minutes, 1764.

Chapter 5

COMMUNITY

JACOB KAUFFMANN HOMESTEAD, Oley Township
This view, across a spring-watered meadow, shows one of Oley Valley's earliest and historically most important farmsteads. The buildings range from the farmhouse on the left (1766) to the large stone 19th-century barn.
Photo by Kenneth LeVan.

The Oley Valley was home to colonists of diverse backgrounds. These people, despite their cultural differences, cooperated to develop institutional structures for community life (governmental and religious) and to provide such accompaniments to settled life as education and roads. Of course, the desire for perceived personal economic benefits occasionally caused considerable friction among persons, and some friction among groups. For example, a person might desire a road to take one's grain and one's neighbors' grain to market, but only a road that caused as little damage to one's own landholding as possible. If not consistently harmonious, however, community life in the colonial Oley Valley did represent a uniquely American mode. The English-speaking public sphere integrated the participation of the various nationalities, while in the private sphere people's right to the retention of their cultural heritage was unchallenged.

FAMILY

The basic social unit underpinning the colonial Oley Valley community was the nuclear family of parents and children, "the little commonwealth" as it was called by at least one early American. The main objective of the great and largely successful economic exertions of the people of the valley was to raise children and send them forth as well prepared for life and work as possible. A homestead was practically a family firm, with the father and mother as officers and the sons and daughters furnishing most, often all, of the labor.

As with the larger community, the little commonwealth sometimes knows disharmony. Despite general accord in family relationships, a few valley families endured painful rifts. Of the fifty-seven colonial-period wills made by fathers with adult children, five showed discord, manifested by denial or severe limitation of a child's expected share in the testator's estate. Of these cases, one was a threat of disownment by a father of a son, rooted in the patriarch's disapproval of his son's religion. This was Johann Dietrich Jungmann's exclusion of his son Jerg in 1745 because the latter had become a Moravian. The other four instances of family trouble, all dating from 1758 onward, had to do with a father's disapproval of a daughter's choice of mate.

Israel Robeson's will of 1771 was one betraying the existence of a clash between father and daughter, rooted in a mating impulse gone awry (in the parent's judgment). His daughter Ann was to receive a cash legacy equal to those due her siblings, £150, but until the death of her disliked husband Solomon Walters, this bequest was to be invested and she to have only the interest, paid directly into her hands. Immediately upon Israel's death, however, Solomon was to be given a silver dollar, a paltry sum customarily granted to legal heirs denied a real share of the estate in order to prevent their bringing a claim. Also to be delivered immediately was Ann's dowry furniture, consisting of a feather bed, bedstead and bed furniture (i.e., bedclothes), "known by the name of her bed," and "the case of drawers marked with the two letters of her maiden name."[1] Apparently Ann had been denied these useful and sentiment-laden items at the time of her marriage to Walters, when she would normally have expected to receive them.

Other disagreements between father and daughter included those between Johannes Lorah and his "unhappily married"[2] daughter Katarina (will of 1768), and between Johannes Geldbach and his daughter Magdalena (1758). Magdalena was to inherit Geldbach's secondary Amity Township farmstead, valued at £1,100, if she was "lawfully wedded."[3] But if she wed a "scandalous, ill-natured man," she was to receive but £50. Magdalena's younger sisters Elisabetha and Katarina were to receive cash bequests of £500 each. Each woman was to be paid £100 when she married and the remaining £400 after the birth of a third child, if the marriage proved "agreeable to her mother's mind." As it happened, Magdalena eventually wed Christian Jaeger and did inherit the Amity plantation.

Sometimes the young woman, about whose marriage her parents were unhappy, may have "had to marry the man." Documents hold clear evidence of the occurrence of premarital sexual activity throughout the colonial period. A young woman named Scheid became pregnant by Isaac Lenhardt in 1720. Little else is known of Lenhardt; he was present in Oley by 1717 and stayed until 1727, when he sold his warranted and surveyed homestead to recently arrived Jean Bertolet. Little is known either of Miss Scheid except that by 1731 English settler John Collins had married her. Johann Heinrich Wolf, another valley resident, had adopted her son by Lenhardt as his own. Wolf gave the boy his own name, Johann Heinrich. Gabriel Falck baptized several other "bastard" children at Molatton Church in the 1730s and 1740s. The Quakers of Exeter Meeting undertook disciplinary actions against ten of their members for premarital sexual activity in the colonial years, and disowned two for extramarital activity.

In addition to the common concern regarding sexual misconduct, Quakers believed that Friends should marry only among their own. A Quaker religious environment could only be created and sustained in a purely Quaker family. "Outgoing in marriage" was severely discouraged, with the threat of disownment from the sect. In 1760 Quaker Anne Boone absconded from her father James's home with non-Quaker Abraham Lincoln (half-brother to the Emancipator's great-grandfather). The two were wed before a minister. Regretting the mode of the wedding but not the union, Anne condemned the elopement to the meeting a year later to regain her membership in the Society of Friends. Lincoln's surviving school book includes a page of his handwriting practice on which the names "Abm. Lincoln" and "Anne Boone" appear side by side. "Anne Boone" is scored through and underneath is written, all in Abraham's hand,

Anne Lincoln
her new name
got by stealth[4]

implying that young Abraham had admired Anne for a time.

The Quaker proscription against "marrying out" was the root of Anne's need to elope; the Boones and Lincolns, extended families with many households in the valley, had longstanding links of friendship. Abraham's sister Sarah had become a Quaker and married Anne's cousin William Boone in 1748. Anne's father James Boone was a devout Friend, but the match between Anne and Abraham, one unforeseen by him, does not appear to have led to lasting hard feelings.

Marriages made between young people from the established families of the valley could turn out badly, whatever the parents' precautions. One such was that between Johannes Joder (the third in the Oley line of that name) and Sarah Schenkel, who wed around 1747. The groom's grandfather and the bride's father, Martin Schenkel, had both been leaders of the New Born sect. The story of Johannes and Sarah is told in detail in Dr. Peter Bertolet's 1860 history of Oley, as received from elderly informants. He relates that, exasperated by her husband's irresponsible drinking, Sarah went to Reading, where she eventually became a woman of "some property."[5] At her death in 1798 she was buried in the family graveyard on the Schenkel homestead in Oley.

Archival documents corroborate Dr. Bertolet's basic account. Joder was an economic failure, though the extended family to which he belonged was able to salvage his children's situation. His father Johannes Joder II, a miller, had deeded Johannes III a 225-acre farm in 1753, but evidently compelled his son to convey the farm to Johannes III's own son Daniel in 1771. Sarah had left Johannes III in 1756; the latter placed a notice in the *Pennsylvanische Berichte* informing readers that his wife had run away and that he was not responsible for her debts. On the 1771 deed to son Daniel, Sarah was referred to as wife and co-owner, but her signature does not appear.

Catherine Berger left her husband Friedrich, to return with her daughter Susanna to the home of her parents, John and Catherine Sands. In his 1774 will her father bequeathed Catherine £20, a cow, and use of a room of her own in the house left to her mother. This room, with food to be provided by her brothers Joseph and Daniel, the inheritors of John Sands's mills and plantation, was to be Catherine's "until she marries again."[6] John Sands left his granddaughter Susanna £10, and directed Joseph and Daniel to send the girl to school at their expense "until she can read and write." Friedrich Berger was to receive a shilling as safeguard against his making any claim on John Sands's estate, though Catherine's father also specified that Berger could keep the £66 that the young couple had been given to start life together.

One unhappy woman known to have left her husband and set up an independent household was Deborah Reiff, wife of Philip Reiff. She took up residence on a six-and-a-half-acre homestead on the High Road from Maiden Creek to Oley, owned jointly with her husband, for a few years in the 1770s. Philip's large plantation was adjacent. By 1779 she purchased and moved to a twenty-five acre

COMMUNITY

homestead a short distance down the same road, where she evidently spent the rest of her days. Perhaps she ran a tavern, a means of survival often adopted by widows. She may have left her husband due to bouts of mental instability on his part. He spent a year or so confined as a "lunatic" in the Pennsylvania Hospital around 1786, though he claimed this treatment was unwarranted. A letter of attorney made in 1786 by Philip to his friend Balthaser Gehr authorized the payment of £20 per annum support to Deborah. Tax assessments from 1786 until Philip's death in 1815 listed "Philip Reiff's Estate," suggesting that he was not in control of his assets, with a separate (and low) assessment for Deborah.

The one other woman known to have lived as head of her own household during the colonial period, who was not a widow, was Mary Jones. She was a spinster. Around 1774-1775 Mary, known to her family as Molly, purchased a half-acre lot from John Sands, Jr., a stone's throw from the plantation of her father Jonas Jones. The latter's 1777 will bequeathed Molly £40 and the use of two acres of meadowland from the Jones farm on which to graze a cow. Jonas Jones also instructed the recipient of the farmstead, Jonas, Jr., to deliver to Molly as much firewood as she needed. How Mary Jones decided to live on her own is not known.

Family life for most inhabitants appears to have been relatively stable and peaceful. Many wills dictated by residents of the valley testified about the respect and affection between husbands and wives, and between parents and children. Fathers with many children, like Johannes Keim (sire of sixteen offspring by successive wives), often could not raise the wherewithal to set up every child with a farm, craft business, or ample dowry. In his will of 1747 Keim set down his appreciation of the willing acceptance of this fact by his children by his first wife:

> All my children from my first wife leave me as soon as them comes to their age saying to me, "Father, what you have you have occasion for, your own self. We will go and see to get our living for *our* own self."[7]

Three of these six children married into well-established Oley families, one becoming a prosperous storekeeper in Reading; the other three moved away.

Jerg Kelchner left for Germany to visit his father in 1747. Before departing, Kelchner made a will directing that his wife Margareta should have full power over his estate to dispose of as she saw fit, "knowing well that she as a good and true mother will never wrong my children."[8] The drafting of a last testament proved a sensible precaution on Kelchner's part as, true to his premonition, he died while abroad. Martin Weiler, unlike Kelchner, lived to see his children come of age. To his son Jacob in 1756 he left all his lands, livestock, and movable goods, "in retaliation of his many kindnesses, care, and great charge he has had in maintaining his aged and feeble father and mother for many years by passed."[9]

DEPARTED WIVES

Whereas Anne, the wife of John Harry of the township of Amity, in Philadelphia County, is eloped from her husband. These are therefore to forwarn all persons not to trust her on her husband's account, for he will pay no debts by her contracted after the date hereof.
—*American Weekly Mercury*, February 3, 1737/38

Jerg Dietrich Held in Oley makes known, that his wife often takes the opportunity to run away from him, and behaves as if it were normal for the likes of her. He warns everybody that she is now run away again, that no one should lend to her on his account, from this time forward he will not pay, and whoever shelters her, offends those in authority.
—*Pennsylvanische Berichte*, June 16, 1746

Ludwig Fillinger in Amity Township in Berks County makes known, that his wife Katarina has gone away from him, and has taken with her many of his things without his permission. No one should lend her anything on his account, he will not pay.
—*Pennsylvanische Berichte*, January 2, 1761

RELATIONS AMONG NATIONALITIES: "GOOD NEIGHBORING"

The plethora of European regional identities among Oley Valley settlers soon coalesced into just two camps: those who spoke German as their primary language for everyday use, and those who spoke English. These two large divisions of inhabitants each formed as amalgams of many varieties of people. The German-speakers included former citizens of a number of German principalities, each with its own cultural identity, as well as "Switzers," and a few Alsatians and "Huguenots" (people with at least some French ancestry whose families had been living for a generation or two in Germany). Among the English-speaking people were immigrants, or more likely children of immigrants, who had come to Pennsylvania during the late seventeenth century in the largely Quaker migration from the North, West, and Midlands of England. Also in the valley were people of English heritage whose families had hopscotched from the early New England coastal settlements to Pennsylvania via Long Island or New Jersey. English-speaking people also included those from Wales, Ireland, Scotland, and Sweden. Each of these European areas, including many regions within Germany and England, held a distinctive cultural heritage. These folk cultures were quite different from one another in speech, farming, food, architecture, and many other aspects of life and custom.

It may at first seem odd that the Swedes came to be counted among the English-speaking settlers. But the Delaware Valley Swedes, always few in number, had had extensive contact with British settlers for several decades before German immigrants arrived in Pennsylvania in any numbers. Although these relations had not been entirely without friction, a tendency for Anglicans and Swedish Lutherans to worship together (continued in the Oley Valley at Molatton Church) had helped reconcile the Swedes to the massive English presence. Unlike the Molatton Swedes, the Holland Dutch (i.e, Netherlandic) people of the valley, mostly migrants from older settlements in New Jersey but including a few who had joined the stream of German emigrants surging through Holland's ports, do not seem to have made the clear-cut alignment with either English- or German-speakers in the valley.

The division of the valley community into German-speakers and English-speakers was *not* a hostile segregation. Relations between the two groups were amicable, sometimes affectionate. Hans Mirtel Gerick named as executor (with Gerick's wife Katarina) his "trusty friend" John Hughes.[10] Marriages between members of opposite groups took place, though infrequently in the colonial years. There was a definite apartness, a sense of two communities living somewhat apart, though geographically mingled. Simply put, the situation was this: a member of one or the other camp tended to have much more extensive and intimate relations with speakers of his language group than with those of the opposite group. But he probably would be well-acquainted with neighbors belonging to the other group.

This major internal division of Oley Valley society was not based on language alone. It also had roots in the settlers' background and cultural orientation. Although there were exceptions, the "English people" who came to the Oley Valley were generally children of immigrants, sometimes grandchildren or even great-grandchildren. They were heirs, not just to the traditions of their European forebears, but to an evolving Delaware Valley culture (or central New Jersey culture, in some cases). The relative ease with which the Molatton Swedes fit into the valley's English-speaking community exemplifies the nature of that community as one composed largely of American-born people. The Swedes, like most of their English neighbors, had not had the experience of forsaking European homelands. Their parents, and they themselves, were participants in the creation of an American regional culture integrating elements from disparate European national and regional cultures, Lenape Indian lifeways, and responses to distinctly American conditions. This process had been advancing for a generation or more when settlement of the Oley Valley commenced. The minority of English-speakers who were immigrants were absorbed into the English community of the valley with little difficulty.

The Germans who came to the valley, on the other hand, were united in being immigrants, though a few had lived in Germantown, or elsewhere among the older Pennsylvania settlements, for some years. Although the need to learn "the ways of the country" must have been self-evident, and most of these pilgrims willing and eager to learn, the German settlers came to the Oley Valley as true Europeans.

There was also a geographical influence on the development of the valley's European community as one divided into social halves. The inhabitants of the northern valley were overwhelmingly German-speakers, while the southern part of the valley was home to significant numbers of both groups, living somewhat mingled. Hence, the upper valley was something of a German enclave. In the lower valley a German farmer was likely to have English neighbors, to have the nearest tavern run by an English person, or to worship in Molatton Church alongside English people. Even a northern valley German would have had a difficult time avoiding all contact with English people, however. The nearest justice of the peace, to whom the German speaker might have to go for a variety of purposes, such as obtaining a marriage license, would be English. The farmer probably would have had to go to an English person occasionally for some business reason, especially in the settlement's early decades, when the number of mills and craftsmen was limited.

Several powerful factors operated to keep the two language-defined communities apart. There was the language barrier itself. There were differences in lifeways that may well have made members of one group seem somewhat peculiar to members of the other. For example, most German settlers employed cast-iron stoves, fed with hot coals from the cooking hearth, to create a house environment much warmer than that in which their English neighbors resided. Some of the English in the valley did take up the use of stoves for heating late in the colonial period.

Religious observance was another strong factor keeping the two camps apart. The various churches and sects to which the valley's European inhabitants belonged were all naturally offshoots of churches and sects back in the European homelands. These faiths, such as German Lutheranism or British Quakerism, had evolved and been defined amidst conditions in particular nations. Church or meetinghouse was an important point of social contact, and the valley's religious gatherings were generally composed exclusively of English- or German-speakers. The one exception was Molatton Church, where German Lutherans cooperated with British Anglicans and Swedish Lutherans. Even there, in the 1750s, most German members withdrew to form a Lutheran congregation at New Store.

Although there was a basic separation between English and Germans, there was much contact across this invisible barrier. There were many differences in ways of doing things, but members of the two groups also had much in common. There does not seem to have been any real difference in economic orientation; the flour-export trade held equal attraction for English and German farmers. Historians of early Pennsylvania have often remarked on the immediacy with which almost all German immigrants seem to have taken to the dispersed-farmstead settlement pattern that was traditional to the colony's Swedish and British settlers. The Rhine Valley, from where most of the Germans had come, was dominated by a settlement pattern consisting of concentration in compact villages surrounded by open fields. In German-speaking Europe, the dispersed-farmstead (*Einzelhof*) settlement pattern had been confined to Switzerland and the hilliest areas of the Palatinate and the adjacent states.

The community life of the valley required English and German people to cooperate in a variety of areas. It provided many settings in which the two groups would naturally rub shoulders. English and German persons came together to form township government and to build new roads. When serving in a township post such as constable or tax collector, a man would be dealing with all his neighbors. Farmers and tradespeople of substance were frequently called on to serve on juries to review the course of a new road or to appraise the real estate of a man who had died intestate (i.e., without having made a will). These juries were usually of mixed composition.

People need social contact. At mills and taverns English and German patrons would mingle. A wedding or a funeral in

COMMUNITY

rural colonial Pennsylvania generally was attended by practically all the people living within a given distance. Many contemporaries have commented on the mixing of nationalities and religious groups at these occasions. At the 1753 funeral for Philip Beyer, Heinrich Melchior Muhlenberg followed his German sermon with an English one due to the presence of many of Beyer's English neighbors.

Gottlieb Mittelberger, organist and schoolmaster at Muhlenberg's home congregation (the Augustus Church at Trappe) from 1750 to 1754, noted the social importance of funerals in regional society.

> At times at such formal country weddings or funerals, it is possible to count up to four hundred or five hundred persons on horseback.... When someone has died, especially in the country, where people live far apart from one another, separated by plantations and forests, the actual time of burial is first announced only to the four closest neighbors of the deceased, each of whom in turn passes the information along to his closest neighbor. In such a manner the news of that kind of a funeral spreads through a radius of more than fifty English miles within twenty-four hours. Then, whenever possible, each family sends at least one representative, riding on horseback, to the funeral at the proper time. While these people are assembling, those present are handed pieces of good cake on a large tin platter. Aside from that everyone gets a goblet of well-warmed West Indian rum, to which are added lemons, sugar, and juniper berries, which makes a good combination. After this the guests are also offered warmed sweet cider.... When almost all the people are there and the time of the funeral approaches, the corpse is carried to the general burial ground. When that is too far away, burial takes place in the dead person's own field. Those people who have previously assembled ride silently behind the coffin.[11]

Exeter Friends, considering the state of the meeting in 1756, had to admit that

> Some amongst us have been guilty of the unnecessary frequenting of taverns, and some of drinking to excess; and some we fear have taken too great latitude in making entertainments at marriages and burials as well as upon some other occasions.[12]

Muhlenberg noted with disapprobation the fondness of most of the Swedish and English parishioners of Molatton Church for "*Fressen, Saufen, Tanzen,*"[13] and the alarming contagion of this way of life among Molatton vicinity Germans. ("Gorging, drinking, [and] dancing" was a phrase frequently applied by pietists when referring to the frivolity of worldly people.) A variety of social recreations were popular, especially contests of skill such as horse races and shooting matches, which young Exeter Meeting Quakers several times faced communal discipline for attending. The urge to have the best possible competition would have made these contests multinational gatherings.

Language, after all, was not an impenetrable barrier. Most male valley landowners (English and German) were literate. About half the document signatures made by German citizens of the colonial Oley Valley were in English script rather than in Old German script. This high proportion, much larger than that in exclusively German districts of the county, implies that many Germans were acquiring at least the rudiments of English. It appears that the presence of a sizable number of settlers of British heritage did have some effect on the extent to which their German neighbors learned English. Of German women's linguistic attainments little is known. Most, evidently illiterate, affixed marks to their deeds and wills, as did most English women.

The onus of learning an unfamiliar tongue was on the Germans. The legal language of the province was English, some mastery of which must have appeared essential to any person with aspirations to be a man of affairs. There is no hard evidence that the English people in the valley shook off their then oft-remarked stubbornness regarding the learning of foreign languages. But some Anglo-American lawyers and officials in Reading, the county seat, did so. The frequency of contact should have imparted knowledge of at least a little spoken German to many English people. It would have behooved an English miller or tanner who wanted his German neighbors' business to study German.

Schools built and supervised by Oley Valley residents probably provided rudimentary exposure to English for many German children, depending on the language skills of the schoolmasters serving at a given time. English children could have absorbed some German at the "English German school" begun in southwestern Amity Township in 1774, a notable example of cooperation between the nationalities.[14] The eight neighbors serving as trustees in 1774 included four Germans, three English persons, and a Swede. This school was exceptional for not being attached to a local religious body. Probably all the local churches and the Exeter Meeting conducted schools during the final two decades of the colonial era (1755-1775). Interruptions due to lack of suitable masters appear to have been fairly frequent, however.

Little is known about what subjects were taught, or how, in Pennsylvania country schools of the period, about how the parents' economic means may have affected a child's ability to attend, or about attitudes regarding the schooling of girls. Many colonial-period wills from the valley charged widows with the responsibility of "educating the children," but only those of farmer Peter Jones (1772) and miller John Sands (1774) gave more explicit directions. Jones ordered that his son Ezekiel should have two years' schooling at the estate's expense before the boy was bound to a trade of Ezekiel's choice. Sands's granddaughter Susanna was to attend school "until she can read and write."

Conspicuous consumption was a form of communication with no language barrier. Imported goods were mostly British in origin. The gentry of the province, concentrated in Philadelphia and environs, were mostly of English heritage. The few Pennsylvania Germans of similar status tended to follow the lead of their English fellows in matters of fashion. These people set styles, some of which not only the ironmasters and biggest landowners of the valley but also the more prosperous among the farmers and tradespeople could emulate. In the late colonial years, tea services generally appeared in the estate inventories of more substantial citizens, whether English or German. Such imported innovations in ways of living, shared by members of both groups, could have made people seem less foreign to each other, at least among the better-off citizens in the valley.

The considerable contact between English- and German-speaking people was generally of an amicable, cordial character. Helping to make it so was the pervasive influence of the then-powerful ethic of "neighboring." A good neighbor is still appreciated today, but it is difficult to convey the importance that this virtual institution held for the rural inhabitants of colonial Pennsylvania. It was considered one's duty to act as a safeguard for the well-being of one's neighbors. This function took on a quasi-legal status. It was not happenstance that a neighbor from within two properties' distance almost always was among the witnesses to an ailing man's will or among the appraisers of a deceased man's estate. Attorney Edward Biddle led off his successful summation of the case against the deathbed will of Benjamin Longworthy, which would have kept the latter's young slaves in bondage, with the assertion that "Not one of his neighbors [was] a witness to his will."[15] That alone called the will into question. Two of Englishman Longworthy's three immediate landowning neighbors, who were all Germans, were summoned to testify in the case.

Relations between neighbors could go sour, and such feuding was likely to be particularly bitter. But these squabbles were the exception to the rule. For "neighboring" to function, a family had to maintain good relations with other households in its proximity. This in turn ensured good general relations between German- and English-speakers. The safety or well-being of one, or of one's family, might someday depend on this person so different from oneself. Attendance at a neighbor family's wedding or funeral takes on added importance when viewed in this light. "Paying respects" mattered.

OLEY VALLEY HERITAGE

LOCAL GOVERNMENT

Discussion of government in the colonial Oley Valley must begin with the township. The township was the form of immediate local government decreed in William Penn's charter for his colony. If citizens were to have the king's peace upheld in their community, the poor cared for, stray livestock controlled, or public roads provided and maintained, they had to form a township. Then they would have a constable, a tax collector, a supervisor of highways, a keeper of the pound (an official who rounded up and secured stray livestock), and an overseer of the poor. A road was the ultimate goal for the "several inhabitants of Oley" who petitioned the Philadelphia County Court of Quarter Sessions in 1735 for the creation of a new township in the area between Amity Township and New Hanover Township. "Nothing as yet has been done [about the desired road] because no overseers have been as yet appointed . . . although there is at least thirty families settled on the said land."[16] The township was granted, and named "Douglass."

Amity Township was the first one in the Oley Valley. It was created by the year 1716 as a township of Philadelphia County. (Berks County came into existence in 1752.) Before the creation of Oley Township in 1722, the names Amity and Manatawny were used interchangeably by both officials and laymen. Afterward, "Manatawny" was used for a time in referring to the overall Oley Valley settlement.[17] Amity probably was named either for the good relations among the settlers, who were of many different nationalities, or for the origin of the Swedes' Tract, the ten-thousand-acre grant that was the root of the first settlement of the valley. William Penn had given the tract to a group of Swedish colonists in 1701 in an attempt to restore amicable relations between the English and the Swedes. The Swedes had complained that grasping proprietary officials had defrauded them of much of the original land (located in the Philadelphia vicinity) that they had received from their old colonial government.

Township government was a zealously sought, and jealously guarded, privilege. The township provided services, such as roads and crime control, but these required taxes and, probably more onerous, labor. Any suitable man, generally a young one but of adequate means, was liable to serve in township office. The constable, the overseer of the poor, and (until 1762) the supervisor of highways were appointed by the justices of the county court; the tax collector, by the county commissioners. The keeper of the pound was elected in an annual township meeting, as well as the supervisors of highways after 1762.

The qualification to vote in colonial Pennsylvania was ownership of fifty acres of land, with twelve acres cleared, or of personal property worth £50. Most heads of households could meet these standards. The term for all township offices was one year, and only hardship could excuse one from service. The officer received a small stipend not commensurate with the hours worked or the miles traveled. Appointment to a township post was no doubt more annoyance than boon to a busy young farmer or craftsman, unless (what was unlikely) he had ambitions regarding county-level office, in which case township-level experience was almost prerequisite. A township official was liable to a stiff fine if the county justices determined that he had been negligent in the performance of duty. This happened to Amity Supervisor of Highways Johannes Lorah, and Exeter Supervisors of Highways George Henton and George Carey in 1767, to Amity Constable Isaac Boone and Exeter Constable Johannes Bishop in 1770, and to Exeter supervisors of highways Abraham Lincoln and Peter Schneider in 1771. As for the much-sought roads, until 1762 their construction and maintenance was the work of the entire community, as supervised by the road overseers. Each land owner contributed two days of road work per year.

As settlement progressed, filling the valley itself and proceeding to climb up into the surrounding hills, there arose a trend toward defining permanent boundaries for the townships. By so doing, a limit was fixed on the taxes, labor, and travel necessitated by township governmental activities. There was a period of a few years, approximately the late 1730s and early 1740s, during which longer-established valley floor residents in effect provided township services for their lately-arrived hill country neighbors.

COMMUNITY

Amity Township always was defined officially as having the same bounds as the original Swedes' Tract of 1701. However, the early tax, road, and land records show that, in practice, before 1735, Amity also took in the southern part of what became Douglass Township, and before 1741, the southern part of Exeter Township. At first, even the settlers on the Chester County bank of the Schuylkill River, a narrow strip of valley land, counted themselves, and paid taxes, as citizens of Amity Township, Philadelphia County. They were cut off from the heart of Chester County by the "rocks and mountains"[18] to their south, with no road through to the main Chester County settlements. Most of them worshiped at Molatton Church in Amity, and they all considered themselves part of the Amity community. In 1723, though, jealous Chester justices lassoed them, and thereafter they were counted in Chester County (in Coventry Township) until Berks County was created in 1752. As for Oley Township in its first years (around 1722-1740), it appears that it included everything in the Oley Valley north of Amity. Until 1740, Oley Township lacked a definite boundary.

Between about 1716 and 1722, Amity was the only township, and evidently whatever governmental functions happened in any part of the valley during those pioneer days did so under the auspices of Amity. In 1720 thirty-two "inhabitants of Oley" made petition to the Philadelphia County Court of Quarter Sessions for a township for the northern half of the valley. The upper valley was now "pretty thick settled . . . and the distance and extent . . . makes it very inconvenient and too large to be comprehended in one township and therefore it's hoped for the conveniency of the inhabitants the said request may be granted."[19] The central concern here was "the conveniency of the inhabitants" (i.e., the distance an official would have to travel to perform a duty, or perhaps the distance one would have to travel to get the constable's assistance). The court created Oley Township in 1722.

The years 1740 through 1745 were transforming ones for the governmental structure of the valley. During those years the Philadelphia County segment of the rich valley floor (some 90 percent of it) was carved into three townships with defined boundaries. It is not a coincidence that in 1741 and 1742 Philadelphia County created the first public roads crossing over the Oley Hills from the Oley Valley eastward to the Colebrookdale and Goshenhoppen vicinities. With the better low-lying lands of eastern Berks County pretty much taken up, settlers were moving into hill country such as that of present-day District, Earl, and Pike townships, through which these roads ran. This was land of marginal value at best. The people claiming it were people of marginal economic status, immigrants not as well provided for as those who had taken up the excellent lands of the Oley Valley earlier. The logical course for better-off new arrivals was westward across southern Pennsylvania, or down into western Maryland and Virginia, to reach newly opened lands of high quality.

The new settlements in the hills to the west, north, and east of the valley needed township services, and the valley townships' lack of effective boundaries seemed to invite requests for such services. The valley people quickly responded by correcting the earlier omission of set boundaries. Paying township taxes and having the money spent for the distant hill settlements was "inconvenient," not to mention having to journey up there to perform a constable's duties. Gone was the easygoing attitude that extended Amity Township's *de facto* scope to include an area twice the size of the Swedes' Tract. The first action taken was to define the bounds of Oley Township, in September 1740. The Philadelphia County Court did so in answer to a petition, by fifty-three Oley inhabitants, stating that "they had petitioned this court about fifteen years past for a township which was granted by the name of Oley, but the bounds thereof were never yet ascertained."[20]

The next step was the erection of Exeter Township a year or so later, December 1741. Seventeen "inhabitants of the south part of Oley" had brought a petition to the court bemoaning that "more than fifty families were left out" of Oley Township.[21] The new township included that area outside and to the west of the proper bounds of Amity Township that had been administered as if it were in Amity. The name Exeter was chosen in deference to the Boone family, so influential in the affairs of that part of the valley, who hailed from the vicinity of the town of Exeter in Devonshire, England.

Last came certification of the boundaries of Amity Township in March 1745. The boundaries were established as those of the original Swedes' Tract. Neither the Philadelphia County Court's clerks nor the concerned settlers could find any documents related to the township's erection or its boundaries. The petition in this instance asserted that "by reason of large bodies of land that lie without the bounds of the said ten thousand acres [the Swedes' Tract], not as yet erected into any township," "we have suffered great hardships and they are like still to continue."[22] This is no doubt a reference to the hill people's annoying demand for township service. The Amity people's request was granted, and not until after the creation of Berks County in 1752 would the hill country itself receive township government.

Township constables and overseers carried out most of the day-to-day drudgery of local government. There was another level to local administration, though, that of the county, which encompassed the townships. County officials included the sheriff (chief officer for law enforcement), the coroner (then an assistant to the sheriff whose duties included the supervision of juries investigating cause of death), three commissioners (supervisors of taxation), six tax assessors, the treasurer, and the clerkships of the five county courts (generally held by just one man).

The most important local office was that of justice of the peace. Sitting in aggregate as the county court, the resident justices of the peace ran county government. They supervised the other county officers and the township officers in their duties, in addition to being the judges in the legal system. The justices had the ultimate power of decision on the creation of townships and roads. There was no set number of justices per county, rather there were as many as the population seemed to require and the governor deemed worthy of appointment. Nor was there any set geographical zoning for their distribution, but they seem to have been stationed so that every locality had one.

Besides his duties at the county seat, a justice of the peace had other responsibilities of a less formal, more localized sort. He issued arrest warrants to constables, and organized posses, if the king's peace was threatened. Sitting alone, he gave judgment over civil cases involving small claims. He certified deeds and issued marriage licenses, a lucrative business. Justices were usually well off to begin with, men of experience and ability. Personal connections played a role in their selection too, though, as the justiceship of the peace was a post appointed by the governor.

Crime did raise its head in the valley from time to time. Theft occurred. A 1773 court of quarter sessions condemned John Kerr for stealing miller John Sands's silver watch (valued at £5). Sands got his watch back; Kerr still had it when he was caught. Kerr had to pay a fine of £5, and to receive twenty-one "lashes on the bare back, well laid on, tomorrow between the hours of ten and twelve in the forenoon at the public whipping post,"[23] in Reading.

The Oley Valley received its first justice appointment, that of George Boone, Jr., in 1728. Boone served the valley alone until 1745 (except for a brief period, 1733-1736, when his friend Mordecai Lincoln occupied a justice's post until Lincoln's death). In 1745 Boone was joined by fellow Exeter Meeting member Anthony Lee, and from then through 1775, there were always at least two justices resident in the valley.

Following the creation of Berks County in 1752, and until 1761, there were four Oley Valley justices, more than necessary for the valley. Evidently senior provincial officials tended to prejudice against German settlers' participation in government at the higher levels. This anti-German attitude hung on, though weakening, through the remainder of the colonial period. In 1752, only two of Berks County's twelve justices of the peace were of German origin, and in 1775 still only four of fourteen. The Oley Valley had a disproportionate share of Berks County's small English-speaking element, though by 1752 valley people of British Isles origins were outnumbered by Germans by a noticeable margin.

As the result of the provincial establishment's tendency toward the exclusion of Germans from office, the English people of the Oley Valley enjoyed a brief "golden period" of political leadership in Berks County during the 1750s and early 1760s. During the Philadelphia County years, they had been too far from the center of political activity, and comparatively too low in socioeconomic status to make more than a ripple in the political pond, aside perhaps from George Boone, Jr. Their brief surge in the early Berks County years applied to elected offices, such as those of sheriff, coroner, and commissioner, as well as appointed ones like that of justice of the peace. During the years 1752-1767, Oley Valley Englishmen (a group numbering five percent or so of the county's population) served ten of the county's thirty-six justice terms, four of the fifteen sheriff terms, six of the fifteen coroner terms, and twenty of the forty-five commissioner terms.

For their part, German-speaking Berks Countians appear to have submitted contentedly to government by their English neighbors, endorsing the latter's leadership with their votes. Until late in the colonial years, rural Pennsylvania Germans had little tendency to seek office compared to that of their British countrymen. Most men who ran successfully for the more important county offices were encouraged and aided by powerful province-level political interests. Relatively wealthy men tended to seek and win these offices (and at this time comparatively few Berks Germans had this relative wealth). The four Oley Valley Germans who served as Philadelphia County assessors (1743-1752), and the three who attained county-level political office higher than that of assessor during the Berks County phase of the colonial period (1752-1775), were all among the more prosperous people in the valley. These were Johannes Lesher (assessor 1743-1745), Abraham Levan (assessor 1746-1750), Samuel Guldin (assessor 1750-1751), Isaac Levan (assessor 1751-1752), Jacob Weber (sheriff 1759-1761 and 1763-1765), Samuel Hoch (commissioner 1760-1762), and Jacob Schneider (commissioner 1768-1771).

English-speaking men related to or connected with George Boone, Jr., seem to have constituted a local political network in the 1750s and 1760s. Boone himself retired from his justiceship in 1749 and died in 1753. His "loving friend" Mordecai Lincoln had served beside him as justice during the years 1733-1736. Active in the early Berks County years were George Boone, Jr.'s brother James (justice 1752-1761, delegate to the provincial assembly 1758-1759); George Boone, Jr.'s son William (coroner 1752-1755, sheriff 1755-1757); George Boone, Jr.'s son-in-law John Hughes (collector of excise 1752-1763, commissioner 1762-1763); William Boone's brother-in-law Thomas Lincoln (son of Mordecai), sheriff 1757-1759; George Boone, Jr.'s probable cousin William Maugridge (justice 1752-1766); and Maugridge's son-in-law Edward Drury (commissioner 1752-1756). Anthony Lee, like George Boone, Jr., a prominent member of Exeter Friends Meeting, was the Oley Valley's other justice of the peace beginning in 1745. He continued in the post until 1761.

During this period, which was also that of the French and Indian War (1754-1763), Pennsylvania's politicians were divided into two factions, the Proprietary party and the Quaker party. (Neither of these would qualify as a "party" in the sense of our modern Republicans and Democrats.) The Boone clique was aligned with the Quaker party, which accused Proprietary officials of seeking to establish mandatory militia service for all citizens. Quakers, and many Berks Germans, were committed pacifists, while British and Provincial troops waged war on the Pennsylvania frontier against Indian tribes allied with France. A letter from Proprietary supporter Conrad Weiser to Proprietary Secretary Richard Peters sheds some light on the Berks election of October 1755. During colonial times, the county election was held in Reading, and citizens had to journey there to vote. The procedure in colonial Pennsylvania, in electing sheriffs, was for the voter to cast ballots for *two* candidates. Then the two names with the most votes were submitted to the governor, who had the privilege of ultimate selection. Governors almost always chose the one with the most votes, however, as happened in this instance. The office of county sheriff was fought over with special vehemence by the two factions because sheriffs oversaw the election process. Weiser described this election as follows:

> I attended once more an election in this town in order to assist my friend Jonas Seely [an ironmaster from southern Berks] to get the sheriff's office. But he lost it notwithstanding the whole body of people seemed to be for him when

they came to town. But the opposite party went about to almost every man and reported that Jonas Seely was a Governor's man and did associate [i.e., join in forming a militia organization] with the people of Reading and exercised them but a few days ago, that he would certainly bring things about that they must all take up a musket and exercise, which our foolish Germans did believe, without any further consideration, and turned against Seely so that William Boone and John Hughes are upon the returns. The latter was but a few votes before Seely. A great many people are sorry for the foolish behavior of the Germans and would be pleased to give the sheriff's office to John Hughes in order to bring that spiteful little fellow William Boone to some disappointment.[24]

The vestry of Saint Gabriel's Church may have been another center of influence in local politics during the colonial era, perhaps with some association with the Boone clique. Molatton vestrymen active in government included, besides Boone relations Maugridge and Drury, William Bird (justice 1752-1761), Bird's son Mark (justice 1770-1776), John Godfrey (commissioner 1752-1761), John Warren (coroner 1758-1760), and George Douglass (justice 1764-1776). The officeholding by these men may simply reflect the tendency for positions to go to the English and the prosperous, rather than a role for Saint Gabriel's as a local link in a system of political patronage.

Men following certain commercial occupations had some tendency to fill county-level office. Such was the case for millers George Boone, Jr., William Boone, and Joseph Millard (justice 1761-1770), storekeepers George Douglass and Edward Drury, and innholder-tanner John Hughes. Their businesses, with people coming and going constantly, no doubt provided them with the political gossip of the county and province, made them widely known in the community, encouraged sociability on their part, and served as easily found locations at which to transact official business.

COMMUNITY

STOLEN

Samuel Hoch in Oley in Berks County makes known, that on the morning of Sept. 10, 1759, a red-colored stallion was stolen out of the stable, a driving or wagon horse, which was still fairly fresh. The said stallion is 12 years old, has a white tail and mane, is shod in front, 15 hands tall, is unusually well set and strong, and is branded on the left rear shank with a very large and distinct S H, so that one can see it well 10 rods distant. One supposes, that the one who has stolen it, is the one who has recently broken out of jail in Reading, on whom the sheriff has already put 10 or 15 pounds reward. His name is David Jones, he is about 25 years old, 6 feet tall, is clean of countenance, and dresses himself neatly; also wears at times a peruke with a long plait of hair, also speaks a little German. Whoever takes up and keeps the said stallion and thief, so that one can have them, shall have 5 pounds, or for the stallion alone 3 pounds, from me, SAMUEL HOCH
—*Pennsylvanische Berichte*, September 28, 1759

ROAD AND RIVER

One chief task of government in colonial times was the provision of the best possible means of transportation. An Oley Valley farmer might not devote much of his attention to great issues deliberated at the State House in Philadelphia, but he knew that roads mattered. Rural Pennsylvania was a prosperous place by the standards of the Western world in that age. Flour made from wheat, and exported to the Caribbean, New England, the British Isles, and Spain and Portugal, was the basis of this prosperity. Huge quantities of wheat had to be moved from farm to gristmill, and huge quantities of flour from mill to market.

The first of many petitions for roads drafted by citizens of the Oley Valley, made in 1717, was clear about the nature of the problem:

> Your petitioners having for some years labored under the necessity of convenient roads to the market and corn mills, which hath rendered their passing much more dangerous and troublesome than otherwise it would be, . . . a road should be laid out to the King's Road to Philadelphia, and one to Schuylkill over against the Swedes' Tract in the most convenient place for repairing to Thomas Miller's [Millard's] mill.[25]

The need to travel to "mill and market" long remained a common theme in petitions for roads. Churches and meetinghouses were sometimes road petition targets, though three of the valley's six colonial religious gatherings (Molatton, Schwarzwald, and New Store) were established at existing road junctions.

The need for roads was not only economic but also social. Our forebears evidently got around a good bit more than generally thought. In 1725 a group of Oley Valley settlers first presented an ambitious plan (then refused) to the Philadelphia County Court for a road that would go from the Schuylkill River through the Oley Valley to Colebrookdale Furnace, and then on to northern Bucks County. Among other justifications, the proposed road would "be very beneficial to those great numbers of people that are settled amongst us from the Jerseys, Esopus [today the vicinity of Kingston, New York], Albany, etc., and are of times agoing between those their present settlements and their former habitations."[26] Even with a good horse, to go from Oley to Albany, New York, must have been a considerable undertaking. It is likely that long-range visiting took place over the winter, when most people had less work to do.

There was probably also a good deal of short-range travel for other than business reasons. By the late colonial years, many families had relatives living in one or more of the neighboring localities of Maiden Creek, Moselem, Maxatawny, the Oley Hills, Goshenhoppen, and Colebrookdale, as well as (beginning in 1751) the town of Reading. The first three of the preceding communities were to some degree offspring of the Oley Valley settlement, with many first-generation Oley Valley children numbering among their pioneers. Reading also drew valley people to quarterly court sessions, semian-

OLEY VALLEY HERITAGE

nual fairs (starting in 1766), and annual elections. Before the existence of Reading (the first houses in the town went up in 1751), people occasionally visited Germantown and Philadelphia. The latter city was the county seat for Philadelphia County, and so was where most Oley Valley people went to vote prior to 1752. Eight Oley people contributed to a subscription in 1738 to build a new Lutheran church in Germantown, and Philadelphia was the necessary resort for business concerning land, estates, and the law.

Roads did not come free. They were paid for with labor until 1762, and afterward with revenue. In fact, the Philadelphia County justices maintained a conservative attitude about road creation throughout the period during which they had oversight over the Oley Valley. They refrained from ordering new roads unless they were certain that enough people lived in the area through which the road was to pass so that it would receive proper maintenance. A group of inhabitants from Oley and Tulpehocken made petition in 1727 for a road from the "Lutheran Meeting House at Tulpehocken" to "the High Road from Oley to Philadelphia" (via ferry over the Schuylkill). They included among their arguments one that posited that, "as a great part of the land [is] at present not settled through which the hereby petitioned road is naturally designed to go . . . there will be no opposition made in the laying it out."[27] As will be seen, disputes over damage to people's land by roads *was* a problem. But maintaining the road seemed a bigger problem to the Philadelphia County Court without workers in the empty Exeter area (in which lay much of the proposed route). The petition was denied.

The most important early roads were all either delayed or reduced in length from the original request, and in some cases both. A perhaps extreme but illustrative example is the road that went from Finney's Ferry (now Reading) to New Store (Amityville), where it connected with the High Road from Oley to Philadelphia (Route 662). First known as the High (or Great) Road from Tulpehocken to Philadelphia, it became before long the High Road from Reading to Philadelphia. This highway was not granted until 1736, eleven years after the first petition. The petitions from 1725 and 1727 cited above are but two variations among the *five* it took to get this road. The Philadelphia County Court refused it repeatedly, evidently because of the lack of inhabitants. The Exeter area filled with homesteads much later than Oley and Amity townships, evidently due to its farther distance from Philadelphia and lesser desirability of soil. Even in 1736, the ambitious target of two of the petitions (1725 and 1736), for the road to extend from present-day Stonersville past Colebrookdale Furnace to northern Bucks County, was turned down. This would have required the justices to put a road through another area still thinly settled (southern Earl and northern Douglass townships today). Such a road had to wait until 1752, another sixteen years.

There were unofficial roads as well as publicly maintained ones, tracks running through districts with few settlers. These were no doubt often based on Indian trails and were only as smooth as the repeated application of boot, horseshoe, and cartwheel could make them. For example, the stretch of road described above, denied in 1736 but granted in 1752, *was* traveled as an unofficial route during the interim and probably earlier.

Such roads of happenstance and footwear must have made tough traveling, as the inadequacy even of the official highways was frequently remarked on by travelers. The leading Lutheran minister Heinrich Melchior Muhlenberg added Molatton Church to his many pastoral responsibilities during the years 1748-1752. He lived at Trappe, sixteen miles farther down in Philadelphia County. Muhlenberg gave service to Molatton only from April through November, "since the impassable roads . . . make visitation impossible during the winter."[28]

For most of the colonial period in Pennsylvania, the maintenance of the road system was the direct responsibility of the populace. A township supervisor of highways, appointed by the county justices, directed the statutory (and unavoidable) labor of the local men. Each property owner was required to provide two days' road labor per annum. In 1762 the road maintenance procedure was completely overhauled. Thenceforward a township road tax was levied, two supervisors of highways were elected rather than appointed in each township, and the statutory labor requirement was abolished. The township hired laborers to maintain the roads instead. The reform of 1762 was evidently a response to the ongoing flour industry boom that had taken off in the late 1740s. Better roads were desired; hence a more efficient maintenance system was needed. Those farmers who were raising large wheat crops for the market were willing to pay a road tax to obtain better roads. The hiring of township road workers from among the then-increasing body of landless men also saved the wheat farmers the two days' labor that would otherwise have been tapped for the roads.

An alternative to road travel was the Schuylkill River. This water route antedated any land one; the Swedes, the first European settlers, were nautical people. A descendant of the Molatton Swedes recalled in the early 1800s what he had heard from his grandmother, Magdalena Huling Holstein. "They then did all their traveling by canoes, on the Schuylkill. When married, she and her wedding friends came down to Swedes Ford, in their canoes. In the same manner they always made their visits to Philadelphia."[29] The British settlers of Amity and Exeter quickly adopted the use of these "canoes," probably instructed in watercraft by their friends the Swedes.

"Canoe" is evidently a misnomer. These vessels probably were Scandinavian-derived boats with "double ends" (i.e., with a stern similar to the bow instead of having a right-angled shape). According to Richard Hulan, an authority on the material culture of the Delaware Valley Swedes, the term "canoe" was used in common parlance because of this superficial resemblance to the double-ended Lenape Indian canoe.[30] The colonists in the lower Oley Valley employed these boats to haul substantial loads of wheat and flour. Ironmaster William Bird was using "canoes" in 1760 to move loads of iron on the river. Canoes such as those built by the region's Indians would not have had the necessary capacity.

The Schuylkill had its limitations. The river's shallow depth and rock-studded bed made it navigable only when freshets (i.e., rain- or thaw-fed waterflows that came mainly at springtime) raised the water level above normal. As laden boats could not run the river at most times, those who preferred that mode of transport generally had to wait a period. In 1774 Amity miller John Sands was partner in a "lot of land, storehouse and boat

144

COMMUNITY

on the Schuylkill,"[31] probably at George Douglass's store by Saint Gabriel's Church at Molatton. Sands's mill was four miles from the river. He moved his flour to the storehouse, then waited for the right moment to dispatch it downriver.

Besides the natural impediments to river-borne travel, there were those of human origin. People living on the Schuylkill below the Berks County area made weirs and dams to aid in catching fish. They were most active, and their works most prominent, when the shad ran in the early spring, just when freshets made the Schuylkill high enough for navigation with much greater consistency and predictability than at any other time of year. These weirs greatly exacerbated the trickiness and hazard of running the river. In March 1732 thirteen Swedes and Englishmen from the lower Oley Valley made depositions before Justice George Boone, Jr., "touching some of the hazards and hardships by them sustained, on fish dams and racks in the Schuylkill."

> Marcus Huling saith, that as he was going down Schuylkill with a canoe loaded with wheat, that striking on a fish dam, she took in a great deal of water into the wheat, by means whereof his wheat was much damaged, and that it was in great danger of being all lost. . . .
> Jonas Jones saith, that in the month of February it being extreme cold, he struck fast on a fish dam, and to save his load of wheat was obliged to leap into the river to the middle of his body, and with all his labor and skill could not get off in less than half an hour. Afterwards proceeding on his journey with the said wet clothes, they were frozen stiff on his back, by means whereof he underwent a great deal of misery. . . .
> Isaac Smally saith, that going down the said river with 140 bushels of wheat in a canoe, they struck fast on a rack dam, and in order to save the load from being all lost, he was, much against his mind, obliged to leap into the river. The water, being to his chin, frequently dashed into his mouth, [so that only] between whiles he breathed, and both he and his partner held the canoe with great labor, whilst a young man there present ran above a mile to call help to get off. . . .
> Jonas Yocom and Richard Dunklin say, that they got fast on a fish dam with their canoe loaded with 60 bushels of wheat, and the said Dunklin's wife and a young child in the canoe, and were for more than an hour in great danger of being overset into the river, where if they had, undoubtedly the woman and child would have been lost. . . .
> George Boone, John Boone, Joseph Boone, James Boone, and Samuel Boone say, that they have been sundry times fast on the said fish dams and rack dams, and to preserve the loads of wheat have been forced several times to leap into the river, and have very narrowly escaped with their lives and loads.[32]

The presence of George Boone, Jr.'s father and four of his brothers among the men whose depositions the justice sent to the governor's council, suggests that Boone already had determined to put a stop to weir fishing on the Schuylkill. The practice had been outlawed by the provincial assembly in 1730.

The struggle between the upcountry people and the fishermen went on through the eighteenth century, apparently never resolved until settled by a permanent dearth of fish. The issue involved both government's duty to ensure the best possible means of transportation and its duty to make just settlement of disputes between citizens. In colonial Pennsylvania, where the scope of the government's activities was somewhat limited, transportation was a major object for official attention. The supervision of the road system was ultimately the responsibility of the county justices, and they spent much of their time in court considering and acting on proposed roads. The need for better means to move goods and people led to frequent disputes between individuals and the larger community. Everyone wanted roads; no one (except tavernkeepers, millers, and the like) wanted them running across his property.

Such disputes could arise between different communities, as happened in the long-lived contest between the lower Oley Valley people and the fishermen. A struggle between two localities was the most intractable sort. The government of the province was neither a successful arbiter nor an effective ruler. "The powers that be" recognized that the business of Pennsylvania was wheat, not shad. Both the executive and the legislative branches placed their weight nominally on the side of the upland people, but this weight was not of adequate tonnage. The assembly passed an ordinance banning "weirs, dams, etc. within the Schuylkill" in 1730. Still, in 1734, petitions arrived at the State House complaining that "notwithstanding the laws already made to the contrary, the navigation of the River Schuylkill is still obstructed by weirs, racks and other devices for catching fish, . . . from whence . . . have arisen many enmities, breaches of the peace, and troublesome suits at law."[33] In response the assembly approved what seemed a stronger anti-weir law. All such measures came to naught, however. The fishermen's local authorities were on their side, and evidently this was what counted. In colonial Pennsylvania, the most effective governmental power may well have been that exercised by local officials.

In 1738 a frustrated Justice George Boone, Jr., took on the fishermen alone, acting in his community's interest, and lost. Boone lacked the support of his counterparts from the fishermen's neighborhood, and perhaps had those officers' active opposition instead. William Richard, who was constable for Amity Township at the time, told the story in a deposition before the governor's council:

> On the twentieth day of this instant, April, he received a warrant from George Boone, Esq., one of His Majesty's justices of the peace of the county [of Philadelphia], requiring him . . . to take to his assistance such persons as this deponent should think proper, and go down the river Schuylkill and remove all such obstructions as should be found in the river. In obedience to which warrant this deponent took several persons . . . as his assistants, and together with one Robert Smith, constable of the Township of Oley, who had received a warrant to the same purpose, went down the river in three

canoes, to Mingo Creek [French Creek?] where they found a large number of racks and obstructions in the river, and saw four men upon an island near the racks. This deponent and company removed the racks without any opposition. From thence they proceeded down the river to the mouth of Pickering's Creek, near which they found several racks which reached across the river to an island, which racks this deponent and company also removed. Immediately after the racks were removed, about the number of two hundred men came down on both sides of the river, and were very rude and abusive, and threatened this deponent and his company. The deponent expecting from the ill language and threats given that some mischief or a quarrel would ensue, he took his staff in his hand and his warrant and commanded the men in the King's name to keep the peace, and told them that he came there, in a peaceable manner and according to law, to move the racks and obstructions in the river. Upon which some of the men damned the laws and the law makers, and cursed this deponent and his assistants. One James Starr knocked this deponent down in the river with a large club or stake, after which several of the men attacked this deponent and company with large clubs, and knocked down the said Robert Smith, the constable, as also several of this deponent's assistants. One John Wainwright, in company with this deponent, was struck down with a pole or staff, and lay as dead with his body on the shore and his feet in the river. This deponent and company finding that they were not able to make resistance, were obliged to make their best of their way in order to save their lives.[34]

The injured Wainwright recovered. Among the "company" were Timothy and Benjamin Millard, sons of the Oley Valley's first miller Thomas Millard, who lived on the Chester County side of the Schuylkill and thus were outside Justice Boone's jurisdiction. They were not liable to be ordered to participate in the weir-removal posse, hence their willing presence suggests that the cause was a popular one in the lower Oley Valley.

There was much anti-fishing bluster by the governor and assembly in the aftermath of this riot. The following spring the weirs and dams were there, and so every spring through the remainder of the century. The fishing-weir controversy was not an issue so vital that it prodded the provincial authorities to make the fishermen's local officials toe the mark instead of protecting them. After all, a great deal of the Oley Valley's wheat, flour, and iron managed to get down the river.

Government was more effective in sorting out transportation-related disputes that cropped up *within* the Oley Valley. Citizens routinely appeared before the county court of quarter sessions to protest condemnation of their land as road right-of-way. Proprietor William Penn had specifically allowed a 6-percent addition to every land purchase (one paid for one hundred acres but received one hundred and six) in an effort to ameliorate such damage before it occurred. Still, if one could prove to a jury's satisfaction that the injury to one's holdings was greater than could be covered by the six percent, one would receive an award. This happened frequently. In a typical example from 1769, Johannes Kerlin of Amity and Peter Haas of Union protested the new road that ran through their lands. Kerlin claimed that he would "sustain great damage" because the road ran through his "improved lands the distance of between seventy and eighty perches."[35] (A "perch," synonymous with a rod, is sixteen and one half feet.) Haas complained that the road went through his orchard and meadow. A jury awarded Kerlin £36 15s and Haas £10.

Land owners wanted to avoid having roads run across their properties, unless they ran the sort of service or retail business for which a highway's proximity would be an asset. Not having a public road meant all of the land could be used as the owner saw fit, including that 6 percent bonus. The owner would not have the road surveyors determining that the best course ran through an orchard that had only recently been created. The owner would not have to build long, additional fences to ensure that herded animals did not ruin the crops. The ongoing patrons of a "customary" road, a track through an area theretofore unsettled, often petitioned for their route to be taken on the public charge once newly established homesteaders commenced putting up barriers to their passage.

Lack of courtesy by one's neighbors could be a serious problem, as Anders Lycon found. Unfortunately for Lycon, "an ancient Swede living in Amity Township," he lived directly across the Schuylkill from Thomas Millard's gristmill. Millard's mill was the Oley Valley's first, and in 1727, the year of Lycon's plaintive petition to the Philadelphia Court of Quarter Sessions, was still one of just three or four in the valley. Lycon had been enduring the road and its traffic for eight years. Andrew Robeson, the former chief justice of the provincial supreme court who had resigned his post and moved to the Oley Valley in 1714 to reign briefly as the valley's leading citizen, had been influential in the creation of the road.

> Some of my neighbors do daily throw down my fence to go across [my] meadow to the aforesaid mill, by reason that Andrew Robeson in his lifetime forced a road through this meadow (I being a very poor man), and ever since my neighbors will take a privilege to pass and repass and throw my fence down, and leave it to my great damage.[36]

Lycon wanted the court's protection, but a petition was brought by Millard to the same session, protesting against inhabitants blocking the road to his mill with fences. The miller and his patrons won.

Deciding the best possible route for a road sometimes occasioned disagreeable disputes among neighbors. One of the most rancorous of these was that over the High Road from Moselem to Oley. This dispute pitted headstrong Oley Forge ironmaster Johannes Lesher against almost everyone else in the north end of the valley and dragged on for four years. It may well have been Lesher who fired the initial volley (with fences for ammunition), in an attempt to fend off the creation of a public road through his land. The March 1747-1748 petition from "sundry inhabitants near Moselem" praying that a public road be established running "over the hills into Oley Township and . . . into the great road leading

COMMUNITY

to Philadelphia'' related that the Moselem people had been using a track in that direction "only on sufferance" of the property owners and that this way was "lately stopped."[37] To chart the road through this purely German vicinity the Philadelphia County Court selected a road jury on which all but one of the six jurors were Quakers of Exeter Monthly Meeting. (The laying out of a given road was always assigned to "six sufficient housekeepers of the neighborhood,"[38] whose work was then reviewed and allowed or disallowed by the justices.) For the Moselem-to-Oley road, the Philadelphia County justices seemed to think that the Friends' renowned talent for conciliation was required.

Despite the presence of the seasoned and respected Friends, the first version of the road, or at any rate the first version returned to the court, met with a hostile reception. Both Oley and Moselem sent angry petitions. The latter said that the road as surveyed took them far out of their way, and asked that it be laid out as originally planned. The Oley people complained "That upon petition of John Lesher the road had been reviewed and laid out in a manner prejudicial to several, . . . particularly Frederick DelaPlank, through whose orchard it is now laid, and a graveyard belonging to the family."[39] Accordingly the court appointed two justices (incidentally both also Exeter Monthly Meeting members) to review the road course and suggest alterations. These men, Francis Parvin and John Potts, did so, but their recommendation was not acted on. Frustrated, the Oley and Moselem people loosed another petition.

> By a draft hereby annexed will plainly appear, how we have been abused by some of the reviewers to the admiration of some understanding persons, to see how jurors could be so blind as to lay out the road so unaccountably crooked, and in such bad ground that there must of necessity be a causeway made one hundred and ninety perches, when there is good ground for a road, and much nearer, and will not do one tenth part the damage to the neighbors.[40]

The court responded to this petition with an order to the original jury to meet again. Still there was delay, Exeter men James Boone, Ellis Hughes, and Thomas Ellis reporting to the court that their Maiden Creek colleague Moses Starr was "resolute to do nothing otherwise than what he had first done."[41] Starr, an influential and relatively wealthy Quaker farmer who would become Berks County's first delegate to the provincial assembly in 1752, used his clout in 1748 to keep the High Road from Maiden Creek to Finney's Ferry off his own 550-acre home tract. He appears to have been a staunch ally of Johannes Lesher in the Moselem-to-Oley road struggle.

Ultimately the court and jury acted without Starr's participation, and the road was certified in the form recommended by justices Parvin and Potts in December 1750, almost three years after the original petition. But the saga was not over. Lesher and one other neighbor, Johannes Barto, sought damages. The first jury assigned to this matter, which included original road jurors Boone, Hughes, and Anthony Lee, could not agree on a proper settlement. Another jury was called, which in December 1751 awarded Lesher £10 and Barto £5.

A tenacious contender, Lesher was indicted twenty years later (August 1771) for a criminal misdemeanor on the charge that he, "a certain fence of the height of five feet upon the [Moselem-to-Oley] highway did erect and place."[42] Witnesses against Lesher were his fellow substantial Oley residents Jacob Kauffmann, Caspar Griesemer, Tychicus Weidner, and Samuel Lee. Whatever the facts and contributing circumstances in the case (they being unavailable for modern readers), Lesher emerged acquitted.

Of course other disputes arose among citizens for the legal authorities to untangle. Johannes Lesher seems to have had a penchant for contention. His name makes a profoundly disproportionate number of appearances in the fragmentary surviving court records. Wealthy ironmaster Lesher had started his career described as "blacksmith." He may have alienated his neighbors and fellow Germans by his affectation of aristocratic airs, shown in his baronial mansion at Oley Forge. In 1766 the ironmaster was sued by rich Oley farmer Conrad Reiff for £60 because Reiff's slave Joe died while on rent to Lesher. In 1770 a Berks jury of the Court of Nisi Prius found for Reiff, but awarded him only £3. (Nisi Prius was the name under which the provincial supreme court heard appeals from the judgment of the counties' courts of common pleas.) That year Lesher's neighbor Caspar Griesemer took him to court because the Oley Forge dam caused Manatawny Creek to overflow Griesemer's land. In 1773 the Nisi Prius jury acquitted Lesher. Litigation could be just as time-consuming and profitable for lawyers then as now.

The incomplete court papers that fortunately survive from the final decade or so of the colonial period suggest that serious quarrels involving neighbors or business associates were not uncommon. One Nisi Prius case, from 1770, involved Exeter neighbors Christoph Beyer and Johannes Bishop. The real issue may have been one of precise property boundaries, but all that is definitely known is that Beyer charged Bishop with felling Beyer's trees: ten hickories worth 15s. each, six white oaks worth 10s. each, five black oaks at 10s., and a walnut at 40s.

Quarrels could flare into violence. Jacob Cupp of Amity was hauled before the Berks Court of Quarter Sessions, which judged criminal misdemeanors, for assault and battery on Jost Sees in 1773. The two men lived on adjoining farms from 1770 to 1797. Among several other such known cases was an instance in 1767 in which wealthy Oley farmer and innholder Antony Jaeger, his sons Daniel and Henry, and his son-in-law Balthaser Gehr were tried for assault and battery on the Jaegers' lifelong neighbor, miller Heinrich Kerst. Neighbor Jacob Silvius also stood trial for coming to Kerst's defense. Jacob Weber, landlord to Amity innkeeper Martin Becker, was tried for assault and battery on Becker in 1769. Weber pled guilty and got off with a fine of 5s.

Friction between neighbors was inevitable. People argued over where a road should go, but in the end a road enabling access for the neighborhood to the outside world and to markets would still be created. The European American inhabitants of the Oley Valley, people from a variety of cultural backgrounds, cooperated to meet their needs. When this effort at cooperation occasioned a perceived injury for one citizen, or when neighbors quarreled, governmental institutions strove to settle such matters.

OLEY VALLEY HERITAGE

OLEY TOWNSHIP SUPERVISORS OF HIGHWAYS RECORD 1774-1775

Kept by Samuel Lee. Original in the Don Yoder Collection.

1774

8th mo., 29th — To myself 1 day working on the road, 4s. To 4 hands 1 day, one being 2s. 6d., the others 3s., total 11s.6d.

9th mo., 16th — To myself 1 day, 4s.

29th — To myself 1 day, 4s. To Peter Joder's team [of workhorses], 7s. 6d. To 2 hands 1 day, 6s.

11th mo., 5th — To myself 1 day, 4s. To 4 hands 1 day, 12s. To 1 man & boy with 2 horses and a sled part of a day, 6s.

29th — To myself 1 day, 4s. To Martin Schenkel's and Daniel Guldin's teams 1 day each, 7s. 6d., 15s.

To [cash] paid Daniel Hunter [Jaeger] for digging in a hollow road and ditching, 10s.
To 3 hands 1 day, 9s.
To Samuel Lee, Jr. 3/4 of a day, 2s. 3d.
To a boy 1 day, 2s.
To cash paid Judah Boone, hauling 20 wagon loads of stone & dirt, & making a bridge over the Limekiln Creek, £1

1775

2nd mo., 28th — To myself and three men one day, 13s. To [cash] paid Henry Leinbach and son for hauling stone a half a day into the hollow road, 3s. 9d.

3rd mo., 7th — To myself and six men one day, widening and mending the road from Frederick Meyerly's toward Reading, £1 2s.

11th — Myself and 4 men one day, 16s. Peter Joder's and William Reider's teams one day each, 7s. 6d., 15s. To 27 feet of plank for a bridge, 2s. 5d.

3rd mo., 17th — To [cash] paid John Stitzel for hauling stone into two muddy places in the furnace road, 12s. 6d. To myself and 5 men one day mending the road from Henry Kerst's mill upwards, 19s. To [cash] paid John Lesher for hauling stone into a hollow road by the tile place, 8s. 4d.

18th — To commissions for gathering the [road] tax, £1 19s.

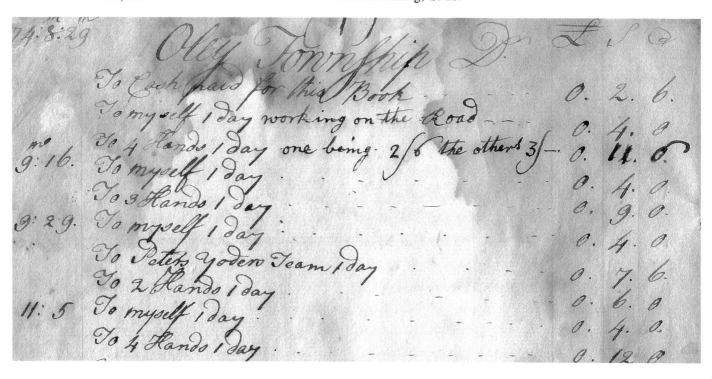

COMMUNITY

CONCLUSION

By 1775 the European families living in the Oley Valley—German, British, and Swedish—had created an American community. In many areas of ordinary life, they did things in ways quite different from those of their European forebears. These peoples had adapted elements of their European heritage to American conditions. They also had learned from one another. As a result of adaptive, experimental, idea-sharing processes, the European heritage continued but was transformed.

Examples of adaptation, experimentation, and the adoption of other groups' practices are abundant, especially in the realms of agriculture and architecture. Particularly influential was the embracement by valley agrarians of the wheat-dominated Pennsylvania agricultural system. Many families had had little or no experience growing wheat in their homelands. Some forms of agriculture that had been prominent on European farms, such as winemaking, were left behind. Farmers employed traditional implements such as the plow, the harrow, and the sickle, while overexploiting the fresh American soil to a degree that would have shocked European farmers. The adoption of the Pennsylvania agricultural system by all settler groups was the essential factor underlying the evolution of a regional culture that blended various European and American elements.

Creative adaptation of European tradition to the American environment, and a relative openness to forms from outside the builder's cultural heritage, characterized the vernacular architecture constructed by Oley's people. Settlers built many of their houses and other buildings of log, a construction method familiar to the people of Scandinavia and the mountainous regions of German-speaking Europe but not to those of the British Isles. Some prosperous settlers of British heritage built houses on the double-parlor plan of three rooms, a house type developed in America. Many Germans chose a jamb stove-fitted three-room counterpart that had just recently been adopted in the homeland when Germans began migrating to Pennsylvania. Some English took up the German practice of heating with stoves. The introduction of the stair passage as an element in the Palladian architectural repertoire resulted in the stair passage's incorporation into existing house types to make new ones. An outstanding architectural example of immigrant adaptability was the further development by German settlers of the ancillary house tradition, with a wide range of functions and a variety of forms in the Oley Valley and in other communities. At the end of the colonial era, the evolution was well advanced of a regional vernacular architecture equally the province of both major cultural groups.

For German-speaking settlers, other adaptations came in language and government. Germans learned English to ease business and social contact with Anglo-Pennsylvanians. By performing the duties of township officers and serving on juries, immigrants from the German principalities gained the experience of participating in local administration. With the Revolution, Pennsylvania Germans would emerge as county-level governmental leaders. The Oley Valley settlers' loyal attachment to their European heritage was most apparent in their devotion to the Christian religion they had brought to America. Even in this area they displayed a resilient adaptability to American conditions. Church people surmounted the challenge presented by the scarcity of ordained ministers. They carried on their devotions without the reassuring presence of officially ordained clergymen.

In 1775 the organized religious congregations in the Oley Valley included three of German Reformed worshipers, two of Lutherans, one of Quakers, and one of Anglicans, with small gatherings of Moravians, Mennonites, and German Baptists. The Oley Valley community was representative of various religions and nationalities. These different people were generally good neighbors to one another, even if local life included some social, economic, and personal friction. At Saint Gabriel's Church, Swedish, English, and German people joined in worship and in the maintenance of congregational life, a notable example of cooperation among nationalities and faiths. The funerals of well-regarded people like Philip Beyer and Ellis Hughes were attended by friends and neighbors of differing national background and creed.

As of 1775, the extent of intermarriage between English-speakers and German-speakers was limited, but it was far from unknown. The well-advanced mixing of Britons and Swedes was serving as a precedent. Marriages between the two large divisions of inhabitants would become increasingly common after the Revolution. Eventually most British and Swedish families in the valley would move on, as would some Germans. Those English-speaking families who stayed would be absorbed into a Pennsylvania German community possessing a rich culture of complex origin.

The generally warm relations among Oley Valley Germans, English people, and Swedes in the colonial years are worth noting. Colonial Pennsylvania's distinctive and lasting contribution to American life was the prevailing tolerance among diverse groups of people. The Oley Valley of the colonial years was not a utopia: The Lenape had to leave, slavery existed, and even many European servants took flight. But in Oley and other early Pennsylvania communities the democratic ideals of William Penn were progressively realized.

NOTES

[1] Will of Israel Robeson, 1769 (codicil 1771), Berks County Wills, vol. 2, 165. Office of the Berks County Register of Wills, Berks County Courthouse, Reading, Pennsylvania.

[2] Will of John Lorah, 1768, Berks County Wills, vol. 2, 4.

[3] Will of John Gelbach, 1758, Berks County Wills, vol. 1, 51.

[4] Exeter Township 225th Anniversary Historical Committee, *Exeter: the Forgotten Corner* (1967), 55.

[5] Peter G. Bertolet, *Fragments of the Past: Historical Sketches of Oley and Vicinity* (Oley: The Women's Club of Oley Valley, 1980), 75.

[6] Will of John Sands, 1774, Berks County Wills, vol. 2, 184.

[7] Will of John Keim, 1747, Berks County Wills, vol. 1, 8.

[8] Will of George Kelchner, 1747, Philadelphia County Wills, Bk. I, 243.

[9] Will of Martin Weiler, 1756, Berks County Wills, vol. 1, 105.

[10] Will of Hans Martel Gerick, 1757, Berks County Wills, vol.1, 44.

[11] Gottlieb Mittelberger, *Journey to Pennsylvania*, translated and edited by Oscar Handlin and John Clive (Cambridge, Mass.: Harvard University Press, 1960), 43-44.

[12] Exeter Monthly Meeting Men's Minutes, July 29, 1756.

[13] *The Journals of Henry Melchior Muhlenberg*, edited by Theodore G. Tappert and John W. Doberstein (Philadelphia: The Evangelical Lutheran Ministerium of Pennsylvania and Adjacent States, 1945), vol. 1, 186.

[14] Berks County Deeds, vol. 7, 23. Office of the Berks County Register of Wills, Berks County Courthouse, Reading, Pennsylvania.

[15] Minutes of hearing on the will of Benjamin Longworthy, 1765, Probate Files, Office of the Berks County Register of Wills.

[16] Philadelphia County Road Docket, vol. 2, 246, Philadelphia City Archives, Philadelphia, Pennsylvania.

[17] The generally accepted dates for the formation of Amity and Oley townships are 1719 and 1722, respectively. There is no Philadelphia County township formation docket for the years before 1730. The name Amity is used in three early deeds: (1) May 18, 1716, from John and Charity Campbell of "Amity Township, also called Manatawny," to Gershan Mott, for land "in the Swedes' Tract"; (2) December 10, 1717, from John Theodorick and Dorothy Greiner "of Amity" to John Jacob Roth, for land "in Amity"; and (3) January 16, 1718-1719, from Andrew Robeson, "gentleman of Amity," to Hans Stult "of Manatawny," for land "near Manatawny," that is known to have been located within the Swedes' Tract, and hence in Amity. In the 1718-1726 volume of the Philadelphia County Commissioners' Minutes, reference was made to the 1718 taxes for "Manatawny Township," evidently meaning Amity. Reference was to Amity Township from 1719 onward. Philadelphia County Deed Book E-7/9, 386, and Book F-8, 30; Berks County Deed Book B-2, 34; Philadelphia County Commissioners' Minutes, 1718-1726, Philadelphia City Archives, Philadelphia, Pennsylvania.

Regarding Oley Township's date of formation, the commissioners' minutes first referred to the taxes for "Oley Township" in 1722. A surviving 1720 petition from Oley residents asked that a township of that name be established. The 1740 petition requesting that the township's boundary be surveyed, referred to the township's having been formed "about fifteen years past." Philadelphia County Township Petitions, Philadelphia City Archives.

[18] Petition of Upper Inhabitants of the West Side of the Schuylkill to the Provincial Council, 1720, copy in Minutes of the Chester County Court of Quarter Sessions, Chester County Archives, West Chester, Pennsylvania.

[19] Petition for Oley Township, 1720, Philadelphia County Township Boundary Papers, Philadelphia City Archives.

[20] Philadelphia County Road Docket, vol. 2, 355.

[21] Petition for Exeter Township, 1741, Philadelphia County Township Boundary Papers.

[22] Petition for Amity Township, 1744, Philadelphia County Township Boundary Papers.

[23] Minutes of the Berks County Court of Quarter Sessions, 1767-1775, Local Government Records Collection (microfilm), Pennsylvania State Archives.

[24] J. Bennett Nolan, *The Foundation of the Town of Reading in Pennsylvania* (Reading: School District of Reading, 1929), 90.

[25] Philadelphia County Road Petitions, 19-314, B-1, Philadelphia City Archives.

[26] Philadelphia County Road Petitions, 19-315, B-2.

[27] Philadelphia County Road Petitions, 19-319, B-6.

[28] *The Journals of Henry Melchior Muhlenberg*, vol. 1, 208.

[29] I. Daniel Rupp, *History of the Counties of Berks and Lebanon* (Lancaster: G. Hills, 1844), 82.

[30] Richard H. Hulan, "The Swedes Were Like Ducks: Baltimore Clippers, Ohio Keelboats, and Several Facts," paper presented at "New Sweden in America" conference, University of Delaware, Newark, Delaware, March 3-5, 1988.

[31] Will of John Sands, 1774, Berks County Wills, vol. 2, 184.

[32] *Pennsylvania Archives*, First Series, vol. 1, 315-16.

[33] *Pennsylvania Archives*, Eighth Series, vol. 3, 222.

[34] *Pennsylvania Archives*, First Series, vol. 1, 553-54.

[35] Berks County Court of Quarter Sessions Docket, February 1769, Office of the Berks County Clerk of Courts, Berks County Courthouse.

[36] Philadelphia County Road Docket, vol. 2, 146.

[37] Philadelphia County Road Docket, vol. 3, 87.

[38] John F. Walzer, "Transportation in the Philadelphia Trading Area, 1740-1775," unpublished Ph.D. diss., University of Wisconsin, 1968, 150.

[39] Philadelphia County Road Petitions, 20-338.

[40] Philadelphia County Road Petitions, 20-340.

[41] Philadelphia County Road Docket, vol. 3, 150.

[42] Miscellaneous Court Papers, Berks County Court of Quarter Sessions, Office of the Berks County Clerk of Courts.

COMMUNITY

JACOB KEIM HOMESTEAD, 1753, Pike Township
View showing main house (1753) and ancillary house, used as Keim's turner's workshop. Property of the Historic Preservation Trust of Berks County.
Photo by Jerry Orabona.

APPENDIX 1

COLONIAL-PERIOD SCHOOLS IN THE OLEY VALLEY

William Bird at Pine Forge:

1741-1744: The account ledger Bird kept for the general store that he ran at Pine Forge recorded charges to many Molatton vicinity residents for "schooling their children" by "my schoolmaster."

George DeBenneville:

1743: DeBenneville arrived in Oley. He is said to have taught school at one or more times during his residence there. He moved to the Germantown vicinity in 1757.

Oley Moravian Church:

1743: The Moravians opened a school for local children, which they operated continuously until 1770.

1748: The Moravians built a large half-timbered house and opened a boarding school in it. This boarding school incorporated their school for local children. The boarding school closed in 1751 but reopened 1755-1761 (with fifty-three boarding students in 1756). For detailed accounts of the Moravian educational establishment at Oley, see J. Taylor Hamilton, "The Moravian Work at Oley, Berks County, Pennsylvania," in *Transactions of the Moravian Historical Society*, vol. 13 (1944); and Mabel Haller, "Early Moravian Education in Pennsylvania," in *Transactions of the Moravian Historical Society*, vol. 15 (1953).

New Store Union Church:

1754: Heinrich Melchior Muhlenberg noted that the New Store union congregation had built a schoolhouse.

1756: Twenty residents of the New Store vicinity, probably affiliated with the union church there, advertised in a Germantown newspaper for someone to fill the position of schoolmaster at their recently constructed schoolhouse.

Oley Reformed Church:

1759: Johannes Lesher advertised in the *Pennsylvanische Berichte* that he desired to hire a schoolmaster. This was probably placed for the benefit of the school at Oley Reformed Church.

1765: The Oley Reformed Church register noted that money was still owing on the construction of the schoolhouse.

Saint Gabriel's Church:

1762: Carl Magnus Wrangel noted conversations with the schoolmaster of an "English school" at Saint Gabriel's.

1767 and 1768: "Robert Campbell, schoolmaster" was listed on the Amity tax list—probably employed at Saint Gabriel's. Campbell was the sole Oley Valley schoolmaster referred to in the 1767 and 1768 Berks County tax lists, which are the only surviving colonial-period tax lists that divulge the taxpayers' occupations. Alexander Murray, pastor, referred to a Saint Gabriel's schoolmaster in 1768, though not by name.

Lee Family (northeastern Oley Township):

1762-1763: Records in minutes of Exeter Monthly Meeting of requests by Lee Family members, for privilege of holding separate weekly meetings for worship during winter and summer, refer to holding these meetings "at a schoolhouse near Samuel Lee's." Nothing else is known of this school, at which both English and German children may have been taught.

English-German School in Amity Township (independent):

1774: William Winter gave the trustees "of an English-German school" a free lease for ninety-nine years on a quarter-acre piece of his land abutting the property of Moses Bower, in southwest Amity. (Berks County Deed Book, vol. 7, 23).

Other schools:

No concrete evidence has been found of schools associated with Schwarzwald Union Church or Exeter Meeting during the colonial years, though such schools were probably in existence by the end of the period.

APPENDIX 2

COLONIAL-PERIOD MINISTERS AND PREACHERS IN THE OLEY VALLEY

Heinrich Antes, charismatic German Reformed lay preacher (later a Moravian minister), visits to Oley, around 1736-1743

Matthias Baumann, "New Born" preacher, lived in Oley, 1714-1727

Johann Philip Boehm, German Reformed (began without ordination but eventually received it), intermittent pastor at original Oley Church, 1736-1739

Deborah Boone, Quaker, minister in Exeter Meeting, around 1721-1758

Paul Daniel Brycelius, Moravian, visits to Molatton, 1743-1748

George DeBenneville, nondenominational preacher and early advocate of "universalism," lived in Oley, 1743-1757, occasional visits to Oley Valley, 1757-1775

Andreas Eschenbach, Moravian lay preacher (ordained 1741), missionary and then pastor at Oley, 1740-1742

Gabriel Falck, Swedish Lutheran, pastor at Molatton, 1735-1745

Johann Heinrich Goetschy, unordained German Reformed, pastor at original Oley Church, 1737-1739

Johann Christoph Hartwick, German Lutheran, visits to Saint Gabriel's, 1757-1758

Bernard Michael Hausihl, German Lutheran, visits to Saint Gabriel's, 1758

Samuel Hesselius, Swedish Lutheran, pastor at Molatton, 1720-1722

Alexander Howie, Anglican, visits to Molatton, about 1732

Ellis Hughes, Quaker, minister in Exeter Meeting, about 1731-1764

Jacob Kuhn, Moravian, pastor at Oley Moravian, 1743-1744

John Abraham Lidenius, Swedish Lutheran, pastor at Saint Gabriel's, 1752-1755

Jonas Lidman, Swedish Lutheran, regular visitor to Molatton, about 1722-1730

Abraham Meinung, Moravian, pastor at Oley Moravian, 1744-1745

Philip Jacob Michael, unordained German Reformed, pastor or frequent visitor at Schwarzwald, Oley, and New Store Reformed churches, about 1753-1764

Wolfgang Michler, Moravian, pastor at Oley Moravian, about 1745-1748 and 1761

Friedrich Casimir Miller, unordained German Reformed, in Oley Valley in 1746

Johann Heinrich Moeller, Moravian, pastor at Oley Moravian, 1754-1759

Heinrich Melchior Muhlenberg, German Lutheran, pastor at Molatton/Saint Gabriel's, 1748-1752 and 1755-1757, occasional visits at Schwarzwald and New Store, 1744-1775

Alexander Murray, Anglican, pastor at Saint Gabriel's, 1762-1778

Jerg Neisser, Moravian, pastor at Oley Moravian, 1759-1761

Jerg Nitschmann, Moravian, pastor at Oley Moravian, 1770

Moses Roberts, Quaker, minister in Exeter Meeting, 1768-1775

Andreas Sandel, Swedish Lutheran, visits to Molatton settlement, 1708-1710 (possibly up to 1719)

Johann Helfrich Schaum, German Lutheran, occasional visits to Schwarzwald and New Store, about 1745-1775

Michael Schlatter, German Reformed, visit to Oley Valley, 1746

Daniel Schumacher, independent German Lutheran, pastor at Schwarzwald, 1754-1758

August Gottlieb Spangenberg, leading Moravian, visit to Oley, 1737

Johann Caspar Stoever, German Lutheran (began without ordination but eventually received it), visits to Oley settlement and Molatton, 1731-1734

Johann Ludwig Voigt, German Lutheran, occasional visits to Schwarzwald and New Store, about 1764-1775

Jerg Michael Weiss, German Reformed, visit to Oley settlement, 1729

Carl Magnus Wrangel, Swedish Lutheran, visits to Saint Gabriel's, 1762 and 1763

Count Nicolaus Ludwig von Zinzendorf, leading Moravian, visits to Oley (including holding of "Third Synod"), 1741

APPENDIX 3

COUNTY-LEVEL OFFICIALS RESIDENT IN THE OLEY VALLEY DURING THE COLONIAL PERIOD

This list includes county tax assessors from the Philadelphia County period (pre-1752), but omits those from the Berks County period (1752-1775). This is because identification of Berks assessors is not possible for many years, but the appointment of an assessor from the Oley Valley to the government of so extensive and populous a county as Philadelphia is too significant to omit. Three men served together as commissioners, and six as assessors, for each county, but the number of justices of the peace a county might have was never prescribed. Other county-level offices (sheriff, coroner, treasurer, collector of excise, and the various court clerkships) were solitary posts. Until 1771 Berks County elected but one delegate to the provincial assembly; from then until 1776, two. Unlike other county offices, which were up for contest every October, commissioners served three-year terms. One of the triumvirate of commissioners was elected each year, so that their terms were staggered.

Mark Bird	Justice of the peace 1770-1776
William Bird	Justice of the peace 1752-1761
George Boone, Jr.	Justice of the peace 1728-1749
James Boone	Justice of the peace 1752-1761; Assembly delegate 1758
William Boone	Coroner 1752-1755; Sheriff 1755-1757
George Douglass	Justice of the peace 1764-1776
Edward Drury	Commissioner 1752-1756
John Godfrey	Commissioner 1752-1761
Samuel Guldin	Assessor 1750-1751; Commissioner 1752-1753
Samuel Hoch	Commissioner 1760-1762
John Hughes	Collector of excise 1752-1763; Commissioner 1762-1764
Anthony Lee	Justice of the peace 1745-1761
Johannes Lesher	Assessor 1743-1745
Abraham Levan	Assessor 1746-1750
Isaac Levan	Assessor 1751-1752; Commissioner 1765-1768
Richard Lewis	Commissioner 1764-1767
Abraham Lincoln	Commissioner 1772-1778
Mordecai Lincoln	Justice of the peace 1733-1736
Thomas Lincoln	Sheriff 1757-1759
William Maugridge	Justice of the peace 1752-1766
Joseph Millard	Commissioner 1753-1756; Justice of the peace 1761-1770
Thomas Rutter, Sr.	Assembly delegate 1729
Jacob Schneider	Commissioner 1769-1772
John Warren	Coroner 1758-1760
Jacob Weber (Weaver)	Sheriff 1759-1761 and 1763-1765

APPENDIX 4

NOTEWORTHY COLONIAL-PERIOD BUILDINGS IN THE OLEY VALLEY

The following list refers to buildings that have received preservation attention from government agencies or nonprofit historic-preservation organizations. This attention has taken the form of registration as an important cultural resource, restoration followed by maintenance as a museum or study building, or that of detailed recording of architectural data. The work of the Historic American Buildings Survey and the National Register are far from complete regarding deserving structures both in the Oley Valley and throughout the nation.

HABS: Historic American Buildings Survey—an agency within the National Park Service that documents America's architectural landmarks. HABS recording may include measured architectural drawings, large-format photography, and research in written sources. HABS operates in conjunction with the Historic American Engineering Record. HABS records are available for public use at the Library of Congress (Prints and Photographs Division), Washington, D.C.

HPTBC: Historic Preservation Trust of Berks County—a non-profit organization that acquires selected examples of Berks County's architectural heritage for preservation under the trust's ownership.

HOBAS: Historic Oley Building Archive and Survey—a program undertaken by the Oley Valley Heritage Association to record deserving examples of the early architecture of the valley.

NRHP: National Register of Historic Places—the official list of the significant historic sites, landmarks, and examples of historic architecture in the United States, supervised by the National Park Service.

Oley Township: In 1983 this township was taken onto NRHP in its entire extent, due to its nature as a well-preserved representation of the historic rural landscape. Notable colonial-period (before 1776) buildings, in addition to those in Oley Township listed farther below, include:

George DeBenneville Homestead (house, around 1750, small barn, mid-1700s)
Gregory-Weidner Homestead, settled by 1719 (early house/ancillary house, main house)
Johannes Hoch (John High), Jr., House-Mill, 1761
Antony Jaeger (Hunter) Homestead, settled by 1739 (main house, ancillary house)
Johannes Jaeger (Hunter) Inn, 1768
Johannes Joder (Yoder), Sr., Homestead, small wing of main house, 1741
Johannes Lesher House (Oley Forge Mansion), around 1750-1755
Abraham Levan House, around 1753
Moses Roberts House, 1769
Martin Schenckel House, 1766
Schiffer-Knabb House, log section of house, mid-1700s
Jacob Schneider (Snyder) House, 1767
Robert Stapleton House, around 1730-1735, enlarged about 1740-1745

Abraham Bertolet House, 1736, Oley, HOBAS (drawings)

Bertolet-Herbein Cabin, around 1720-1750, moved from Oley Township, reassembled with accompanying bakehouse (date unknown) on Daniel Boone Homestead State Historic Site, Exeter, HABS (photos, floorplan)

William Bird House, around 1746-1751, Birdsboro, HABS (photos)

Johannes (John) Bishop House (Bishop's Hall), around 1774, Exeter, NRHP

George Boone, Sr., House (Boonecroft), 1733, Exeter, NRHP

Judah Boone Homestead (Mill Tract Farm), around 1770, Exeter, NRHP (house, gristmill, and stable), HABS (house: drawings, photos)

Johannes DeTurk Ancillary House, 1767, Oley Township, HPTBC (lease), HABS (photos, floorplan). The earliest section of the much altered main house on the farmstead is said to have been built around 1740, and is possibly even older.

George Douglass House, 1763, Amity, HPTBC (drawings), NRHP

Ellis-Bertolet Homestead (bakehouse), Oley Township, HOBAS (drawings)

Exeter Friends Meeting House, 1759, Exeter, HABS (photos, floorplan)

Johannes Hoch (John High) Homestead (springhouse, bakehouse), Oley Township, HOBAS (drawings)

Samuel Hoch (High) Tenancy Ancillary House (HABS), Oley Township, HABS (photo), mid-1700s

OLEY VALLEY HERITAGE

Mounce Jones House (Old Swede's House), 1716, Amity, HPTBC, NRHP, HABS (photos, drawings)

Kauffmann (Coffman) Homestead, Oley Township, HABS (main house, 1766, photos), HOBAS (outbuildings, drawings)

Jacob Keim Homestead (house and ancillary house), around 1753, Pike, HPTBC (drawings), NRHP, HABS (photos)

Leinbach-Knabb Homestead (early house/ancillary house, first stage of construction around 1735, log barn, mid-1700s), Oley Township, HOBAS (drawings)

Mordecai Lincoln House, 1733, Exeter, NRHP

Jerg (George) Lotz Ancillary House, 1762, Amity, HABS (photos, drawings)

Maugridge-DeTurk House (Daniel Boone Birthplace: part of house is built on earlier foundation of Squire Boone House), around 1752-1755, Exeter, NRHP, HABS (photos), central feature of Daniel Boone Homestead State Historic Site

Daniel Reiff Homestead (outbuildings), Oley Township, HOBAS (drawings)

Daniel Reiff Tenancy Ancillary House (HABS), late-1700s, Oley Township, HABS (photos)

Schneider (Snyder) Gristmill, mid-1700s, Exeter, NRHP

White Horse Inn, mid-1700s, Amity, HPTBC, NRHP

JOHANNES JODER HOUSE, 1741, Oley Township
The 1741 section is to the left. The central portion of the house was rebuilt in 1782, on a foundation predating 1741. The porch (renewed 1994) overlooks the Manatawny Creek, the adjacent meadowlands, and the covered bridge at Pleasantville.
Photo by Jerry Orabona.

APPENDIX 5

ARCHITECTURAL GLOSSARY

The following list of architectural terms referring to the colonial-period vernacular architecture of southeastern Pennsylvania defines those terms as they are used in this book. Terms for cross reference are given in **bold**.

For more comprehensive reference, especially to the interior elements of early American domestic architecture and to architectural hardware, see the following works: Carl R. Lounsbury, *An Illustrated Glossary of Early Southern Architecture & Landscape* (Oxford: Oxford University Press, 1994), the most comprehensive and the most instructive work of this sort for early America, though its geographical frame of reference extends from Maryland and Delaware southward; Steven J. Phillips, *Old House Dictionary: An Illustrated Guide to American Domestic Architecture, 1600 to 1940* (Washington: The Preservation Press, 1992); and Robert F. Ensminger, *The Pennsylvania Barn: Its Origin, Evolution, and Distribution in North America* (Baltimore: The Johns Hopkins University Press, 1992), useful in this regard for its glossary of terms in barn architecture. Virginia and Lee McAlester, *A Field Guide to American Houses* (New York: Alfred A. Knopf, 1986), despite its failure to cover the Pennsylvania German house-building tradition as a discrete architectural style, is of value for the clarity of its many drawings of architectural elements. The McAlester *Field Guide* is noteworthy in general as an initial handbook for survey and research in American vernacular architecture (whether pursued as profession or avocation). Also recommended in the latter regard are Hugh Howard, *How Old Is This House?: A Skeleton Key to Dating and Identifying Three Centuries of American Houses* (New York: The Noonday Press [Farrar, Straus and Giroux], 1989); and Sally Light, *House Histories: A Guide to Tracing the Genealogy of Your Home* (Spencertown, New York: Golden Hill Press, 1989), which delineates methods of research into a property's history via deeds and other records. Gabrielle M. Lanier and Bernard L. Herman, *A Field Guide to Delaware Architecture* (Baltimore: The Johns Hopkins University Press, forthcoming) promises on the basis of the initial manuscript to emerge as an essential handbook with application to a region much wider than that state. The reader should be able to order the above books via any good bookstore.

Ancillary house — A form of building developed by colonial-period Pennsylvania Germans that combined the functions of a variety of German **outbuildings** under one roof. **Bank siting** is practically universal among structures built to be ancillaries. (Small, early houses were occasionally converted to the ancillary function.) The first or upper floor was most often designed to serve as retirement living quarters or **grandfather house** for aging parents who had turned over the homestead and main house to younger family members, but occasionally as a craft workshop. The **cellar** usually contained a spring or stream in a lined trench and was fitted with a large fireplace, which enabled this space to be used for food and drink storage, laundering, distilling, dairying activity such as cheesemaking, and rendering of butchered meat. The garret of the ancillary house was often employed as **granary** space. Due to this variety of possible functions, an ancillary's cellar or the entire structure might be referred to in period documents as **spring-house**, **wash house**, **milk house**, or **still house**. An ancillary house was most often built in association with a larger main house, but it appears that by the end of the colonial period (i.e., 1775) the form was being built as the principal or only dwelling on some homesteads, e.g., **tenant homesteads** or homesteads in the initial process of development.

Ashlar — Stone masonry work consisting of squared, cut stones of uniform height laid in straight rows, also known as **coursed ashlar** or as **cut stone work**. If also of uniform breadth, then referred to as **dressed ashlar**.

Bakehouse-smokehouse — A form of outbuilding designed for food preparation that appears to have been built fairly frequently in the Oley Valley vicinity during the eighteenth and early nineteenth centuries. The bakehouse, also commonly built as a freestanding structure, typically consisted of an oblong-shaped oven structure with a **gable-roofed** shelter built around the oven's main aperture, with two full side walls but open-sided at the front. When combined with a smokehouse, a vent in the oven permits the entry of smoke into the smokehouse section. **Smokehouses** were also often built as small freestanding structures.

Balcony — An external platform positioned against the house wall with door access to a house's interior, located at a level above that of the first story. A feature only occasionally seen in the architecture of colonial-period Pennsylvania, a balcony was generally supported by cantilever (i.e., by horizontal timbers, elements in the building's internal structure, built to extend outward).

Bank(ed) or bank-sited building — A structure, generally located on a site with a noticeable slope, in which one portion of the exterior wall of the **basement** story is completely below grade (for at least all of one **elevation** or side), and another portion is completely above grade. "Banking" a building enabled easy access to the **cellar** from the exterior. See also **Story and floor level**.

Barn type — See **Type**. See the index for a list of colonial-period Oley Valley barn types and text references to discussion.

Basement — See **Foundation**.

Bay — Three definitions in reference to early Pennsylvania vernacular architecture: 1) A horizontal spatial division in an **elevation** (i.e., side) of a building, centered on an opening (door or window) in the wall. The number of bays in an elevation is the same as the number of openings in whichever floor of the elevation has the greatest number. Hence the **facade** of the standard "Georgian" house, with five windows on the second story aligned over four windows and a centrally-positioned door on the first story, is spoken of as having five bays. The term "bay," most often employed in reference to a building's facade, is useful for describing the design and size of the elevation (or of the building as a whole). 2) In reference to **timber-frame construction**, a "bay" on the facade or rear elevation is denoted as the space between two **bents**. 3) In describing the plan of a barn's first floor, a bay is the space between two bents or between a bent and a **gable-end wall**.

Bead — A rounded **molding** running along the edge of a wooden element, e.g., on the bottom face of a floor **joist** (one intentionally left exposed to the view of persons in the room below.)

Bent — In **timber-frame construction**, a major, complex element in the structure of the rectangular-shaped frame, running its full depth, generally consisting of two or more vertical **posts**, two **rafters**, and a horizontal **girt** for each floor level. A bent would frame each **gable-end wall**, with additional internally-located bents positioned at intervals (often regular) between the ends of the building.

Boxed staircase — See **Winder stairway**.

Brace — A timber, usually short in length, employed to stiffen and thus further strengthen the building's or roof system's overall structure. Positioned to connect two other timbers by making a third side of a triangle among the three, and thus generally in a diagonal relation to either of the other two timbers. Common examples include a **corner brace** at a corner of a frame building's box-like structure, or a **wind brace** connecting a **purlin** and a **principal rafter**.

Buhr stone or buhr — A kind of **millstone**, available only from a small cluster of quarries in northern France, essential for the proper grinding of wheat into flour, and so exported to the rest of northern Europe and North America in large numbers during the eighteenth and nineteenth centuries.

Building type — See **Type**.

Butt purlin — See **Purlin**.

Casement window — A window in which a one-piece frame swings horizontally, open and shut.

Cell — A bounded area (i.e., a room), used in reference to a building's **plan**.

Cellar — Space within a house, at the level of the **foundation** wall or **basement** and thus partly or entirely below grade, suited for food storage due to its relative immunity to external changes in temperature. **Fenestration** was generally limited to small vertical vent slits (giving rise to the legend that cellars were also designed to serve as fortifications), or to small **casement windows** with wooden shutters in place of **glazing**. A cellar might also be constructed solely for storage purposes as a separate subterranean building, generally called a **root cellar**.

Chamber — In eighteenth-century parlance, a room for sleeping and the keeping of personal effects. In German or in Pennsylvania German, *Kammer*. The *Kammer* was the smallest room, and usually an unheated one, in the classic three-room **plan** of the Pennsylvania German **stove-room** house type, generally serving as a first-floor master bedroom.

Chinking — Infill, consisting of wooden slats or small stones and generally covered with a mortar composed mostly of mud or clay, placed to fill the relatively narrow spaces between logs in a building constructed of **hewn logs**.

Cladding — Exterior wall covering, such as **clapboard** or **weatherboard**, or in modern times, aluminum or vinyl siding.

Clapboard — A thin board, generally about four feet long, used in cladding a wood-constructed building. Each **course** of clapboard is applied so as to slightly overlap the course below.

Clipped-gable roof — Another term for a **half-hipped roof**.

Collar beam — A timber extending between and bracing a pair of **rafters**, generally positioned about half to two-thirds of the way from **garret** floor to roof peak.

Common rafter — See **Rafter**.

Common-rafter roof system — A roof structure employing only common rafters (as opposed to one including **principal rafters**). The more traditional variation of the common-rafter system also employs **through purlins**, on which the rafters rest.

Common shingle — See **Shingle**.

Corner fireplace — A fireplace built at an angle against a corner made by two walls, an advantageous arrangement for the radiation of heat.

Corner-notching log construction — The more common method in log construction for fastening the timbers at the building's corners, consisting of cutting and fitting corresponding notches at the ends of the logs.

Corner-post log construction — The less common method in log construction for fastening the timbers at the building's corners, in which the ends of the logs are shaped into **tenons** that are fitted into vertical posts at the corners.

Cornice — On the exterior of a building, the element that projects from the top of the wall to provide a base for that segment of a roof slope that overlaps the **eaves**. On the interior, the uppermost discrete segment of a wall's **finish work** if the wall treatment features demarcation into sections. In either location, the cornice is often the recipient of decoration.

Course — In reference to **masonry** such as brick, cladding such as **clapboard**, or roof coverings such as **shingles**, a horizontal row of similar pieces.

Custom mill — See **Gristmill**.

Cut stone work — See **Ashlar**.

Dormer — A structure built over an opening in a building's roof, with a discrete roof of its own and usually with side walls and a window at its front. Dormers provide a greater measure of light and head room to the **garret** level.

Double-beveled shingle — See **Shingle**.

Double-hung sash — See **Vertical sash window**.

Double-pile construction — Refers to two-room-deep design. See **Pile**.

Dovetail notching — In **corner-notching log construction**, shaping of the end of each log with angled notches on top and bottom edges, conferring a particularly strong lock between logs. Also known as **full-dovetail notching**. In **half-dovetail notching**, just one edge on each end of a log is angled, with the other nearly square. In dovetail notching, the joinery as well as simple gravity act to hold the building together.

Drip course — A **course** of **masonry**, whether bricks or narrow stones, positioned to slightly overlap the joint between the building's wall and the upper edge of some attached structure, such as a **pent roof**, intended to protect the joint from water damage.

Eaves — The place where the roof slope meets the top of the wall. "Eaves" is a singular noun, not a plural one.

Eaves wall or elevation — In reference to a **side-gable** building, a wall aligned with the roof ridge, and hence a front or rear wall. Also known as the **lateral wall**.

Elevation — What can be seen of a building, as viewed from a perspective aligned with one of the main block's four sides; often used to refer to the physical side of a building itself. A building has four elevations.

Ell — A dependent part of a house, smaller and often lower than the **main block**, and which extends rearward from the main block.

English stove — See **Six- and ten-plate stoves**.

Entry — Doorway, the principal entry being the main front doorway.

Entry floor — The space that adjoins the principal **entry**, in the split-level arrangement that characterized both the **basement** and the first floor of an eighteenth-century **gristmill** building. In a mill with an **internal waterwheel**, the basement entry floor was the highest level on that floor, but the middle level on the first floor, lower than the **stone floor** and higher than the floor over the **wheelpit**.

External waterwheel — See **Waterwheel**.

Facade — In common parlance, the principal or front **elevation** of a building. The facade is generally the one that receives the most architectural decoration. In architectural parlance, used in reference to any face of a building (or section thereof).

Fachwerk — See **Timber-frame construction**.

False plate — A horizontal board that runs the length of the building resting on the ends of the **garret**-floor **joists**, generally positioned overlapping or outside the top of the building's wall, and carries the **rafter feet**. See also **Plate**.

False rafter — A board attached to the **rafter foot** so that it overlaps and projects beyond the end of the rafter, employed to give a **kick** to the lower roof line.

Fenestration — Openings in a building's **elevations**, i.e., doors and windows.

Fieldstone work — See **Rough stone work**.

Finish work — The final treatment of a surface, a term generally used in reference to house interiors, where it might include woodwork, **plaster**, paint, etc.

Five-plate stove — See **Jamb stove**.

Floor level — See **Story and floor**.

Flue stove — See **Six- and ten-plate stoves**.

Forebay — The section of the first or upper story of a bank barn of the Swiss barn type, positioned along the **lateral elevation** opposite the up-bank first-story **entry**, that overlaps the basement story, generally by about five to eight feet. The forebay (*Vorbau* in German) provided shelter to livestock in the barnyard, and the animals could be fed via trapdoors in the floor of the forebay. In the Swiss barn type, the forebay is generally supported by cantilever (i.e., by horizontal timbers, elements in the building's internal structure, built to extend outward). The forebay is also an essential architectural element in the Pennsylvania barn type that developed from the Swiss barn around the close of the eighteenth century, though it is usually supported by means other than cantilever, e.g., by intrinsic two-story extensions of the barn's **gable-end walls**.

Foundation — The lowest section of a building's wall, of sturdy construction so as to support the rest of the structure, the weight of which the foundation serves to transmit to the earth. In southeastern Pennsylvania during the colonial period, the foundation wall was generally raised to a few feet above grade, was usually constructed of **rubble stone work**, and would encompass the **cellar** if such space was present. The height of the foundation makes that term practically synonymous with the term basement in regard to early Pennsylvania buildings. Basement refers to the story below the first floor.

Frame construction — See **Timber-frame construction**.

Front-gable orientation — Design of a building so that the **front elevation** is a **gable-end wall or elevation**. In colonial-period southeastern Pennsylvania, front gable orientation appears to have been rare in regard to most kinds of buildings, probably even churches, though it was common in small outbuildings and in Pennsylvania German **ancillary houses**.

Front wall, elevation, or facade — The wall in which is positioned the building's principal **entry**. The most "public" of the elevations, the front generally faces the direction from which the builder expected visitors or patrons to approach, and hence is usually the most decorative wall. Also referred to as the **principal facade**.

Full-dovetail notching — See **Dovetail notching**.

Gable — The triangular-profiled end of a **gable roof**.

Gable-end wall or elevation — The wall that is topped by the roof **gable**. In the **side-gable orientation** that characterized most kinds of buildings in southeastern Pennsylvania during the colonial period, a gable-end wall would be a side wall of the building (rather than the front and rear walls).

Gable roof — A ridged or peaked roof in which roof slopes rise from two opposing walls.

Garret — The attic floor level of a building, for which the roof acts as the ceiling. Also referred to in the eighteenth century as the **loft**.

Gear pit — The area in the split-level floor arrangement of an eighteenth-century **gristmill** building's **basement** floor in which was located the **hurst frame** with the machinery that transmitted and modified power from the **waterwheel** to the **millstones**. The gearpit was situated next to the **wheelpit** and directly beneath the **stone floor**. In a mill with an **internal waterwheel**, the gearpit occupied a central position between the wheelpit and the **entry floor**. The floor of the gearpit was lower than the entry floor, but higher than the deep wheelpit.

Georgian architecture — The name by which the Anglo-American manifestation of **Palladian architecture** is generally known, coined in reference to the then-reigning English kings George I (1714-1727), George II (1727-1760) and George III (1760-1820).

Girt — An element in **timber-frame construction**—a horizontal beam, which serves as a bridging connection between **posts**.

Glazing — The fitting of glass into windows. Often used by architectural historians as a collective noun referring to a colonial-period building's overall window glass.

Granary — An area for the storage of grain. **Granary** might refer to a freestanding building constructed solely for that purpose, probably a relatively small single-**cell** structure in the eighteenth-century Oley Valley vicinity, or to a space within a barn, on the second floor of a **merchant mill** building, or in the **garret** of a house or **ancillary house**.

Grandfather house — See **Ancillary house**.

Gristmill — This term can refer to grain-milling machinery, or to a building constructed to house such machinery. Gristmill buildings of two types were erected in eighteenth-century Pennsylvania: the **custom mill** type and the **merchant mill** type. Both terms also refer (in their original meanings) to distinct ways of conducting the mill business. A custom mill business operated as an artisanal service, i.e., the miller received a "toll" (share) of the grain ground. At a merchant mill business, the miller purchased outright all of the farmer's grain, the flour representing a major market commodity. In architectural reference, the custom mill and merchant mill building types were related to the business forms, in that the merchant mill type was developed in northern Delaware around 1760 in response to the prior evolution of the merchant mill form of business. Either kind of mill business might be conducted in either type of mill building, however. The custom mill type was a structure of one-story-plus-basement height, commonly with its principal **entry** on a the first story of a **lateral wall** but with additional entries on the garret, first story and **basement** of one **gable-end wall**. The merchant mill type was a **front-gable** structure of two-story-plus-basement height, the additional floor level having been developed to serve as **granary**, with entries on three or four levels on the front end wall. No buildings of the merchant mill type are known to have been built in the Oley Valley vicinity prior to 1790. Both the basement and the first floor of colonial-period mill buildings were generally split into two or three levels, due to the presence of the machinery. On the basement were the **entry floor**, the **gearpit** and the **wheelpit** (if the mill was fitted with an **internal waterwheel**). On the first floor were another entry floor, the **stone floor** and the floor over the wheelpit. An office room with a fireplace often occupied a portion of the entry floor area on the first floor, and another fireplace might be located in the basement entry floor.

Half-dovetail notching — See **Dovetail notching**.

Half-hipped roof — A "hipped roof" is a ridged roof with roof slopes rising from all four walls, as opposed to a **gable roof**, one with just two opposing slopes. Buildings with true or full hipped roofs appear to have been rare in rural colonial-period Pennsylvania, but there is evidence that the related half-hipped roof form may have been common in areas of Pennsylvania German settlement. In a half-hipped roof, the roof slopes at the two ends of the building do not extend downward from the roof ridge as far as do those of the two principal slopes. Also known as **jerkin head roof**, **clipped-gable roof**, or, in German, *Walmdach*.

Half-story — A term used in describing the height of a house (e.g., one-and-a-half stories) when the **garret** level has been built with **knee wall** or **dormers** to provide a greater measure of head room.

Half-timber work — See **Timber-frame construction**.

Hall — As the term was generally used by Britons and Anglo-Americans in the eighteenth century, a room for cooking, work, family fellowship and informal entertaining, and quite often, especially in small houses, for sleeping as well. Since in medieval England many houses had been of just one room in size, "hall" had come to be practically synonymous with "house."

Hallway — See **Passage**.

Hay mow — See **Mow**.

Headrace — See **Millrace**.

Hewn-log construction — See **Log construction**.

Homestead — An inhabited property.

Horizontal sash window — A "sash" or two-part sliding window arrangement in which the two segments are positioned side-by-side, instead of vertically (up-and-down). Only one of the two parts moved.

House type — See **Type**. See the index for a list of colonial-period Oley Valley house types and text reference to discussion.

Hurst frame — The heavy **timber-frame** structure built within a **gristmill** building apart from the building's structure to hold the mill machinery, due to the strong vibration of the mill's operation. The hurst frame stands in the gearpit and is topped by the **millstone** arrangement.

Innholder — One who holds a license for the operation of an inn or tavern on his or her premises, possibly renting this privilege to someone other than himself or herself.

Innkeeper — One who operates an inn.

Internal waterwheel — See **Waterwheel**.

Jack arch — See **Straight arch**.

Jamb stove — A heating stove usually constructed of five flat cast-iron plates (making a "box" with one side missing), designed to be placed with the open side positioned directly against an aperture in the rear wall of hearth-and-chimney structure, enabling the easy transfer of hot coals into the stove. Evidence suggests that some colonial-period Pennsylvania Germans employed jamb stoves with a large tile-made structure fitted above a cast-iron five-plate stove base.

Jerkin-head roof — Another term for a **half-hipped roof**.

Joint — The place where two surfaces meet, or the connection fastening two architectural elements together.

Joist — A beam which carries floorboards.

Kammer — See **Chamber**.

Keystone — A wedge-shaped stone that fills the central position in an arch.

Kich — See **Kitchen**.

Kick — An outward flare to the bottom of the roof slope, created by attaching **false rafters** to extend beyond the **rafter feet**. The kick was apparently intended to afford a greater measure of protection from the effects of wet weather to the building's wall.

Kitchen — A room for cooking, though in the eighteenth century it might also be the site of laundering and other work activities. Known in German as *Küche* and in Pennsylvania German as *Kich*, the kitchen was the room in the classic three-room plan of the Pennsylvania German stove-room house type that ran the full depth of the house.

Kitchen building — A structure separate from the main house in which a kitchen is located. Although during the eighteenth century the kitchen building does not appear to have been a common architectural feature in the Pennsylvania countryside, it became a mainstay of rural domestic architecture in the nineteenth century, generally referred to as the **summer kitchen**.

Knee wall — In reference to a house's **garret**, a wall rising to about knee height above the floor, enabling a greater measure of head room so that the garret is considered to add a **half-story** to the building's height.

Küche — See **Kitchen**.

Lateral wall or elevation — In reference to a **side gable** building, a wall aligned with the roof ridge, and hence a front or rear wall. Also known as the **eaves wall**.

Lath — Short, narrow boards, typically two feet or so long, one to two inches wide and less than a half-inch deep, nailed between timbers or larger boards to serve as a surface to which **plaster** would adhere, or to the top face of **rafters** to serve as a support on which to lay a roof covering of **shingles**, **roof tiles**, or **thatch**. Lath was made in the colonial period by splitting boards along the grain by hand with a froe or a hatchet, a process known as "riving."

Lean-to — A **shed-roofed** section of a building, generally one-room deep, that is positioned against a taller part of the building.

Liegender Dachstuhl roof system — See **Strut-supported roof system**.

Lintel — An element laid horizontally to bridge the top of an opening, and thus bear the gravitational force of elements above the opening.

Load-bearing wall — A wall that supports the weight of other building elements positioned above it, generally of relatively sturdy construction. Also known simply as a **bearing wall**.

Loft — Term with two relevant meanings in the colonial period: 1) an alternative term to **garret** as referring to the floor level immediately below the roof, and 2) in a barn, a second-floor-level platform for hay storage built over part of the first floor.

Log construction — A method of building in which the exterior walls (which function as the structure's main supporting element) are built of timbers made from trees that have been felled and often shaped more or less **square**, with the timbers fastened at the building's corners to their fellows by means of **corner notching** or the **corner-post** method. There were two variations as regards the manner in which logs were shaped. In **hewn-log construction**, the logs were hewn (i.e., hand cut along the log) to be roughly square. In **plank or sawn-log construction**, the lumber was cut at a **sawmill** into planks typically three to five inches broad, with properly squared edges. Use of hewn logs required **chinking**; use of planks required caulking with **oakum**. **Rough- or round-log construction**, which entailed very little shaping of the logs, was often used for outbuildings.

Main block — The principal (i.e., largest) discrete section of a building.

Masonry construction — A method of building in which the exterior walls (which function as the structure's main supporting element) consist of stones or of bricks, held together by **mortar**.

Merchant mill — See **Gristmill**.

Milk house — An **outbuilding** in which dairy work and storage takes place. See **Ancillary house**.

Mill dam — A dam erected to control the flow of water necessary for the operation of a water-powered mill. A **millseat's** main dam is situated on a natural downward-flowing watercourse, from which the dam channels water into the **millrace**. An additional dam might be positioned on the race close by the mill to create a **mill pond**.

Mill pond — A pond created on a **millrace** by means of a dam, to store water to enable mill operation during periods of lesser natural waterflow, or to better control waterflow and thus reduce the possibility of flood damage to the mill. Not all millers built ponds as part of their mill-and-waterworks arrangement.

Millrace — The walled ditches constructed by millers to carry waterflow from the natural watercourse to the mill and from thence back to the watercourse. The **headrace** conveys water from the **milldam** at little rate of decline in height, so that there is a pronounced fall of water at the mill. The water returns to its natural stream via the **tailrace**.

Millseat — A property on which one or more mills and the necessary waterworks (**mill dam** and **millraces**) are located.

Millstone — A circular stone with sharpened edge, used to grind grain into flour or meal. Stones are arranged in pairs, one atop the other though positioned apart by little more than a hair's breadth, and powered by the movement of the **waterwheel** (in the eighteenth century) as transmitted by the gearing system. See also **Buhr stone**.

Molding — Decorative trim along the edge of an element, such as a **cornice** or **summer beam**. In the vicinity of the Oley Valley during the colonial period, the elements so decorated were virtually all wooden, and the molding was generally made by cutting with a carpenter's plane.

Mortar — The substance employed to bind a **masonry** wall, applied while in a viscous state. In colonial-period southeastern Pennsylvania, mortar was concocted of lime, water, and sand. A softer mortar made mostly of mud or clay was used to cover the chinking between logs in **hewn-log construction**.

Mortise — Along with the **tenon**, one of the two components of a joint fastening two members in timber-frame construction. A mortise is a recess cut into a beam, designed to receive the **tenon** of another beam.

Mow — A part of a barn's first-floor level devoted to hay storage, often floored with boards and raised slightly above the **threshing floor** area. In the three-**bay** arrangement of the first floor common in barns of various types, the threshing floor generally occupies the center **bay**, with mows in one or both of the end bays.

Oakum — Tar-like substance used to caulk the very narrow spaces between the planks in **plank or sawn-log construction**.

Office house — Term often used in colonial-period America to denote **outbuildings**.

Original section — Used in reference to the oldest part of a standing building that has been constructed in more than one stage and period.

Outbuilding — Any building on a **homestead** apart from the main dwelling house. This term was rarely used by colonial-period Americans though it is the one generally used today; instead, **office house** and **outhouse** were oft-used expressions.

Outhouse — Term often used in colonial-period America to denote **outbuildings**. To colonists, a privy, i.e., a building to shelter the activity of disposing of human waste, was just one of many varieties of outhouse.

Outlooker — See **Pent roof**.

Outshut — "An extension of a building under a **lean-to** roof"—Eric Mercer, in the Glossary section of *English Vernacular Houses: A Study of Traditional Farmhouses and Cottages* (London: Royal Commission on Monuments, 1975), 231.

Palladian architecture — The architectural movement that originated in the Italian architect Andrea Palladio's (1508-1580) adaptation of Roman classical forms, and that developed through the late sixteenth and seventeenth centuries as the dominant current in European Renaissance architecture. The Palladian influence spread gradually from southern Europe to northern Europe (including Germany and the Netherlands), then to England, and eventually to the British North American colonies, where it has since generally been referred to as **Georgian architecture**. Symmetrical balance and order were among Palladian architecture's defining characteristics.

Parlor — In eighteenth-century parlance, a room for formal entertaining, the display of prized possessions and the enactment of familial rituals such as wedding rites. In many Anglo-American houses, especially before circa 1760, the first-floor parlor would also serve as the master bedroom. A house might have two parlors, one serving as a less formal sitting room or as an office.

Partition wall — A wall that serves to divide space and is not intended to help carry the weight of the building above it, hence generally of relatively light construction.

Passage — A space in a building's plan designed to function chiefly as a corridor for movement and as a buffer between rooms. In regard to modern American houses, what is generally referred to as a **hallway**.

Pent eaves — A narrow **shed roof** structure positioned against a **gable-roofed** building's **gable-end** wall at **eaves** level, the intention evidently to protect the lower wall's masonry.

Pent roof — A **shed roof** structure projecting from a building's exterior wall at a level just above the second story's floor, usually supported by external extensions of the floor **joists** and **summer beam** called **outlookers**. Thought by many scholars to have been intended to protect the masonry (or log-building mortar) at the first-floor level.

Pile — A term used in reference to the depth of a building, hence "single-pile," i.e., one room deep, or "double-pile," i.e., two rooms deep.

Pipe stove — See **Six- and ten-plate stoves**.

Plan — The configuration of spaces within a building.

Plank or sawn-log construction — See **Log construction**.

Plaster — Substance used for wall finish, concocted in the colonial period of lime, water, animal hair, an earthen component such as mud, clay or sand, and sometimes straw. Applied ("keyed") in a viscous state to **lath**, roughened timbers or masonry walls, and then smoothed, plaster becomes hard as it dries.

Plate — A major horizontal beam that runs the length of a building, atop a **lateral wall**, and which supports the roof structure. See also **False plate**.

Post — A vertically-positioned beam in **timber-frame construction**, placed as a major supporting element in a **bent**. "The principal means by which the structure remains upright"—Abbott Lowell Cummings, in *The Framed Houses of Massachusetts Bay, 1625-1775* (Cambridge: Harvard University Press, 1979), 52.

Post-and-beam construction — See **Timber-frame construction**.

Post-supported roof system — A roof structure in which pairs of vertical posts support **through purlins** which in turn carry **common rafters**. Traditionally known in England as a **queen-post roof system**, or in German-speaking Europe as a *stehender Dachstuhl* roof system.

Principal entry — See **Entry**.

Principal facade — See **Front wall, elevation or facade**.

Principal rafter — See **Rafter**.

Purlin — A horizontal beam in a roof structure, running lengthwise, which supports **common rafters**. A **through purlin** is a major structural element (i.e., one essential to the support of the overall structure) and runs the full length of the roof as a single timber. A **butt purlin** is a shorter timber running just from one **principal rafter** to the next, and is thus a minor structural element.

Queen-post roof system — See **Post-supported roof system**.

Quoin — In reference to stone **masonry**, the stone placed at the corner of the building, generally relatively large and cut relatively square. Stacked atop one another and alternating as to the building wall with which each is aligned, the function of the quoins is to lock the stone-built structure together.

Race — See **Millrace**.

Rafter — A sloping vertical beam in a roof structure. A **principal rafter** is an element in a **roof truss**. A **common rafter** merely supports **roof-cover boards** or **lath**.

Rafter foot — The bottom end of the **rafter**. A rafter generally tapers from a narrower top end, which connects with the top end of its mate at the roof peak or ridge, to a broader foot. A rafter is referred to as being "footed" in the **plate** or **false plate** that supports it, generally by means of a **mortise-and-tenon** joint in the colonial period.

Rauchkammer — See **Smoke chamber**.

Reciprocating sawmill — See **Sawmill**.

Relieving arch — An arch built over an opening to support the weight of the wall above the opening.

Roof-cover board — Nailed to the top surface of **rafters** to provide a surface on which to lay **shingles**, the roof-cover board was an alternative to **lath**.

Roof ridge — The continuous peak or apex of a **gable** or **half-hipped roof**.

Roof tile — A flat piece made from an earthen or stone substance and used for roof covering. In the colonial-period Oley Valley vicinity, tiles were made of clay and fired for hardness in kilns.

Roof truss — See **Truss**.

Root cellar — See **Cellar**.

Rough- or round-log construction — See **Log construction**.

Rough stone or fieldstone work — A form of stone **masonry** in which irregularly shaped stones are employed.

Rubble stone work — A form of **rough stone work** in which the stones, mostly relatively small ones, are laid randomly, without an attempt to form **courses**.

Sash sawmill — See **Sawmill**.

Sawmill — A mill at which natural timber is cut into lumber, typically scantling (i.e., framing timber), board, and plank (i.e., board of greater than two-inches-by-eight-inches in dimension). In colonial-period Pennsylvania, a sawmill ran on waterpower via **waterwheel** and gearing, and consisted of a vertical saw blade mounted in a frame. The machinery drives the blade up and down, and also pulls the timber head-on against the blade. Such a sawmill is known as a **reciprocating**, **sash**, or **up-and-down sawmill**. The sawmill building is generally a long rectangular structure with stone-built **basement** level and open-sided first story, sheltered by a **gable roof**. The saw itself is mounted in the center, with the **external waterwheel** to the side.

Schtupp — See **Stove room**.

Segmental arch — A relieving arch, built to bridge the top of an opening, composed of several bricks or stones.

Service wing or building — A general term referring to the movement of domestic service functions (e.g., cooking) to house sections or outbuildings separate from the more formal part of the house where polite aspects of living (the family's mutual recreation, dining, entertaining, etc.) took place. The banishment of service functions from the formal area was an aspect of the influence of Palladian architecture in early America.

Shed roof — A roof with a single slope.

Shingle — A narrow board employed as roof cover, made in the colonial period by splitting a larger board along the grain by hand with a froe or a hatchet, a process known as "riving," and then trimming the piece into shape with a drawknife. Shingles are laid aligned from **roof ridge** downward along the roof slope, and to overlap each other. **Single-beveled** or **common shingles** are beveled (i.e., tapered) for their upper two-thirds to enable the overlapping of two consecutive courses of shingles just above them on the roof slope. In addition, **double-beveled** or **side-lapped shingles**, identified in colonial-period Pennsylvania with German-speaking people, are beveled along one side so that the shingles next beside them can overlap them, creating a more tightly-covered roof.

Side-beveled shingle — See **Shingle**.

Side-gable orientation — Design of a building so that the **front elevation** is the **lateral wall or elevation**. This was the standard orientation for most kinds of buildings in southeastern Pennsylvania during the colonial period.

Sill — In a wood-constructed building, a major horizontal beam that rests on an exterior foundation wall, supporting the structure above.

Single-beveled shingle — See **Shingle**.

Single-hung sash — See **Vertical sash window**.

Single-pile construction — Refers to one-room-deep design. See **pile**.

Six- and ten-plate stoves — Two forms of heating stove, assembled from the respective number of cast-iron plates, designed to be situated in a freestanding position, although connected to a chimney by a flue pipe. "Six-plate" refers to the number of plates needed for the top, bottom and four sides of the stove's box. In a ten-plate stove, there were also four movable cast plates that functioned as doors. Both forms were also known as flue, pipe, or English stoves.

Smithy or smith shop — A structure housing a blacksmith's hearth and workshop area.

Smoke chamber — A closet-like space in a house, usually in the **garret**, positioned against the chimney stack and fitted with vents into the chimney to enable the smoking of meat. In German, a **Rauchkammer**.

Smokehouse — A building in which meat is smoked for cooking and preservation. See also **Bakehouse-smokehouse**.

Springhouse — A building in which a spring or stream is enclosed in a lined trench in the floor, providing cool water for food and drink storage. In the parlance of colonial-period Pennsylvania, **springhouse** might be used in reference to two kinds of buildings: 1) a small single-**cell** structure built specifically for this purpose, or 2) an **ancillary house**.

Squared timber — A beam or log with right-angled edges.

Stair passage — A **passage** in which is located an open flight of stairs, an architectural element introduced to early America as an element in **Palladian architecture**.

Stehender Dachstuhl — roof system—See **Post-supported roof system**.

Still house — An **outbuilding** in which distilling takes place. See **Ancillary house**.

Stone-ender — Expression used in reference to a house in which one or both **gable-end walls**, holding the fireplace-and-chimney arrangement, is built of stone while the other walls are built of log or frame. Stone-ender houses in southeastern Pennsylvania are generally of the hall (i.e., single-room) or hall-parlor types.

Stone floor — The area in the split-level floor arrangement of an eighteenth-century **gristmill** building's first floor on which were positioned the pairs of **millstones**, situated over the **gearpit**. The stone floor lay between the floor over the **wheelpit** (if present within the building) and the **entry floor**, and was the highest of the first-floor areas.

Stoop — A small porch structure, generally built in colonial-period southeastern Pennsylvania so as to adjoin a house's front **entry**.

Story and floor level — The term **story** is used in reference to a building's height (e.g., "two stories in height"), or to a level of the building ("second story"), generally in describing the structure from the perspective of the exterior. **Floor** (as in "second floor") is generally used in describing the interior. In a **bank-sited** building, such as a bank barn, a **gristmill**, or an **ancillary house**, the lowest level is referred to as a **basement**, and the first story or floor is that next above the basement.

Stove room — Known in German as *Stube* and in Pennsylvania German as *Schtupp*, the stove room was the room in the classic three-room plan of the Pennsylvania German stove-room house type that held the stove. Generally the largest room in such a house, and approximately square in shape, the stove room was the scene for dining, family fellowship and religious devotions, entertaining, the enactment of familial rituals such as wedding rites, the display of prized possessions, and some work activities. In comparison to Anglo-Pennsylvanian room usage, the Pennsylvania German stove room might be said to have combined aspects of the **hall** and the **parlor.**

Straight arch or jack arch — Three-part segmental **lintel**, in colonial-period southeastern Pennsylvania generally built of cut stone with a **keystone** flanked by smaller blocks.

Strut-supported roof system — Strongly braced, heavy timbered roof support structure, of German origin, which confers a steep pitch to the roof and is of adequate strength to easily support the weight of a roof covering of clay tiles. In German, a **liegender Dachstuhl** system.

Stube — See **Stove room.**

Stud — A relatively light timber that is an element in wall construction, but not a major element in a building's structure. A stud is positioned vertically and in a row with its fellows. In an exterior wall for a **timber-frame** building, the studs hold **cladding** such as horizontal **clapboard** or **weatherboard**. In a building's interior **partition wall**, studs would be used to hold wall **finish** such as **plaster**-and-**lath.**

Summer beam — A major horizontal beam, in a position internal to the building, which helps to support the weight of the overall structure. In colonial-period Pennsylvania buildings, the summer beam generally directly carried the **joists**. The summer beam was often finished, perhaps with a **bead**, and left exposed to view from below in colonial-period Pennsylvania German houses. The word "summer" was apparently an English adaptation of the French term *"sommier,"* for girder.

Summer kitchen — See **Kitchen building.**

Tailrace — See **Millrace.**

Tavern stand — A property on which a tavern business is conducted.

Ten-plate stove — See **Six- and ten-plate stoves.**

Tenancy or tenant homestead — A rented **homestead.**

Tenon — Along with the **mortise**, one of the two components of a joint fastening two members in **timber-frame construction**. The tenon is a projection on the end of a beam, designed to fit into the **mortise** in another beam.

Thatch — A roof covering made by binding straw, generally rye straw in colonial-period Pennsylvania, to the roof. Thatch was particularly favored to shelter barns.

Threshing floor — An area on the first-floor level of a barn used for threshing grain, but also generally serving as a passage for movement. In the three-**bay** arrangement of first-floor common in barns of various types, the threshing floor generally occupies the center bay.

Through purlin — See **Purlin.**

Tie beam — A horizontal beam running the depth of a building, in which are set the feet of a pair of **principal rafters**, and thus an element in a **roof truss**. In **timber-frame construction**, a **girt** might also function as tie beam.

Timber-frame construction — A method of building, also known as **post-and-beam**, in which a box-shaped skeleton of large, squared timbers functions as the structure's main supporting element. The major constituent timbers of this box or skeleton, assembled by fitting the timbers together with **mortise-and-tenon** joints, include the **post**, the **sill**, the **plate**, the **girt**, and the **summer beam**. Posts and girts are tied together with roof **rafters** in a complex component of the overall building frame structure known as a **bent**, which thus serves to unite the timber-frame box with the roof structure. The exterior walls are composed of wooden cladding, i.e. **weatherboard** or **clapboard**, or consist of **half-timber** work. In half-timber, the outer faces of the structural timbers themselves served to make up part of the exterior surface, with an intervening infill such as **wattle and daub** or stone masonry. In German, half-timber is referred to as *Fachwerk*. In the course of the nineteenth century, traditional timber-frame construction was gradually supplanted in America by modern light- or balloon-frame construction, in which relatively light timbers are nailed together. The long transitional period was also characterized by the presence of construction that combined the timber-frame and light-frame techniques, the more essential structural elements being heavier and mortised-and-tenoned. Timber-frame construction long persisted in buildings that required an extra degree of sturdiness, such as gristmills and large barns.

Treenail — A wooden peg hammered through a **mortise**-and-**tenon** joint to secure it; pronounced "trunnel."

Truss or roof truss — A triangular structure consisting of a pair of **principal rafters** and a **tie beam**, employed to confer rigidity to the roof structure. In a building employing a truss system, the weight of the roof is carried by the trusses, of which there are a limited number (perhaps four in a large house). A roof structure could also be composed of **common rafters**, with no trusses.

Type — Term used in reference to the classification of buildings by **plan**, e.g.,

"Swiss barn type" or "hall-parlor house type". Scholars of **vernacular architecture** have identified building type as a physical embodiment of people's ways of living, and hence a form that carries cultural memory and expression.

Up-and-down sawmill — See **Sawmill**.

V notching — In **corner-notching log construction**, the cutting of the end of each log into the shape of an upside-down "V" on its top edge, with a similar cut on the bottom edge but aligned to the building's other wall. With this relatively simple form of notching, gravity is the primary force acting to hold the log walls together.

Vaulted cellar — A cellar space with an arched ceiling.

Vernacular architecture — A term generally used to denote construction methods and building forms derived from traditional practice as opposed to those designed and built with direct and explicit adherence to academic architectural thought and practice. The traditional practice often incorporates a considerable though indirect influence from academic architecture. The impact of **Palladian** architectural design on the development of vernacular house types in eighteenth-century America represents a prominent example of this mingling of the academic with the traditional. **Vernacular architecture** is also used in reference to a growing body of scholarship that considers architecture, including that academically-inspired, as evidence in the study of cultural, social, and economic life.

Vertical sash window — A "sash" or two-part sliding window arrangement in which the two segments are positioned vertically (to move up-and-down). During the colonial period in America, almost all such window elements were constructed so that only the lower one of the two parts moved. Such windows are referred to as **single-hung sash**, as opposed to **double-hung sash**, which only became common in the nineteenth century, and in which both halves were movable.

Walmdach — See **Half-hipped roof**.

Wash house — An **outbuilding** in which laundering takes place. See **Ancillary house**.

Water race — See **Millrace**.

Waterwheel — A wheel that is moved by waterflow and transmits that motive power to mill machinery. The tall wheel, a few feet broad and made of wood during the colonial period, was positioned vertically so as to catch a fall of water. Horizontal boards fitted into the wheel's structure in effect created buckets to catch, carry, and then deposit the water in the course of the wheel's rotation. Wheels of varying design were built according to the dynamics of the particular mill's waterflow. The **wheelpit**, in which the waterwheel was situated, might be in a location **external** or **internal** to a **gristmill** building.

Wattle and daub — A method of making infill for **half-timber work**, consisting of woven sticks (the **wattle**) coated with a thick, plasterlike substance (the **daub**).

Weatherboard — A long, wide board (larger than a **clapboard**) used in cladding a wood-constructed building. Each **course** of weatherboard is applied so as to slightly overlap the course below.

Wheelpit — The enclosure within which a **waterwheel** is mounted. In an eighteenth-century **gristmill** building fitted with an **internal** wheel, the deep wheelpit had the lowest floor of the three areas in the split-level floor arrangement of the **basement** floor. The **lateral walls** of the mill were pierced by arched entry and exit openings for the water to flow into the wheelpit from the **headrace** and out into the **tailrace**.

Winder stairway — A stairway with two or more ninety-degree, right-angle turns, usually enclosed or **boxed** within its own compartment.

Wing — A dependent part of a house, smaller and often lower than the **main block**, and which extends to either side from the main block. In Pennsylvania vernacular houses, the **facade** of the wing might be flush with, or somewhat set back from the facade of the main block.

APPENDIX 6

ISOMETRIC PROJECTIONS OF OLEY VALLEY HOUSE-TYPES

ABRAHAM BERTOLET HOUSE, 1736,
Oley Township
Isometric projection of the plan.
Drawing by Hope M. LeVan, from field measurements by Kenneth LeVan and Hope M. LeVan.

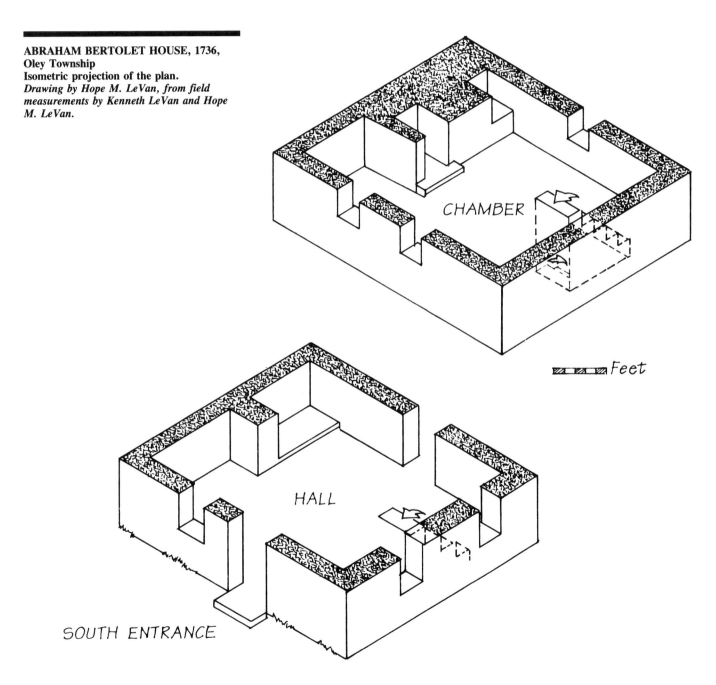

Chambered Hall
Abraham Bertolet House, 1736

167

OLEY VALLEY HERITAGE

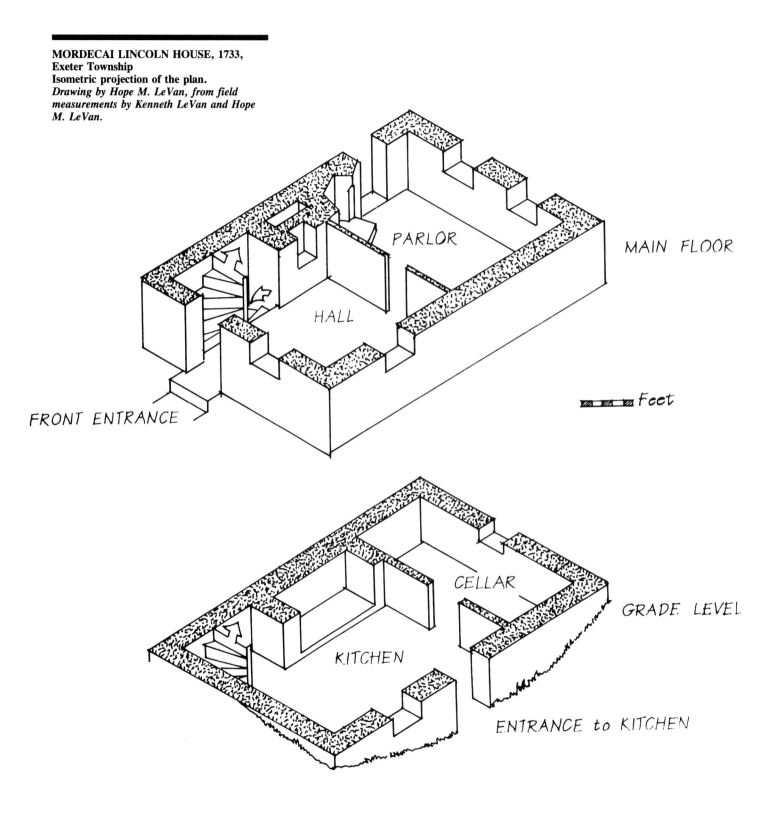

MORDECAI LINCOLN HOUSE, 1733,
Exeter Township
Isometric projection of the plan.
Drawing by Hope M. LeVan, from field measurements by Kenneth LeVan and Hope M. LeVan.

Double Cell (Penn plan)
Mordecai Lincoln House 1733

OLEY VALLEY HERITAGE

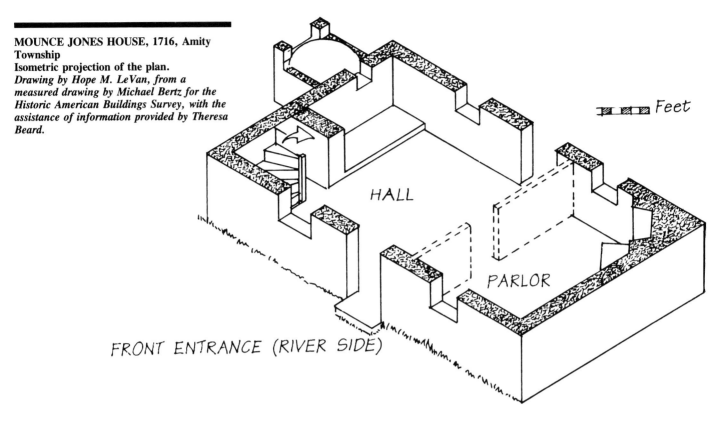

MOUNCE JONES HOUSE, 1716, Amity Township
Isometric projection of the plan.
Drawing by Hope M. LeVan, from a measured drawing by Michael Bertz for the Historic American Buildings Survey, with the assistance of information provided by Theresa Beard.

Hall - Parlor
Mounce Jones House, 1716

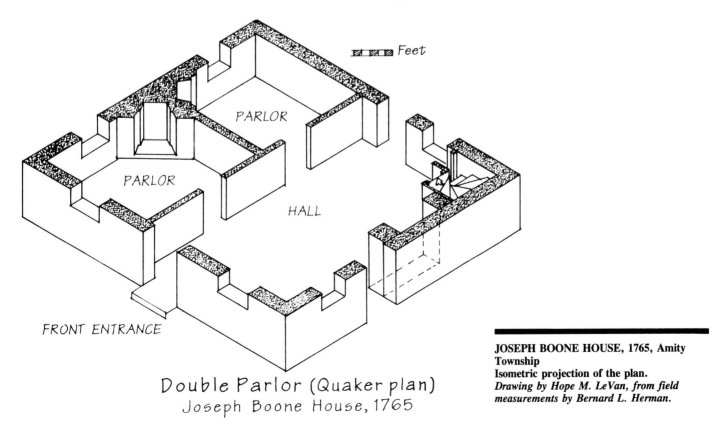

Double Parlor (Quaker plan)
Joseph Boone House, 1765

JOSEPH BOONE HOUSE, 1765, Amity Township
Isometric projection of the plan.
Drawing by Hope M. LeVan, from field measurements by Bernard L. Herman.

OLEY VALLEY HERITAGE

BERTOLET-HERBEIN HOUSE, Circa 1720-1750, Oley Township
Isometric projection of the plan.
Drawing by Hope M. LeVan, from a measured drawing by J. Michael Everett for the Historic American Buildings Survey.

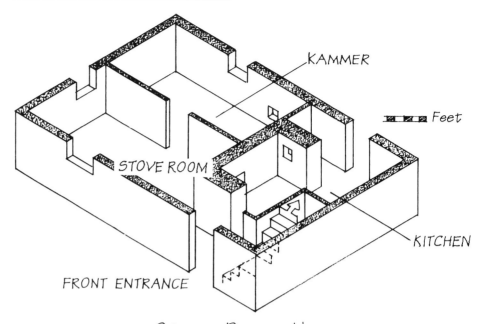

Stove Room House
story and a half log construction
Bertolet - Herbein House c.1720-1750

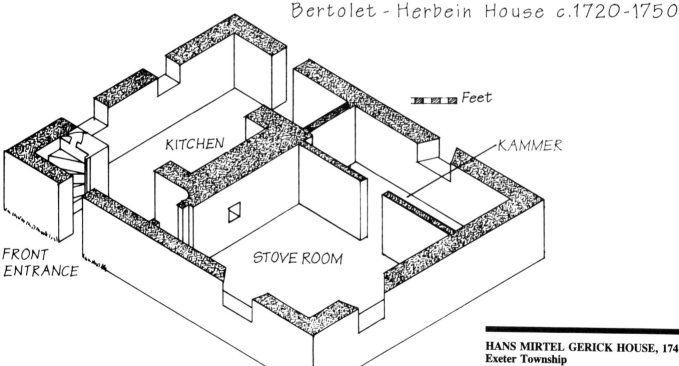

Stove Room House
two-story stone construction
Hans Mirtel Gerick House .1741

HANS MIRTEL GERICK HOUSE, 1741, Exeter Township
Isometric projection of the plan.
Comparison to the isometric projection of the plan of the roughly contemporary but much smaller Bertolet-Herbein House gives some idea of the importance that this three-room configuration of domestic space seems to have held for many colonial-period Pennsylvania Germans. Houses of widely differing size were constructed on the same basic plan, while among Anglo-Pennsylvanians larger dwelling size was likely to result in a greater number of rooms.
Drawing by Hope M. LeVan, from field measurements by James Lewars.

OLEY VALLEY HERITAGE

JOHANNES JAEGER (JOHN HUNTER) INN, 1768, Oley Township
Isometric projection of the plan.
Drawing by Hope M. LeVan, from a measured drawing by G. Edwin Brumbaugh.

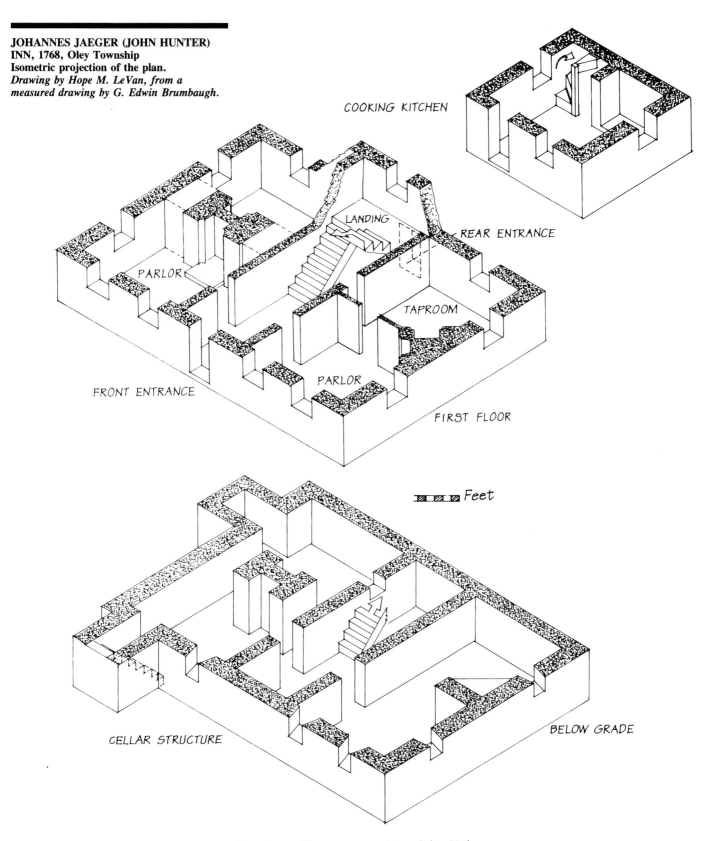

Center-Passage Double Pile
Georgian Palladian
Johannes Jaeger Inn, 1768

OLEY VALLEY HERITAGE

JOHANNES LESHER HOUSE (Oley Forge Mansion), Circa 1750-1755, Oley Township Isometric projection of the plan.
Drawing by Hope M. LeVan, from field measurements by Kenneth LeVan and Hope M. LeVan

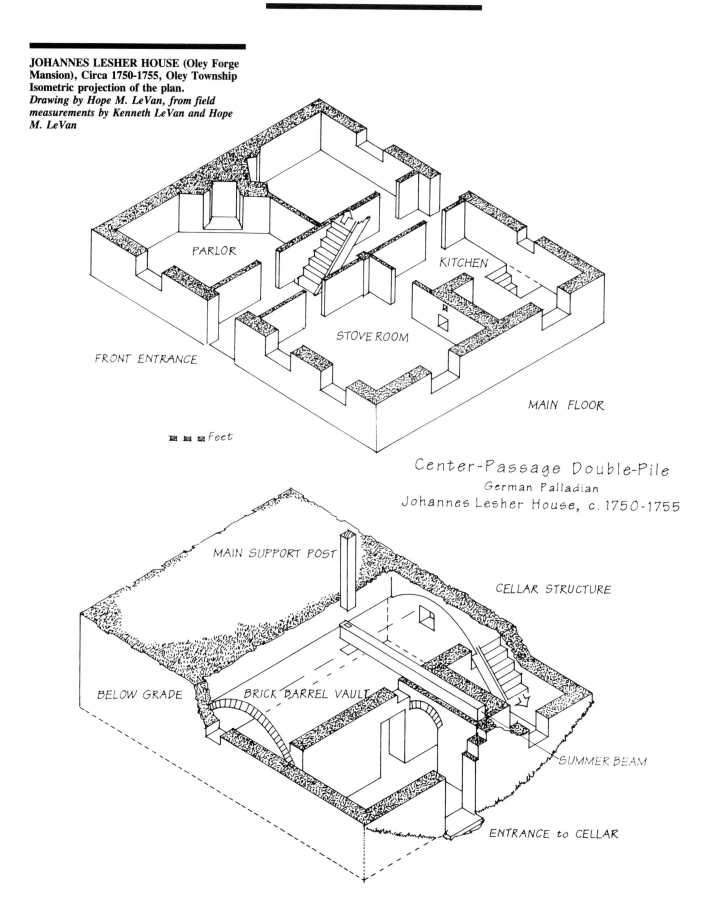

OLEY VALLEY HERITAGE

JOHANNES BISHOP HOUSE (Bishop Hall), Circa 1774, Exeter Township
Isometric projection of the plan. In the nineteenth century, the house received the addition of a smaller wing, which would extend to the lower right.
Drawing by Hope M. LeVan, from a measured drawing by Richard Levengood.

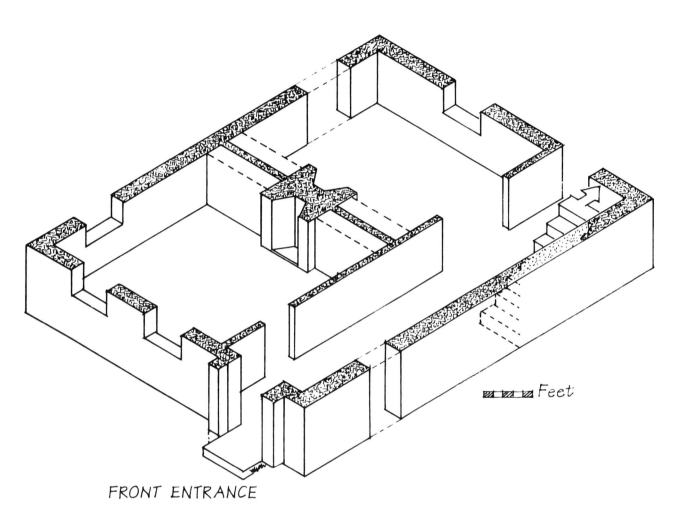

FRONT ENTRANCE

Side-Passage Double-Pile c.1774
Johannes Bishop House,

OLEY VALLEY HERITAGE

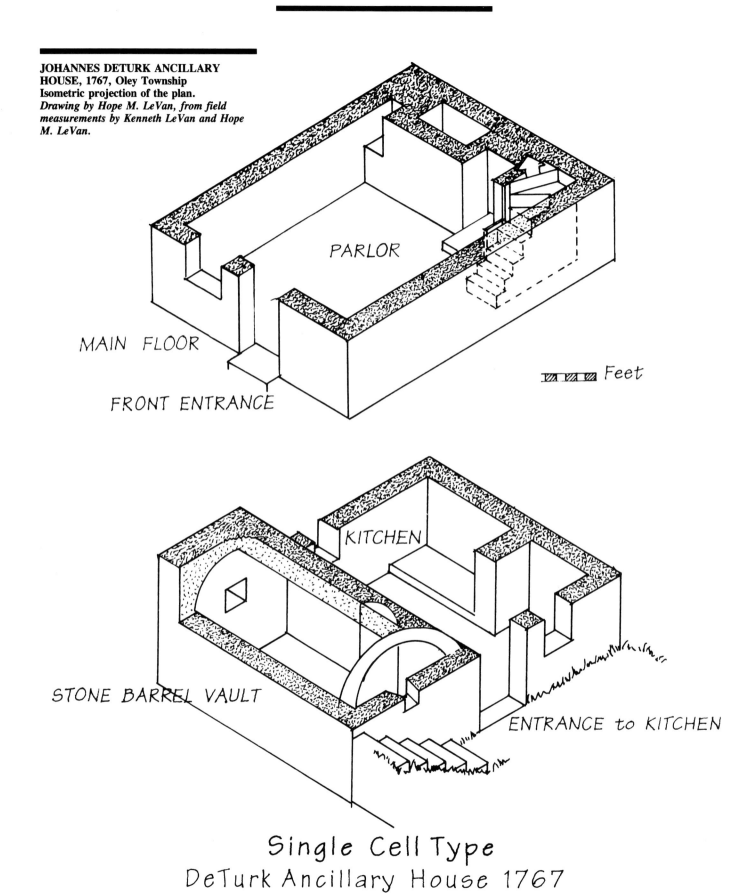

JOHANNES DETURK ANCILLARY HOUSE, 1767, Oley Township
Isometric projection of the plan.
Drawing by Hope M. LeVan, from field measurements by Kenneth LeVan and Hope M. LeVan.

Single Cell Type
DeTurk Ancillary House 1767

OLEY VALLEY HERITAGE

JERG LOTZ ANCILLARY HOUSE, 1762,
Amity Township
Isometric projection of the plan.
Drawing by Hope M. LeVan, from a measured drawing by Philip E. Pendleton.

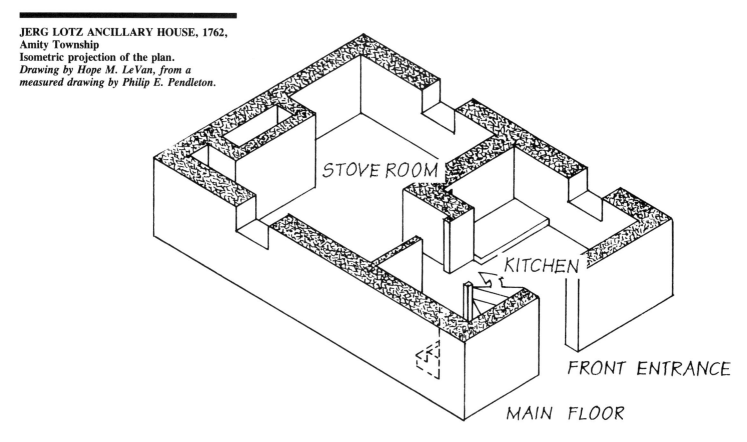

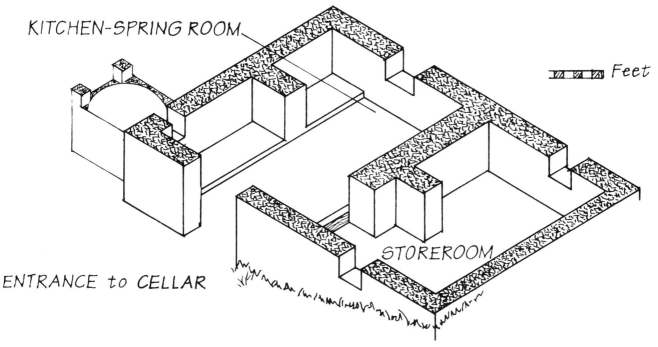

Stove Room House
Lotz Ancillary House c.1762

APPENDIX 7

KNOWN HEADS OF HOUSEHOLDS AND SINGLE FREEMEN RESIDING IN THE OLEY VALLEY 1701-1741

This list was compiled from land office records, deeds, probate records, tax records, petitions for townships and roads, church records, newspapers, and business ledgers. Many of the men named never acquired land. The dates indicated are the earliest that the subjects are known to have been living in the valley, or in sons' cases the earliest they are known to have had their own households. The date 1741 was chosen because in that year the last of the study area's three major townships (Exeter) was created. (The other two were Amity and Oley.) The geographical area researched for this list is that which was studied for this book, and which is depicted in the maps that appear in the book. The list indicates the modern township(s) in which the subject is known to have resided up to 1741.

*   Owned land within the study area (not necessarily at the date indicated)

Am	Amity
Do	Douglass
El	Earl
Ex	Exeter
Ol	Oley
Pi	Pike
Ro	Robeson
Un	Union

John Adams 1738
Johannes Albrecht (John Albright, Alprick) 1731
Johann Martin Altstadt (Alstatt) 1733 Ex *
George Anders (Andrew, Anderson, Enders) 1715 Am *
Wendel Andreas (Andrew) 1729 Am *
Abraham Aschmann (Ashman, Eshman, Ishman) 1720 Ol *
Friedrich Becker (Frederick Baker) 1739 Ex *
Heinrich Becker (Henry Baker) 1720
John Ball 1732 Am *
Andreas Ballie (Andrew Bally) 1727 Ol *
Peter Ballie (Bally) 1721 Ol *
John Banfield 1723 El, Am, Un *
Thomas Banfield (Benfield) 1728 Am
Joseph Barlow 1720
James Barnet 1731
Robert Barnet 1731
Dewald Baum 1729
Matthias Baumann (Bauman, Bowman) 1714 Ol *
Christopher Bechtel 1730 Ex *
Charles Bell 1725 Am *
Henry Bell 1719 Un, Am *
John Bell 1725 Am *
Friedrich Berger (Burger) 1727
Abraham Bertolet 1736 Ol *
Jean (John) Bertolet 1726 Ol *
Pierre (Peter) Bertolet 1720 Ol *
Gabriel Beyer (Boyer) 1733 Ol *
Philip Beyer (Boyer) 1735 Am *
William Bird 1728 Am, Ro *
William Blackford 1733
John Blair (Blare) 1721 Un *
Benjamin Boone 1728 Ex *
George Boone, Sr. 1718 Ex *
George Boone, Jr. 1718 Ex *
James Boone 1734 Ex *
John Boone 1731 Ex *
Joseph Boone 1731 Am *
Samuel Boone 1734 Ex *
Squire Boone 1730 Ex *
Andrew Bord (Burd, Bird) 1727 Ro *
Burgund Bord (Burd, Bird) 1735 Ex *
Jacob Bortzler (Borstler) 1741 Ol *
Johannes Bowman 1741 Ol *
Alexander Brindley 1736 Am *
John Brown 1734 Ro *
Joseph Browne (Brown) 1731 Ex
William Browne (Brown) 1731 Ex
Thomas Brumfield (Bromfield) 1720 Am *
James Burroughs 1727
John Burroughs 1731
Richard Caine 1718
Andrew Caldwell 1731 Am *
John Campbell (Camell, Cambell) 1712 Am *
John Campbell (Camell, Cambell) 1720 Am
Walter Campbell (Camell, Cambell) 1723 Am *
Nicolaus Carber 1740 Un *
Michael Chipp 1731
Ludwig Clapp 1733 Ex *
William Clark 1733
John Cocklin 1732
Daniel Cole 1741 Ex *
Solomon Cole 1734 Ex *
John Collins 1727 Ex *
Caspar Creager 1737 Pi *
David Davis 1729 Am *
William Davis 1720 Am *
Richard Dean 1720
Aaron Dehart 1732
Elias Dehart 1729 Am *
Gilbert Dehart 1731 Am *
James Dehart 1737
Simon Dehart 1731 Am *
Jacob DelaPlank (James DePlank, Delaplaine, Plank) 1720 Ol *
Isaac DeTurk 1712 Ol *
Johannes DeTurk 1734 Ol *
Ludwig Dibler 1736 Am *
Johannes Dillbork 1738
John Dollin 1738
Timothy Donner 1738
Robert Doughty 1723 Am *
Robert Dudley 1733
Peter Dunkelbach (Dunkleback) 1729
Johannes Dunkelberg (Dunklebery) 1732
Richard Dunkley 1718 Am *

OLEY VALLEY HERITAGE

John Ellis 1726 El, Ex *
Thomas Ellis 1729 Ol *
Christopher Engelhart (Engelhard) 1738
Nicolaus Engelhart (Englehard) 1733 Ol *
Philip Erhard (Azard) 1735 Un *
William Evans 1736 Un
Thomas Everett 1740 Am *
Jacob Everson 1736
Thomas Farrell 1729 Ex
Peter Faust 1733 Ex *
Jacob Fetter (Vetter) 1733 Ol *
Johann Adam Filbert (John Adam Philpert) 1731
Joseph Finney 1712 Am *
Thomas Finney 1721 Am
William Finsell 1731
Johannes Fischer (John Fisher) 1727 Ol *
Nicolaus Foos 1738 Do
John Foster 1733
Johannes Friedrich (John Frederick) 1738 Ol *
Jacob Fuge 1727
Andreas Fulk (Andrew Faulk, Folk) 1723 Am
Karl Fulk (Charles Faulk, Folk) 1731 Am *
Jacob Fulk (Faulk, Folk) 1731 Am *
William Furlong 1738
David Garrad 1733 Ol, Ex *
Johannes Geldbach (John Gelbach, Gelback) 1739 Ol *
John George 1728
Hans Mirtel (Martel, Mirtle) Gerick 1730 Ex *
George Gibson 1731
Henry Gibson 1712 Am *
Owen Gilbreath 1738
Thomas Godfrey 1739 Un *
Johann Heinrich Gouker (John Henry Cowger, Gowker) 1734 El *
Sebastian Greff (Graff) 1733 Ol *
Richard Gregory 1719 Ol *
Johann Theodorick Greiner 1717 Am *
Edward Griffith 1721
Ellis Griffith 1741 Am *
Samuel Guldin (Golden, Golding) 1734 Ol *
Ulrich Haggeman (Hageman) 1720 Ol
Samuel Harris 1732 Un *
Michael Harrison 1729
David Harry 1719 Am *
William Harverd (Harford, Harvard) 1730 Am *
Johannes Heagle 1722
Rudolph Heckler 1733 Ex *
Johann Leonard Heit 1733 Pi *
George Henton 1718 Am, Ex *

Abraham Herbein (Herbine, Harpin) 1733 Ol *
Jonathan Herbein (Herbein, Harpin) 1720 Ol *
Morgan Herbert 1731 Ex *
Peter Heygo (Higo, Hygo) 1734 Ex *
Jacob Hill 1735 El *
Johannes Hilsewick (Hilsebeck, Hilseweek) 1720 Ol *
Peter Hilton (Helton) 1725 Ex *
Richard Hilton (Houlton) 1729 Am *
Johannes Hoch (John High) 1727 Ol *
Samuel Hoch (High) 1727 Ol *
Lenhardt Hochgenug (Leonard Heighnoff, Hickenough) 1735 Ex *
Johannes Hodel 1731 Ol *
John Holder 1730
Johannes Hooveracker 1728
Enoch Hower 1738
Johann Arnoldt Huffnagel (Arnold Hufnagle) 1717 Ol *
Ellis Hughes (Hugh) 1731 Ex *
Francis Hughes 1720 Ro *
John Hughes 1741 Ex *
Marcus Huling (Hulings, Hulin) 1716 Am *
Peter Huyet (Huet, Huyett) 1741 Ex *
Antony Jaeger (Hunter) 1738 Ol *
Johann Jerg Jaeger (John George Hunter) 1730 Ol *
Nicolaus Jaeger (Hunter) 1739 Ol *
John James 1738 Am *
Johannes Joder, Sr. (Yoder) 1714 Ol *
Johannes Joder, Jr. (Yoder) 1734 Ol *
Jost Joder (Yost Yoder) 1717 Ol *
Philip John 1735 Un *
Andrew Jones 1727 Am *
Bariah Jones 1731
David Jones 1731
John Jones (Jonasson) 1709 Am *
John Jones 1736
Jonas Jones 1727 Am *
Mounce Jones (Magnus Jonasson) 1704 Am *
Peter Jones 1727 Am *
Samuel Jones 1731
Johann Dietrich Jungmann (Youngman) 1733 Ol *
John Justus (Justice) 1709 Am *
David Kauffmann (Coffman, Coughman, Kaufman) 1727 Ol *
Johannes Kauffman (Coffman, Coughman, Kaufman) 1733 Am
Johannes Keim (John Kime, Kyme) 1719 Ol *
Johann Jerg (George) Kelchner 1733 Ol *
Andreas Kepler 1733 Am *

Johann Heinrich Kersten (Kerst) 1714 Ol *
Johannes Kerst (Kersten) 1734 Ol *
Johannes Koch 1737 Ol *
Philip Kühlwein (Coolwine) 1709 Ol *
Christopher Lanire 1727
George Lanire 1727
Johannes Lebo 1739 Ex *
Jean LeDee 1709 Ol *
Anthony Lee 1713 Ol *
Friedrich Leinbach (Frederick Lineback) 1741 Ex, Ol *
Johannes Leinbach (John Lineback) 1723 Ol *
Isaac Lenhardt (Leonard) 1717 Ol *
Philip Leondekasy (Lesundegavy) 1736 El *
Johannes (John) Lesher 1735 Ol *
Nicolaus Lesher "Sr." 1729 Ol *
Nicolaus Lesher "Jr." 1735 Ol (not a son to the one above) *
Abraham Levan (Levant) 1727 Ol *
Isaac Levan (Levant) 1730 Ex *
Jacob Levan (Levant) 1729
James Lewis 1725 Cu *
John Lewis 1735 Ro *
Thomas Lewis 1719 Am *
Mordecai Lincoln 1727 Ex *
John Lloyd (Loyd) 1740 Un *
Benjamin Longworthy 1720 Ol *
Johann Frank Loodginer 1738
William Looth 1738
Johannes Lorah 1741 Am *
Michael Luckenbill (Lookingbill) 1736
Anders (Andrew) Lycon (Likens, Lykon, Leiken) 1709 Am
Peter Lycon (Likens, Lykon, Leiken) 1731
Alexander McGee (Magee) 1731
Charles McGrew (Magrew) 1737 Un *
Joseph McGuire 1734
Francis McManus 1731
Robert Mathews 1734 Ex *
Silvanus Maybery 1733
Friedrich Meinert (Frederick Meinhart) 1734 Ol *
Stephen Messerschmidt (Messersmith) 1725 Ex *
Thomas Millard (Miller) 1709 Un *
Adam Miller 1736 El *
Stephen Miller 1729 Am *
Hugh Mitchell 1736 Am *
William Morgan 1718 Ex *
William Morgan 1730
Friedrich Moyer (Meyer) 1738
Jacob Neas 1729
Victor Neely (Nealy, Neily) 1731 Ro *
Walter Newman 1708 Am *
Job Noble 1719 Am

James Norrill 1733 Ol *
James Old 1731
Johannes Oyster (John Eyster) 1734 Pi *
Thomas Palmer 1731 Ex, Am *
Jerg (George) Passler 1738
Robert Patterson 1731 Ex *
Engelhard (Engle, Engel) Peter (Poeter) 1719 Ol *
John Phillips 1731 Am *
Wilhelm (William) Pott 1739 Pi *
John Price 1734 Ro *
Francis Pummill 1720
Edward Rees 1726 Am *
George Rees 1740 Un *
Griffith Rees 1736 Ro *
Thomas Rees 1728 Un, Am *
Conrad Reiff (Rife) 1737 Ol *
Anders Reinberg (Andrew Ringberry) 1730 Do, Am *
Peter L. Reiss (Rice) 1729
Robert Rew 1731
James Richard 1725 Am *
Owen Richard 1718 Am *
Owen Richard, Jr. 1733 Ex, Am *
William Richard 1731 Am *
Rowland Richards 1741 Ex, Am
John Richardson 1738
Henry Ridner 1738
Franz Ritter (Francis Rutter) 1733 Ex *
Jerg Ritter (George Rutter) 1725 Ex *
William Roberts 1727 Ex *
Andrew Robeson 1714 Ex *
Israel Robeson 1718 Ro *
Jonathan Robeson 1725 Ex *
Peter Robeson 1733 Ex *
Samuel Robeson 1737 Ro *
Johann Conrad Rodt 1732
Johann Jacob Rodt (Jacob Roth, Roads, Rhoads) 1717 Am *
Roger Rogers 1740 Ro *
Francis Rouse (Rew, Rowe, Ruse) 1734 Am *
John Rumford 1713 Un *
Joseph Rutter 1729 Do *
Thomas Rutter 1715 Do *
Conrad Sadler 1737 Ex *
Antony Sadowski (Sadowsky) 1712 Am *

Abijah Sands 1733 Am *
John Sands 1734 Am *
Samuel Savage 1716 Am *
John Scarlet, Jr. 1740 Ro *
Samuel Schall (Shall, Sholl, Saul) 1717 Ex *
Martin Schenckel (Shenkel, Shankle) 1719 Ol *
Ulrich Scherer (Sherer) 1733 Ex *
Maximillian Schiffer (Shiffer, Sheffer) 1733 Ol *
Johannes Schneider (John Snyder, Snider, Sneyder) 1717 Ol *
Johann Jacob Schneider 1741 Ol *
Johann Nicolaus Seehang 1733 Ex *
Jacob Seltzer (Selzer) 1738 Ol *
Peter Shilbert (Shilpert) 1733 Ol *
John Showell 1738
John Sinclair 1718 Un *
John Sleder 1731
Isaac Smaily (Smally) 1731
John Smith 1720
Robert Smith 1734
Thomas Smith 1731
Daniel Spencer 1736
Robert Stapleton 1727 Ol *
Jacob Stauber (Stover) 1713 Ol *
Thomas Steel 1736
David Stephens 1728 Un *
Thomas Stone 1720
Hans Stult (Stolt) 1718 Am *
Ralph Sutton 1719 Ol *
Martin Sweetner 1738
Heinrich Thomas 1733 Ol *
Lewis Thomas 1718 Am *
James Thompson 1720 Ex *
John Tribby 1719 Am, Un *
Richard Truman (Trewman, Trueman) 1719 Ex *
Caspar Trump 1724 Am *
Anthony Turner 1731 Am *
John Turner 1734 El *
Thomas Turner 1732 Am *
Elias Wagner (Wagoner) 1740 Ex *
Benjamin Wainwright 1727
John Wainwright 1730 Ex
Jacob Warren (Waren) 1730 Am *
James Warren (Waren) 1719 Am *

John Warren, Sr. (Waren) 1731 Am *
John Warren, Jr. (Waren) 1719 Am *
Michael Warren (Waren) 1733 Am, Ex *
Daniel Warlick (Warlich) 1738 Ol *
Evan Watkins 1729 Am *
John Webb 1734 Ex *
Jacob Weber (Weaver) 1724 (probably circa 1714) Am *
Christian Weicks (Wicks, Wix) 1734 Ex *
Adam Weidner 1727 Ol *
Jerg (George) Adam Weidner 1735 Pi, El *
Johannes Weidner 1738
Peter Weidner Before 1734 Pi *
Johannes Weiler 1737 Ex *
Martin Weiler 1730 Ex *
David Weiser 1740 Ol *
Isaac Weisman (Wiseman) 1725
Aaron Werner (Vernon, Warner) 1733 Un *
Heinrich Werner (Henry Vernon, Warner) 1733 Ex *
Samuel Whitacre (Whitaker) 1725 Am *
Daniel Wilkinson 1734
Samuel Wilkinson 1741 Ex
Thomas Willits 1737 Am *
John Williams 1741 Ex
Owen Williams 1731 Am *
James Winter 1729 Am *
Heinrich Winterberg (Henry Winterberry) 1734 Un, Ro *
Johann Heinrich Wolf 1731 Ex *
Daniel Womelsdorff (Wummelsdorf, Womelsdorf) 1731 Am *
Richard Wood 1720
Thomas Wyatt 1736 Ex *
Peter Yarnell (Yarnall) 1730 Ex *
John Yocom (Yocum, Yokom, Jochim) 1726 Do *
Jonas Yocom (Yocum, Yokom, Jochim) 1714 Do *

APPENDIX 8

TOWNSHIP ZONE MAPS FOR 1725, 1750, AND 1775 SHOWING BUSINESSES, SOCIAL ORGANIZATIONS, AND NATIONALITIES

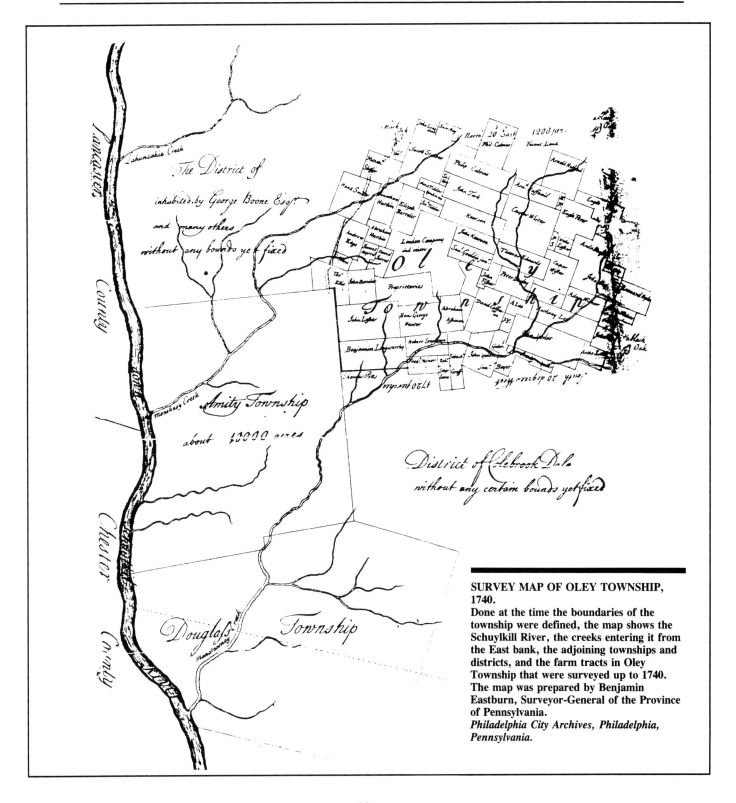

SURVEY MAP OF OLEY TOWNSHIP, 1740.
Done at the time the boundaries of the township were defined, the map shows the Schuylkill River, the creeks entering it from the East bank, the adjoining townships and districts, and the farm tracts in Oley Township that were surveyed up to 1740. The map was prepared by Benjamin Eastburn, Surveyor-General of the Province of Pennsylvania.
Philadelphia City Archives, Philadelphia, Pennsylvania.

OLEY VALLEY HERITAGE

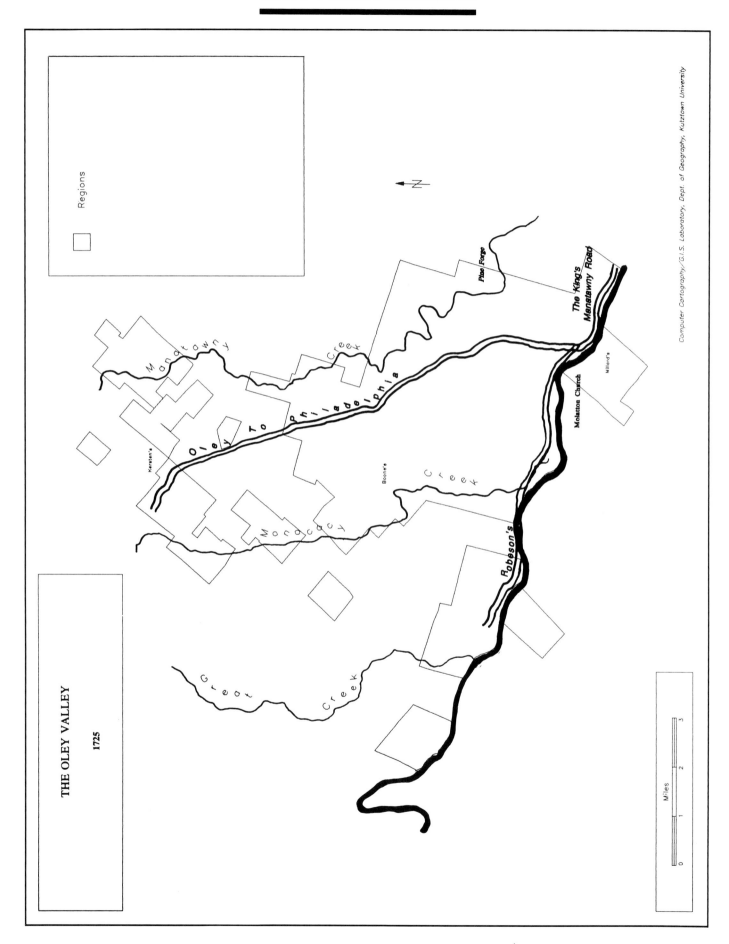

OLEY VALLEY HERITAGE

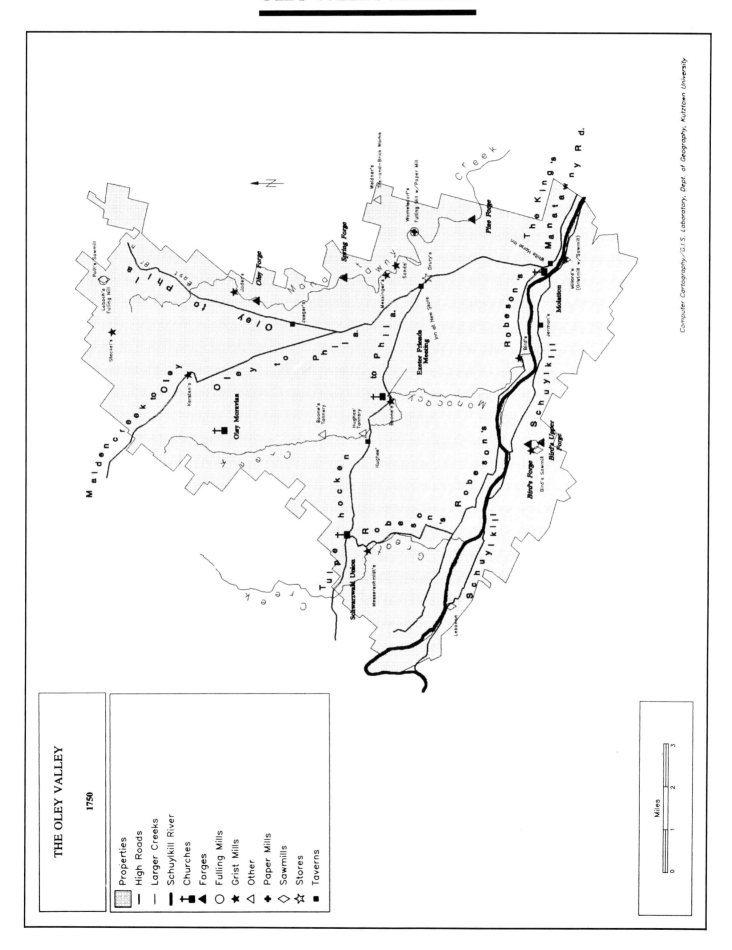

OLEY VALLEY HERITAGE

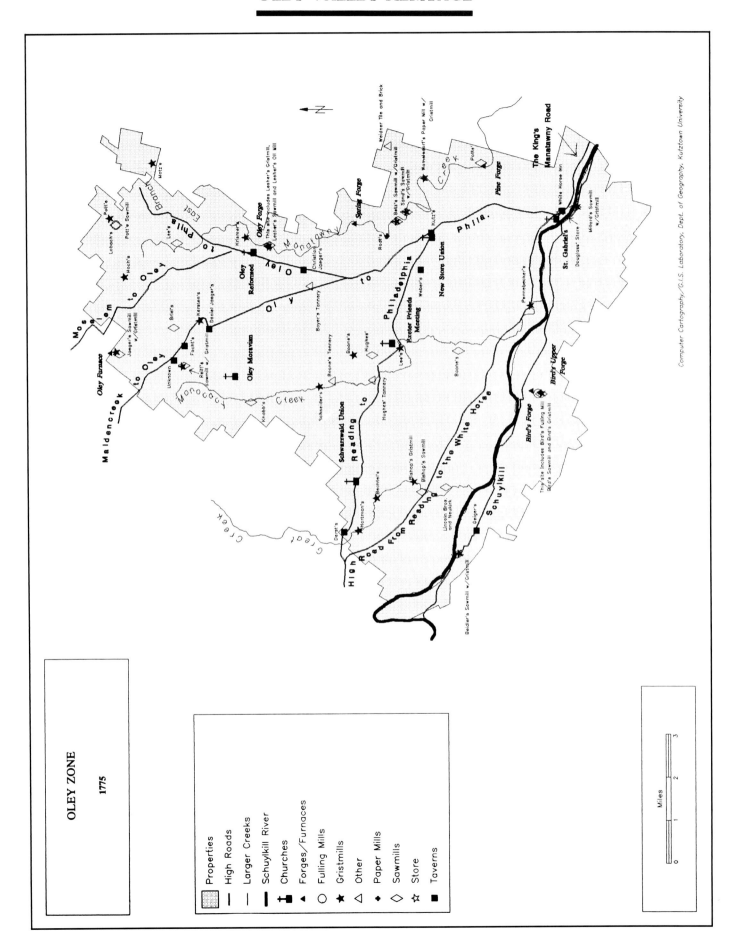

OLEY VALLEY HERITAGE

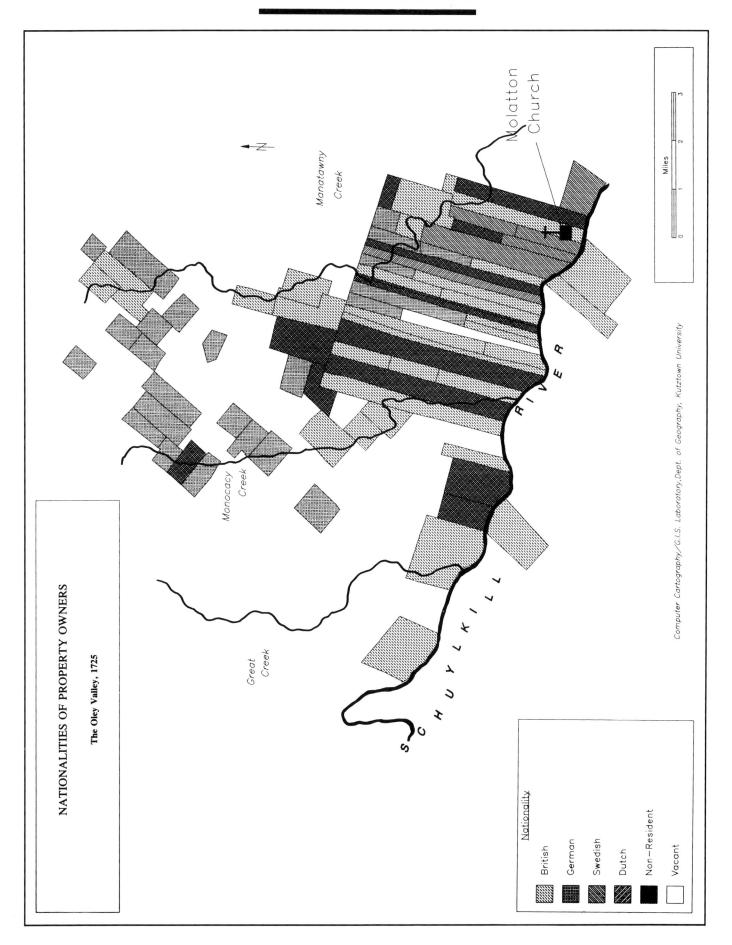

OLEY VALLEY HERITAGE

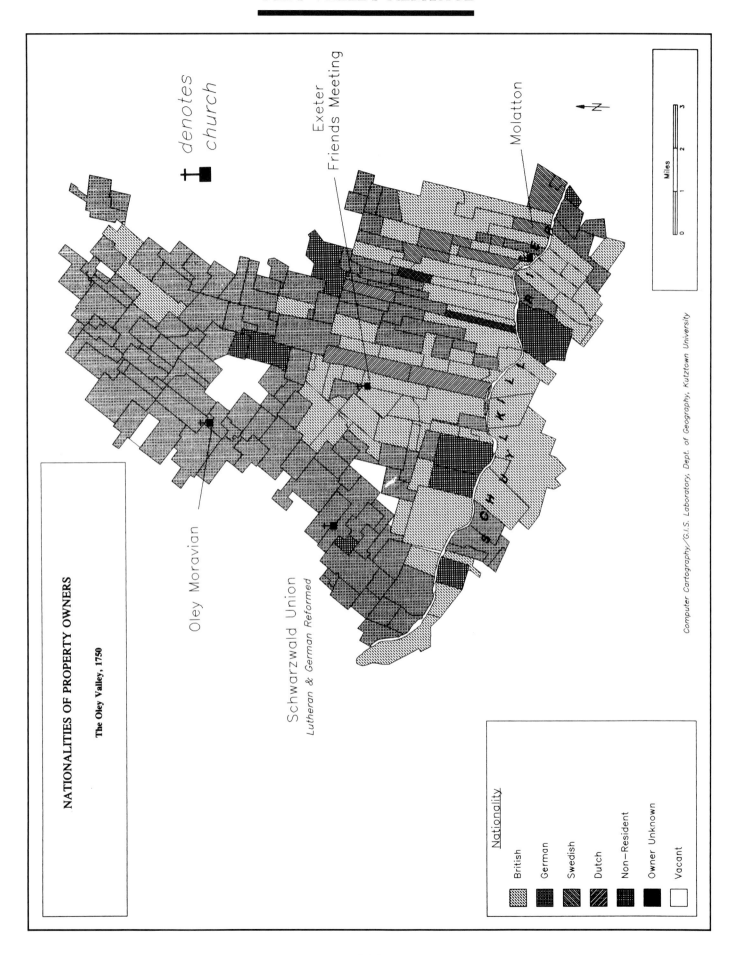

OLEY VALLEY HERITAGE

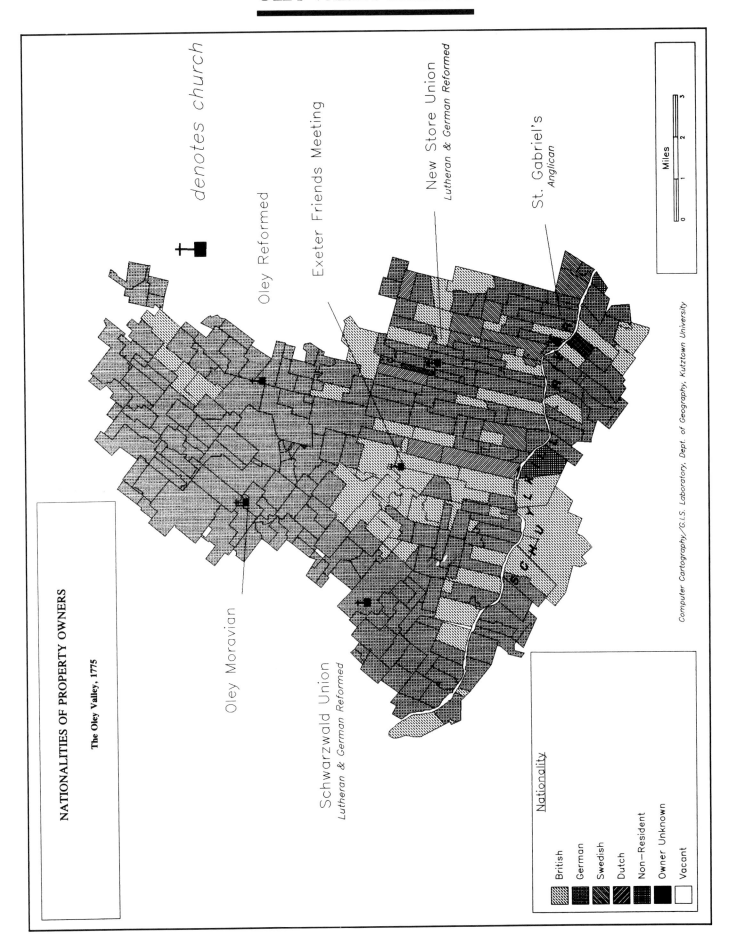

APPENDIX 9

TOWNSHIP ZONE MAPS FOR 1725, 1750, AND 1775, WITH PROPERTY OWNERSHIP KEY

Occupation of the valley by Europeans began by 1704, but the initial, "pioneer" stage persisted for three or four decades. As of 1725, only the fringe of the Exeter Township area had been claimed, and much of the fertile upper valley ("Oley proper") and the great bulk of the south bank of the Schuylkill were unclaimed. Because Amity Township had originated as a land grant, and thus was claimed in its entirety, its thinly settled nature is veiled. The valley's industrial works comprised Thomas Rutter's exploratory iron-refining effort at Pine Forge, and three gristmills. Two spur roads had been run into the valley, their junction in the earliest settled precinct making a logical site for Molatton Church, the valley's first established church congregation. Sometime within the next two decades Marcus Huling established the White Horse Inn, the valley's first house of public entertainment and accommodation.

At this early date, claimed or owned properties in the valley did not compose one great, contiguous block. Instead, early settlers and outside real-estate investors took up tracts in various parts of the valley, according to their preferences. At the onset of settlement, Germans tended to gravitate toward the northern end of the especially fertile upper valley (or "Oley proper"). This concentration possibly represents a cluster of New Born adherents who settled together. British settlers and non-resident owners tended to claim or buy land along the Schuylkill, in the immediate watershed of Monocacy Creek, or in the southern end of the upper valley (i.e., on these maps the southern fringe of the Oley Zone and the northern fringe of the Amity Zone). The Swedes, the valley's initial pioneers and founders of Molatton Church, maintained a relative enclave in the southeast corner of the valley.

The pattern of land ownership in 1725 gives a slightly misleading idea of the pattern of actual European settlement in the valley. In reality, a few additional German homesteaders, who had not yet claimed land, enlarged the extent of settlement in the north end of the upper valley (Oley Zone) somewhat. Amity Township, the distinctly rectangular southeastern subdivision of the valley, had originated as one large private property, the Swedes' Tract. Settlers clustered along its northern boundary (at the lower end of the rich, limestone-floored upper valley area), and along the Schuylkill. The broad central section of Amity was left nearly empty (though owned by non-resident individuals).

During the colonial years the valley was gradually and discontiguously surveyed into properties of varying size, but generally in shapes as nearly rectangular as possible. The bounds of each new property were set out on one of two basic alignments, as decreed by circumstance. In the southeastern part of the valley, surveys were run in a direction roughly twenty compass degrees east of North (N20*E), almost perpendicular to the course of the Schuylkill River. Tracts were laid out to fall straight back from the river. This pattern was initiated in the Swedes' Tract, the first claim in the valley (1701). The seventeen Delaware Valley Swedes, initial grantees, desired river frontage for every separate parcel within the tract. Although only one of the original Swedish patentees (Mounce Jones) actually settled on the tract, at the planning stage the Swedes evidently anticipated a period of adherence to their traditional nautical mode of transportation. Early properties extending contiguously along the north bank of the Schuylkill to the west of the Swedes' Tract, and farther into the upper Oley Valley to the north, were surveyed on the same twenty-compass-degrees-east-of-North alignment. In the remainder of the valley (i.e., in its north and northwest areas and on the south bank of the Schuylkill), surveys were run on a northeast-southwest axis.

In 1750 the development process was well underway. Settlement had reached every corner of the valley. There were more religious congregations, more high roads, more ironworks and gristmills, and a plethora of industrial sites and commercial businesses: sawmills, taverns, tanneries, stores, fulling mills, a paper mill and a tile-and-brick works. The immediate watershed of Manatawny Creek had emerged as a veritable "industrial corridor," a role in which it would soon be joined by Monocacy and Great (or Antietam) creeks.

The large, irregularly shaped "vacant" tract just north of the center of the valley evidently represented a tacit reservation, the shrunken domain of the local Lenape. A tendency to form neighborhoods based on nationality was apparent, with churches of corresponding national origin at the center of these neighborhoods. Due to the somewhat easy use of the Schuylkill as a transportation route for light, day-to-day travel, Molatton Church's neighborhood extended well up- and downriver.

By 1775 the development process, with steady increase in overall population and in the number of properties, and with further economic growth and diversification, had led to a slight move toward urbanization. Churches and business sites formed hamlets at the road junctions at Molatton (Saint Gabriel's Church), New Store, and the vicinity of the modern village of Oley (the mile along the High Road from Maidencreek to Oley, from Daniel Jaeger's tavern northward). The industrial concentrations built by Johannes Lesher at Oley Forge and by the Bird family at Bird's Forges had created what might be called "company hamlets." From these modest concentrations of settlement would evolve, respectively, modern Douglassville, Amityville, Oley, Spangsville, and Birdsboro.

Most of the large initial tracts patented before 1740 had been subdivided. Migration into the valley during the latter half of the period (about 1740-1775) had been predominantly by German-speaking people. British and Swedish children had exhibited a greater tendency to leave the valley for other parts as they matured. Throughout the period the proportion of inhabitants who were transients, staying a few years and then moving on, as opposed to permanent settlers, had been higher among the British than among the Germans. These factors resulted in an ongoing trend toward the conveyance of land from British sellers to German buyers. In 1775 the neighborhoods of Exeter Meeting and Saint Gabriel's persisted to some degree as English-speaking enclaves, but German, British, and Swedish homesteads were increasingly intermingled.

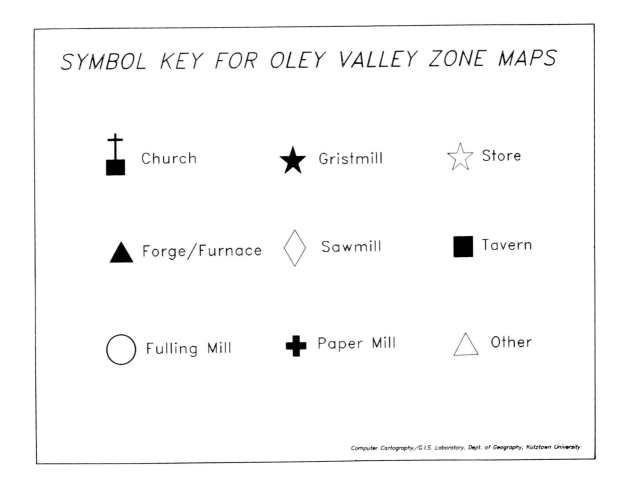

OLEY VALLEY HERITAGE

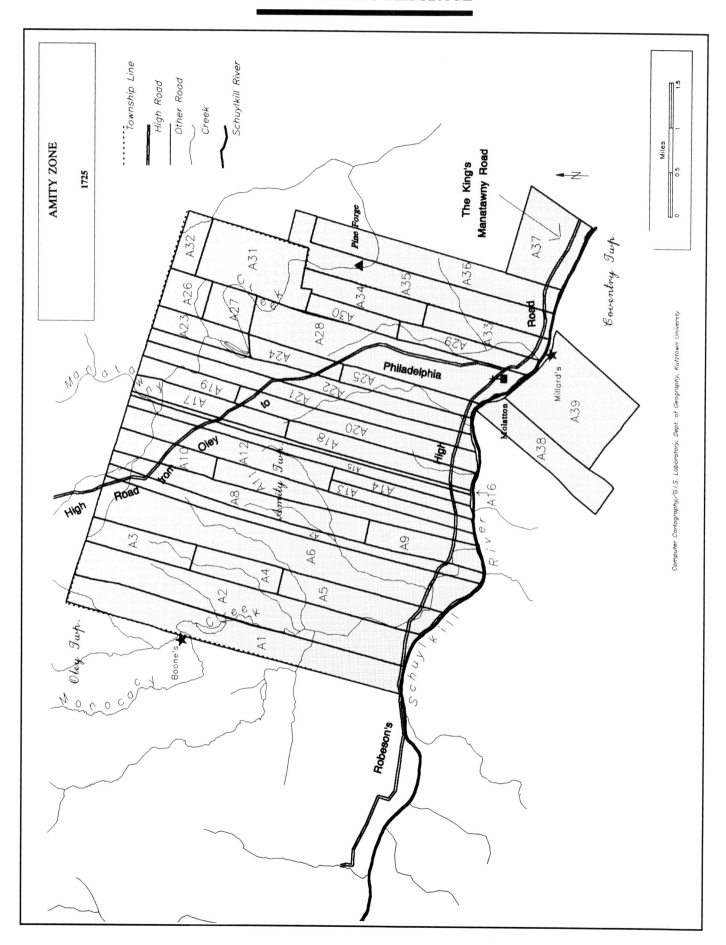

Landowners of Amity Township, Philadelphia County, and Adjacent Area 1725

1. George Boone, Sr.
2. Benjamin Borden (resident in Freehold, Monmouth County, East New Jersey)
3. Thomas Brumfield
4. James Warren
5. John Warren, Jr.
6. Gershan Mott (resident in Middletown, Monmouth County, East New Jersey)
7. Estate of John Campbell
8. Owen Richard
9. Stephen Miller
10. Jacob Weber (Weaver)
11. VACANT
12. Andreas Fulk
13. Charles Bell
14. John Bell
15. Estate of Peter Boon (resident in Penn's Neck, Salem County, West New Jersey)
16. Stephen Brush (location of residence unknown, but probably not in Oley Valley)
17. David Harry
18. William Davis
19. George Anders
20. Joseph Finney
21. Antony Sadowsky
22. Thomas Edwards (resident in Freehold, Monmouth County, East New Jersey)
23. Johann Theodorick Greiner
24. Johann Jacob Rodt (Roth, Rhoads)
25. Henry Gibson
26. Caspar Trump
27. Robert Doughty
28. Magnus Jonasson (Mounce Jones)
29. Marcus Huling
30. Estate of George Savage (resident in Roxborough Township, Philadelphia County)
31. Estate of Samuel Savage
32. Estate of George Savage (resident in Roxborough Township, Philadelphia County)
33. Anders Lycon
34. Magnus Jonasson (Mounce Jones)
35. Thomas Rutter, Sr.—"Pine Forge"
36. Thomas Rutter, Jr. (resident in Philadelphia)
37. Jonas and John Yocom
38. John Rumford, *Coventry Township, Chester County*
39. Thomas Millard (Miller), *Coventry Township, Chester County*

OLEY VALLEY HERITAGE

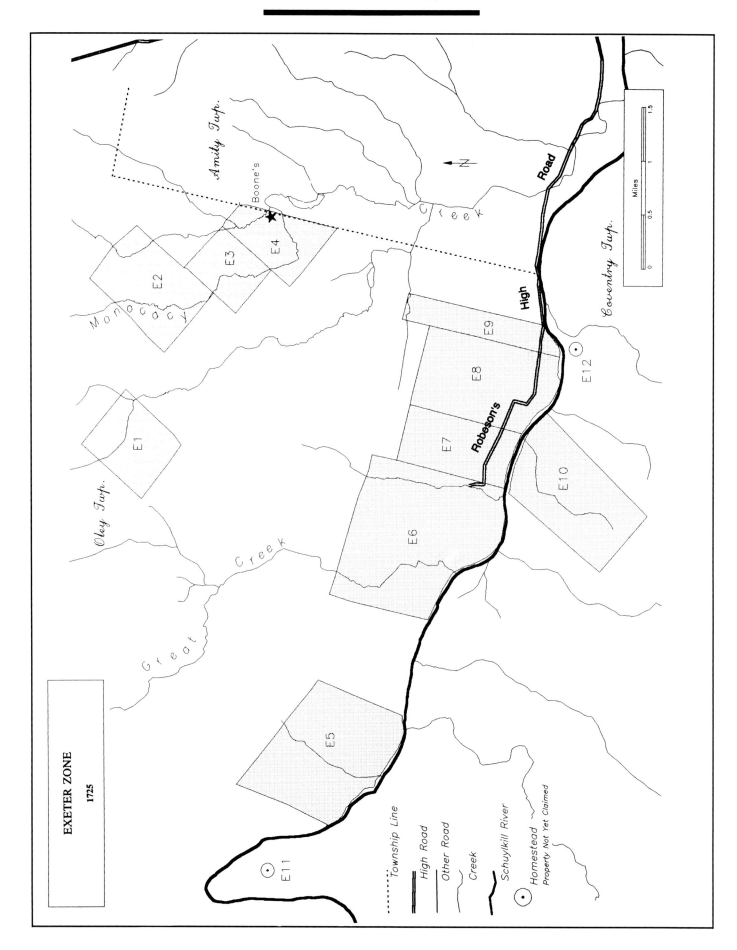

Landowners of Oley Township (Southwestern Section), Philadelphia County, and Adjacent Area 1725

1. Jerg Ritter (George Rutter)
2. George Boone, Sr.
3. Richard Trueman
4. George Boone, Jr.
5. Estate of Andrew Robeson
6. Estate of Andrew Robeson
7. John Jones (resident in Philadelphia)
8. Joseph Kirkbride (resident in Falls Township, Bucks County)
9. William Morgan
10. Israel Robeson, *Coventry Township, Chester County*

Residents with homesteads settled but land not yet claimed:

11. James Lewis
12. Francis Hughes

OLEY VALLEY HERITAGE

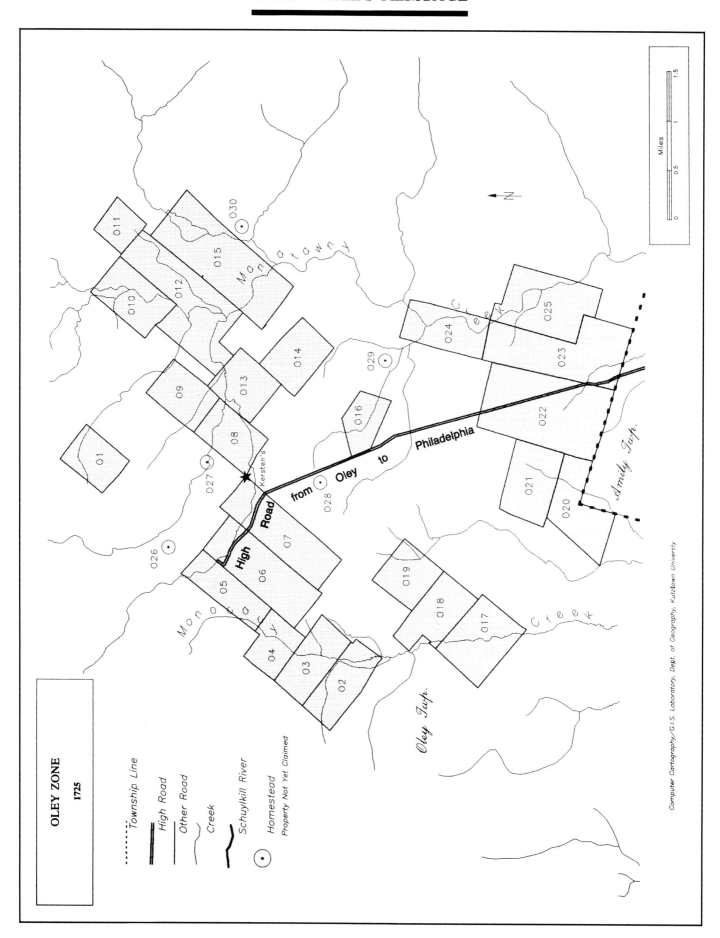

Landowners of Oley Township (Northeastern Section), Philadelphia County, 1725

1. Engelhard Peter
2. Johannes Leinbach (Lineback)
3. Edward Evans (resident in Abington Township, Philadelphia County)
4. Matthias Baumann (Bowman)
5. Philip Kühlwein (Coolwine)
6. Isaac DeTurk
7. Johann Heinrich Kersten
8. Esther DeTurk
9. Katarina Weimer
10. Richard Gregory
11. Johannes Keim (Cime)
12. Anthony Lee
13. Peter Ballie
14. Jonathan Herbein
15. Johannes Joder (John Yoder)
16. Martin Schenkel (Shankle)
17. Johannes Schneider (Snyder)
18. Jonathan Herbein
19. Pierre Bertolet
20. David Evans (resident in Philadelphia)
21. Isaac Lenhardt (Leonard)
22. John Shiers (resident in Plymouth Township, Philadelphia County)
23. Benjamin Longworthy
24. Thomas Millard (Miller)
25. John Banfield

Residents with homesteads settled but land not yet claimed:

26. Johann Arnoldt Huffnagel
27. Jacob DelaPlank
28. Johannes Hilseweck
29. Abraham Aschmann
30. Johann Jost Joder

OLEY VALLEY HERITAGE

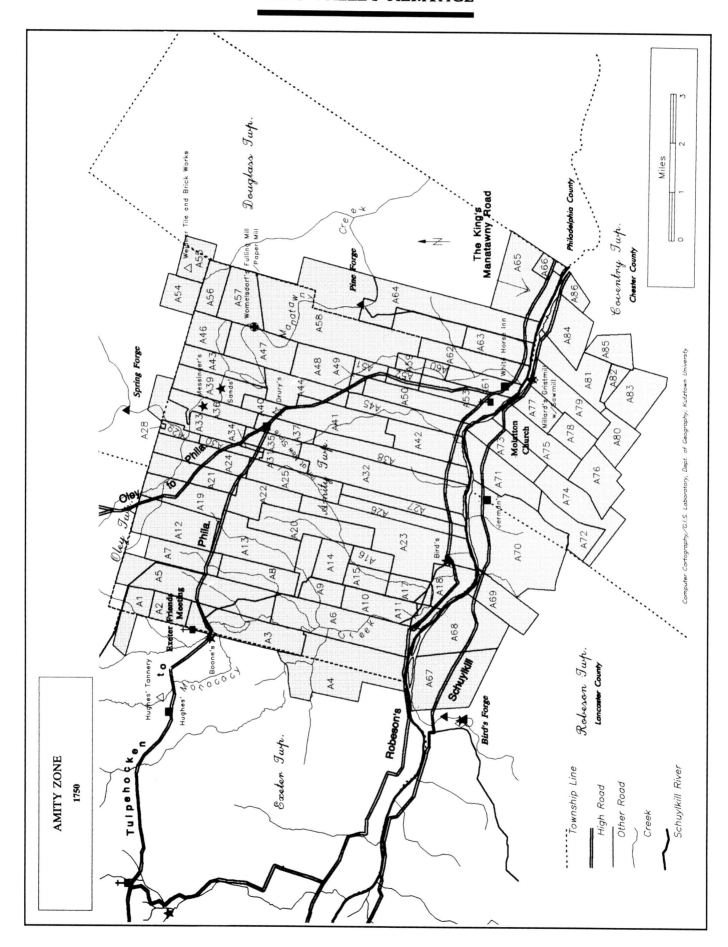

OLEY VALLEY HERITAGE

Landowners of Amity Township, Philadelphia County, and Adjacent Area 1750

1. Morris Ellis, *Exeter Township*
2. Estate of Samuel Boone
3. John Boone
4. Joseph Boone
5. Gilbert Dehart
6. William Winter
7. Thomas Brumfield
8. John Warren
9. John Ball
10. Jacob Warren
11. Hugh McCafferty
12. Anthony Lee
13. Johannes Lorah
14. Jerg (George) Lotz
15. Ellis Griffith
16. Adam Wartman
17. Adam Wartman
18. John Campbell
19. Jacob Rodt (Roth, Rhoads)
20. Peter Weber (Weaver)
21. Peter Weber (Weaver)
22. Jacob Weber (Weaver)
23. William Bird
24. Cornelius Dehart
25. Daniel Andreas
26. OWNER UNKNOWN—Charles Bell in 1725; Eidel Gerhard in 1767
27. Estate of Stephen Miller
28. Daniel Froelich
29. Reinhold Aubenshein
30. Martin Becker
31. Michael Trump
32. William Bird and John Potts
33. Philip Beyer
34. Michael Messinger
35. Estate of Johann Jerg Bechtel
36. Michael Messinger
37. Nicolaus Jaeger (Hunter) or George Anders (Andrew)—Jaeger renewed license for public house on property in June 1750; Anders renewed license in September 1751.
38. Hugh Mitchell
39. John Sands
40. Edward Drury
41. James Warren
42. George Boone
43. Johann Theodorick Greiner
44. Jonas Jones
45. Henry Gibson
46. Daniel Ludwig
47. Abijah Sands
48. Jonas Jones
49. Moses Heyman
50. Peter Jones
51. Nicholas Jones
52. Owen Richard
53. Thomas Banfield
54. Johann Heinrich Gouker (Cowger), Jerg (George) Adam Weidner
55. Heinrich VanReed
56.
57. Daniel Womelsdorff
58. John Potts—Pine Forge, *Douglass Township, Philadelphia County*
59. Johannes Raifschneider
60. John Huling
61. Philip Balzer Cressman
62. Benjamin Boone
63. Mounce Huling, *Douglass Township*
64. Thomas Potts, *Douglass Township*
65. Jonas Yocom, *Douglass Township*
66. Anders Reinberg (Ringberry), *Douglass Township*
67. John Harrison, *Robeson Township, Lancaster County*
68. Caleb Harrison, *Robeson Township*
69. John Lincoln, *Robeson Township*
70. Anthony Morris, *Robeson Township* (resident in Philadelphia)
71. Jacob Stover, *Coventry Township, Chester County*
72. John Thomas, *Coventry Township*
73. Thomas Godfrey, *Coventry Township*
74. John Godfrey, *Coventry Township*
75. Thomas Millard, *Coventry Township*
76. Samuel Harris, *Coventry Township*
77. Benjamin Millard, *Coventry Township*
78. Timothy Millard, *Coventry Township*
79. Thomas Millard, *Coventry Township*
80. Isaac Adams, *Coventry Township*
81. Daniel Joder (Yoder), *Coventry Township*
82. VACANT
83. Charles McGrew, *Coventry Township*
84. Abraham Wanger, *Coventry Township*
85. Andrew Wolf, *Coventry Township*
86. James Ingles (resident on an adjoining property in Coventry Township outside study area)

OLEY VALLEY HERITAGE

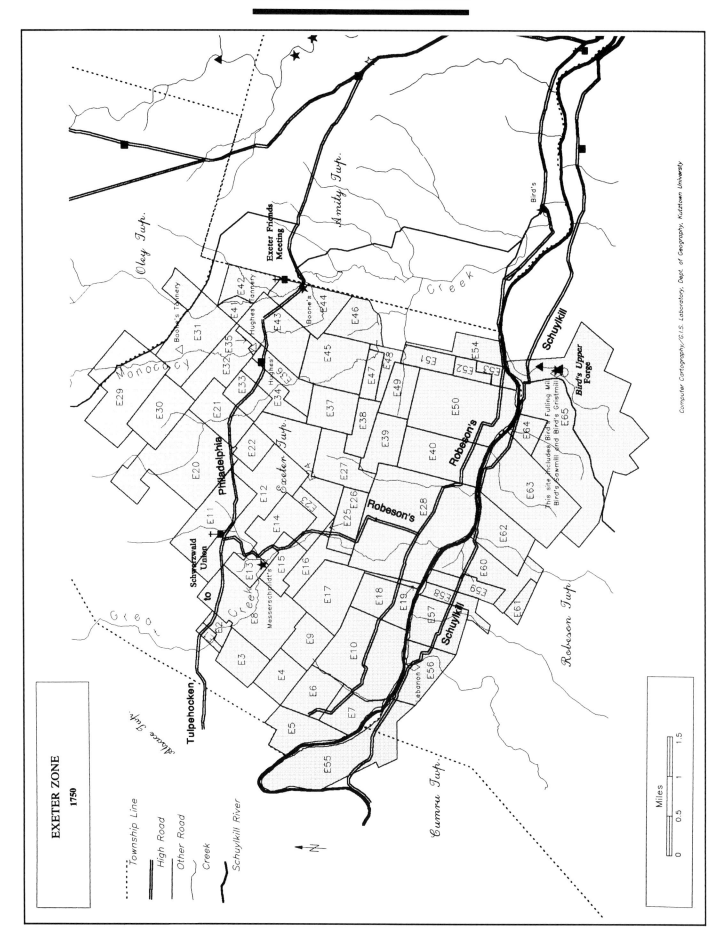

OLEY VALLEY HERITAGE

Landowners of Exeter Township (Part), Philadelphia County, and Adjacent Area 1750

1. Isaac Levan (Levant)
2. Estate of Johannes Kerst
3. Michael Zeister
4. Heinrich Werner (Vernon)
5. Isaac Levan (Levant)
6. Elias Wagner
7. Daniel Messerschmidt (Messersmith)
8. Isaac Levan (Levant)
9. Johannes Bishop
10. Johannes Lebo
11. Johann Martin Alstadt
12. Hans Mirtel Gerick
13. William Allen (resident in Philadelphia)
14. Valentine Messerschmidt (Messersmith)
15. Martin Weiler
16. Christopher Beyer
17. Christopher Bechtel
18. James Thompson
19. VACANT
20. Franz Ritter (Rutter)
21. Friedrich Becker (Baker)
22. Lenhard Hochgenug (Highenough)
23. Peter Faust
24. VACANT
25. George Henton
26. George Henton
27. Peter Huyet
28. Estate of Mordecai Lincoln
29. Estate of Johannes Schneider (Snyder), *Oley Township*
30. Rudolph Heckler
31. James Boone
32. John Webb
33. Lenhard Hochgenug (Highenough)
34. Nicolaus Keim
35. John Hughes
36. Benjamin Boone
37. Ludwig Clapp
38. Michael Ludwig
39. Daniel Cole
40. Samuel Massey (resident in Philadelphia)
41. Estate of Samuel Boone
42. Caspar Stahl
43. Ellis Hughes (Hugh)
44. George Boone
45. Benjamin Boone
46. William Maugridge
47. David Garrad
48. Henry Thompson
49. Jacob Beyer
50. Joseph Kirkbride (resident in Falls Township, Bucks County)
51. Daniel Cole
52. Robert Patterson
53. Clement Cherington
54. Estate of Conrad Sadler
55. James Lewis, *Cumru Township, Lancaster County*
56. George Boone, *Robeson Township, Lancaster County*
57. Antony Geiger, *Robeson Township* (resident in Douglass Township, Philadelphia County)
58. Roger Rogers, *Robeson Township*
59. Elias Retge (Redcay), *Robeson Township*
60. Heinrich Winterberg (Winterberry), *Robeson Township*
61. Elias Retge (Redcay), *Robeson Township*
62. Johann Adam Neidig (Nidy), *Robeson Township*
63. Israel Robeson, *Robeson Township*
64. Samuel Robeson, *Robeson Township*
65. William Bird—"Bird's Forge," *Robeson Township*

OLEY VALLEY HERITAGE

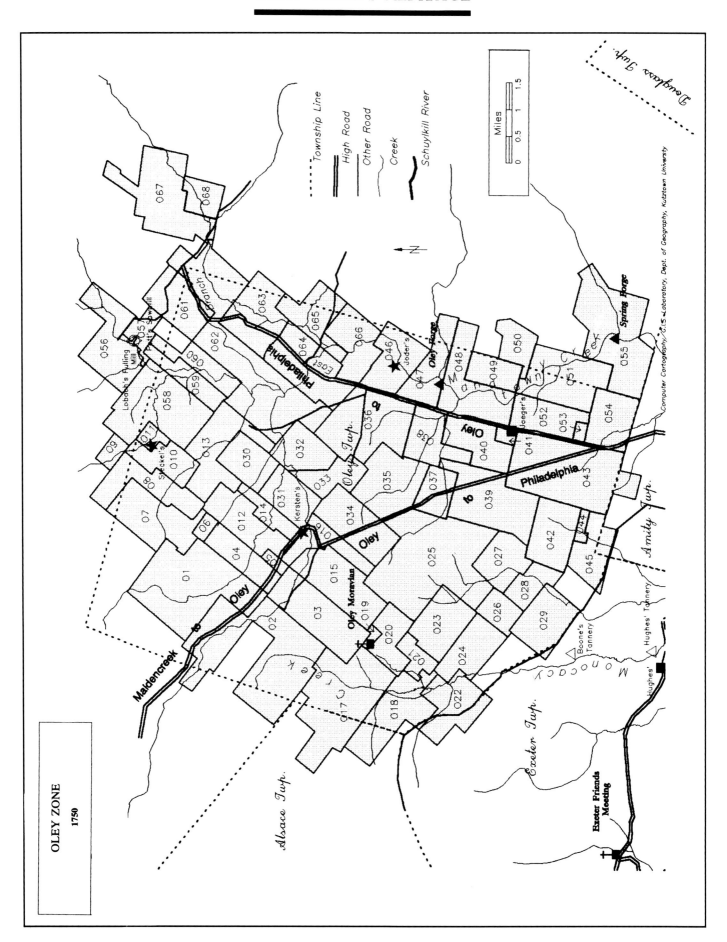

Landowners of Oley Township, Philadelphia County 1750

1. Johann Arnold Huffnagel
2. Conrad Reiff (and the Estate of Philip Kühlwein)
3. Johannes DeTurk
4. Daniel Warlick
5. Johann Jerg (George) Kelchner
6. Johannes Friedrich (Frederick)
7. Abraham Peter
8. Johannes Barto
9. Dietrich Hilt
10. Nicolaus Lesher
11. Valentine Steckel
12. David Weiser
13. Johannes Lesher
14. Jacob DelaPlank (James DePlank, Delaplaine, Plank)
15. Antony Jaeger (Hunter)
16. Estate of Johannes Kerst
17. Samuel Hoch (High)
18. Estate of Johannes Leinbach
19. Oley Moravian Church and School
20. Johann Dietrich Jungmann (Youngman)
21. Johannes Baumann (Bowman)
22. Maximillian Schiffer
23. Jonathan Herbein
24. Jonathan Herbein
25. VACANT (evidently the domain of the Lenape Indians)
26. Philip Herbein
27. Jean Bertolet
28. Valentine Reiss
29. Jacob Selzer (Seltser)
30. Abraham Levan (Levant)
31. Abraham Bertolet
32. Johannes Bertolet, Jr.
33. Johannes Fischer (Fisher)
34. Samuel Guldin
35. Estate of Martin Schenkel
36. David Kauffmann
37. Caspar Wistar (resident in Philadelphia)
38. Caspar Griesemer (Krismer)
39. Mary Shewbart (resident in Philadelphia)
40. Nicolaus Jaeger (Hunter)
41. Johannes Jaeger (John Hunter)
42. Jean Bertolet
43. Johannes Lesher
44. Rowland Ellis
45. Thomas Ellis
46. Johannes Joder (Yoder)
47. John Ross (resident in Philadelphia) and Johannes Lesher—Oley Forge
48. Robert Stapleton
49. Friedrich Meinert (Meinhart)
50. George Boone
51. Jacob Hill
52. Benjamin Longworthy
53. Jacob Kines
54. Johannes Geldbach
55. Thomas Potts (resident in Colebrookdale Township, Philadelphia County), Samuel Mickle (resident in Philadelphia), and George Mifflin (resident in Philadelphia)—Spring Forge
56. Wilhelm Pott
57. Peter Lobach
58. Johannes Hoch (John High)
59. Tychicus Weidner
60. Lazarus Weidner
61. Johannes Keim
62. Anthony Lee
63. Johannes Joder (John Yoder)
64. Daniel Joder (Yoder)
65. Johann Jost Joder (Yoder)
66. Gabriel Beyer
67. Johannes Oyster (Eister)
68. Caspar Creager

OLEY VALLEY HERITAGE

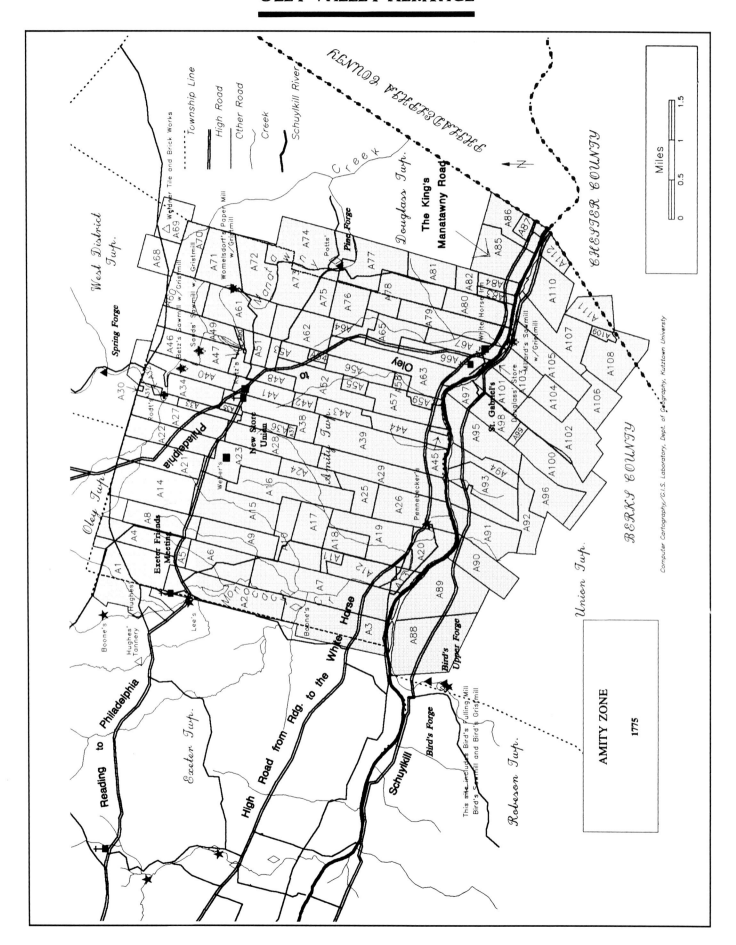

Landowners of Amity Township, Berks County, and Adjacent Area 1775

1. Samuel Lee, *Exeter Township*
2. Isaac Boone
3. Hugh Boone
4. Lorentz Strunk
5. Lawrence Rattican
6. William Dehart
7. William Winter
8. Solomon Brumfield
9. Estate of John Warren
10. Johannes Dieter
11. Jerg (George) Lotz
12. Moses Bower
13. Peter Fischer
14. Christian Jaeger (Hunter)
15. Jerg (George) Lorah
16. Peter Weber (Weaver)
17. Jerg (George) Lotz
18. Estate of Ellis Griffith
19. Mounce Jones
20. Heinrich Lehr (Lear)
21. Jacob Rodt (Roth, Rhoads)
22. Peter Weber (Weaver)
23. Jacob Weber (Weaver)
24. Benjamin Williams
25. Heinrich Lehr (Lear)
26. Derick Pennebecker
27. Cornelius Dehart
28. Michael Ludwig
29. David Davis
30. Daniel Froehlich (Fraylig)
31. Jacob Klein
32. Jacob Rodt (Roth, Rhoads)
33. Location of dividing line unknown: Cornelius Dehart (36 acres to north) and Michael Ludwig (20 acres to south)
34. Johannes Beyer
35. Nicolaus Beyer
36. Peter Mock
37. Nicolaus Beyer
38. Jerg (George) Lanciscus
39. Peter Dehaven
40. Johannes Betz
41. Thomas Kutz
42. Heinrich Herner
43. Samuel Hoch (High)
44. Peter Gruenwald (Greenwalt)
45. Samuel Hoch (High)
46. Estate of John Sands
47. Mary Jones
48. Balthasar Leffel
49. Johannes Greiner
50. Nicholas Jones
51. Jonathan Bell
52. Johann Nicolaus Seidel
53. Nicholas Jones
54. Jonathan Bell
55. Samuel Reinberg (Ringberry)
56. Abraham Beidler
57. David Davis
58. Estate of Andrew Gibson
59. Samuel Reinberg (Ringberry)
60. Michael Ludwig, Jr.
61. Estate of Abijah Sands
62. Jonas Jones
63. Estate of Peter Jones
64. James Bowen
65. Martin Marquart (Markwert)
66. Johannes Kerlin
67. George Douglass
68. Johannes Motzer, *West District Township*
69. Jerg (George) Adam Weidner, *West District Township*
70. Henry VanReed
71. Estate of Daniel Womelsdorff
72. Estate of John Potts
73. Peter Bunn
74. David Potts—Pine Forge, *Douglass Township*
75. Jacob Lebengut (Levergood, Lebengood)
76. Peter Yocom
77. Heinrich Egle, *Douglass Township*
78. Jacob Wenger, *Douglass Township*
79. Jacob Cupp
80. Jost Sees, *Douglass Township*
81. Karl and Johannes Lubold, *Douglass Township*
82. Heinrich Egle, *Douglass Township*
83. Johannes Hoffmann, *Douglass Township*
84. Peter Moser, *Douglass Township*
85. Estate of Jonas Yocom, *Douglass Township*
86. Peter Yocom, *Douglass Township*
87. Nicolaus Bunn, *Douglass Township*
88. John Harrison, *Union Township*
89. Caleb Harrison, *Union Township* (resident in Middletown Township, Chester County)
90. Jacob Retge (Redcay), *Union Township*
91. Johannes Steiner (Stoner), *Union Township*
92. Jerg (George) Kerst, *Union Township*
93. Thomas Parry, *Union Township*
94. Johannes Umsted, *Union Township*
95. Jerg (George) Kerst, *Union Township*
96. Johannes Dehaven, *Union Township*
97. Jerg (George) Ax (Acks), *Union Township*
98. Abraham Wistler, *Union Township*
99. Jerg (George) Ax (Acks), *Union Township*
100. Johannes Umsted, *Union Township*
101. John Godfrey, *Union Township*
102. Johannes Wanger, *Union Township*
103. Location of dividing line unknown: John Godfrey (northwestern half) and Joseph Millard, Jr. (southeastern half), *Union Township*
104. Owen Reinhard, *Union Township*
105. Mordecai Millard, *Union Township*
106. George Douglass, *Union Township*
107. Daniel Joder (Yoder), *Union Township*
108. Jane Millard, *Union Township*
109. Mordecai Harris, *Union Township*
110. Abraham Wanger, *Union Township*
111. Jacob Switzer, *Union Township*
112. James Ingles, *Union Township* (resident on an adjoining property in Coventry Township, Chester County)

OLEY VALLEY HERITAGE

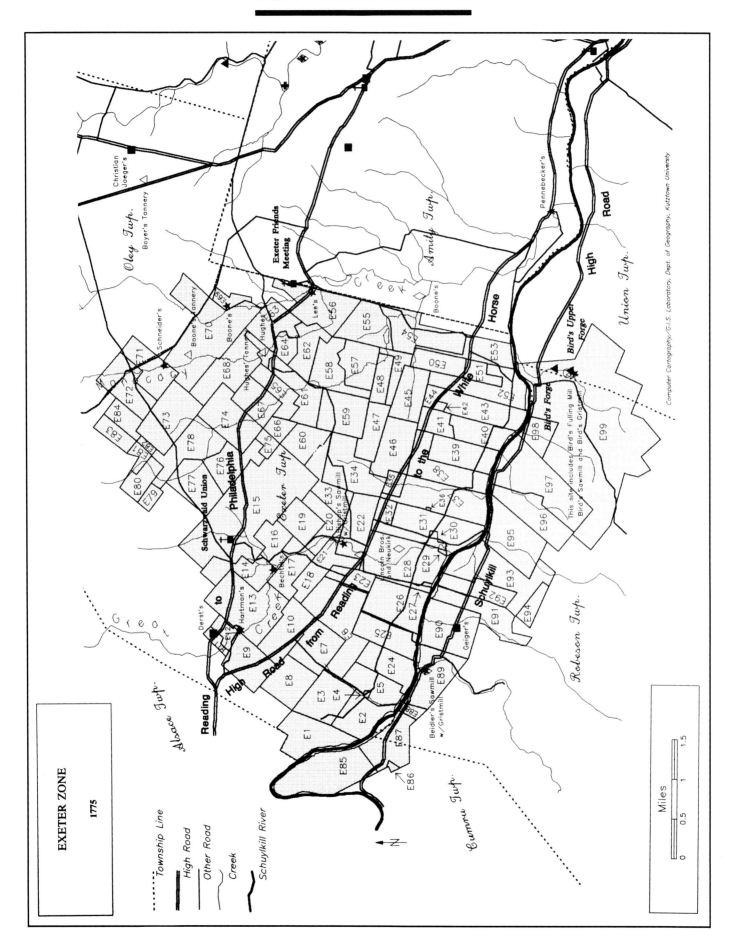

OLEY VALLEY HERITAGE

Landowners of Exeter Township (Part), Berks County, and Adjacent Area 1775

1. Abraham Levan
2. Daniel Messerschmidt
3. Abraham Levan
4. OWNER UNKNOWN (William Miller in 1760)
5. Lenhard Lebo
6. Jacob Bechtel
7. Paul Derst
8. Abraham Levan
9. Paul Derst
10. Daniel Levan
11. Paul Derst
12. Johannes Hartmann
13. Jacob Levan
14. Heinrich Kerst
15. Adam Altstadt
16. Johannes Bechtel
17. Jacob Weiler
18. Christopher Beyer
19. Paul Ritter (Rutter)
20. Johannes Bishop
21. Johannes Bishop
22. Johannes Bishop
23. Johannes Bechtel
24. Friedrich Guthard (Goodhart)
25. Johannes Bechtel
26. John Thompson
27. VACANT
28. Abraham Lincoln
29. Benjamin Tallman
30. Jacob Bechtel
31. Johannes Neukirch
32. James Millard
33. Jacob Weiler
34. Heinrich Kloss (Close)
35. Philip Kaub
36. Thomas Lincoln
37. Mordecai Lincoln
38. Johann Jacob Huyet
39. Benjamin Tallman
40. Michael Christ
41. Nicolaus Herner
42. Michael Christ
43. Friedrich Herner
44. Jonathan Millard
45. Johannes Beyer
46. Matthias Dieter
47. Michael Ludwig
48. Michael Ludwig
49. Henry Thompson
50. Nicolaus Herner
51. Robert Patterson
52. Matthias Herner
53. Estate of Conrad Sadler
54. Joseph Boone, Jr.
55. Johannes DeTurk, Jr.
56. John Lee
57. Benjamin Boone
58. Samuel Boone
59. Johannes Beiler
60. Robert Henton
61. Peter Bechtel
62. Abel Thomas
63. Samuel Hughes
64. George Hughes
65. Edward Hughes
66. Benjamin Boone
67. William Collins
68. Samuel Webb
69. Judah Boone
70. James Boone
71. Peter Schneider (Snyder)
72. Johann Jacob Schneider (Snyder), *Oley Township*
73. Johannes Heckler
74. Adam Jung (Young)
75. William Collins
76. Israel Ritter (Rutter)
77. Franz Ritter (Rutter)
78. Jerg Ritter (Rutter)
79. Jerg Ritter (Rutter)
80. Israel Ritter (Rutter)
81. Franz Ritter (Rutter)
82. VACANT
83. Johann Jacob Schneider (Snyder)
84. Peter Schneider (Snyder)
85. Richard Lewis, *Cumru Township*
86. Richard Lewis, *Cumru Township*
87. Sebastian Morian, *Cumru Township*
88. Richard Lewis, *Robeson Township*
89. Conrad Beidler, *Robeson Township*
90. Christopher Geiger, *Robeson Township*
91. Valentine Hahn, *Robeson Township*
92. Elias Retge (Redcay), *Robeson Township*
93. Heinrich Pennebecker, *Robeson Township*
94. Elias Retge (Redcay), *Robeson Township*
95. Estate of Valentine Eames (Embs, Aims), *Robeson Township*
96. Herman Umsted, *Robeson Township*
97. Moses Robeson, *Robeson Township*
98. Robert Patterson, *Robeson Township*
99. Mark Bird—Bird's Forges, *Robeson Township*

OLEY VALLEY HERITAGE

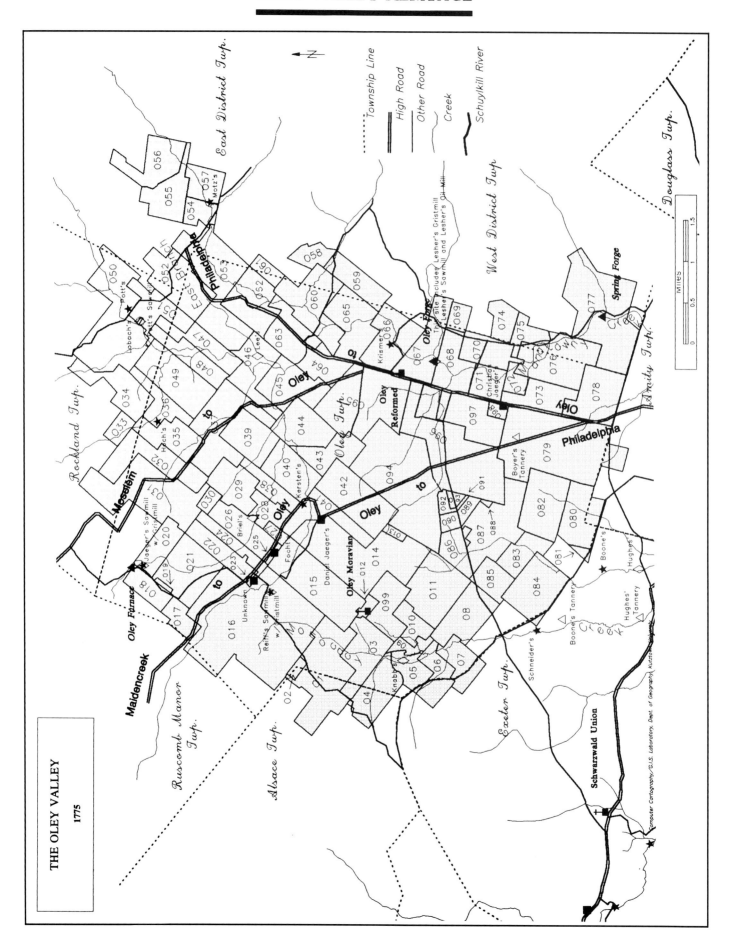

OLEY VALLEY HERITAGE

Landowners of Oley Township, Berks County, and Adjacent Area 1775

1. Daniel Hoch (High)
2. VACANT
3. Estate of Samuel Hoch (High)
4. Heinrich Leinbach (Lineback)
5. Peter Knabb
6. Johannes Schiffer
7. Daniel Schneider, *Exeter Township*
8. Jacob Herbein
9. Ulrich Mohn
10. Jacob Wiest
11. Peter Herbein
12. Oley Moravian Church
13. Johannes Stoetzel (Stitzel)
14. Daniel Jaeger (Hunter)
15. Johannes DeTurk
16. Conrad Reiff and the Estate of Philip Kühlwein
17. Daniel Wentzel
18. Jacob Winey (resident in Philadelphia), Christian Lower (resident in Tulpehocken Township) and Henry Smith—Oley Furnace
19. Elias Huffnagel
20. Friedrich Jaeger (Hunter)
21. Johannes Stoetzel (Stitzel)
22. Elias Huffnagel
23. Deborah and Philip Reiff
24. Estate of Benjamin Huffnagel
25. Jerg (George) Focht
26. Peter Briel
27. Matthias Sauermilch (Sowermilk)
28. David Weiser
29. Christian Weiser
30. Isaac Barto
31. Daniel Peter
32. Isaac Barto
33. Estate of Johannes Hoch (John High), Jr., *Rockland Township*
34. Jacob Keim, *Rockland Township*
35. Nicolaus Lesher
36. Estate of Johannes Hoch (John High), Jr.
37. Johannes Lesher
38. Daniel Rothermel
39. Daniel Levan
40. Daniel Bertolet
41. Heinrich Kerst
42. Daniel Guldin
43. Estate of Johannes Reppert
44. Johannes Bertolet
45. Thomas Lee
46. Samuel Lee
47. Lazarus Weidner
48. Tychicus Weidner
49. Abraham Hoch
50. TWO TRACTS, *Rockland Township*: Jacob Joder (Yoder) on west side, Johannes Pott on east side (with gristmill and sawmill), location of dividing line between them unknown. Tax list of 1780 reported 200 acres for Joder, 235 acres for Pott.
51. Peter Lobach, *Rockland Township*
52. Jerg (George) Keim
53. John Lee
54. Estate of Samuel Oyster (Eister), *East District Township*
55. Jerg (George) Oyster (Eister), *East District Township*
56. Johannes Oyster (Eister), *East District Township*
57. Matthias Motz, *East District Township*
58. Lenhard Schoefer, *East District Township*
59. Philip Hartmann, *West District Township*
60. Johann Jost Joder (Yoder)
61. Peter Joder (Yoder)
62. Daniel Joder (Yoder)
63. Peter Joder (Yoder)
64. Jerg Joder (Yoder)
65. Johannes Lesher
66. Caspar Griesemer (Krismer)
67. Johannes Lesher—Oley Forge
68. John Stapleton
69. William Stapleton, *West District Township*
70. Johannes Hill
71. William Stapleton
72. Christian Jaeger (Hunter)
73. Moses Roberts
74. Christian Jaeger (Hunter), *West District Township*
75. Jacob Hill, *West District Township*
76. Jacob Hill, *West District Township*
77. Samuel Mickle (resident in Philadelphia), John Fishbourne Mifflin (resident in Philadelphia) and John Old—Spring Forge, *West District Township*
78. Jacob Geldbach
79. Johannes Lesher
80. Johannes Bertolet
81. Estate of Rowland Ellis, *Exeter Township*
82. Friedrich (Frederick) Bertolet
83. David Reiss
84. Michael Knabb
85. David Herbein
86. Caspar Neun
87. Michael Knabb
88. OWNER UNKNOWN (Samuel Lee in 1773)
89. William Stapleton
90. Jacob Wiest
91. Johannes Faber
92. Nicolaus Lesher
93. Martin Schenkel
94. Martin Schenkel
95. Jacob Kauffmann (Coffman)
96. Caspar Griesemer (Krismer)
97. Nicolaus Jaeger (Hunter)
98. Christian Jaeger (Hunter)

OLEY VALLEY HERITAGE

Photo by James Lewars.

APPENDIX 10

DANIEL BOONE HOMESTEAD

Daniel Boone Homestead State Historic Site is a history museum portraying the eighteenth-century heritage of the Oley Valley. The site, which comprises many buildings and over five hundred acres of parkland, is a cultural and recreational resource for the citizens of the valley as well as visitors. Two annual festivals, an annual dinner, other smaller-scale events, and monthly lectures, devoted to eighteenth-century Pennsylvania history and folklife, are sponsored by the Friends of the Daniel Boone Homestead, a private nonprofit organization.

The many buildings include the Maugridge-DeTurk House, a nineteenth-century barn, a reconstructed blacksmith shop, the Bertolet-Herbein House, and the Bertolet Sawmill. The Maugridge-DeTurk House is furnished with an impressive collection of period Anglo-Pennsylvanian and Pennsylvania German pieces, mostly from the collection of the Philadelphia Museum of Art. The Bertolet-Herbein House, moved to the site from Oley Township, is a log stove-room house of the early-to-middle eighteenth century. The Bertolet Sawmill, also moved from Oley, is from the early nineteenth century.

The Kentucky pioneer Daniel Boone was born on this homestead in 1734, though all that is left from his father Squire Boone's occupancy is part of the foundation of the house. William Maugridge built the main section, a large hall-parlor house, circa 1752-1755. Such a substantial dwelling, by the standards of the time, was appropriate to Maugridge's status as justice of the peace (1752-1766), the principal office in local government. Maugridge was an interesting figure in the colonial period of the Oley Valley. A Philadelphia master shipbuilder and a member of Benjamin Franklin's "Junto," a club consisting of intellectually inclined artisans and tradesmen, Maugridge left the city around 1746 to take up country life in the Oley Valley. Maugridge numbered among his acquaintances Franklin and Heinrich Melchior Muhlenberg, the leading German Lutheran minister, who for a time was the justice (and church vestryman's) pastor at Saint Gabriel's Church. Muhlenberg tended to be a rather sardonic skeptic regarding his fellow man's character, but he considered Maugridge an "awakened" man of devout Christianity and integrity. To his friend Franklin, Maugridge was an "excellent sensible man." It is possible that in the Oley Valley the master shipbuilder turned his contracting talents to the construction of substantial buildings (such as his house) and was responsible for many houses built in the settlement between 1746 and 1766, the date of his death.

The Maugridge-DeTurk House was completed by Johannes DeTurk, Jr., who purchased the property in 1770. In putting their stamp on the house, DeTurk and his wife Elisabetha added such Pennsylvania German features as a five-plate jamb-stove arrangement. They did this by building the addition at the kitchen-hearth end of the Anglo-Pennsylvanian hall-parlor house and knocking an aperture for the stove through the back of the hearth wall. The house thus exemplifies the mingling of the two cultures in the Oley Valley. This characteristic of the valley is reflected in the museum interpretation of the house, which incorporates material objects from each cultural tradition in respective sections of the building.

BIBLIOGRAPHY

I PRIMARY SOURCES

A. Published

1. Newspapers

American Weekly Mercury, 1719-1746.

Hoch-Deutsch Pennsylvanische Geschicht-Schreiber/Pennsylvanische Berichte, 1743-1762.

Pennsylvania Chronicle, 1767-1774.

Pennsylvania Gazette, 1728-1775. The CD-ROM edition of the *Gazette*, 1728-1765, created by Accessible Archives, Inc. of Malvern, Penn., greatly facilitates use of this important source. Compiled on two folios (1728-1750 and 1751-1765), it is available for use at many major libraries.

Wöchentliche Pennsylvanische Staatsbote, 1767-1775.

2. *Pennsylvania Archives*. Governmental records published in Harrisburg by the State.

Colonial Records. Volumes 1-10, Minutes of the Provincial Council, 1683-1776. 1852.

Pennsylvania Archives. First Series. Edited by Samuel Hazard. Volumes 1-4, Papers of the Provincial Government, 1644-1776. 1852-1853.

Second Series. Edited by John B. Linn and William Henry Egle. Volume 2, pages 345-486, Naturalizations, 1740-1773.

Volume 9, County Officers. Pages 697-741, Philadelphia County, 1682-1776. Pages 784-87, Berks County, 1752-1776.

Volume 19, Minutes of the Pennsylvania Board of Property, 1685-1739.

Third Series. Edited by William Henry Egle.
Volume 1, Minutes of the Pennsylvania Board of Property, 1732-1791.

Volume 18, Berks County Tax Lists, 1767-1785.

Volume 24, Land Warrantees. Pages 3-58, Philadelphia County, 1733-1866. Pages 61-106, Chester County, 1733-1858. Pages 349-568, Lancaster County, 1733-1896.

Volume 26, Land Warrantees. Pages 241-335, Berks County, 1752-1890.

Volumes 27-30, Index to the Third Series.

3. Other Published Primary Sources

Acrelius, Israel. *A History of New Sweden.* Translated and edited by William M. Reynolds. *Memoirs of the Historical Society of Pennsylvania* 11 (1874).

Aland, Kurt, ed. *Die Korrespondenz Heinrich Melchior Mühlenbergs.* 3 vols. Berlin: Walter DeGruyter, 1986-1990.

Berky, Andrew S., ed. *Journals and Papers of David Shultze.* 2 vols. Pennsburg, Penn.: Schwenkfelder Library, 1952.

"The Certificate Given to Jean Bertolet in 1726." *Historical Review of Berks County* 3, no. 3 (April 1938): 80-81.

DeBenneville, George. *Some Remarkable Passages in the Life of Dr. George DeBenneville.* Translated by Elhanan Winchester. Germantown: Converse Cleaves, 1890. Reprint of 1800 edition.

Dewees, Samuel. *A History of the Life and Services of Captain Samuel Dewees.* Baltimore: Robert Neilson, 1844.

Gruber, M. A., ed. "The Newborn." *The Penn Germania* 13 (1912): 336-63.

Hinke, William J., ed. *Minutes and Letters of the Coetus of the German Reformed Congregations in Pennsylvania 1747-1792.* Philadelphia: Reformed Church Publication Board, 1903.

———, ed. *Life and Letters of the Rev. John Philip Boehm.* Philadelphia: Publication and Sunday School Board of the Reformed Church in the United States, 1916.

Kalm, Pehr. *Peter Kalm's Travels in North America.* Edited by Adolph B. Benson. New York: Dover Publications, Inc., 1987. Reprint of 1937 edition; New York: Wilson-Erickson.

Kelsey, R. W., ed. "An Early Description of Pennsylvania: Letter of Christopher Sower, Written in 1724." *Pennsylvania Magazine of History and Biography* 45 (1921): 243-54.

Mann, W. J., and B. M. Schmucker, eds. *Halle Reports: New Edition.* Philadelphia: Globe Printing House, 1882.

Mittelberger, Gottlieb. *Journey to Pennsylvania.* Edited and translated by Oscar Handlin and John Clive. Cambridge: Harvard University Press, 1960.

Perry, William Stevens, ed. *Historical Collections Relating to the American Colonial Church* (Church of England). Volume 2: Pennsylvania. Hartford, Conn.: The Church Press, 1871.

"Records of Indentures of Individuals Bound Out in the Office of the Mayor of Philadelphia, 1771 to 1773." *Pennsylvania German Society Proceedings* 16 (1907).

Reichel, William C., ed. "Annals of Early Moravian Settlement in Georgia and Pennsylvania" [1734-1742]. In *Memorials of the Moravian Church*, vol. 1. Philadelphia: J. B. Lippincott & Co., 1870.

Rink, Franz, and Frederick S. Weiser, eds. "Genealogical Data from the Registers of the Moravian Congregation in the Oley Valley, Berks County, Pennsylvania." *Der Reggeboge* 14 (1980): 1-13.

Schoepf, Johann David. *Travels in the Confederation 1783-1784*. Translated and edited by Alfred J. Morrison. New York: Bergman Publishers, 1968. Reprint of 1911 edition; Philadelphia: W. J. Campbell.

Schulze, John Ludwig, ed. *Reports of the United German Evangelical Lutheran Congregations in North America*. Reading: Pilger Bookstore, 1882.

"Servants Bound Before James Hamilton, Mayor of Philadelphia, 1745 to 1746." *Pennsylvania Magazine of History and Biography* 30 (1906), 348-352, 427-436; 31 (1907), 83-102, 195-206, 351-367, 461-473; 32 (1908), 88-103, 237-249, 351-370.

Stoudt, John Joseph, ed. "Matthias Baumann: The New Born." *Historical Review of Berks County* 43, no. 4 (Fall 1978): 136-38, 142-44, 147.

Tappert, Theodore G., and John W. Doberstein, eds. *The Journals of Henry Melchior Muhlenberg*. 3 vols. Philadelphia: The Evangelical Lutheran Ministerium of Pennsylvania and Adjacent States, 1945-1958.

Weiser, Frederick S., ed. "Donors to the Lutheran Church in Germantown in 1738 and Records of Baptisms There in 1741 and 1742." *Der Reggeboge* 19, no. 1 (1985), 1-13.

OLEY VALLEY HERITAGE

B. Unpublished Sources

1. Governmental Records

Amity Township. Tax list, 1731 (held at Historical Society of Berks County, Reading).

Berks County Commissioners.
Tax lists, bound (held at Historical Society of Berks County).
Tax lists, unbound (held at Historical Society of Berks County).
Tax and Exoneration lists (held at Pennsylvania State Archives, Harrisburg; available on microfilm at Historical Society of Berks County).

Berks County Court of Nisi Prius.
Records (held in Record Group 33 [Pennsylvania Supreme Court, Eastern District], Pennsylvania State Archives).

Berks County Court of Oyer and Terminer.
Records (held in Record Group 33 [Pennsylvania Supreme Court, Eastern District], Pennsylvania State Archives).

Berks County Court of Quarter Sessions.

Court dockets, 1767-1770 and 1773. Office of the Clerk of Courts, Berks County Courthouse.
Court dockets, 1767-1775. Archives, Historical Society of Berks County.

Miscellaneous papers. Office of the Clerk of Courts.
Road dockets and draft book, 1752-1775. Office of the Clerk of Courts.

Berks County Recorder of Deeds, Berks County Courthouse.
Deed Books.
Mortgage Books.

Berks County Register of Wills, Berks County Courthouse.
Orphans Court Records.
Probate files (original estate documents, including wills, inventories, accounts, and other records).
Will Books.

Chester County Court of Quarter Sessions. (records held at Chester County Archives, West Chester).

Lancaster County Court of Quarter Sessions, Lancaster County Courthouse, Lancaster.

Oley Township Road Supervisors' Book, 1774-1820 (Don Yoder Collection).

Pennsylvania General Loan Office.
Mortgage books 1724-1732, 1735-1756 (held at Philadelphia City Archives, Philadelphia, and at Historical Society of Pennsylvania, Philadelphia).

Pennsylvania Provincial Secretary.
Public House Licenses, 1747-1752 (held in Record Group 21 [Records of the Proprietary Government], Pennsylvania State Archives).

Philadelphia County Commissioners (records held at Philadelphia City Archives).
Minutes.

Philadelphia County Court of Quarter Sessions (records held at Philadelphia City Archives).
Road docket.
Road petitions.
Township formation papers.

Philadelphia County Recorder of Deeds.
Deeds and Mortgages (available on microfilm at Historical Society of Pennsylvania, Philadelphia).

Philadelphia County Register of Wills, Philadelphia.
Probate files (including wills and estate inventories).
Will Books (available on microfilm at Historical Society of Pennsylvania).

Proprietary Land Office.
Warrants, Surveys and Patents (held at Pennsylvania Bureau of Land Records, Pennsylvania State Archives).
Miscellaneous papers (held in Manuscripts Division, Historical Society of Pennsylvania).
Letter books of James Steel, 1715-1741 (James Logan Papers).
Letters of John Georges, 1733-1734 (Society Miscellaneous Collection).
Notebooks of Nicholas Scull (Deputy Surveyor for Philadelphia County), 1733-1738.

List of Quitrents Due at Manatawny, 1734 (Miscellaneous Manuscripts of Berks and Montgomery Counties).

2. Records of Religious Organizations

Exeter Monthly Meeting (available on microfilm at Friends Historical Library, Swarthmore College, Swarthmore, Penn.).
Men's Minutes.
Women's Minutes.

Nicholas Garrison Drawings. Moravian Archives, Bethlehem, Penn.

Gwynedd Monthly Meeting (available on microfilm at Friends Historical Library).
Men's Minutes.

Oley Moravian Church. Churchbooks and miscellaneous papers, 1755-1761. Moravian Archives.

Report of the Congregation of Bethlehem. Includes memoirs regarding deceased church members. Moravian Archives.

Saint Gabriel's Protestant Episcopal Church, Douglassville, Penn. Churchbook.

Papers of the Society for the Propagation of the Gospel (Church of England) (available on microfilm at Manuscript Division, Library of Congress, Washington, D.C.).

Stille, C. J., ed. Census of Wicacoa Parish, 1753. In Archivum Americum: Upsal Documents Relating to the Swedish Churches on the Delaware (available at Manuscripts Division, Historical Society of Pennsylvania).

3. Miscellaneous Unpublished Primary Sources

William Bird Store Account Book, 1741-1747. Forge and Furnace Collection, Manuscripts Division, Historical Society of Pennsylvania.

Boone Family Collection. Archives, Historical Society of Berks County.

George Douglass Store Day Book, 1767-1769 (available on microfilm at Historical Society of Berks County).

James Logan Letter Books. Logan Papers, Manuscripts Division, Historical Society of Pennsylvania.

Pine Forge Account Books. Forge and Furnace Collection, Manuscripts Division, Historical Society of Pennsylvania.

Journal of Carl Magnus Wrangel. Translated by Richard H. Hulan.

II SECONDARY SOURCES

Alderfer, E. G. *The Ephrata Commune: An Early American Counterculture*. Pittsburgh: University of Pittsburgh Press, 1985.

Allen, David Grayson. *In English Ways: The Movement of Societies and the Transferral of English Local Law and Custom to Massachusetts Bay in the Seventeenth Century*. Chapel Hill: The University of North Carolina Press, 1981.

Bailyn, Bernard. *The Peopling of British North America: An Introduction*. New York: Alfred A. Knopf, 1986.

———. *Voyagers to the West: A Passage in the Peopling of America on the Eve of the Revolution*. New York: Alfred A. Knopf, 1986.

Ball, Duane E. "Dynamics of Population and Wealth in Eighteenth-Century Chester County, Pennsylvania." *Journal of Interdisciplinary History* 6 (1976): 621-44.

Becker, Laura Leff. "The American Revolution as a Community Experience: A Case Study of Reading, Pennsylvania." Ph.D. diss., University of Pennsylvania, 1978.

———. "The People and the System: Legal Activities in a Colonial Pennsylvania Town." *Pennsylvania Magazine of History and Biography* 106 (1982): 135-49.

———. "Diversity and Its Significance in an Eighteenth-Century Pennsylvania Town." In *Friends and Neighbors: Group Life in America's First Plural Society*, edited by Michael Zuckerman, 196-221. Philadelphia: Temple University Press, 1982.

Becker, Marshall J. "The Okehocking Band of Lenape: Cultural Continuities and Accommodations in Southeastern Pennsylvania." In *Strategies for Survival: American Indians in the Eastern United States*, edited by Frank W. Porter, III, 43-83. Contributions in Ethnic Studies, no. 15. New York: Greenwood Press, 1986.

———. "A Summary of Lenape Socio-Political Organization and Settlement Pattern at the Time of European Contact: the Evidence for Collecting Bands." *Journal of Middle Atlantic Archaeology* 4 (1988): 79-83.

Becker, Marshall Joseph. "Shingle Making: An Aspect of Early American Carpentry." *Pennsylvania Folklife* 25, no. 2 (Winter 1975-1976), 2-19.

Beeman, Richard R. "The New Social History and the Search for 'Community' in Colonial America." *American Quarterly* 29 (1977): 422-43.

Benes, Peter, ed. *The Dublin Seminar for New England Folklife Annual Proceedings 1987: Early American Probate Inventories*. Boston: Boston University, 1989.

Bergengren, Charles. "The Cycle of Transformation in the Houses of Schaefferstown, Pennsylvania." Ph.D. diss., University of Pennsylvania, 1988.

———. "The Cycle of Transformation in Schaefferstown, Pennsylvania, Houses." In *Perspectives in Vernacular Architecture, IV*, edited by Thomas Carter and Bernard L. Herman, 98-107. Columbia: University of Missouri Press, 1991.

Bertolet, Daniel H. *A Genealogical History of the Bertolet Family: The Descendants of Jean Bertolet*. Harrisburg: Press of the United Evangelical Publishing House, 1914.

Bertolet, Peter G. *Fragments of the Past: Historical Sketches of Oley and Vicinity*. Oley: The Woman's Club of Oley Valley, 1980.

Bining, Arthur Cecil. *Pennsylvania Iron Manufacture in the Eighteenth Century*. 2nd ed. Harrisburg: Pennsylvania Historical and Museum Commission, 1973.

Birch, Edith White. "Barricke Mariche, Mountain Mary." *Historical Review of Berks County* 4, no. 1 (October 1938): 6-10.

Bockelman, Wayne L. "Local Politics in Pre-Revolutionary Lancaster County." *Pennsylvania Magazine of History and Biography* 97 (1973): 45-74.

Boorstin, Daniel J. *The Americans: The Colonial Experience*. New York: Random House, 1958.

Borie, Beauveau, IV. *Farming and Folk Society: Threshing among the Pennsylvania Germans*. Ann Arbor: UMI Research Press, 1986.

Borkowski, Joseph A. "Anthony Sadowski: Polish Pioneer, Indian Messenger and Trader." *Historical Review of Berks County* 32, no. 1 (Winter 1966-67): 13-16.

Boyer, Charles C. *American Boyers*. Kutztown, Penn.: Kutztown Publishing Co., 1915.

Breen, T. H. "Creative Adaptations: Peoples and Cultures." In *Colonial British America: Essays in the New History of the Early Modern Era*, edited by Jack P. Greene and J. R. Pole, 195-232. Baltimore: The Johns Hopkins University Press, 1984.

———. *Imagining the Past: East Hampton Histories*. Reading, Mass.: Addison-Wesley Publishing Company, Inc., 1989.

Brown, Frank M., ed. *Amity: First in Berks*. Amity Township 250th Anniversary Executive Committee, 1969.

Brumbaugh, G. Edwin. "Colonial Architecture of the Pennsylvania Germans." *Pennsylvania German Society Proceedings* 41 (1933).

Brumbaugh, Martin Grove. *A History of the German Baptist Brethren in Europe and America*. Mount Morris, Illinois: Brethren Publishing House, 1899.

Buchanan, Jane Gray. *Thomas Thompson and Ann Finney of Colonial Pennsylvania and North Carolina*. Published privately, 1988.

Bucher, Robert C. "Meadow Irrigation in Pennsylvania." *Pennsylvania Folklife* 11, no. 2 (Fall 1960), 24-32.

———. "Steep Roofs and Red Tiles." *Pennsylvania Folklife* 12, no. 2 (Winter 1961-62): 18-25.

———. "The Continental Log House." *Pennsylvania Folklife* 12, no. 4 (Summer 1962): 14-19.

———. "Grain in the Attic." *Pennsylvania Folklife* 13, no. 2 (Winter 1962-63): 7-15.

———. "The Swiss Bank House in Pennsylvania." *Pennsylvania Folklife* 18, no. 2 (Winter 1968-1969): 2-11.

———. "The Long Shingle." *Pennsylvania Folklife* 18, no. 4 (Summer 1969): 51-56.

Bucher, Robert C. and Alan G. Keyser. "Thatching in Pennsylvania." *Der Reggeboge* 16, no. 1 (1982): 1-23.

Bushman, Richard L. "American High-Style and Vernacular Cultures." In *Colonial British America: Essays in the New History of the Early Modern Era*, edited by Jack P. Greene and J. R. Pole, 345-83. Baltimore: The Johns Hopkins University Press, 1984.

———. *The Refinement of America: People, Houses, Cities*. New York: Alfred A. Knopf, 1992.

Butler, Jon. *Awash in a Sea of Faith: Christianizing the American People*. Cambridge: Harvard University Press, 1990.

Carson, Cary. "Doing History with Material Culture." In *Material Culture and the Study of American Life*, edited by Ian M. G. Quimby, 41-64. New York: W. W. Norton & Company, for the Henry Francis DuPont Winterthur Museum, 1978.

Chappell, Edward A. "Looking at Buildings." *Fresh Advices: A Research Supplement* (November 1984).

———. "Germans and Swiss." In *America's Architectural Roots: Ethnic Groups that Built America*, edited by Dell Upton, 68-73. Washington, D.C.: The Preservation Press, 1986.

———. "Acculturation in the Shenandoah Valley: Rhenish Houses of the Massanutten Settlement." In *Common Places: Readings in American Vernacular Architecture*, edited by Dell Upton and John Michael Vlach, 27-57. Athens: The University of Georgia Press, 1986. Reprinted from *Proceedings of the American Philosophical Society* 124 (1980): 55-89.

Claussen, William E. "Violent Incident along the Manatawny, 1728." *Historical Review of Berks County* 42, no. 3 (Summer 1977): 95-97, 119.

Clay, Jehu Curtis. *Annals of the Swedes on the Delaware*. Philadelphia: H. Hooker & Co., 1858.

Clemens, Paul G. E., and Lucy Simler. "Rural Labor and the Farm Household in Chester County, Pennsylvania, 1750-1820." In *Work and Labor in Early*

America, edited by Stephen Innes, 106-43. Chapel Hill: University of North Carolina Press, 1988.

Cooper, Patricia Irvin. "Some Misconceptions in American Log Building Studies." *Material Culture* 23, No. 2 (Summer 1991), 43-61.

Cott, Nancy F. "Eighteenth-Century Family and Social Life Revealed in Massachusetts Divorce Records." *Journal of Social History* 10 (1976): 20-43.

Craig, Peter Stebbins. "The 1693 Census of the Swedes on the Delaware." *Swedish American Genealogist* 9, no. 1 (March 1989): 1-9; no. 3 (September 1989): 97-113; 10, no. 1 (March 1990): 1-16; no. 3 (September 1990), 127-45; 11, no. 1 (March 1991): 34-51, 67-88; no. 3 (September 1991): 177-96.

Craig, Peter Stebbins, and Henry Wesley Yocom. "The Yocums of Aronameck in Philadelphia, 1648-1702." *National Genealogical Society Quarterly* 71, no. 4 (1983): 243-79.

Croll, P. C. *Annals of the Oley Valley in Berks County, Pa.* Reading: Reading Eagle Press, 1926.

DeChant, Alliene Saeger. *Down Oley Way.* Kutztown, Penn.: published privately, 1953.

Deetz, James. *In Small Things Forgotten: The Archaeology of Early American Life.* Garden City, N.Y.: Anchor Press, 1977.

DeTurk, Eugene P. *History and Genealogy of the DeTurk Family.* Reading, Penn.: DeTurk Family Association, 1934.

Doerflinger, Thomas M. *A Vigorous Spirit of Enterprise: Merchants and Economic Development in Revolutionary Philadelphia.* Chapel Hill: University of North Carolina Press, 1986.

———. "Farmers and Dry Goods in the Philadelphia Market Area, 1750-1800." In *The Economy of Early America: The Revolutionary Period, 1763-1790*, edited by Ronald Hoffman, John J. McCusker, Russell R. Menard, and Peter J. Albert, 166-95. Charlottesville: University Press of Virginia, 1988.

Dornbusch, Charles H., and John K. Heyl. *Pennsylvania German Barns.* Pennsylvania German Folklore Society Proceedings 21 (1958); i-xxiv, 1-299.

Ducoff-Barone, Deborah. "Marketing and Manufacturing: A Study of Domestic Cast Iron Articles Produced at Colebrookdale Furnace, Berks County, Pennsylvania, 1735-1751." *Pennsylvania History* 50: 20-37.

DuHamel, William. "An Historical Sketch of William Bird: Founder of Birdsboro, Pennsylvania, 1703-1761." *Historical Review of Berks County* 47, no. 2 (Spring 1982): 58, 70, 72.

Durnbaugh, Donald F., ed. *The Brethren in Colonial America: A Source Book on the Transplantation and Development of the Church of the Brethren in the Eighteenth Century.* Elgin, Illinois: The Brethren Press, 1967.

Edgerton, Samuel Y. "Heat and Style: Eighteenth-Century House Warming by Stoves." *Journal of the Society of Architectural Historians* 20 (1961): 20-26.

———. "Heating Stoves in Eighteenth-Century Philadelphia." *Bulletin of the Association for Preservation Technology* 3 (1971): 15-104.

Ensminger, Robert F. *The Pennsylvania Barn: Its Origin, Evolution, and Distribution in North America.* Baltimore: The Johns Hopkins University Press, 1992.

Eshelman, John E. "The Society of Friends, and Their Meeting Houses, in Berks County." *Historical Review of Berks County* 1, no. 2 (January 1936): 34-40.

———. "The Journal of Moses Roberts—Quaker Minister of Oley." *Historical Review of Berks County* 8, no. 3 (April 1943): 70-74.

———. "Quaker Marriage Certificate of 1736." *Historical Review of Berks County* 14, no. 3 (April 1949): 77-79.

———. "The Keim Family of Lobachsville." *Historical Review of Berks County* 21, no. 1 (October 1955): 2-7, 27-29.

Exeter Township 225th Anniversary Historical Committee. *Exeter: The Forgotten Corner.* 1967.

Fischer, David Hackett. *Albion's Seed: Four British Folkways in America.* Oxford: Oxford University Press, 1989.

Frankhouser, Earle M. "The Origin of Land Titles in Berks County." *Historical Review of Berks County* 30, no. 4 (Autumn 1965): 102-05, 126-27.

———. "The London Company and the Ancestors of Abraham Lincoln." *Historical Review of Berks County* 34, no. 4 (Autumn 1969): 137-39.

Friesen, Steve. "Home Is Where the Hearth Is." *Pennsylvania Folklife* 40 (1991): 98-118.

———. "The Five-Plate Stove Revisited." *Pennsylvania Folklife* 41 (1991): 20-24.

Frost, J. William. *The Quaker Family in Colonial America: A Portrait of the Society of Friends.* New York: St. Martin's Press, 1973.

Gehret, Ellen J., and Alan G. Keyser, "Flax Processing in Pennsylvania From Seed to Fiber." *Pennsylvania Folklife* 22, no. 1 (Autumn 1972): 10-34.

Gerhard, Elmer Schultz. "The First Preacher of Universalism in Pennsylvania." *Historical Review of Berks County* 14, no. 1 (October 1948): 15-19.

Glass, Joseph W. *The Pennsylvania Culture Region: A View from the Barn.* Ann Arbor: UMI Research Press, 1986.

Glassie, Henry. *Pattern in the Material Folk Culture of the Eastern United States.* Philadelphia: University of Pennsylvania Press, 1968.

———. "The Types of the Southern Mountain Cabin." In *The Study of American Folklore: An Introduction*, edited by Jan Harold Brunvard, 338-70. New York: W. W. Norton & Company, 1968.

———. "A Central Chimney Continental Log House." *Pennsylvania Folklife* 18, no. 2 (Winter 1968-69): 32-39.

———. "Eighteenth-Century Cultural Process in Delaware Valley Folk Building." In *Common Places: Readings in American Vernacular Architecture*, edited by Dell Upton and John Michael Vlach, 394-425. Athens: The University of Georgia Press, 1986. Reprinted from *Winterthur Portfolio* 7 (1972): 29-57.

———. "The Variation of Concepts within Tradition: Barn Building in Otsego County, New York." In *Man and Cultural Heritage: Papers in Honor of Fred B. Kniffen*, edited by H. J. Walker and W. G. Haag, 177-235. *Geoscience and Man* 5 (1974).

———. *Folk Housing in Middle Virginia: A Structural Analysis of Historic Artifacts*. Knoxville: The University of Tennessee Press, 1975.

Glatfelter, Charles H. *Pastors and People: German Lutheran and Reformed Churches in the Pennsylvania Field, 1717-1793*. 2 vols. Publications of the Pennsylvania German Society 13 (1980) and 15 (1981).

Grant, Phyllis S. "Exeter Friends' Meeting 1737-1787." *Historical Review of Berks County* 47, no. 2 (Spring 1982): 62-63, 71, 74-80.

Greene, Jack P. *Pursuits of Happiness: The Social Development of Early Modern British Colonies and the Formation of American Culture*. Chapel Hill: University of North Carolina Press, 1988.

Greene, Jack P., and J. R. Pole, eds. *Colonial British America: Essays in the New History of the Early Modern Era*. Baltimore: The Johns Hopkins University Press, 1984.

Gross, Robert A. *The Minutemen and Their World*. New York: Hill and Wang, 1976.

Grubb, Farley. "The Market Structure of Shipping German Immigrants to Colonial America." *Pennsylvania Magazine of History and Biography* 111 (1987): 27-48.

———. "Morbidity and Mortality on the North Atlantic Passage: Eighteenth-Century German Immigration." *Journal of Interdisciplinary History* 17 (1987): 565-85.

———. "German Immigration to Pennsylvania, 1709 to 1820." *Journal of Interdisciplinary History* 20 (1990): 417-36.

Guenther, Karen. " 'A Garden for the Friends of God:' Religious Diversity in the Oley Valley to 1750." *Pennsylvania Folklife* 33, no. 3 (Autumn 1983): 138-44.

Haberlein, Mark. "German Migrants in Colonial Pennsylvania: Resources, Opportunities, and Experience." *William and Mary Quarterly* 50 (1993): 555-74.

Haller, Mabel. "Early Moravian Education in Pennsylvania." *Transactions of the Moravian Historical Society* 15 (1953).

Hamilton, J. Taylor. "The Moravian Work at Oley, Berks County, Penna." *Transactions of the Moravian Historical Society* 13 (1944): 8-18.

Heath, Kingston W. "Defining the Nature of Vernacular." *Material Culture* 20, No. 2 (Summer-Fall 1988), 1-8.

Henderson, Rodger C. "Demographic Patterns and Family Structure in Eighteenth-Century Lancaster County, Pennsylvania." *Pennsylvania Magazine of History and Biography* 114 (1990): 349-84.

Henretta, James A. "Farms and Families: Mentalité in Pre-Industrial America." *William and Mary Quarterly* 41 (1978): 1-32.

Herman, Bernard L. *Architecture and Rural Life in Central Delaware 1700-1900*. Knoxville: The University of Tennessee Press, 1987.

———. *The Stolen House*. Charlottesville: University Press of Virginia, 1992.

Historical Methods 13, no. 1 (Winter 1980), "Special Issue: Early America."

Hofstra, Warren R. "The Opequon Inventories, Frederick County, Virginia, 1749-1796." *Ulster Folklife* 35 (1989): 42-71.

———. "Land, Ethnicity, and Community at the Opequon Settlement, Virginia, 1730-1800." *Virginia Magazine of History and Biography* 98 (1990): 423-48.

———. "Adaptation or Survival?: Folk Housing at Opequon Settlement." *Ulster Folklife* 37 (1991): 36-61.

———. "Land Policy and Settlement in the Northern Shenandoah Valley." In *Appalachian Frontiers: Settlement, Society & Development in the Preindustrial Era*, edited by Robert D. Mitchell, 105-126. Lexington, Kentucky: University of Kentucky Press, 1991.

———. "The Virginia Backcountry in the Eighteenth Century: The Question of Origins and the Issue of Outcomes." *Virginia Magazine of History and Biography* 101, No. 4 (October 1993), 485-508.

———. "Private Dwellings, Public Ways, and the Landscape of Early Rural Capitalism in Virginia's Shenandoah Valley." In *Perspectives in Vernacular Architecture, V*, edited by Elizabeth Cromley and Carter Hudgins. Knoxville: University of Tennessee Press, forthcoming.

Hopkins, Phoebe B. "The DeTurk House of Oley." *Historical Review of Berks County* 31, no. 2 (Spring 1966): 56-58, 69-72.

Horvath, Arlene. "Vernacular Expression in Quaker Chester County, Pennsylvania: The Taylor-Parke House and Its Maker." In *Perspectives in Vernacular Architecture, II*, edited by Camille Wells, 150-60. Columbia: University of Missouri Press, 1986.

Howell, Charles. "Colonial Watermills in the Wooden Age." In *America's Wooden Age*, edited by Brooke Hindle, 120-59. Tarrytown, N.Y.: Sleepy Hollow Press, 1975.

Howell, Charles, and Allan Keller. *The Mill at Philipsburg Manor Upper Mills and a Brief History of Milling*. Tarrytown, N.Y.: Sleepy Hollow Restorations, 1977.

Hulan, Richard. "New Sweden and Its Churches." *Lutheran Quarterly* 2 (1988): 3-33.

Hutslar, Donald A. *The Architecture of Migration: Log Construction in the Ohio Country, 1750-1850*. Athens: Ohio University Press, 1986.

Illick, Joseph E. *Colonial Pennsylvania: A History*. New York: Charles Scribner's Sons, 1976.

Innes, Stephen, ed. *Work and Labor in Early America*. Chapel Hill: The University of North Carolina Press, 1988.

Isaac, Rhys. *The Transformation of Virginia, 1740-1790*. Chapel Hill: University of North Carolina Press, 1982.

Jensen, Joan M. *Loosening the Bonds: Mid-Atlantic Farm Women 1750-1850*. New Haven: Yale University Press, 1986.

Jones, Henry Z., Jr., and Annette K. Burgert. "A New Emigrant List: Bonfeld, 1710-1738." *Der Reggeboge* 14, no. 4 (October 1980): 3-19.

Jordan, Terry G. *American Log Buildings: An Old World Heritage*. Chapel Hill: The University of North Carolina Press, 1985.

Jordan, Terry G., and Matti Kaups. *The American Backwoods Frontier: An Ethnic and Ecological Interpretation*. Baltimore: The Johns Hopkins University Press, 1989.

Kennedy, Dean. "Farmhouses of Oley Valley, Berks County, Pennsylvania." In *Colonial Architecture of the Mid-Atlantic*, edited by Lisa C. Mullins, 103-18, vol. 4 in the series: Architectural Treasures of Early America. Harrisburg: The National Historical Society, 1987.

Kessel, Elizabeth Augusta. "Germans on the Maryland Frontier: A Social History of Frederick County, Maryland, 1730-1800." Ph.D. diss., Rice University, 1981.

Keyser, Alan G. "Gardens and Gardening among the Pennsylvania Germans." *Pennsylvania Folklife* 20, no. 3 (Spring 1971): 2-15.

———. "Beds, Bedding, Bedsteads and Sleep." *Der Reggeboge* 12, no. 4 (October 1978): 1-28.

Keyser, Alan G., and William P. Stein. "The Pennsylvania German Tri-Level Ground Barn." *Der Reggeboge* 9, no. 3/4 (December 1975): 1-25.

Kindig, Stephen, Carol Epler, Phoebe Hopkins, Kenneth LeVan, and Philip Pendleton. *Gristmills of Berks County*. Wyomissing, Penn.: Berks County Conservancy, forthcoming.

Kniffen, Fred B., and Henry Glassie. "Building in Wood in the Eastern United States: A Time-Place Perspective." In *Common Places: Readings in American Vernacular Architecture*, edited by Dell Upton and John Michael Vlach, 159-81. Athens: The University of Georgia Press, 1986. Reprinted from *Geographical Review* 56 (1966): 40-66.

Lanier, Gabrielle. "Samuel Wilson's Working World: Builders and Buildings in Chester County, Pennsylvania, 1780-1827." In *Perspectives in Vernacular Architecture, IV*, edited by Thomas Carter and Bernard L. Herman, 23-30. Columbia: University of Missouri Press, 1991.

Lawton, Arthur J. "The Pre-Metric Foot and Its Use in Pennsylvania German Architecture." *Pennsylvania Folklife* 19, no. 1 (Autumn 1969): 37-45.

———. "The Ground Rules of Folk Architecture." *Pennsylvania Folklife* 23, no. 1 (Autumn 1973): 13-19.

Lea, J. Henry, and J. R. Hutchinson, *The Ancestry of Abraham Lincoln*. Boston: Houghton Mifflin Company, 1909.

Lemon, James T. "The Agricultural Practices of National Groups in Eighteenth-Century Southeastern Pennsylvania." *Geographical Review* 56 (1966): 467-96.

———. "Household Consumption in Eighteenth-Century America and Its Relationship to Production and Trade: the Situation among Farmers in Southeastern Pennsylvania." *Agricultural History* 41 (1967): 59-70.

———. *The Best Poor Man's Country: A Geographical Study of Early Southeastern Pennsylvania*. Baltimore: The Johns Hopkins Press, 1972.

———. "The Weakness of Place and Community in Early Pennsylvania." In *European Settlement and Development in North America: Essays on Geographical Change in Honour and Memory of Andrew Hill Clark*, edited by James R. Gibson, 190-207. Toronto: University of Toronto Press, 1978.

———. "Comment on James A. Henretta's 'Families and Farms: Mentalité in Pre-Industrial America.'" *William and Mary Quarterly* 37 (1980): 688-700.

———. "Early Americans and Their Social Environment." *Journal of Historical Geography* 6 (1980): 115-31.

———. "Spatial Order: Households in Local Communities and Regions." In *Colonial British America: Essays in the New History of the Early Modern Era*, edited by Jack P. Greene and J. R. Pole, 86-122. Baltimore: The Johns Hopkins University Press, 1984.

———. "Agriculture and Society in Early America." *Agricultural History Review* 35 (1987): 76-94.

Lemon, James T., and Gary B. Nash. "The Distribution of Wealth in Eighteenth-Century America: A Century of Change in Chester County, Pennsylvania, 1693-1802." *Journal of Social History* 2 (1968): 1-24.

Levengood, Richard L. "Bishop's House." *Historical Review of Berks County* 51, no. 3 (Summer 1986): 96-98, 106.

Levy, Barry. *Quakers and the American Family: British Settlement in the Delaware Valley*. Oxford: Oxford University Press, 1988.

Lewars, James A. "Pennsylvania German Kicked Roofs." *Historical Review of Berks County* 47, no. 1 (Winter 1981-82): 10-15, 28.

Long, Amos, Jr. *The Pennsylvania German Family Farm*. Publications of the Pennsylvania German Society 6 (1972).

McCurdy, Linda. "The Potts Family Iron Industry in the Schuylkill Valley." Ph.D. diss., Pennsylvania State University, 1974.

McCusker, John J., and Russell R. Menard. *The Economy of British America, 1607-1789*. Chapel Hill: University of North Carolina Press, 1985.

Makler, Richard. "Fishermen's Revolt." *Historical Review of Berks County* 53, no. 1 (Winter 1987-88): 15, 18, 35.

Magee, James F., Jr. "Berks County Paper Mills, Paper Makers and Watermarks, 1747-1832." *Historical Review of Berks County* 13, no. 3 (April 1948): 76-78.

Marietta, Jack D. *The Reformation of American Quakerism, 1748-1783*. Philadelphia: University of Pennsylvania Press, 1984.

Martindale, Ella Catherine Griesemer. *The Griesemers*. Griesemer Family Association, 1980.

Meiser, George M., IX. "Index to P. C. Croll's *Annals of the Oley Valley*." *Historical Review of Berks County* 31, no. 4 (Autumn 1966): 126-32.

———. "Graveyards of Historic Oley." *Historical Review of Berks County* 33, no. 3 (Summer 1968): 88-90.

Meiser, George M., IX. and Gloria Jean Meiser. *The Passing Scene: Stories of Old-Time Reading and Berks*. 8 vols. Reading: The Historical Society of Berks County, 1982-1992. See especially vol. 4, 120-29, and vol. 6, 201-05.

Mercer, Henry C. *The Bible in Iron: Pictured Stoves and Stoveplates*. 3rd ed., revised by Joseph E. Sandford. Doylestown: The Bucks County Historical Society, 1961.

Michel, Jack. " 'In a Manner and Fashion Suitable to Their Degree:' A Preliminary Investigation of the Material Culture of Early Rural Pennsylvania." In *Working Papers from the Regional Economic History Research Center* 5, no. 1 (1981).

Miller, Daniel. "The Early Moravian Settlements in Berks County." *Transactions of the Historical Society of Berks County* 2 (1910): 309-34.

———. "Maria Young, the Mountain Recluse of Oley." *Transactions of the Historical Society of Berks County* 3 (1923): 209-20.

Miller, Randall M., ed. *Germans in America: Retrospect and Prospect*. Philadelphia: German Society of Pennsylvania, 1984.

Milspaw, Yvonne J. "Reshaping Tradition: Changes to Pennsylvania German Folk Houses." *Pioneer America* 15 (1983): 67-83.

Montgomery, Morton L. *History of Berks County, Pennsylvania*. Philadelphia: Everts, Peck & Richards, 1886.

———. *Historical and Biographical Annals of Berks County, Pennsylvania*. 2 vols. Chicago: J. Beers & Co., 1909.

Moore, Christopher. *Louisbourg Portraits*. Toronto: Macmillan of Canada, 1982.

Murtagh, William John. "The Philadelphia Row House." *Journal of the Society of Architectural Historians* 16 (1957): 3-13.

Nash, Gary B. *Quakers and Politics: Pennsylvania, 1681-1726*. Princeton: Princeton University Press, 1968.

Nolan, J. Bennett. *Early Narratives of Berks County*. Reading: Historical Society of Berks County, 1927.

———. *The Foundation of the Town of Reading in Pennsylvania*. Reading: School District of Reading, 1929.

———. "Ben Franklin's Mortgage on the Daniel Boone Farm." *Historical Review of Berks County* 10, no. 4 (July 1945): 114-16.

Pendleton, Philip E. "The Origin of the Swedish Settlement at Old Morlatton." *Historical Review of Berks County* 53, no. 3 (Summer 1988): 129-33, 141-43.

Pillsbury, Richard. "The Construction Materials of the Rural Folk Housing of the Pennsylvania Culture Region." *Pioneer America* 8 (1976): 98-106.

———. "Patterns in the Folk and Vernacular House Forms of the Pennsylvania Culture Region." *Pioneer America* 9 (1977): 12-31.

Pruitt, Bettye Hobbs. "Self-Sufficiency and the Agricultural Economy of Eighteenth-Century Massachusetts." *William and Mary Quarterly* 41 (1984): 333-64.

Reinberger, Mark. "Graeme Park and the Three-Cell Plan: A Lost Type in Colonial Architecture." In *Perspectives in Vernacular Architecture, IV*, edited by Thomas Carter and Bernard L. Herman, 146-54. Columbia, Mo.: University of Missouri Press, 1991.

Richards, Louis. "The Berks County Ancestry of Abraham Lincoln." *Transactions of the Historical Society of Berks County* 2 (1905-1910): 369-77.

Roberts, Warren E. "The Tools Used in Building Log Houses in Indiana." In *Common Places: Readings in American*

Vernacular Architecture, edited by Dell Upton and John Michael Vlach, 182-203. Athens: The University of Georgia Press, 1986. Reprinted from *Pioneer America* 9 (1977): 32-61.

———. "Some Comments on Log Construction in Scandinavia and the United States." In *Viewpoints on Folklife: Looking at the Overlooked*, by Warren E. Roberts, 273-88. Ann Arbor: UMI Research Press, 1988. Reprinted from *Folklore Today: A Festschrift for Richard Dorson*, edited by Linda Degh, Felix Oinas, and Henry Glassie, 437-50. Bloomington: Indiana University Press, 1976.

Roeber, A. G. "In German Ways? Problems and Potentials of Eighteenth-Century German Social and Emigration History." *William and Mary Quarterly* 44 (1987): 750-74.

———. "The Origins and Transfer of German-American Concepts of Property and Inheritance." *Perspectives in American History* 3 (1987): 115-71.

———. "'The Origin of Whatever Is Not English among Us:' The Dutch-speaking and the German-speaking Peoples of Colonial British America." In *Strangers Within the Realm: Cultural Margins of the First British Empire*, edited by Bernard Bailyn and Philip D. Morgan, 220-83. Chapel Hill: University of North Carolina Press, 1991.

———. *Palatines, Liberty, and Property: German Lutherans in Colonial British America*. Baltimore: The Johns Hopkins University Press, 1993.

Rupp, I. Daniel. *History of the Counties of Berks and Lebanon*. Lancaster: G. Hills, 1844.

———. *A Collection of Thirty Thousand Names*. Philadelphia: Ig. Kohler, 1876.

Rutman, Darrett B. "Community Study." *Historical Methods* 13 (1980): 29-41.

———. "Assessing the Little Communities of Early America." *William and Mary Quarterly* 43 (1986): 163-78.

Sachse, Julius Friederich, *The German Sectarians of Pennsylvania, 1708-1742: A Critical and Legendary History of the Ephrata Cloister and the Dunkers*. Philadelphia: published privately, 1899.

———. *Justus Falckner*. Philadelphia: published privately, 1903.

Salinger, Sharon V. *"To Serve Well and Faithfully:" Labor and Indentured Servitude in Pennsylvania, 1682-1800*. Cambridge: Cambridge University Press, 1987.

Salmon, Marylynn. "The Court Records of Philadelphia, Bucks, and Berks Counties in the Seventeenth and Eighteenth Centuries." *Pennsylvania Magazine of History and Biography* 107 (1983): 249-91.

Schlereth, Thomas J., ed. *Material Culture Studies in America*. Nashville: The American Association for State and Local History, 1982.

———, ed. *Material Culture: A Research Guide*. Lawrence, Kan.: University Press of Kansas, 1985.

Schmauk, Theodore E. "The Lutheran Church in Pennsylvania, 1638-1800." *Pennsylvania German Society Proceedings* 11 (1902).

Schultz, George Winterhalter. "Major General Daniel Udree: Oley Ironmaster, Soldier, Statesman." *Historical Review of Berks County* 1, no. 3 (April 1936): 66-70.

———. "The Old Moravian Boarding School in Oley Township." *Historical Review of Berks County* 6, no. 3 (April 1941): 85.

———. "Colebrookdale: 'Mother' of Pennsylvania's Iron Industry." *Historical Review of Berks County* 10, no. 1 (October 1944).

Schwartz, Sally. *A Mixed Multitude: The Struggle for Toleration in Colonial Pennsylvania*. New York: New York University Press, 1987.

Schweitzer, Mary M. *Custom and Contract: Household, Government, and the Economy in Rural Pennsylvania*. New York: Columbia University Press, 1987.

Shammas, Carole. "How Self-Sufficient Was Early America?" *Journal of Interdisciplinary History* 13 (1982): 247-72.

Shaner, Richard H. "Archaeological Excavation at Oley Forge." *Historical Review of Berks County* 36, no. 2 (Spring 1971), 55-58, 77-79.

Shelley, Donald A. *The Fraktur-Writings or Illuminated Manuscripts of the Pennsylvania Germans*. Pennsylvania German Folklore Society Proceedings 23 (1958-1959).

Shoemaker, Alfred L., ed. *The Pennsylvania Barn*. Lancaster: The Pennsylvania Dutch Folklore Center, Inc., 1956.

Shurtleff, Harold R. *The Log Cabin Myth: A Study of the Early Dwellings of the English Colonists in Early America*. Cambridge: Harvard University Press, 1939.

Simler, Lucy. "The Township: The Community of the Rural Pennsylvanian." *Pennsylvania Magazine of History and Biography* 106 (1982): 41-68.

———. "Tenancy in Colonial Pennsylvania: The Case of Chester County." *William and Mary Quarterly* 43 (1986): 542-69.

———. "The Landless Worker, 1750-1820: an Index of Economic and Social Change in Chester County, Pennsylvania." *Pennsylvania Magazine of History and Biography* 114 (1990): 163-99.

Simler, Lucy, and Paul G. E. Clemens. "The 'Best Poor Man's Country' in 1783: the Population Structure of Rural Society in Late-Eighteenth-Century Southeastern Pennsylvania." *Proceedings of the American Philosophical Society* 133 (1989): 234-61.

Smith, Billy G. *The "Lower Sort": Philadelphia's Laboring People, 1750-1800*. Ithaca: Cornell University Press, 1990.

Snydacker, Daniel. "Kinship and Community in Rural Pennsylvania, 1749-1820." *Journal of Interdisciplinary History* 13 (1982): 41-61.

Soderlund, Jean R. *Quakers and Slavery: A Divided Spirit*. Princeton: Princeton University Press, 1985.

———. "Women's Authority in Pennsylvania and New Jersey Quaker Meetings, 1680-1760." *William and Mary Quarterly* 44 (1987): 722-49.

Spraker, Hazel Atterbury. *The Boone Family*. Rutland, Vt.: The Tuttle Company, 1922.

St. George, Robert Blair, ed. *Material Life in America 1600-1860*. Boston: Northeastern University Press, 1988.

Stoudt, John Baer. *The Children and the Children's Children of Rudolph Hoch and Melchior Hoch*. Published privately, 1949.

Stoudt, John Joseph. "Daniel and Squire Boone." *Historical Review of Berks County* 1, no. 4 (July 1936): 108-12.

———. "The Date of the Arrival of Matthias Baumann." *Historical Review of Berks County* 3, no. 3 (April 1938): 79.

———. "Yost Yoder and George DeBenneville." *Historical Review of Berks County* 21, no. 2 (January 1956): 48-49.

———. "Was America's First Autobiography Written in Oley?" *Historical Review of Berks County* 26, no. 3 (Summer 1961): 87.

Strassburger, Ralph Beaver, and William John Hinke, eds. *Pennsylvania German Pioneers*. 3 vols. Pennsylvania German Society *Proceedings* 42-44 (1934).

Swank, Scott T., ed. *Arts of the Pennsylvania Germans*. New York: W. W. Norton & Company, 1983; copublished with Pennsylvania German Society as Publications, vol. 17.

Sweeney, Kevin M. "Gravestones." In *The Great River: Art and Society of the Connecticut Valley, 1635-1820*, edited by Gerald W.R. Ward and William N. Hosley, 485-523. Hartford: Wadsworth Atheneum, 1985.

Trommler, Frank, and Joseph McVeigh, eds. *America and the Germans: An Assessment of a Three-Hundred-Year History*. 2 vols. Philadelphia: University of Pennsylvania Press, 1985.

Tully, Alan. *William Penn's Legacy: Politics and Social Structure in Provincial Pennsylvania, 1726-1755*. Baltimore: The Johns Hopkins University Press, 1977.

———. "Englishmen and Germans: National-Group Contact in Colonial Pennsylvania, 1700-1755." *Pennsylvania History* 45 (1978): 237-56.

Turner, Frederick Jackson. "The Significance of the Frontier in American History." *Annual Report of the American Historical Association for the Year 1893*, 197-227.

Turner, Robert P., ed. *Lewis Miller: Sketches and Chronicles*. Introduction by Donald A. Shelley. York: The Historical Society of York County, 1966.

Upton, Dell. "The Power of Things: Recent Studies in American Vernacular Architecture." In *Material Culture: A Research Guide*, edited by Thomas J. Schlereth. Lawrence: University Press of Kansas, 1985.

Upton, Dell, and John Michael Vlach, eds. *Common Places: Readings in American Vernacular Architecture*. Athens, Ga.: The University of Georgia Press, 1986.

VanDolsen, Nancy. *Cumberland County: An Architectural Survey*. Carlisle: Cumberland County Historical Society, 1990.

Vickers, Daniel. "Competency and Competition: Economic Culture in Early America." *William and Mary Quarterly* 47 (1990): 1-29.

Waciega, Lisa Wilson. "A 'Man of Business': The Widow of Means in Southeastern Pennsylvania, 1750-1850." *William and Mary Quarterly* 44 (1987): 40-64.

Wacker, Peter O. *The Musconetcong Valley: A Historical Geography*. New Brunswick: Rutgers University Press, 1968.

———. *Land & People: A Cultural Geography of Preindustrial New Jersey: Origins and Settlement Patterns*. New Brunswick: Rutgers University Press, 1975.

Walker, Joseph E. *Hopewell Village: A Social and Economic History of an Ironmaking Community*. Philadelphia: University of Pennsylvania Press, 1966.

Walsh, Lorena S. "Community Networks in the Early Chesapeake." In *Colonial Chesapeake Society*, edited by Lois Green Carr, Philip Morgan, and Jean Russo, 200-41. Chapel Hill: University of North Carolina Press, 1988.

Walzer, John Flexer. "Transportation in the Philadelphia Trading Area, 1740-1775." Ph.D. diss., University of Wisconsin, 1968.

Warren, Louis A. "The Lincolns of Berks County." *Historical Review of Berks County* 14, no. 3 (April 1949): 83-85.

Waterman, Thomas Tileston. *The Dwellings of Colonial America*. Chapel Hill: The University of North Carolina Press, 1950.

Weaver, William Woys. "Pennsylvania German Architecture: Bibliography in European Backgrounds." *Pennsylvania Folklife* 24, no. 3 (Spring 1975): 36-40.

———. "The Pennsylvania German House: European Antecedents and New World Forms." *Winterthur Portfolio* 21 (1986): 243-64.

Wegman, Harold C. *A History of Schwarzwald Lutheran Church 1737-1987*. Reading: Schwarzwald Lutheran Church, 1987.

Wellenreuther, Hermann. "Image and Counterimage, Tradition and Expectation: The German Immigrants in English Colonial Society in Pennsylvania, 1700-1765." In *America and the Germans: An Assessment of a Three-Hundred-Year History*, edited by Frank Trommler and Joseph McVeigh, vol. 1, 85-105. Philadelphia: University of Pennsylvania Press, 1985.

Wertenbaker, Thomas Jefferson. *The Founding of American Civilization: The Middle Colonies*. New York: Charles Scribner's Sons, 1938.

Wokeck, Marianne Sophia. "The Flow and the Composition of German Immigration to Philadelphia, 1727-1775." *Pennsylvania Magazine of History and Biography* 105 (1981): 249-78.

———. "A Tide of Alien Tongues: The Flow and Ebb of German Immigration to Pennsylvania, 1683-1776." Ph.D. diss., Temple University, 1983.

———. "Promoters and Passengers: The German Immigrant Trade, 1683-1775." In *The World of William Penn*, edited by Richard S. Dunn and Mary Maples Dunn, 259-78. Philadelphia: University of Pennsylvania Press, 1986.

Wolf, Stephanie Grauman. *Urban Village: Population, Community, and Family Structure in Germantown, Pennsylvania, 1683-1800*. Princeton: Princeton University Press, 1976.

———. "Hyphenated Culture: The Creation of an Eighteenth-Century German-American Culture." In *America and the Germans: An Assessment of a Three-Hundred-Year History*, edited by Frank Trommler and Joseph McVeigh, vol. 1, 66-84. Philadelphia: University of Pennsylvania Press, 1985.

———. *As Various as Their Land: The Everyday Lives of Eighteenth-Century Americans*. New York: Harper Collins Publishers, 1993.

Yeich, M. A. "A Lincoln Interlude." *Historical Review of Berks County* 3, no. 3 (April 1938): 71-72.

Yoder, Don. "Origins of the Pennsylvania Yoders." In *The Yoder Family Reunion Book*. Published privately, 1954.

———. "Through the Traveler's Eye." In *The Pennsylvania Barn*, edited by Alfred L. Shoemaker, 12-21. Lancaster: The Pennsylvania Dutch Folklore Center, Inc., 1956.

———, ed. *Rhineland Emigrants: Lists of German Settlers in Colonial America*. Baltimore: Genealogical Publishing Co., Inc., 1981. See especially pp. 97-107.

———. "The Palatine Connection: The Pennsylvania German Culture and Its European Roots." In *Germans in America: Retrospect and Prospect*, edited by Randall M. Miller, 92-109. Philadelphia: German Society of Pennsylvania, 1984.

———. "The Origins of the Oley Valley Yoders." *Yoder Newsletter*, no. 5 (April 1985) 1, 3-6.

———. "The Pennsylvania Germans: Three Centuries of Identity Crisis." In *America and the Germans: An Assessment of a Three-Hundred-Year History*, edited by Frank Trommler and Joseph McVeigh, vol. 1, 40-65. Philadelphia: University of Pennsylvania Press, 1985.

———. *Discovering American Folklife: Studies in Ethnic, Religious, and Regional Culture*. Ann Arbor: UMI Research Press, 1990.

Zink, Clifford W. "Dutch Framed Houses in New York and New Jersey." *Winterthur Portfolio* 22, No. 4 (Winter 1987), 265-294.

ACKNOWLEDGMENTS

The present work is, first and foremost, an outgrowth of the enduring commitment on the part of the Oley Valley Heritage Association to the study of the history and architectural history of the Oley Valley community. I would like to thank the board of the Heritage Association, as well as the membership at large, for their support of this project over the years. I hope that this work will make a contribution to the fulfillment of the association's mission: "Protecting Our Future by Preserving Our Past." A series of Local History Grants from the Pennsylvania Historical and Museum Commission funded most of the research undertaken for this book. I wish to express my gratitude to the Board of the Pennsylvania German Society for the honor I have received in choosing my book for their series of publications.

My more personal thanks go to Laurel Miller, Donald Shelley, Hilda Fisher, Marsha Chappell, Richard Druckenbrod, Don Yoder, John Diefenderfer, William Rupp, and Willard Wetzel for their assistance over the years in making arrangements with the two publishing organizations.

This text has passed under the gaze of quite a few pairs of reviewing eyes, and has benefited every time. I would like to give my thanks to all the readers: James Lewars, Nathaniel Alcock, Bernard Herman, Donald Shelley, Ruth Baker, and a careful reader at the PHMC who contributed much but who was never identified to me. In addition, the manuscript has enjoyed the eminently insightful guidance of Don Yoder as scholarly editor. I also wish to thank Willard Wetzel for his editorial labors.

The research for the book was undertaken at a wide array of libraries and agencies. In particular, the staffs of the Historical Society of Berks County, the Berks County Register of Wills, the Historical Society of Pennsylvania, the Pennsylvania State Archives, the Friends Historical Library at Swarthmore College, the Schwenkfelder Library, the Historical Society of the Cocalico Valley, the Moravian Archives, and the State Museum of Pennsylvania have been generous in their assistance. Joyce O'Brien, Dennis Moyer, Cynthia Marquet, Vernon Nelson, and Clare Messimer have gone out of their way to be helpful. Barbara Gill has personally made the library of the Historical Society of Berks County an especially enjoyable and easy place to work.

Much of the research was done in the field, at colonial-period homesteads. The Historic Preservation Trust of Berks County generously permitted examination, photography, and measuring at its outstanding collection of eighteenth-century Oley Valley buildings, as did the Daniel Boone Homestead State Historic Site, Exeter Friends Meeting, and the Pine Forge Academy. Among those Oley Valley residents who graciously and patiently opened their homes to the author and illustrators were Dante and Honora Bertagna, Severin Fayerman, William and Susan Buoni, Walter and Emily Diener, David Kaufman, James and Cathy Coker, Donald and Esther Shelley, Joseph and Mary Ann Griffin, Howard Stoltzfus, Ajay Shah, Elizabeth Levandowski, Rosamund and the late John Moxon, and Charles and Frances Rasweiler. My apologies go to the many residents whose properties I have photographed or surveyed and whom there is not the opportunity to thank by name here.

I am indebted to a number of people who contributed historic photographs, architectural measurements or historic documents from their private collections: Robert Ensminger, Christopher Witmer, James Lewars, Bernard Herman, Jane Levan, Donald Shelley, Don Yoder, Richard Levengood, and especially Robert Bucher. Tim Noble, Gabrielle Lanier, and Stephen Kindig kindly assisted with the transmission of these materials. Laurel Miller and Peter Stebbins Craig generously shared their research, and in particular, Richard Hulan kindly permitted the use of his unpublished translation of Carl Magnus Wrangel's journal. Accessible Archives, Inc., of Malvern, Pennsylvania, lent assistance by identifying the libraries in possession of their recently published CD-ROM edition of the colonial-period *Pennsylvania Gazette*, a refinement of this important source that promises to be of immeasurable assistance to students of early American history and material culture. The Geography Department of Kutztown University made possible the computer-generated maps of the Oley Valley settlement; Petra Zimmermann did the computer cartography, often going the extra mile to provide her time.

Studying the surviving colonial-period architecture of the Oley Valley has truly been a learning process, and I have been fortunate to have the benefit of many fine teachers. They bear no responsibility for any misinterpretations that may be contained in this text, however. The formal as well as informal instruction and advice I have received from Bernard Herman and Myron Stachiw has been of immense value. Edward Chappell, never formally one of my teachers, has contributed as much as anyone to my education in architectural history. David Ames, Christopher Witmer, Norman Glass, Gabrielle Lanier, Stephen Kindig, Jerry Clouse, Nora Pat Small, Jeanne Whitney and, especially, Kenneth LeVan have all shown me much. My fieldwork was much facilitated by Edward Stokes, Howard Stoltzfus, Stephen and Felicitas Kindig, and Kenneth and Hope LeVan, who it seemed were always ready at the end of the day with a shady or warm place at their Oley Valley homes to chat and reflect.

Undertaking a project on the scale of the researching and writing of this book is bound to "make life more interesting," in a number of ways. I owe great thanks to my co-workers at Louis Berger & Associates, Inc., as well as to my friends and to all my family, for their patience with the influence "The Book" has exerted on seemingly every aspect of my life. I am especially grateful to my wife Deborah, to my son Nathaniel, and to my mother, Mary V. Pendleton, for their understanding.

Having now written one, this author wonders whether a non-fiction book can ever truly be said to be essentially the work of one person. Don Yoder, Stephen Kindig, James Lewars, Bernard Herman, Myron Stachiw, Edward Chappell, and especially my mother and Deborah have conveyed an encouragement that has sustained the work over a period of years. At the head of this group of supporters should be placed Phoebe Hopkins, who could be said to have originated the idea of the book. I have always thought of this as "Phoebe's book." I also think of it often, though, as "Ken and Hope's book." Aside from their tireless advice, encouragement, patience and hospitality, the many hours of work Kenneth and Hope M. LeVan have put into the architectural field measurements, Ken's photography, and Hope's luminous maps and drawings have taken my little history book and made it into a thing of beauty.

ABRAHAM LEVAN HOUSE, Circa 1753, Oley Township
A view from the rear across the fields, showing later additions to the original structure.
Photo by Kenneth LeVan.

INDEX

SUBJECT INDEX

Abingdon Friends Meeting (see also Quakers), 18, 129
African-American people, 33, 46, 50-51, 100, 147
Agricultural system of the Oley Valley, 29-37, 47, 53, 149
Agricultural system of the Oley Valley, decline of soil fertility, 34
Agricultural year, 32-33
Albany, New York, 143
Alsace Township, 13, 95, 119
Alsatian people, 15, 21, 137
Amity Township, 13, 16, 18, 20, 23, 24, 25, 33, 42, 45, 49, 56, 57, 58, 59, 66, 68, 69, 70, 72, 73, 77, 83, 87, 93, 94, 99, 100, 103, 105, 120, 136, 137, 139, 140, 141, 144, 145, 146, 147, 152, 155, 156, 169, 175, 176-178, 186, 189, 195, 201
Amity Township, maps of, 188, 194, 200
Amityville, Pennsylvania (see also New Store), 119, 120, 144, 187
Ancillary house building type, 22, 68, 84-93, 157, 160, 162, 164, 165, 166
Anglicans, 18, 24, 103, 120, 121, 122-123, 124-125, 137, 143, 149, 152, 153
Anglo-Pennsylvania house types, 67, 68-70
Antietam Creek, 35, 187
Apples, 36-37
Apprentices, 48
Artisans and tradesmen, 37-38, 45, 46, 47, 207
Ashlar, 59, 157
Bakehouses, 58, 65, 96, 157
Balconies, 67, 73, 77, 91, 157
Ballie House, Peter, 22
Bank barn (without forebay) type, 94, 95
Bank-sited buildings, 22, 40, 87-88, 98, 157, 165
Barley, 32, 33
Barns, 27, 34, 56, 58, 65, 86, 94-96, 98, 99, 100, 158, 207
Basements, 157, 159, 160, 164, 165, 166
Basket, Pennsylvania, 95
Bays, 19, 20, 22, 44, 68, 75, 77, 80, 81, 82, 84, 90, 158, 207
Beads (construction), 158, 165
Bearing walls (see also load-bearing walls), 161
Beer, 33
Bees, 37
Bents, 158, 163, 165
Berks County, 14, 16, 71, 137, 140, 141, 142, 154, 201, 203, 205
Bertolet-Herbein House or Cabin, 57, 58, 67, 71, 72, 80, 155, 170, 207
Bertolet House, Abraham, 65, 66, 68, 83, 90, 155, 167
Bertolet Sawmill, 98, 207

Bethlehem, Pennsylvania, city of, 113, 114, 117, 118
Bieber's Mill, 86
Bird House, William (see also Birdsborough Forge Mansion), 44, 69, 82-83, 155
Bird's Forges, 187
Birdsboro, Pennsylvania, 13, 43, 44, 49, 69, 82-83, 155, 187
Birdsborough Forge Mansion (see Bird House, William)
Bishop Hall (see Bishop House, Johannes)
Bishop House, Johannes, 59, 74, 75, 81, 155, 173
Black Bear Tavern, 11
Black Horse Tavern, 11
Black people (see African-American people)
Blacksmith shop buildings (see smithies)
Bohemia, 111
Bonfeld, Germany, village of, 20
Boone Gristmill, William, 11
Boone Homestead, Judah, 155
Boone Homestead State Historic Site, Daniel, 20, 57, 58, 61, 71, 93, 98, 155, 156, 207
Boone House, George, Sr., 66, 69-70, 155
Boone House, Joseph, 24, 59, 70, 169
Boone House, Judah, 81-82
Boone Mill, Judah, 40, 98
Boxed staircases, 74, 158, 166
Braces, 158
Brandy, 36, 37
Brick masonry construction (see also masonry construction), 56, 58, 60, 63
Brickmaking, 59-60
British people, 137, 183-185
Bucks County, 144
Buckwheat, 32, 33
Buhr stones, 98, 158, 162
Butt purlins (see purlins)
Cacoosing, Pennsylvania, 26
Cattle, 34-35
Cellars, 22, 55, 60, 61, 62, 63, 72, 82, 88, 93, 99, 100, 157, 158, 159
Cells (construction), 158, 160, 164
Center-passage double-pile house type, 67, 73-79, 100, 112, 116, 171, 172
Center-passage single-pile house type, 44, 82-83
Chambered hall house type, 65, 68, 167
Chambered halls, 68
Chambers, 158
Chester County, 95, 141
Chestnut trees, 62
Chinking, 57, 61, 158, 162
Christina (Wilmington), Delaware, 122
Church buildings, 57, 110, 114, 120, 121, 123, 125, 128

Church ministers, unofficial or irregular, 110, 120-121, 130-131, 153
Church of England (see Anglicans)
Church of Sweden (see Swedish Lutherans)
Cider, 33, 36-37, 93
Cider mills, 36-37
Cider presses, 37, 97
Cidermaking, 36
Cladding, 158, 165
Clapboard, 158, 159, 165, 166
Clipped-gable roofs (see also half-hipped roofs), 72, 158, 161
Clothing, 35-36
Coal houses, 99
Cocalico Valley, Pennsylvania, 107
Colebrookdale Furnace, 42, 143, 144
Colebrookdale, Pennsylvania, 26, 43, 100, 141, 143
Collar beams, 64, 158
Common rafters (see also rafters), 64-65, 66, 158, 163, 165
Common shingles (see also shingles), 158
Construction methods employed in Oley Valley architecture, 56-67
Consumer goods (see domestic material environment) Continental house type (see stove-room house type) Corner braces (see also braces), 158
Corner fireplaces, 69, 70, 77, 78, 158
Corner-notching log construction, 56, 58, 158, 159, 162, 166
Corner-post log construction, 56-57, 115, 162
Cornices, 59, 81, 158-159, 162
County courts, role of as governmental unit, 140, 141-142, 145, 146, 147, 154
County, function and organization of as governmental unit, 141-142, 154
Coursed ashlar (see also ashlar), 157
Courses (construction), 158, 159, 164, 166
Coventry, Pennsylvania, 43
Craftsmen (see artisans and tradesmen)
Credit, role of in Oley Valley economy, 47-48
Cribs, 96
Crime, 51, 141-142, 143
Cumru Township, 13
Custom mills (see also gristmills), 159, 160
Cut-stone work, 24, 55, 59, 88, 157, 159
Darra House (see DeHart House, Cornelius)
DeBenneville Homestead, George, 155
DeBenneville-Knabb Barn, 94, 95
DeHart House, Cornelius, 18, 73, 83
DeTurk Ancillary House, Johannes, 64, 88, 89, 155, 174
DeTurk House, Johannes, 83, 113
Devonshire, England, 128, 141
Disputes regarding property, 147

Disputes regarding transportation routes, 144-147
District Township, 141
Dogs, 35
Domestic material environment, 83-84
Dormers, 77, 94, 159, 161
Double-cell house type, 19, 39, 55, 68, 72, 81, 84, 93, 168
Double-hung sash (see windows, vertical sash)
Double-parlor house type, 24, 70, 72, 77, 84, 149, 169
Double-pile construction, 61, 70, 159
Douglass House, George, 77, 155
Douglass Township, 13, 42, 66, 69, 100, 140, 141, 144, 152, 176-178
Douglassville, Pennsylvania, 187
Dovetail notching, 57, 159
Drip courses, 61, 159
Drury Store, Edward, 11
Dunkers (see German Baptist Brethren)
Dutch or Netherlandic people, 18, 121, 137-138, 183-185
Dutch Reformed Church, 105, 110
Earl Township, 13, 42, 60, 141, 144, 176-178
Eave walls, 159, 161
Eaves, 159
Economic goals of Oley Valley people, 31, 44-45
Elderly people, 46, 85
Elections, 142-143
Elevations, 157, 158, 159
Ellis-Bertolet Homestead, 155
Ellis-Lee House, 132
Ells, 81, 159
Entries (construction), 159, 160, 164
Entry floors, 159, 160, 164
Ephrata Cloister, 107
Ephrata, Pennsylvania, 107
Eppstein, Germany, town of, 106
Esopus, New York, 143
Exeter Friends Meeting (see also Quakers), 11, 33, 51, 127, 129, 136, 139, 147, 152, 155, 184, 185, 187
Exeter Township, 13, 19, 20, 23, 35, 39, 40, 42, 48, 55, 57, 59, 61, 66, 67, 68, 69, 70, 71, 72, 73, 74, 75, 81, 82, 87, 97, 98, 99, 120, 127, 129, 140, 141, 144, 147, 152, 155, 156, 168, 170, 173, 176-178, 186, 197, 203
Exeter Township, maps of, 196, 202
Exeter Zone, map of, 190
Facades, 19, 24, 44, 59, 67, 75, 77, 81, 82, 83, 88, 158, 159, 166
Fachwerk (see timber-frame construction) False plates (see also plates), 159, 163
False rafters (see also rafters), 65, 159, 161
Family cemetary plots, 109, 111, 147
Family groups, immigration by, 15-16, 18-20
Family life, 127, 130, 135-137
Farm tools, 29, 32, 149
Farmstead organization, 97-98
Fences, 35, 97
Fenestration, 42, 60, 66, 81, 83, 158, 159
Fieldstone work (see also rough stone work), 59, 159, 163
Finish, interior of houses, 62-63, 74, 81, 83, 159

Finney's Ferry (see also Reading, city of), 144
First Purchase rights, 25
Flax, 35-36
Forebays, 27, 95, 159
Forges, 98, 181, 182
Forges, bloomery, 42
Forges, finery, 42
Forges, iron-refining, 43
Foundations, 63, 158, 159-160
Four-over-four house type, 18, 83, 113
Frankenthal, Germany, town of, 106
French and Indian War, 15, 26, 130, 142
French Creek, 146
French people, 15, 18, 137
Friends (see Quakers)
Front elevations, 160, 164
Front facades, 160
Front-gable orientation, 160
Front walls, 160
Fruit, cultivation of (see orchards)
Full-dovetail notching, 159, 160
Fulling mills, 40, 92, 98, 181, 182
Funerals, 123, 131, 139, 140
Furnaces, ironmaking, 41, 42, 71, 98
Furniture (see domestic material environment)
Gable-end doors, 98
Gable-end walls, 22, 40, 77, 79, 84, 86, 88, 158, 159, 160, 164
Gable-end windows, 72, 94
Gable roofs, 157, 160, 163, 164
Gables, 56, 61, 160
Gardens, 37, 97
Garrets, 55, 64, 66, 68, 73, 77, 86, 88, 96, 158, 159, 160, 161, 164
Gearpits, 160, 164
General Loan Office of Pennsylvania, 47
Georgian architecture (see also Palladian architecture), 56, 59, 160, 163
Gerick House, Hans Mirtel, 66, 72, 87, 170
German Baptist Brethren, 107, 109, 149
German church people, 15, 105, 106, 108, 109-111, 119-121
German immigration to Pennsylvania, 15-16, 27, 48-50, 105, 106, 138
German Lutherans (see also German church people), 15, 18, 24, 109, 121, 124, 138, 149, 153
German Palladian houses, 75, 77-79, 112, 116
German people, 183-185
German Reformed Church (see also German church people), 15, 103, 105, 109-111, 114, 130-131, 149, 153
German sectarians, 15, 105, 109
Germantown, town of, 38, 47, 48, 49, 74, 78, 105, 109, 118, 144
Gibraltar, Pennsylvania, 42
Girts, 58, 158, 160
Glazing, 66, 158, 160
Gloria Dei Church (see also Wicacoa), 104, 121
Gnadenhutten, Pennsylvania, 118
Goshenhoppen, Pennsylvania, 26, 118, 141, 143
Governmental and political activity, 108, 127, 128-129, 130, 138, 140-148, 149, 154
Granaries, 84, 86, 88, 95, 96, 157, 160
Grandfather houses, 85, 88, 92, 157, 160

Gravestones, 103, 104, 105, 110, 120, 122
Great Creek (see also Antietam Creek), 187
Gregory-Weidner Homestead, 68, 90, 155
Gristmills, 11, 31, 33, 38-40, 56, 84, 85, 98, 99, 128, 138, 143, 144-145, 146, 155, 156, 159, 160, 161, 164, 165, 166, 181, 182, 186
Ground-level barn type, 94
Grumblethorpe (see Wister House, John)
Gwynedd Friends Meeting (see also Quakers), 18, 129
Half-dovetail notching, 57, 159, 160
Half-hipped roofs, 72, 160, 163
Half-story, 68, 161
Half-timber work, 58, 161, 165, 166
Hall house type, 67-68, 87, 90
Hall-parlor house type, 16, 20, 44, 68-69, 70, 82, 93, 132, 169, 207
Halls, 161
Hallways, 163
Harrows, 32, 33, 100
Harvest, 33
Hay, 35
Hay barracks, 97
Hay mows (see also mows), 95, 161
Headraces (see also millraces), 98, 161, 162, 166
Herner Tavern, Nicolaus, 73-74
Herrnhut, Germany, town of, 111, 112
Hewn-log construction, 56, 158, 161, 162
High Road from Maiden Creek to Finney's Ferry, 147
High Road from Maiden Creek to Oley, 97, 136, 187
High Road from Moselem to Oley, 146-147
High Road from Oley to Philadelphia, 120, 122, 144
High Road from Reading to Philadelphia, 144
High Road from Tulpehocken to Philadelphia, 120, 144
Historic American Buildings Survey, 155
Historic Oley Building Archive and Survey, 155
Historic Preservation Trust of Berks County, 16, 39, 77, 90, 155
Hoch Homestead, Johannes, 155
Hoch Homestead, Samuel III, 86
Hoch House-Mill, Johannes, Jr., 61, 84, 85, 98, 155
Hoch Tenancy Ancillary House, Samuel, 155
Hochstadt, Germany, 114
Homesteads, 161, 162
Horses, 32, 33, 34-35, 100
House-mill building type, 61, 84, 85
House types, general discussion of, 67, 161, 165-166
House types, Oley Valley, 167-175
Hughes Tavern, John, 11
Huguenots (see French people)
Hunter Inn, John (see Jaeger Inn, Johannes)
Hurst frames, 98, 160, 161
Indian corn, 32, 33
Indians (see Lenni Lenape)
Industry, refining and manufacturing, 38-43
Innholders, 161
Innkeepers, 161
Inns and taverns, 11, 33, 37, 57-58, 74-75, 76, 77, 100, 135, 137, 138, 143, 145, 147, 155,

156, 181, 182, 186
Internal waterwheels (see also waterwheels), 159, 160, 161
Irish people, 48-49, 124, 137
Iron, cast, 42
Iron, wrought, 42
Iron industry, 42-43
Ironmasters, 11, 42-43, 45, 46, 49-50, 67, 73-74, 77, 122, 144, 146-147, 152
Irrigation, meadow, 35
Jack arches, 59, 161
Jacksonwald, Pennsylvania, 119
Jaeger Homestead, Antony, 135, 155
Jaeger Inn, Johannes (see also Hunter Inn, John), 74-75, 76, 77, 100, 155, 171
Jerkin head roofs (see also half-hipped roofs), 72, 160, 161
Joder House, Johannes, Sr., 19, 68, 155, 156
Joints, 58, 61, 64, 161
Joists, 58, 61, 63, 64, 158, 159, 161, 163, 165
Jones House, Mounce, 16, 66, 69, 156, 169
Justices of the peace (see also county courts), 142
Kammers (see chambers)
Kauffmann Ancillary House, Jacob, 88
Kauffmann Homestead, 156
Kauffmann House, Jacob, 23, 56, 60, 62, 63, 73, 74, 75, 134-135
Keim Ancillary House, Jacob, 64, 90-92
Keim Homestead, Jacob, 63, 90, 151, 156
Keim House, Jacob, 37, 73, 75, 82, 83, 91
Kemp's Tavern, 135
Keystones, 59, 161, 165
Kicks (construction), 65, 98, 159, 161
King's High Road to Philadelphia, 122, 143
Kingston, New York, 143
Kitchen buildings, 161
Kitchens, 161
Knee walls, 161
Kuhlwein House, 58
Laborers, 16, 33, 46, 48
Lambsheim, Germany, town of, 106
Lancaster County, 107
Land dealers (see land speculators)
Land, process of claiming for settlement, 24-25
Land speculators, 24-25
Language, 139, 149
Lateral elevations, 93, 95, 159, 161, 164
Lateral walls, 159, 160, 161, 163, 166
Laths, 161, 163, 165
Lean-to structures, 22, 70, 161, 162
Lebanon Sawmill, 42, 128
Lee House, Thomas, 69
Leinbach-Knabb Homestead, 68, 90, 95, 156
Lenni Lenape, 13, 25-27, 109, 138, 149, 187
Lesher House, Johannes, 63, 64, 67, 71, 76, 77, 78, 79, 155, 172, 231
Levan House, Abraham, 21, 73, 155, 220
Liegender Dachstuhl (see also strut-supported roof systems), 63-64, 161
Limekiln Creek, 148
Limestone soil (see soil types, effects of)
Lincoln House, Abraham, 70
Lincoln House, Mordecai, 19, 55, 66, 68, 81, 156, 168
Lintels, 59, 88, 161, 165
Livestock, 33, 34-35, 95, 96

Load-bearing walls, 161
Lofts, 67, 96, 160, 161
Log construction, 38, 56-58, 61, 63, 69, 73-74, 92, 94, 95, 101, 115, 149, 162
London Company, The (see Pennsylvania Land Company, London)
Long Island, New York, 25
Lotz Ancillary House, Jerg, 87, 93, 156, 175
Lumber trade, 42
Lutheran Church, German (see German Lutherans)
Lutheran Church, Swedish (see Swedish Lutherans)
Lutheran Ministerium, 120
Maiden Creek, Pennsylvania, 143, 147
Main blocks, 159, 162, 166
Manatawny Creek, 20, 25, 40, 100, 122, 147, 186-187
Manatawny, Pennsylvania, 39, 140
Mariner's Compass Tavern, 11
Masonry construction, 159, 162, 163
Material life, general, e.g. furniture and consumer goods, 136, 139-140
Matzong, Pennsylvania, 122
Maugridge-DeTurk House, 20, 61, 69, 93, 156, 207
Maxatawny, Pennsylvania, 143
Mennonites, 109, 149
Merchant milling, 41-42, 98, 160, 162
Milk houses, 86, 97, 157, 162
Milldams, 98, 162
Millers (see gristmills)
Millponds, 98, 162
Millraces, 162
Millseats, 40, 98, 162
Millstones, 158, 160, 161, 162, 164
Mill Tract Farm (see Boone Homestead, Judah)
Mingo Creek, 146
Mining, iron, 43
Molatton Church, 18, 24, 103, 109, 136, 137, 139, 141, 183, 184, 186, 187
Molatton, Pennsylvania, 25-26, 69, 104, 122, 143, 145
Moldings, 158, 162
Money (see credit, role of in Oley Valley economy)
Monocacy Creek, 23, 25, 128, 186, 187
Montgomery County, 124
Moravia, 111
Moravian Boarding School (see Oley Moravian Boarding School)
Moravians, 71, 97, 108, 111-118, 123, 126, 135, 149, 152, 153
Mortar, 59, 162
Mortise, 58, 61, 63, 162, 163, 165
Moselem, Pennsylvania, 43, 143, 146-147
Mows, 162
Moxon Farm (see Reiff Homestead, Daniel)
National Register of Historic Places, 155
Nationalities of the Oley Valley, 15, 17, 23-24, 31, 32, 33, 46, 61, 62, 63-64, 65, 66-67, 68-73, 74, 79-81, 93, 121, 142, 149, 183-185, 186, 187
Nationalities of the Oley Valley, relationships between, 137-140
Neighbors, relationships between, 140, 147
Neshaminy, Pennsylvania, 122

Netherlandic people (see Dutch people)
New Born sect, 18, 106-108, 109, 111-112, 118, 153, 186
New England people, 18, 25, 121, 137
New Hanover Township, 119, 123, 124, 140
New Jersey settlers, 18, 25, 121, 137
New Store, Pennsylvania (see also Amityville), 33, 119, 138, 143, 144, 152, 187
New Store Union Church, 119, 120, 121, 124, 125, 152, 185
New Sweden (see Swedes, Delaware Valley)
Newspaper advertisements, 39, 40, 48, 51-52, 57, 99-100, 136, 137, 143
Northumberland County, 125
Oak trees, 62
Oakum, 57, 162
Oats, 31, 32, 33
Office houses, 162
Oil mills, 40, 98
Old Swedes' Church, Philadelphia (see Gloria Dei Church) Old Swede's House (see also Jones House, Mounce), 156
Oley Forge, 43, 45, 47, 50, 64, 119, 146, 147, 187
Oley Forge Mansion (see Lesher House, Johannes)
Oley Furnace, 41, 43, 80
Oley Hill Church, 119
Oley Hills, Pennsylvania, 43, 141, 143
Oley Huguenots, 18, 20-21
Oley Moravian Boarding School, 58, 78, 79, 112, 116
Oley Moravian Church, 184, 185
Oley Moravian Mission, 112-116
Oley Reformed Church (first congregation), 110-111, 114, 119
Oley Reformed Church (second congregation), 103, 119, 120, 152, 185
Oley Township, 13, 19, 21, 23, 37, 38, 41, 43, 45, 48, 49, 56, 57, 58, 60, 61, 62, 63, 64, 65, 66, 67, 68, 69, 71, 72, 73, 74-75, 76, 77, 78, 79, 80, 81, 83, 84, 85, 86, 88, 89, 90, 93, 94, 95, 96, 97, 98, 100, 103, 108, 111, 112, 113, 114, 115, 116, 120, 140, 141, 143, 144, 145-147, 152, 155, 156, 167, 170, 171, 172, 174, 176-178, 191, 193, 199, 205
Oley Township, maps of, 179, 192, 198, 204
Oley Valley, differences between upper and lower sections, 13, 23, 25, 72, 138
Oley Valley, geographical description, 13
Oley Valley, heads of households and single freemen, 176-178
Oley Valley, maps of, 11, 14, 17, 30, 179-185, 188-205
Oley Valley, origin of name, 13
Oley Valley, population of, 1767, 45
Oley Valley settlement, development of, 30, 186-187
Oley, village of, 187
One-room house type (see hall house type)
Orchards, 36, 98, 99, 100
Original sections (construction), 162
Outbuildings (of types smaller than barns), 58, 63, 96-97, 157, 164, 166
Outhouses, 162
Outlookers (see also pent roofs), 162, 163

223

Outshuts, 70, 162
Oxen, 32
Palatinate, Germany, 15, 18, 105, 106, 138
Palladian architecture, 56, 59, 149, 160, 162-163, 164, 166
Palladian-influenced house types, 67, 73-83
Papermills, 42, 181, 182
Parlors, 163
Partition walls, 62, 163, 165
Passages, 163
Peaches, 36
Penn family (see Proprietors of Pennsylvania)
Penn-plan house type (see double-cell house type)
Pennsylvania farmhouse type (see four-over-four house type)
Pennsylvania German house types, 22, 67, 70-73, 77-79
Pennsylvania Land Company, London, 26
Pent eaves, 18, 65, 163
Pent roofs, 18, 24, 61, 65, 73, 159, 162, 163
Perkiomen, Pennsylvania, 122
Peter's Mill (see Hoch House-Mill, Johannes, Jr.)
Philadelphia, city of, 11, 13, 16, 25, 29, 31, 33, 41, 42, 43, 47, 48, 51, 58, 67, 68, 74, 78, 99, 100, 107, 113, 121, 122, 123, 125, 128, 143, 144, 147, 207
Philadelphia County, 99, 108, 128, 137, 140, 141, 142, 144, 145-146, 147, 154, 189, 191, 193, 195, 197, 199
Pickering's Creek, 146
Pietism, 106, 111, 123
Pigs, 34-35, 96, 97
Pike Township, 13, 17, 63, 67, 73, 75, 82, 83, 84, 90, 91, 92, 98, 141, 156, 176-178
Pile (construction), 163
Pine Forge Mansion (see Rutter House, Joseph)
Pine Forge, 11, 20, 42, 43, 45, 47, 51, 69, 152, 186
Pintels, 66
Plan (construction), 158, 163
Plank-log construction, 57, 162, 163
Plaster, 62, 63, 76, 83, 159, 161, 163, 165
Plates (construction), 58, 62, 64, 71, 159, 163, 165
Pleurisy, 123-124
Plows, 32, 100
Politics (see governmental and political activity)
Poor people, 46, 47, 68
Post-and-beam construction, 58, 163, 165
Post-supported roof systems, 65-66, 163
Posts, 158, 160, 163, 165
Pott House, Wilhelm, 67, 92
Pott House-Mill, Johannes, 84, 98
Pottsgrove (Pottstown), Pennsylvania, 43, 65, 100
Poultry, 35
Poverty (see poor people)
Presbyterians, 121
Pricetown, Pennsylvania, 109
Principal entries (see also entries), 163
Principal facades (see also facades), 160, 163
Principal rafters (see also rafters), 64-65, 158, 163, 165
Proprietors of Pennsylvania, 24
Purlins, 58, 64, 65, 158, 163

Quaker-plan house type (see double-parlor house type)
Quakers, 18, 24, 33, 50, 51, 69, 70, 80, 97, 126-132, 136, 138, 139, 142, 147, 149, 152, 153
Queen-post roof system (see also post-supported roof systems), 163
Quoins, 59, 163
Raccoon (Swedesboro), New Jersey, 123
Races (see millraces) Rafter feet, 159, 161, 163
Rafters, 58, 64, 158, 161, 163, 165
Rauchkammer (see also smoke chambers), 55, 66, 163
Reading, city of, 11, 13, 33, 38, 99, 100, 124-125, 136, 137, 138, 139, 142, 143-144, 148
Reciprocating sawmills (see also sawmills), 163
Reformed Coetus, 120
Reiff Homestead, Daniel, 37, 96, 97, 98, 156
Reiff Tenancy Ancillary House, Daniel, 156
Relieving arches, 163
Religious life, general fervor of, 126
Religious life, unsettled conditions of early Pennsylvania, 104-105
Rhine Valley or Rhineland, 15, 31, 58, 66, 138
River travel, Schuylkill River (see also disputes regarding transportation routes), 23, 144-145, 186, 187
Road travel (see also disputes regarding transportation routes; roads, public, creation and maintenance of), 143-144, 146
Roads, public, creation and maintenance of, 108, 140, 143-144, 145, 146, 148
Roberts House, Moses, 80, 81, 155
Robeson Township, 13, 42, 72, 99, 128, 176-178
Rockland Church, 119
Roof-cover boards, 163
Roof ridges, 64, 163, 164
Roof tiles, 65-66, 161, 163
Roof tiles, clay, 65, 66, 91
Roof tiles, stone, 66
Roof trusses (see also trusses), 163, 165
Root cellars (see also cellars), 63, 97, 158, 163
Rough-log construction, 162, 163
Rough stone work, 59, 163
Round-log construction, 56, 162, 163
Rubble stone work, 159, 163-164
Rum, 33
Ruscomb Manor Township, 95
Rutter House, Joseph, 42, 66, 69-70
Rye, 31, 32, 33, 96
Saint Gabriel's Church (see also Molatton Church), 18, 103, 105, 119, 120, 122, 143, 149, 152, 185, 187, 207
Saint Lawrence, Pennsylvania, 13
Salem United Church of Christ (see Oley Reformed Church, second congregation), 103, 120
Salem, North Carolina, 118
Sands House, John, 72
Sash sawmills (see sawmills)
Sawmills, 35, 36, 40, 42, 57, 85, 92, 98, 128, 131, 162, 164, 181, 182, 207
Sawn-log construction, 57, 100, 162, 163
Schenkel Homestead, Martin, 38, 60, 98
Schenkel House, Martin, 60, 63, 155

Schiffer-Knabb House, 155
Schneider Homestead, Johannes, 93
Schneider House, Jacob, 155
Schneider Mill, 39, 67, 98, 156
Schools, 57, 100, 112, 115, 116, 117, 123, 136, 139, 152
Schuylkill River, 13, 16, 23, 25, 33, 99, 100, 104, 119, 122, 141, 144-145, 146, 181, 182, 186, 187
Schwarzwald, Pennsylvania, 25, 99, 119, 120, 143
Schwarzwald Union Congregation, 120, 121, 152, 184, 185
Scottish people, 121, 123, 124, 137
Scythes, 32
Segmental arches, 59, 61, 164
Servants, indentured, 15-16, 33, 46, 47, 48-50, 51-52
Service wings, 164
Settlement patterns, 17, 30, 186-187
Settlement process in the Oley Valley, 15, 16-25
Seven Years' War, 15
Sexual activity, illicit, 130, 136
Shale soil (see soil types, effects of)
Shed-roofed buildings, 161, 163, 164
Sheep, 34-36
Shingles, 159, 161, 163, 164
Shingles, double-beveled, 66
Shingles, side-lapped, 66
Shingles, wooden, 65, 66
Side-gable construction, 159, 160, 161, 164
Side-passage double-pile house type, 80, 81, 84, 173
Side-passage single-pile house type, 81-82
Sills, 58, 164, 165
Single cell house type, 174
Single-hung sash (see windows, vertical sash)
Single-pile construction, 68
Sittler Farm Cabin (see Leinbach-Knabb Homestead)
Skippack, Pennsylvania, 111-112
Slaves (see African-American people)
Smithies, 37, 38, 96, 97, 98, 100, 164, 207
Smoke chambers, 56, 164
Smoke channels, 79
Smokehouses, 58, 65, 96, 157, 164
Socializing, community, 117, 123, 138-139
Society of Friends (see Quakers)
Soil types, effects of, 13, 23-24, 31, 72, 97-98
Spangsville, Pennsylvania, 40, 119, 187
Spelt, 31, 32, 33
Spohn's Smithy, 38, 98
Spring Forge, 42, 51
Springhouses, 85, 88, 92, 94, 96, 97, 157, 164
Squared timbers, 164
Stables, 34, 56, 95, 96, 97, 99, 100
Stair passages, 79, 81, 164
Stapleton House, Robert, 60, 72, 93, 155
Stauber-Leinbach Homestead, 114
Stehender Dachstuhl (see also post-supported roof systems), 164
Still houses, 97, 157, 164
Stills, 37
Stone-enders, 69, 164
Stone flag, 66
Stone floors, 159, 160, 164

Stone masonry construction (see also masonry construction), 56, 58-59, 61, 63, 69, 70, 84, 87, 94
Stonersville, Pennsylvania, 144
Stoops, 66, 67, 164
Stores and storekeepers, 11, 33, 36, 47, 77, 83, 143, 145, 152, 181, 182
Stories and floor levels, 164-165
Stove-room house type, 18, 21, 22, 23, 57, 70-73, 77, 82, 87, 88, 90, 92, 93, 113, 114, 149, 158, 165, 170, 175, 207
Stoves, English, 81, 159
Stoves, five-plate, 159
Stoves, flue, 81, 159
Stoves, jamb, 20, 71, 79, 92, 93, 161, 207
Stoves, pipe, 81, 163
Stoves, six- and ten-plate, 79, 80, 90, 164
Strut-supported roof systems, 63-66, 73, 96, 98, 165
Stube (see stove-room house type)
Studs (construction), 165
Summer beams, 61, 62, 63, 87, 162, 163, 165
Summer kitchens (see also kitchens), 85, 161, 165
Surveying of Oley land, process of, 186
Swedes, Delaware Valley, 16, 23, 25, 58, 69, 121-125, 137, 138, 140, 144, 186
Swedes' Tract, 25, 140, 141, 186
Swedish Lutherans, 18, 24, 104, 121-125, 137, 138, 153
Swine (see pigs)
Swiss barn type, 94-95
Swiss people, 15, 18, 21, 58, 85, 94, 95
Switzerland, 138
Synod movement, Zinzendorf's, 113
Tailraces (see also millraces), 98, 162, 165, 166
Tanneries, 38, 98, 128
Tavern stands, 165
Taverns (see inns and taverns)

Taxation, 45, 94, 97, 137
Tenancy or tenant homesteads, 157, 165
Tenants and tenant farming, 44, 46, 92-93, 116
Tenons, 58, 63, 158, 162, 163, 165
Textiles, 35-36
Thatching, of roofs, 65, 66, 101, 161, 165
Thirty Years' War, 15
Three-cell house type, 42, 69-70
Threshing, 33
Threshing floors, 95, 162, 165
Through purlins (see also purlins), 64, 158, 163, 165
Tie beams, 165
Tile making, 59-60
Timber-frame construction, 56, 58, 63, 94, 112, 158, 160, 161, 163, 165
Townships, establishment of Oley Valley, 140-141
Townships, function and organization of, as governmental unit, 140
Tradesmen (see artisans and tradesmen)
Trappe, Pennsylvania, 31, 67, 124, 139, 144
Treenails, 64, 165
Trees, hardwood, used for building construction, 61-62
Trusses, 165
Tulip poplar trees, 62
Tulpehocken, Pennsylvania, 144
Two-room house type, 67
Umsted House, Herman, 72
Union Township, 13, 99, 146, 176-178
Universalism, 118
Up-and-down sawmills (see also sawmills), 166
V notching, 166
Vaulted cellars (see also cellars), 166
Vegetables, 37, 97
Vernacular architecture of the Oley Valley, general comments regarding, 13, 52-53, 55, 58, 60-61, 67, 98-99, 149, 166
Wagon houses, 97

Walmdach (see half-hipped roofs)
Washhouses, 84, 88, 92, 157, 166
Water races (see millraces)
Waterwheels, 160, 162, 164, 166
Wattle and daub, 58, 165, 166
Wealth, comparative of Oley Valley people, 43-47
Weatherboard, 158, 165, 166
Weavers, 36
Weddings, 139, 140
Weiser Homestead, David, 87
Welsh people, 31, 137
Wheat, 29-31, 32, 33, 41, 96, 99, 138, 143, 144, 149
Wheel pits, 98, 159, 160, 164, 166
Whiskey, 33
Whitacre Homestead, Samuel, 69
White Horse Inn, 11, 39, 68, 99, 156, 186
Whitemarsh, Pennsylvania, 122
Whitpain Township, Philadelphia County, 109
Wicacoa, Pennsylvania, 104, 121, 122, 124
Widows (see women, role and experience of)
Wind braces (see also braces), 158
Winder stairways, 166
Windows, casement, 66, 158
Windows, horizontal sash, 59, 66-67, 92, 161
Windows, vertical sash, 69, 66-67, 159, 166
Wine production, lack of in the Oley Valley, 31
Wine, 33, 149
Wings (construction), 19, 23, 65, 70, 81, 166
Winnowing mills, 32
Wister House, John, 78
Women, role and experience of, 16, 33, 37, 45-46, 47, 49, 50, 51, 72, 84, 85-86, 117, 118, 126, 127-128, 129, 135-137, 139
Wool, 35-36
Yocom House, Jonas, 69
Zion Union Congregation, 119

OLEY VALLEY HERITAGE

PERSONAL NAMES

Acrelius, Israel, 32-33, 34, 36-37
Adams, Isaac, 195
Adams, John, 176
Albrecht, Johannes, 176
Allen, William, 197
Allison, Amy, 126
Altstadt, Adam, 49, 203
Altstadt, Johann Martin, 176, 197
Anders, George, 33, 36, 83, 176, 189, 195
Andreas, Daniel, 195
Andreas, Wendel, 176
Antes, Heinrich, 111, 114, 153
Aschmann family, 18
Aschmann, Abraham, 176, 193
Aubenshein, Reinhold, 195
Ax, Jerg, 201
Ball, John, 176, 195
Ballie family, 18, 21
Ballie, Peter, 22, 176, 193
Banfield, John, 176
Banfield, Thomas, 176, 193, 195
Barlow, Joseph, 176
Barnet, James, 176
Barnet, Robert, 176
Barto family, 21
Barto, Isaac, 205
Barto, Johannes, 147, 199
Baum, Dewald, 176
Baumann family, 18
Baumann, Johannes, 199
Baumann, Katarina Kuhlwein, 106
Baumann, Matthias, 106-107, 108, 109, 114, 118, 153, 176, 193
Bechtel, Christopher, 176, 197
Bechtel, Jacob, 35, 203
Bechtel, Johannes, 203
Bechtel, Johann Jerg, 195
Bechtel, Peter, 203
Becker, Friedrich, 176, 197
Becker, Heinrich, 176
Becker, Marshall J., 26
Becker, Martin, 147, 195
Becker, Peter, 109
Beidler, Abraham, 201
Beidler, Conrad, 203
Beiler, Johannes, 203
Beissel, Conrad, 107, 109
Bell, Charles, 96, 176, 189, 195
Bell, Henry, 176
Bell, John, 176, 189
Bell, Jonathan, 201
Berger, Catherine Sands, 136
Berger, Friedrich, 136, 176
Berger, Susanna, 136
Bertolet family, 18
Bertolet, Abraham, 65, 66, 68, 83, 90, 112, 155, 167, 176, 199
Bertolet, Daniel, 25, 205
Bertolet, Esther DeTurk, 25, 26, 193
Bertolet, Friedrich, 205
Bertolet, Jean, 20, 112, 113, 118, 136, 176, 199
Bertolet, Johannes, Jr., 199, 205

Bertolet, Peter G. 10, 25, 26-27, 50, 57, 67, 108, 115, 136
Bertolet, Pierre, 18-20, 176, 193
Betz, Johannes, 201
Beyer, Christoph, 147, 197, 203
Beyer, Gabriel, 176, 199
Beyer, Jacob, 197
Beyer, Johannes, 201, 203
Beyer, Nicolaus, 120, 201
Beyer, Philip, 50, 107, 108, 119, 120, 139, 149, 176, 195
Biddle, Edward, 140
Bird, Mark, 44, 46, 49, 50, 143, 154, 203
Bird, William, 11, 43, 44, 47, 49, 50, 52, 99, 122, 123, 143, 144, 152, 154, 155, 176, 195, 197
Bishop, Elisabetha, 51
Bishop, Johannes, 32, 49, 59, 74, 75, 81, 140, 147, 155, 173, 197, 203
Blackford, William, 176
Blair, John, 176
Boehm, Johann Philipp, 108, 109-111, 153
Boon, Peter, 189
Boone family, 18, 23-24, 42, 114, 128, 141
Boone, Benjamin, Jr., 35, 36
Boone, Benjamin, Sr., 33, 35, 97-98, 176, 195, 197, 203
Boone, Daniel, 13, 20, 61, 71, 155, 156
Boone, Deborah, 24, 127-129, 153
Boone, George, Jr., 24, 99, 127-130, 142, 143, 145-146, 154, 176, 191
Boone, George, Sr., 66, 67, 69, 70, 108, 128, 130, 155, 176, 189, 191, 195, 197, 199
Boone, Hugh, 201
Boone, Isaac, 140, 201
Boone, James, 42, 70, 128, 136, 142, 145, 147, 154, 176, 197, 203
Boone, John, 48, 128, 145, 176, 195
Boone, Joseph, 33, 59, 70, 128, 145, 169, 176, 195
Boone, Joseph, Jr., 203
Boone, Judah, 40, 81-82, 98, 148, 155, 203
Boone, Mary, 128
Boone, Moses, 48
Boone, Samuel, Jr., 131
Boone, Samuel, Sr., 35, 98, 131, 145, 176, 195, 197, 203
Boone, Sarah Lincoln, 136
Boone, Squire, 61, 156, 176
Boone, William, 11, 51, 86, 130, 136, 142, 143, 154
Bord family, 18
Bord, Andrew, 176
Bord, Burgund, 176
Borden, Benjamin, 189
Bortzler, Jacob, 176
Bowen, James, 201
Bower, Moses, 152, 201
Bowman, Johannes, 176
Briel, Peter, 205
Brindley, Alexander, 176
Brooks, George, 52
Brown, John, 176

Browne, Joseph, 176
Browne, William, 176
Brush, Stephen, 189
Brumfield, Solomon, 201
Brumfield, Thomas, 176, 189, 195
Brycelius, Paul Daniel, 123, 153
Bunn, Nicolaus, 201
Burchell, William, 52
Burroughs, James, 176
Burroughs, John, 176
Caine, Richard, 176
Caldwell, Andrew, 176
Campbell family, 18
Campbell, John, 93, 176, 189, 195
Campbell, Robert, 152
Campbell, Walter, 36, 176
Carber, Nicolaus, 176
Carey, George, 140
Chappell, Edward A., 62
Cherington, Clement, 197
Chipp, Michael, 176
Christ, Michael, 203
Clapp, Ludwig, 176, 197
Clark, William, 176
Cocklin, John, 176
Cole, Daniel, 176, 197
Cole, Samuel, 176
Collins, John, 136, 176
Collins, William, 203
Cookson, Samuel, 39
Cox, Susanna, 93
Craesman, Philip Balthasar, 39, 99, 195
Creager, Caspar, 176, 199
Croll, P.C., 10
Cudgeon, Abigail, 51
Cudgeon, Dinah, 51
Cudgeon, Elizabeth, 51
Cudgeon, Jane, 51
Cudgeon, John, 51
Cupp, Jacob, 147, 201
Davis, David, 176, 201
Davis, William, 176, 189
Dean, Richard, 176
De Benneville, Esther Bertolet, 118
DeBenneville, George, 21, 48, 118, 152, 153, 155
DeChant, Aliene, 65
DeHart family, 18
DeHart, Aaron, 176
DeHart, Cornelius, 18, 73, 83, 195, 201
DeHart, Elias, 176
DeHart, Gilbert, 176, 195
DeHart, James, 176
DeHart, Simon, 176
DeHart, William, 201
Dehaven, Johannes, 201
Dehaven, Peter, 201
DelaPlank family, 21
DelaPlank, Frederick, 147
DelaPlank, Jacob, 25, 32, 36-37, 176, 193, 199
DePlank family (see DelaPlank family), 21
Derst, Paul, 203

DeTurk family, 18, 116
DeTurk, Isaac, 20, 106, 176, 193
DeTurk, Johannes, 61, 83, 86, 88, 89, 113, 155, 174, 176, 199
DeTurk, Johannes, Jr., 20, 93, 203, 205
DeTurk, Maria, 106, 107-108, 113
Devlan, Francis Daniel, 57
Dewees, Samuel, 49, 50
Dewees, Thomas, 100
Dewees, William, 100
Dibler, Ludwig, 176
Dieter, Johannes, 201
Dieter, Matthias, 203
Dillbork, Johannes, 176
Dirk (servant), 98
Dollin, John, 176
Donahew, Daniel, 52
Donner, Timothy, 176
Doughty, Robert, 176, 189
Douglass, George, 39, 77, 143, 145, 154, 155, 201
Drexel, Gottlieb, 103
Drury, Edward, 11, 142, 143, 154, 195
Dudley, Robert, 176
Dunkelbach, Peter, 176
Dunkelberg, Johannes, 176
Dunkley, Richard, 176
Dunklin, Richard, 145
Eames, Valentine, 203
Eastburn, Benjamin, 179
Edwards, Thomas, 189
Effert, Martin, 49
Egle, Heinrich, 201
Ellis family, 18
Ellis, John, 177
Ellis, Mordecai, 51
Ellis, Morris, 132, 195
Ellis, Rowland, 199, 205
Ellis, Thomas, 31, 147, 177, 199
Engelhart, Christopher, 177
Englehart, Nicolaus, 177
Ensminger, Robert, 95
Erhard, Philip, 177
Ernst, Christoph von, 52
Eschenbach, Andreas, 112-117, 153
Eshelman, John E., 10
Evans, David, 193
Evans, Edward, 193
Evans, William, 177
Everett, Thomas, 177
Everson, Jacob, 177
Faber, Johannes, 205
Falck, Gabriel, 51, 123, 124, 136, 153
Falckner, Justus, 105
Farrell, Thomas, 177
Faust, Peter, 177, 197
Fetter, Jacob, 177
Filbert, Johann Adam, 177
Fillinger, Katarina, 137
Fillinger, Ludwig, 137
Finney, Joseph, 177, 189
Finney, Thomas, 177
Finsell, 177
Fischer family, 21
Fischer, Johannes, 177, 199
Fisher, Peter, 201
Focht, Jerg, 205

Foos, Nicolaus, 31, 177
Foster, John, 177
Fothergill, Samuel, 130
Franklin, Benjamin, 33, 42
Franklin, Deborah, 33
Friedrich, Johannes, 177, 199
Fritz, Johannes, 49
Froehlich, Daniel, 195, 201
Fuge, Jacob, 177
Fulk, Andreas, 177, 189
Fulk, Karl, 177
Fulk, Jacob, 177
Furlong, William, 177
Garrad, David, 177, 197
Garrison, Nicholas, 97
Gehr, Balthasar, 137, 147
Geiger, Antony, 197
Geiger, Christopher, 203
Geldbach, Elisabetha, 136
Geldbach, Jacob, 34, 51, 205
Geldbach, Johannes, 34, 136, 177, 199
Geldbach, Katarina, 136
Geldbach, Magdalena, 34
George, John, 177
Gerhard, Eidel, 195
Gerick, Hans Mirtel, 31, 66, 72, 86, 87, 97, 99, 138, 170, 177, 197
Gerick, Jerg, 31
Gerick, Katarina, 86, 138
Gibson, Andrew, 201
Gibson, George, 177
Gibson, Henry, 20, 34, 177, 189, 195
Gilbreath, Owen, 177
Glatfelter, Charles, 121
Godfrey, John, 100, 143, 154, 195, 201
Godfrey, Thomas, 177, 195
Goetschy, Johann Heinrich, 110, 114, 153
Gouker, Johann Heinrich, 177, 195
Greff, Sebastian, 177
Gregory, Richard, 177, 193
Greiner, Johann Theodorick, 20, 177, 189, 195, 201
Griesemer, Caspar, 43, 121, 147, 199, 205
Griffith, Edward, 177
Griffith, Ellis, 177, 195, 201
Gruenwald, Peter, 201
Guldin, Daniel, 148, 205
Guldin, Samuel, 142, 154, 177, 199
Guthard, Friedrich, 203
Haas, Peter, 146
Haggeman, Ulrich, 177
Hahn, Valentine, 203
Haller, Mabel, 152
Hamilton, J. Taylor, 10, 117, 152
Harpel, Peter, 43
Harris, Mordecai, 201
Harris, Samuel, 177
Harrison, Caleb, 195, 201
Harrison, John, 62, 195, 201
Harrison, Michael, 177
Harry, Anne, 137
Harry, David, 31, 120, 177, 189
Harry, John, 99, 137
Hartmann, Johannes, 203
Hartmann, Philip, 205
Hartwick, Johann Christoph, 124, 153
Harverd, William, 177

Hausihl, Bernard Michael, 124, 153
Heagle, Johannes, 177
Heckler, Johannes, 203
Heckler, Rudolph, 177, 197
Heilman, Samuel, 37
Heit, Johann Leonard, 177
Held, Jerg Dietrich, 137
Henton, George, 140, 177, 197
Henton, Hannah, 126
Henton, Robert, 203
Herbein family, 18, 21
Herbein, Abraham, 177
Herbein, David, 205
Herbein, Jacob, 205
Herbein, Jonathan, 112, 113, 114-117, 177, 193, 199
Herbein, Peter, 205
Herbein, Philip, 199
Herbert, Morgan, 177
Herner, Friedrich, 203
Herner, Heinrich, 201
Herner, Michael, 203
Herner, Nicolaus, 73
Hesselius, Brigitta Lycon, 122
Hesselius, Samuel, 122, 124, 153
Heygo, Peter, 177
Heyman, Moses, 195
High family (see Hoch family), 18
Hill, Jacob, 177, 199, 205
Hill, Johannes, Jr., 48, 205
Hilsewick, Johannes, 177, 193
Hilt, Derick, 84, 199
Hilton, Peter, 177
Hilton, Richard, 177
Hinke, William J., 111
Hoch family, 18
Hoch, Abraham, 205
Hoch, Daniel, 205
Hoch, Johannes, Jr., 61, 84, 85, 155, 177, 199, 205
Hoch, Samuel III, 86
Hoch, Samuel, Sr., 86, 142, 143, 155, 177, 199, 201, 205
Hochgenug, Lenhardt, 177, 197
Hodel, Johannes, 177
Hoffmann, Johannes, 201
Hoffsess, Margareta, 49
Hoffsess, Maria, 49
Holder, John, 177
Holstein, Magdalena Huling, 143
Holstein, Mr., 26
Hooveracker, Johannes, 177
Hopkins, Susannah, 126
Hopkins, William, 126
Hower, Enoch, 177
Howie, Alexander, 122-123, 153
Huffnagel family, 18, 97-98
Huffnagel, Arnoldt, 108
Huffnagel, Benjamin, 32, 205
Huffnagel, Elias, 205
Huffnagel, Johann Arnoldt, 97, 177, 193, 199
Hughes family, 18
Hughes, Edward, 131, 203
Hughes, Ellis, 31, 131, 147, 149, 153, 177, 197
Hughes, Francis, 99, 177, 191
Hughes, George, 203

Hughes, Jane, 131
Hughes, John, 11, 32, 131, 138, 142, 143, 154, 177, 197
Hughes, Samuel, 203
Hughes, William, 131
Huling family, 16
Huling, John, 195
Huling, Magdalena, 26
Huling, Marcus, 39, 99, 100, 145, 177, 189
Huling, Mounce, 195
Hunter, John (see Jaeger, Johannes)
Huyet family, 21
Huyet, Johann Jacob, 203
Huyet, Peter, 177, 197
Ingles, James, 195, 201
Jaeger, Antony, 43, 44-46, 49, 147, 155, 177, 199
Jaeger, Christian, 136, 201, 205
Jaeger, Daniel, 147, 148, 205
Jaeger, Friedrich, 205
Jaeger, Henry, 147
Jaeger, Johann Jerg, 177
Jaeger, Johannes, 74, 75, 76, 77, 155, 171, 199
Jaeger, Magdalena Geldbach, 136
Jaeger, Nicolaus, 52, 177, 195, 199, 205
James, John, 177
Joder family (see Yoder family), 18
Joder, Anna Rosina LeDee, 106
Joder, Daniel, 136, 195, 199, 201, 205
Joder, Jacob, 205
Joder, Jerg, 205
Joder, Johannes II, 19, 43, 49, 136, 177
Joder, Johannes III, 136
Joder, Johannes, Sr., 40, 68, 106, 108, 155, 177, 193, 199
Joder, Jost, 177, 193, 199, 205
Joder, Peter, 148, 205
Joder, Samuel, 26, 31
Joder, Sarah Schenkel, 136
John, Philip, 51, 177
Jonasson family (see Jones family), 23-24
Jonasson, Ingabo (see Jones, Ingabo), 18, 24
Jonasson, Magnus (see Jones, Mounce), 16, 18, 24, 25, 83, 189
Jones family (see Jonasson family), 23-24, 47
Jones, Andrew, 177
Jones, Bariah, 177
Jones, David, 143, 177
Jones, Ezekiel, 139
Jones, Ingabo (see Jonasson, Ingabo), 122
Jones, John, 177, 191
Jones, Jonas, 47, 124, 137, 145, 177, 195, 201
Jones, Margaret (daughter of Jonas), 47
Jones, Margaret (daughter of Mounce), 39
Jones, Mary, 137, 201
Jones, Mounce (see Jonasson, Magnus), 16, 25, 39, 66, 69, 83, 108, 122, 124, 156, 169, 177, 189, 201
Jones, Nicholas, 195, 201
Jones, Peter I, 83-84, 96
Jones, Peter II, 83-84, 126, 139, 177, 195, 201
Jones, Ruth Henton, 126
Jones, Samuel, 177
Jung, Adam, 203
Jungmann, Jerg, 118, 135
Jungmann, Johann Dietrich, 33, 135, 177, 199

Justus, John, 177
Kalm, Pehr, 34
Kaub, Philip, 203
Kauffmann family, 18
Kauffmann, David, 177, 199
Kauffmann, Jacob, 23, 56, 60, 62, 63, 73, 74, 75, 147, 205
Kauffmann, Johannes, 177
Keemer, James, 52, 99
Keim family, 18, 21
Keim, Jacob, 63, 73, 75, 82, 83, 90-92, 151, 156, 205
Keim, Jerg, 205
Keim, Johannes, 83, 137, 177, 193, 199
Keim, Nicolaus, 197
Kelchner, Jerg, 137, 177, 199
Kelchner, Margareta, 137
Kepler, Andreas, 177
Kerlin, Johannes, 146, 201
Kerr, John, 142
Kerst family (see Kersten family), 18
Kerst, Heinrich, 31, 147, 203, 205
Kerst, Henry, 148
Kerst, Jerg, 201
Kerst, Johannes, 177, 197, 199
Kersten family, 18
Kersten, Johann Heinrich, 32, 177, 193
Kines, Jacob, 199
Kirkbride, Joseph, 191, 197
Klein, Jacob, 201
Kloss, Heinrich, 203
Knabb, Maria Elisabetha, 90
Knabb, Michael, 205
Knabb, Peter, 90, 205
Koch, Johannes, 177
Krebs, Katarina, 50
Kuhlwein family, 19
Kuhlwein, Maria LeDee, 106
Kuhlwein, Philip, 96, 106, 108, 114, 177, 193, 199, 205
Kuhn, Jacob, 153
Kutz, Thomas, 201
Lanciscus, Jerg, 201
Lanire, Christopher, 177
Lanire, George, 177
Lebengut, Jacob, 201
Lebo family, 21
Lebo, Johannes, 177, 197
Lebo, Lenhardt, 203
LeDee, Jean, 20, 106, 177
Lee family, 132, 152
Lee, Anthony, 24, 108, 129, 131, 142, 147, 154, 177, 193, 195, 199
Lee, Eleanor Ellis, 131-132
Lee, John, 203, 205
Lee, Samuel, 51, 147, 148, 152, 201, 205
Lee, Samuel, Jr., 148
Lee, Thomas, 69, 131-132, 205
Leffel, Balthasar, 201
Lehr, Heinrich, 201
Leinbach family, 114, 117-118
Leinbach, Anna Elisabetha, 113, 114, 117-118
Leinbach, Friedrich, 117, 177
Leinbach, Heinrich, 117, 205
Leinbach, Henry, 148
Leinbach, Johannes, 113, 114, 177, 193, 199
Leinbach, Johannes, Jr., 114, 117

Leinbach, Maria Barbara, 118
Lenhardt, Isaac, 136, 177, 193
Leondekasy, Philip, 177
Lesher, Johannes, 43, 44-46, 47, 49, 50, 63, 64, 67, 71, 76, 77, 78, 79, 100, 121, 142, 146-147, 148, 152, 154, 155, 172, 177, 199, 205, 231
Lesher, Nicolaus, Jr., 177
Lesher, Nicolaus, Sr., 177, 199, 205
Levan family, 18
Levan, Abraham, 20, 21, 49, 73, 142, 154, 155, 177, 199, 203, 220
Levan, Daniel, 203, 205
Levan, Isaac, 20, 49, 114, 120, 142, 154, 177, 197
Levan, Jacob, 177, 203
Lewis, James, 177, 191, 197
Lewis, John, 177
Lewis, Richard, 50, 154, 203
Lewis, Thomas, 177
Lidenius, Brigitta Reinberg, 124
Lidenius, John Abraham, 24, 153
Lidman, Jonas, 122, 153
Lightfoot, Benjamin, 131
Lincoln family, 18, 35
Lincoln, Abraham, 35, 70, 136, 140, 154, 203
Lincoln, Anne Boone, 136
Lincoln, Hannah Salter, 104
Lincoln, John, 195
Lincoln, Mary Robeson, 104
Lincoln, Mordecai, Jr., 35, 68
Lincoln, Mordecai, Sr., 19, 55, 66, 68, 81, 104, 142, 154, 156, 168, 177, 197, 203
Lincoln, Thomas, 35, 142, 154, 203
Lloyd, John, 177
Lobach, Peter, 199, 205
Longworthy, Benjamin, 24, 36, 48, 51, 91, 140, 177, 193, 199
Longworthy, John, 51
Longworthy, Maria Meinert, 51, 97
Loodginer, Johann Frank, 177
Looth, William, 177
Lorah, Jerg, 201
Lorah, Johannes, 136, 140, 177, 195
Lorah, Katarina, 136
Lotz, Jerg, 93, 156, 175, 195, 201
Louisa (slave), 51
Lower, Christian, 205
Lubold, Johannes, 201
Lubold, Karl, 201
Luckenbill, Michael, 177
Ludwig, Daniel, 195
Ludwig, Michael, 197, 201, 203
Ludwig, Michael, Jr., 201
Lycon family, 16
Lycon, Anders, 122, 146, 177, 189
Lycon, Peter, 177
Lynch, Thomas, 52
McCafferty, Hugh, 195
McGee, Alexander, 177
McGrew, Charles, 177, 195
McGuire, Joseph, 177
McManus, Francis, 177
Marquart, Martin, 201
Massey, Samuel, 197
Manskul, John or Johannes, 52
Mathews, Robert, 177

Maugridge, William, 20, 33, 93, 123, 142, 143, 154, 197
Maybery, Friedrich, 177
May, Thomas, 46
Meinert, Friedrich, Jr., 51
Meinert, Friedrich, Sr., 49, 51, 177, 199
Meinung, Abraham, 153
Messerschmidt, Daniel, 197, 203
Messerschmidt, Stephen, 177
Messerschmidt, Valentine, 197
Messinger, Michael, 195
Meyerly, Frederick, 148
Michael, Philip Jacob, 121, 130-131, 153
Michael, Sarah Webb, 130
Michler, Wolfgang, 153
Mickle, Samuel, 42, 199, 205
Mifflin, George, 42, 199
Mifflin, John Fishbourne, 205
Millard, Benjamin, 26, 146
Millard, James, 203
Millard, Jane, 201
Millard, Jonathan, 203
Millard, Joseph, 143, 154
Millard, Joseph, Jr., 201
Millard, Mordecai, 201
Millard, Thomas, 99, 143, 146, 177, 189, 193, 195
Millard, Timothy, 146, 195
Miller, Adam, 177
Miller, David, 36
Miller, Friedrich Casimir, 153
Miller, Stephen, 177, 189, 195
Miller, William, 203
Mitchell, Hugh, 177, 195
Mittelberger, Gottlieb, 31, 34, 35, 50, 67, 108
Mock, Peter, 201
Moeller, Johann Heinrich, 153
Mohn, Ulrich, 205
Molther, Sophia, 113, 118
Montgomery, Morton L., 10
Moore, Joseph, 52
Morgan, William, 177, 191
Morian, Sebastian, 203
Morris, Anthony, 195
Moser, Peter, 201
Mott, Greshan, 189
Motz, Matthias, 205
Motzer, Johannes, 201
Moyer, Friedrich, 177
Muhlenberg, Heinrich Melchior, 34, 51, 104-105, 107, 119, 120, 121, 123-125, 126, 139, 144, 152, 153
Muller, David, 49
Murfy, James, 51-52
Murray, Alexander, 125, 152, 153
Murray, Nancy Morgan, 125
Naesman, Magister, 123
Nealy, Victor, 99, 177
Neas, Jacob, 177
Neidig, Johann Adam, 197
Neisser, Jerg, 153
Neukirch, Heinrich, 86
Neukirch, Johannes, 203
Neun, Caspar, 205
Newberry, William, 51
Newman, Walter, 177
Nitschmann, Anna, 113

Nitschmann, Jerg, 153
Noble, Job, 177
Nolan, J. Bennett, 10
Norrill, James, 178
Old, James, 178
Old, John, 46, 49, 205
Oyster, Jerg, 205
Oyster, Johannes, 178, 199, 205
Oyster, Samuel, 32, 205
Palmer, Thomas, 178
Parry, Thomas, 201
Parvin, Francis, 147
Passler, Jerg, 178
Patterson, Robert, 178, 197, 203
Penn, John, 65
Penn, William, 15, 23, 24, 25, 26, 105, 126-127, 140, 149
Pennebecker, Derick, 201
Pennebecker, Heinrich, 203
Peter family, 18
Peter, Abraham, 33, 37, 199
Peter, Daniel, 205
Peter, Engelhard, 178, 193
Peters, Richard, 142
Phillips, John, 178
Plank family (see DelaPlank family), 21
Pott, Johannes, 84, 205
Pott, Wilhelm, 67, 92, 112, 178, 199
Potts, David, 201
Potts, John, 99, 100, 147, 195
Potts, Thomas, 52, 195, 199
Price, John, 178
Pummill, Francis, 178
Raifschneider, Johannes, 195
Rattican, Lawrence, 201
Read, James, 125
Rees, Edward, 178
Rees, George, 178
Rees, Griffith, 178
Rees, Thomas, 178
Reider, William, 148
Reiff, Conrad, 44-46, 48-49, 50, 108, 147, 178, 199, 205
Reiff, Daniel, 37, 96, 97, 98, 156
Reiff, Deborah, 136-137, 205
Reiff, Philip, 136-137, 205
Reinberg, Anders, 124, 178, 195
Reinberg, Samuel, 201
Reinhard, Owen, 201
Reiss, David, 205
Reiss, Peter L., 178
Reiss, Valentine, 199
Reppert, Johannes, 205
Retge, Elias, 197, 203
Retge, Jacob, 201
Rew, Robert, 178
Richard, James, 48, 178
Richard, Owen, 24, 31, 178, 189, 195
Richard, Owen, Jr., 178
Richard, William, 145-146, 178
Richards, Rowland, 178
Richardson, John, 178
Ridner, Henry, 178
Rieger, Bartholomew, 104, 105, 121
Ritter family, 18
Ritter, Franz, 112, 113, 117, 178, 197, 203
Ritter, Israel, 203

Ritter, Jerg, 178, 191, 203
Ritter, Paul, 203
Roberts, Joseph, 51
Roberts, Moses, 51, 80, 81, 153, 155, 205
Roberts, William, 178
Robeson, Andrew, 18, 103-104, 105, 108, 122, 146, 178, 191
Robeson, Israel, 135-136, 178, 191, 197
Robeson, Jonathan, 42, 128, 178
Robeson, Mary, 18, 104
Robeson, Moses, 203
Robeson, Peter, 99, 178
Robeson, Samuel, 178, 197
Rodt family, 42
Rodt, Johann Conrad, 178
Rodt, Johann Jacob, 20, 178, 189, 195, 201
Rogers, Roger, 178, 197
Ross, John, 43, 199
Rothermel, Christian, 97
Rothermel, Daniel, 205
Rouse, Francis, 178
Rumford, John, 178, 189
Rutter, John, 20
Rutter, Joseph, 20, 42, 66, 69, 178
Rutter, Thomas, Jr., 20, 100, 189
Rutter, Thomas, Sr., 20, 42, 51, 154, 178, 189
Sadler, Conrad, 178, 197, 203
Sadowski family, 18
Sadowski, Antony, 178, 189
Sandel, Andreas, 122, 153
Sands, Abijah, 31, 178, 195, 201
Sands, Abijah, Jr., 97
Sands, Catherine, 136
Sands, Daniel, 136
Sands, John, 72, 136, 139, 142, 144-145, 178, 195, 201
Sands, John, Jr., 137
Sands, Joseph, 136
Sands, Susanna, 139
Sauer, Christoph, 118
Sauermilch, Matthias, 205
Savage, George, 189
Savage, Samuel, 20, 178, 189
Scarlet, John, Jr., 178
Schall, Samuel, 178
Schaum, Johann Helfrich, 121, 153
Scheid, Miss, 136
Schenkel family, 18
Schenkel, Magdalena, 37, 97
Schenkel, Martin, 33, 37, 38, 60, 63, 94, 106, 108, 136, 148, 155, 178, 193, 199, 205
Scherer, Ulrich, 178
Schiffer, Johannes, 205
Schiffer, Maximillian, 178, 199
Schlatter, Michael, 121, 153
Schneider family, 18, 21, 109, 111
Schneider, Daniel, 98
Schneider, Jacob, 142, 154, 155
Schneider, Johannes, 93, 96, 109, 110, 178, 193, 197
Schneider, Johann Jacob, 178, 203
Schneider, Katarina, 109, 110
Schneider, Peter, 140, 203
Schoefer, Lenhard, 205
Schoepf, Johann David, 36
Schultman, Widow, 26

Schulze, David, 118
Schumacher, Daniel, 121, 153
Seehang, Johann Nicolaus, 178
Seely, Jonas, 142-143
Sees, Jost, 147, 201
Seidel, Johann Nicolaus, 201
Seltzer, Jacob, 178, 199
Shewbart, Mary, 199
Shiers, John, 193
Shilbert, Peter, 178
Showell, John, 178
Silvius, Jacob, 147
Sinclair, John, 178
Sleder, John, 178
Smally, Isaac, 145, 178
Smith, Henry, 205
Smith, John, 178
Smith, Robert, 145-146, 178
Smith, Thomas, 178
Spangenberg, August Gottlieb, 108, 111-112, 153
Spencer, Daniel, 178
Stahl, Caspar, 197
Stapleton, John, 205
Stapleton, Robert, 60, 72, 155, 178, 199
Stapleton, William, 205
Starr, James, 146
Starr, Moses, 147
Stauber, Jacob, 114, 128, 178, 195
Stauber, Sarah Boone, 114, 128
Steckel, Valentine, 199
Steel, Thomas, 178
Steiner, Johannes, 201
Stephens, David, 178
Stitzel, John, 148
Stoetzel, Johannes, 205
Stoever, Johann Caspar, 109, 110, 153
Stone, Thomas, 178
Stoudt, John Joseph, 10
Strunk, Lorentz, 201
Stult, Hans, 178
Surrey, John, 99
Sutton, Ralph, 178
Sweetner, Martin, 178
Switzer, Jacob, 201
Swope, Benedict, 43
Tallman, Benjamin, 203
Tallman, William, 35
Tamplan, Samuel, 51-52
Thomas, Abel, 203
Thomas, Heinrich, 178
Thomas, John, 195
Thomas, Lewis, 178
Thompson, Henry, 197, 203
Thompson, James, 178, 197

Thompson, John, 203
Tigle, Jacob, 49, 50
Tribby, John, 178
Truman, Richard, 178, 191
Trump, Caspar, 178, 189
Trump, Michael, 195
Turner, Anthony, 178
Turner, John, 178
Turner, Thomas, 178
Umensetter, Johannes, 40
Umsted, Ann, 72
Umsted, Herman, 72, 203
Umsted, Johannes, 201
Unckelbach, Johann Heinrich, 50
VanReed, Heinrich, 195, 201
Violet (slave), 51
Voigt, Johann Ludwig, 121, 153
Wagner, Elias, 178, 197
Wainwright, Benjamin, 178
Wainwright, John, 146, 178
Wall, Patrick, 52
Walters, Ann Robeson, 135-136
Walters, Solomon, 135-136
Wanger, Abraham, 195, 201
Wanger, Johannes, 201
Warren family, 18
Warren, Jacob, 178, 195
Warren, James, 178, 195
Warren, John, 143, 154, 178, 189, 195, 201
Warren, John, Jr., 32, 178, 189
Warren, Michael, 178
Warlick, Daniel, 178, 199
Wartman, Adam, 195
Watkins, Evan, 178
Watson, John Fanning, 26
Weaver family (see Weber family), 18
Webb, John, 178, 197
Webb, Moses, 26
Webb, Samuel, 203
Weber family, 18
Weber, Jacob, 31, 51, 57, 97, 100, 106, 142, 147, 154, 178, 189, 195, 201
Weber, Magdalena, 49
Weber, Peter, 195, 201
Weicks, Christian, 178
Weidner, Adam, 59-60, 178
Weidner, Jerg Adam, 49, 50, 59-60, 66, 178, 195, 201
Weidner, Johannes, 178
Weidner, Peter, 178
Weidner, Lazarus, 109, 199, 205
Weidner, Tychicus, 147, 199, 205
Weiler, Jacob, 137, 203
Weiler, Johannes, 178
Weiler, Martin, 137, 178, 197

Weimer, Katarina, 193
Weiser, Christian, 85, 205
Weiser, Conrad, 142-143
Weiser, David, 85, 87, 178, 199, 205
Weiser, Katarina, 85
Weisman, Isaac, 178
Weiss, Jerg Michael, 109, 153
Welker, Dietrich, 43
Weller, Anna, 50
Weller, Eva Maria, 50
Weller, Peter, 49-50
Wenger, Heinrich, 201
Wentzel, Daniel, 205
Werner, Aaron, 178
Werner, Heinrich, 114, 120, 178, 197
Wertenbaker, Thomas Jefferson, 37
Whitacre, Samuel, 69, 178
Wiest, Jacob, 205
Wilkinson, Daniel, 178
Wilkinson, Samuel, 178
Willits, Thomas, 178
Williams, Benjamin, 201
Williams, John, 178
Williams, Owen, 178
Winey, Jacob, 205
Winter family, 18
Winter, James, 178
Winter, William, 152, 195, 201
Winterberg, Heinrich, 178
Wistar, Caspar, 199
Wister, John, 78
Wistler, Abraham, 201
Wolf, Andrew, 195
Wolf, Johann Heinrich II, 136
Wolf, Johann Heinrich, 136, 178
Womelsdorff family, 42
Womelsdorff, Daniel, 40, 42, 97, 178, 195, 201
Womelsdorff, Elisabetha, 84
Wood, Richard, 178
Wrangel, Carl Magnus, 124-125, 152, 153
Wyatt, Thomas, 178
Yarnell, Peter, 178
Yocom family, 16
Yocom, John, 97, 100, 178, 189
Yocom, Jonas, 69, 145, 178, 189, 195, 201
Yocom, Peter, 201
Yoder family (see Joder family), 18
Yoder, John (see Joder, Johannes), 11, 52
Zeister, Michael, 35, 197
Zinzendorf, Benigna, 114, 118
Zinzendorf, Count Nicolaus Ludwig von, 111-118, 119, 123, 153

OLEY VALLEY HERITAGE

JOHANNES LESHER HOUSE (Oley Forge Mansion), Circa 1750-1755, Oley Township.
Photo by Kenneth LeVan.

THE PENNSYLVANIA GERMAN SOCIETY
P.O. BOX 397
BIRDSBORO, PENNSYLVANIA 19508

OFFICERS (1994)
JOHN P. DIEFENDERFER, President
EDWARD E. QUINTER, Vice President
GEORGE F. SPOTTS, Treasurer
DAVID L. VALUSKA, Secretary
DON YODER, Editor

BOARD OF DIRECTORS (1994)

VERONICA L. BACKENSTOE	ALLEN G. MUSSER
LUKE K. BRINKER	EDWARD E. QUINTER
DORIS K. DAUB	MARK I. ROTHERMEL
JOHN P. DIEFENDERFER	N. DANIEL SCHWALM
RICHARD DRUCKENBROD	CARL D. SNYDER
DONALD F. DURNBAUGH	GEORGE F. SPOTTS
WILLIAM B. FETTERMAN	EUGENE STINE
JOHN B. FRANTZ	DAVID L. VALUSKA
NORMAN HOFFMAN	JANET S. WELSH
ROBERT G. HOSTETTER	CAROLYN C. WENGER
MARION LOIS HUFFINES	WILLARD W. WETZEL
ROBERT M. KLINE	DON YODER

THE OLEY VALLEY HERITAGE ASSOCIATION
P.O. BOX 401
OLEY, PENNSYLVANIA 19547

OFFICERS (1994)
MARSHA CHAPPELL, President
ELEANOR SHANER, Vice President
JANE LEVAN, Treasurer
HILDA FISHER, Secretary

BOARD OF DIRECTORS (1994)
MARSHA CHAPPELL
HILDA FISHER
JANE LEVAN
KENNETH LEVAN
LAUREL MILLER
ELEANOR SHANER
DONALD SHELLEY
CAROL WENTZEL
MICHAEL WENTZEL